ASIA
(202)-   833 - 3410

A CRITIQUE OF CONTEMPORARY
AMERICAN SOCIOLOGY

THE REYNOLDS SERIES IN SOCIOLOGY

Larry T. Reynolds, *Editor*

by **GENERAL HALL, INC.**

A CRITIQUE OF CONTEMPORARY AMERICAN SOCIOLOGY

Edited by

Ted R. Vaughan
Gideon Sjoberg
Larry T. Reynolds

GENERAL HALL, INC.
Publishers
5 Talon Way
Dix Hills, New York 11746

A CRITIQUE OF CONTEMPORARY
AMERICAN SOCIOLOGY

GENERAL HALL, INC.
5 Talon Way
Dix Hills, New York 11746

Copyright © 1993 by Ted R. Vaughan, Gideon Sjoberg,
and Larry T. Reynolds

Publisher: Ravi Mehra
Composition: *Graphics Division,* General Hall, Inc.

LIBRARY OF CONGRESS CATALOG CARD NUMBER: 92-75608

ISBN:1–882289–02–1 [paper]
       1–882289–03–X [cloth]

Manufactured in the United States of America

Dedicated

to

Jack Dodson

and

Rupert Koeninger

who, as practicing critical sociologists,

strove to advance democratic ideals and

courageously suffered the consequences

Contents

PREFACE

This edited book is, in our view, a much needed step toward a critique of contemporary American sociology. This effort strives to sustain the scholarly tradition of, for example, Robert Lynd, Oliver Cox, C. Wright Mills, Pitirim A. Sorokin, Alvin Gouldner, Jessie Bernard, and Patricia Hill Collins.

Contemporary American sociology stands in need of a critical reevaluation and renewal for two reasons. First, sociology has more to offer U.S. society and the emerging world community than the advocates of the natural science model suppose. In recent decades sociologists have become increasingly enamored with techniques and methods. In the process we can observe a growing separation of social theory from research procedures. These patterns, combined with the hyperspecialization in the discipline, have led mainstream sociology away from its classical heritage. We admire the scope and substance of the works of Karl Marx, Max Weber, Emile Durkheim and Talcott Parsons. But their writings must be reconstituted if they are to be relevant to the contemporary world. Social theory and research methodology must be reformulated if sociologists are to confront the issues posed by the onrush of events in the United States and abroad. Although technical research procedures have a place in sociology, they should not become ends in themselves. Such a practice is self-defeating if we are to understand what has occurred, for example, in eastern Europe and the former Soviet Union in the late 1980s and early 1990s. Technical procedures per se are grossly inadequate for analyzing the rise and implications of the European Community (EC) or of Japan as a world economic power.

A second reason for a sustained critique is of a more practical nature. In the late 1980s and early 1990s the discipline of sociology, as has been reported in, for example, the *New York Times* and *Newsweek*, is embattled. The executive officer of the American Sociological Association recently observed that the influence of sociology in the National Science Foundation (NSF) has been declining and then listed departments that have been dissolved or are in particularly difficult straits. Most sociologists believe that issues facing the discipline can be resolved through more effective administrative action or by greater attention to technical scientific procedures. We do not wish to abandon technical expertise, but standardized techniques are not ends in themselves. If sociologists are to legitimate their scholarly endeavors, they must be able to contribute to the intellectual discourse about the great social and moral issues of our day. We must turn, for example, to Robert Bellah, William Julius Wilson, and

1

Immanuel Wallerstein as exemplars of sociological investigation. They demonstrate how sociologists can advance our understanding of empirical phenomena that are of pressing import and how sociological ideas can inform broader civic discourse—well beyond the confines of sociology itself.

We engage in critique not for its own sake but for the sake of renewal. In order to create viable options for the discipline in the future, we must first evaluate critically what exists. We are deeply committed to the search for alternative theoretical and methodological orientations that will enable us to address problems relevant to the end of this century and the beginning of the next one. Nowadays, most sociologists seem willing to adapt to ongoing social changes. But, we must do more than rely on a "bunker mentality"; we must be proactive in staking out new courses of actions for ourselves and our students, as well as for the larger national and international communities in which we exist.

This book contains a set of interrelated themes that highlights some of the serious intellectual (and practical) limitations of contemporary American sociology. While each chapter should be read on its own merits, we, as editors, in the Introductions to Parts I and II have isolated the recurrent themes that pervade this volume.

As should become evident, we disassociate ourselves from the postmodernists. Their perspective, with its built-in relativism and solipsism, is self-destructive, not constructive. In particular, the postmodernists are unable to grasp the implications of the large-scale bureaucratic organizations that shape the lives of people today. To those who manage these organizations, the musings of the postmodernists are merely that—musings.

Unfortunately, the present work, which was initiated in 1987, has had a difficult history. The delay resulted from unforseen events in our respective lives and from a marked change in the focus of this venture in midstream. We apologize to the contributors for the unanticipated delay in getting the book into print.

We also must acknowledge our indebtedness to a loosely structured editorial board that reviewed the manuscripts. The efforts of these reviewers greatly improved the quality of the chapters. Leonard Cain has been especially helpful to us. He devoted numerous hours to evaluating manuscripts not only for their overall argument but for their clarity and precision. He read and reread certain manuscripts as they underwent extensive revisions.

Kathryn Kuhn also spent a great deal of time on a number of the manuscripts. Her incisive criticisms made it possible to improve their arguments and readability. James Otis Smith took a special interest in several chapters, and we are grateful for his significant contributions. So too, Boyd Littrell, who is a contributor, critically commented on selected chapters, and his suggestions greatly aided the authors in producing higher quality manuscripts.

Richard Colvard, Sandy Lemens, and Roger Nett also contributed to this effort. Colvard used his well-honed editorial abilities to great advantage in dissecting an earlier draft of the chapter on ethics and human rights. Although he may not agree with the final version, we learned from his penetrating criticisms. Several other reviewers, who shall remain anonymous, were of major assistance in our editorial work. One person in particular helped the editors to upgrade one set of chapters.

We are grateful for the patience and helpfulness of Judy Elam, who has typed and retyped different versions of this manuscript with care. Jan Allgood is also to be commended for her efforts.

Our hope is that our readers will join in the effort to revitalize the intellectual thrust of American sociology and deal more effectively with the practical problems that currently plague the discipline.

The Editors

PART I

INTRODUCTION

This book represents a wide-ranging effort to evaluate critically the discipline of American sociology. It rests on the premise that sociology is not living up to its potential as a scholarly and intellectual endeavor. Sociologists can (and must) offer students and members of U.S. society, as well as persons in the international community, a fuller understanding of the everyday life in which we are all embedded and of the enormity of the social and cultural changes that are sweeping the world. *Our critique is not for critique's sake. For us, a critique of "what is" becomes the foundation for constructing alternative theoretical frameworks and methodologies that will advance the cause not merely of sociology but especially of the democratic ideal on a societal and worldwide basis.*

In recent years sociology has received considerable negative scrutiny in the mass media. The *New York Times* and *Newsweek*, for example, have published articles about the plight of the field. Moreover, the executive officer of the American Sociological Association has confirmed the existing unease (Felice Levine, "The Executive Officer's Column," *Footnotes*. 19, no. 10: 1992:2). Levine admits that sociologists lost ground in the last decade at the National Science Foundation "in dollars, visibility, and to a certain extent leadership role." She also takes note of a number of problem-plagued departments. Sociologists are keenly aware of the closing of the once highly regarded department at Washington University in St. Louis, but that is only a small part of a larger picture regarding the downsizing of full-time teaching positions in a variety of departments in the United States.

One typical reaction by sociologists to the current crisis or malaise facing the discipline has been that sociologists have failed to "mend their fences" within their college or university. We readily acknowledge that sociologists should not only carry out research but should also be effective teachers and academic citizens. The power base at the local level cannot be ignored. Nonetheless, few sociologists have linked the current crisis to the intellectual or scholarly shortcomings of present-day American sociology. We do. Most sociologists cast the problems of the discipline in practical or political terms. Although the practical and the theoretical realms overlap and interact, sociologists must recast their theoretical and methodological orientations if they are to deal with the major social and cultural issues that are unfolding on the world scene.

4

We are deeply committed to sociology's classical heritage. Karl Marx, Max Weber, Emile Durkheim, George Herbert Mead, Karl Mannheim, and Talcott Parsons, among others, contributed to our basic understanding about the nature of human action and the social order. Yet by and large, those who created this heritage focused on "the great transformation"—on the transition from a preindustrial to a scientific/industrial order, or from a precapitalist to a capitalist mode of production, from feudal to bureaucratic organizations.

As we look to the twenty-first century, we are confronting a new range of social issues and arrangements that must be addressed. While we should build on the classical tradition, theoretical and methodological innovations are called for if we are to interpret the emerging problems of the contemporary world. Look about. Since the late 1980s, eastern Europe and the former Soviet Union have been undergoing a transformation beyond the wildest imagination of most sociologists or other social scientists. While the former Soviet Union and Yugoslavia, for instance, have been fragmenting along ethnic lines, we are onlookers to the integration of western Europe. Although divisive struggles loom on the horizon, the European Community seems on the verge of becoming a reality. This remarkable experiment of merging nation-states that were out to destroy one another during most of the nineteenth and twentieth centuries is surely deserving of intensive sociological investigation. So, too, is the rise of a global economy and of various international organizations, with which most sociologists deal in only a marginal way.

If we look inward and back upon the Reagan era, we stand in wonderment of the long-range consequences of the Iran-contra and Savings and Loan debacles. During the 1980s we lived at a time when greed was worshipped, and a form of the new individualism emerged wherein the larger common good was decried by many in the United States. In the process a few gained great wealth at the expense of the many.

Sociologists have contributed all too little to our understanding of the social patterns mentioned above. Why? Our diagnosis is that over the past several decades the discipline's intellectual contribution has been deeply eroded by the growing dominance of the natural science model. Standardized technical research procedures have been employed at the expense of sustained theoretical analysis of empirical phenomena. This orientation has stifled, rather than advanced, social inquiry.

The dominance of the natural science model in sociology, though not without its detractors, is reflected by, for instance, the prestige rankings in the early 1980s of the department at the University of Wisconsin at Madison as No. 1 in the U.S. But this department is not alone in its emphasis on techniques and methods. Departments at Indiana, Washington (Seattle), Michigan, North Carolina (Chapel Hill), and Harvard (after Parsons's retirement), among others, attest to the power of the natural science model in the discipline.

Sociology will continue to falter if it relies too heavily for its legitimacy on the natural science model. Instead, theoretical analysis of major social issues in the manner of, for instance, Robert Bellah, William Julius Wilson, and Immanuel Wallerstein becomes essential. These sociologists have something important to say about broader moral and political issues within the society and within the emerging world community.

The four chapters in Part I consider various limitations of the natural science model; there are other linkages among these chapters as well. In chapter 1, Vaughan begins with an overview of the discipline since World War II. He does so by using a series of edited handbooks to provide us with an understanding of how sociologists have evaluated the state of sociology. He then utilizes this background as a basis for analyzing the domain assumptions or presuppositions underlying the natural science model. These are seldom, if ever, spelled out. After that, he outlines a new direction for sociological analysis. In the process he questions the narrow definition of "validity" associated with the natural science model and argues that sociologists should become concerned with the construction of alternative futures—not just simply a description of what is.

Sjoberg and Vaughan in chapter 2 proceed to examine how sociology is currently interwoven with bureaucratic structures—in the university setting, in the broader society, and on the international scene. They go further and document how the natural science model has been a product of, and in turn supports, the bureaucratic process. Their conclusion is that many contemporary sociologists have entered Weber's iron cage. The methods of the natural science model do not permit sociologists to examine the larger organizational structures in which they live and work. We must escape from the iron cage to advance sociological, as well as democratic, discourse.

In chapter 3 Sjoberg and Vaughan continue, in a somewhat different vein, to reevaluate the natural science model. A good deal has been written about the ethics of social research, and the American Sociological Association has adopted a Code of Ethics. Unfortunately, no sociologist has critically examined the ethical foundations of the discipline with the goal of setting forth an alternative moral framework—one founded on human rights. Yet sociologists have a compelling contribution to make in rethinking the nature of human rights—a matter of far-reaching practical and theoretical import on the global scene. Sociologists have avoided this problem and will continue to do so if they remain captives of the natural science model.

In chapter 4 Norma Williams and Andrée F. Sjoberg forcefully reevaluate the intersection of race and ethnic issues with those of gender. They adopt a framework that emphasizes the asymmetry between the perspectives of the privileged and nonprivileged within societies and within the world system. This chapter serves at least two distinct purposes. First, it is must reading as a complement, and sometimes a corrective, to the arguments set forth in chapter

2 on the bureaucratization of sociology and in chapter 3 on the analysis of human rights. We are aware, for instance, that a fuller analysis of human rights must address ethnic and gender issues. Second, the essay by Williams and Sjoberg stands on its own. It raises some fundamental questions about theory and research. The asymmetry between the top-down versus bottom-up perspectives indicates that "social units" are not "equal," and serious dangers befall adherents of the natural science model who add up these in order to explain the whole. In more substantive terms, Williams and Sjoberg call attention, in the light of broad cross-cultural analysis, to the need for analyzing gender in the context of race and ethnicity as well as social class. Understanding the interrelationships among race and ethnicity, gender, and the larger stratification system is a major challenge for social scientists—and sociologists are no exception. A firmer grasp of these matters is essential to constructing a more viable democratic order within and among nations.

If we place this book in a larger intellectual framework, we perceive ourselves as sustaining the tradition of Robert Lynd, Oliver Cox, C. Wright Mills, Pitirim A. Sorokin, Alvin Gouldner, Jessie Bernard, and, more recently, Patricia Hill Collins. In one sense, Mills's *Sociological Imagination* (New York: Oxford University Press 1959) contains a number of the ideas on which we build. Mills's career is also instructive. Mills' early intellectual grounding in pragmatism—in the works of Charles Peirce, John Dewey, and George Herbert Mead—informed his later work in a manner most sociologists do not recognize. Mills took seriously the pragmatist's commitment to work toward (if not to achieve) the democratic ideal. Mills saw this ideal as being eroded by the power elite (as well as the emphasis on techniques and methods in sociology). As for Gouldner, we are in agreement with his call for detailing the role of sociologists' domain assumptions. By doing so, we can advance our understanding of theoretical and, we would add, research activities.

Although recognizing the worth of Mills and Gouldner, neither gave sufficient attention to racial and ethnic issues, to say nothing of gender. Gouldner in particular can be faulted for not being more attentive to the implications of the civil rights movement, which had been under way for about fifteen years prior to the publication of his *The Coming Crisis of Western Sociology* (New York: Basic Books 1970). Moreover, his preoccupation with Parsons led him to ignore the rising hegemony of the natural science model. Still, as history heals some of the wounds of those whom Mills and Gouldner so boldly assaulted, we expect their writings will be more widely accepted, even acclaimed, in various subfields of sociology and other disciplines. The same can be said of Sorokin who, to a considerable degree, undercut his powerful intellectual argument in, for instance, his *Fads and Foibles in Modern Sociology and Related Sciences* (Chicago: Regnery 1956) by the harshness and "overstatement" of his attacks.

Jessie Bernard's intellectual journey is also worthy of special mention. Her biographer, Robert Bannister (See *Jessie Bernard* [New Brunswick: Rutgers University Press 1991]) indicates that Bernard turned her back on her deeply ingrained positivist past as she set out to formulate her sociological version of feminism. If sociologists take seriously democratic issues—as Bernard did with regard to gender inequality—they too will reject core assumptions of the natural science model.

We cannot ignore Oliver Cox. After Robert Lynd, he stands as one of the earliest critics of mainstream sociology in the United States—particularly with respect to class and race (See *Caste, Class and Race* [New York: Doubleday 1948]). Cox attacked Robert Park, among others, and this despite the fact he received his doctorate at Chicago. That Cox was one of the first neo-Marxists in sociology in the post-World War II era did not aid his cause, for his most widely recognized book was published just before the rise of McCarthyism. That Cox was black and taught at a small school, without graduate students to champion his position, added to his marginalization. Cox has yet to receive his just deserts by sociologists who claim to discuss conflict theory in sociology.

We find a continuation of a critical stance in American sociology by Patricia Hill Collins (See *Black Feminist Thought* [Cambridge: Allen and Unwin 1990]). Collins relentlessly takes mainstream sociologists to task for ignoring the black women's perspective. Her work underscores the fact that the critical spirit lives on within the discipline.

The sociologists mentioned above have taken up the cudgels of criticizing the dominant worldview in sociology from divergent theoretical foundations. Even so, they share strategic domain assumptions. They have rejected the "value-fact" dichotomy; they are committed to examining more than "what is." The sociologists who are part of the critical heritage in America have been striving to advance, albeit from differing perspectives, the cause of civic discourse and the democratic ideal. Regrettably, this theoretical orientation is ignored in the leading textbooks in sociological theory (to say nothing of those in research methods).

Although we associate ourselves with the critical tradition in sociology, we also perceive differences between ourselves and the sociologists noted above. One significant difference (except perhaps for Sorokin) is that we are convinced that sociologists can (and should) play a role in the construction of alternative futures—that they should engage in "countersystem analysis." Neither Mills nor Gouldner, for instance, emphasized sociology's place in the construction of alternatives. We would incorporate this form of analysis into the critical tradition that is an essential feature of American sociology.

We now insert two caveats with respect to this book. In the first section (and in several chapters in Part II) the contributors are critical of the natural science model. Yet we do not wish to rid sociology of this orientation. Our goal is to provide a competing and viable theoretical and methodological orientation to the natural science model. Research procedures and techniques cannot dictate the kinds of ideas that sociologists address if sociology is to sustain itself intellectually.

Another caveat relates to the nature of critique itself. Today, a number of readers are likely to associate critique with postmodernism—with, for example, some form of "deconstructionism." We strongly disassociate ourselves from this perspective. Sociologists who have bought into postmodernism—be they adherents of Jacques Derrida, Michel Foucault, or others—have entered a dead-end street. Although we do not directly debate with the sociological adherents of this orientation, we believe the postmodernist worldview, with its solipsism and relativism, undermines any effort to construct a more humane world.

If sociology is to sustain its legitimacy within American society and on the international scene, sociologists must grapple with issues that enhance the quality of democratic discourse. We hark back to the likes of Bellah, Wilson and Wallerstein. If we view sociology within this framework, critique is a reasonable, even necessary, undertaking.

Chapter **1**

The Crisis in Contemporary American Sociology: A Critique of the Discipline's Dominant Paradigm

Ted R. Vaughan

In the 1950s, C. Wright Mills (1959) criticized American sociologists for their "abstracted empiricism," the irrelevancy of their general theory, and their failure to confront the moral issues associated with social power. At the time, he was a rather lonely voice in the discipline, for his assessment of the field ran counter to the rising optimism of the era. His critique of the discipline was set forth at a time when U.S. power on the world scene was at its height, when American higher education was expanding rapidly, and when sociologists were caught up in great enthusiasm for the future of the discipline as a scientific enterprise.

As we take stock of American sociology in the 1990s, the broader social context is quite different from that to which Mills was responding. In the intervening decades, the limitations of American military power were exposed—despite the performance in the 1991 Persian Gulf War—in Vietnam. Moreover, Japan and Germany challenged American dominance in the economic arena. At the same time, higher education lost some of the glamour it enjoyed in the early 1960s. In fact, extensive debates regarding the nature and direction of higher education were highlighted in Bloom's (1987) *The Closing of The American Mind*, a conservative attack that attained best-seller status. So, too, we find increased controversy over the role of science, particularly with respect to funding issues.

Within this altered social and cultural context, the heady exhilaration expressed by many sociologists in the 1950s and 1960s has become muted. Although the dominant stance within the discipline continues to be one of optimism and overall satisfaction with respect to the thrust of sociology, a growing number of prominent sociologists, representing divergent theoretical positions, have expressed gnawing doubts concerning the state of the field. There is a heightened, albeit diffuse, sense that the discipline is disoriented and is not making the progress anticipated just a few decades ago. Outside the discipline, Joseph Berger (1989) called attention to this malaise in an article in the *New York Times* titled "Sociology's Long Decade in the Wilderness." Although officials of the American Sociological Association (ASA)—as well as others—challenged this description of the field, the unease continues to be manifest in a variety of ways within the discipline.

The Central Argument and Its Articulation

The sense that "clearly something is wrong with sociology"—to use Rossi's (1990) phrase—has increasingly come to focus on the issue of disciplinary fragmentation. A recurring theme in recent American sociology is that the scientific ideal of continuity, codification, and the accumulation of knowledge is threatened by a growing lack of disciplinary consensus, thereby undercutting the discipline's claim to scientific status.

We readily acknowledge that, in contrast with the 1950s, a wider array of theoretical orientations today competes for attention. In addition, specialization in substantive areas has proceeded at a rapid pace. For example, gender studies, which currently looms large in the discipline, did not exist as recently as the 1960s. We also find new sections being added within the ASA, such as one on "emotions," which has come to be perceived as independent of social psychology. Moreover, within such traditional fields as the family, sociologists are defining themselves as specialists in family violence, divorce, and so on. Further, specialized journals appear, reflecting and reinforcing substantive specialization.

Yet our central thesis challenges the current diagnosis concerning the "ills" that beset American sociology. We reason, instead, that the fundamental crisis in the field exists in the failure of sociologists to engage in, and make significant contributions to, the discourse concerning the major empirical and moral problems confronting humankind as we approach the end of the twentieth century. Moreover, both the marginalization of sociology in relation to large-scale issues and the fragmentation within the discipline have a common source—American sociologists' preponderant reliance on the natural science model to produce scientific knowledge about the social world. The conception of knowledge pursued by advocates of the natural science model emphasizes the discovery of invariant relationships existing in the natural social world through the precise measurement of quantitative variables. In order to produce this form of scientific knowledge, sociologists have come to concentrate heavily on increasingly more sophisticated technical procedures and methods to obtain and analyze data.

Underlying the apparent fragmentation is a pervasive methodological paradigm that stresses the necessity of technical research procedures, primarily quantitative in nature, as the basis for scientific sociology. Technical precision and replicability are the hallmarks of the current methodological hegemony. Yet to achieve these objectives, researchers typically must focus on narrow, manageable research problems, thereby furthering the fragmentation in the discipline.

Equating technical procedures with methodology has undermined the traditional conception of methodology, which was concerned with the "logic of inquiry"—that is, of the interrelation of theory, methods, and data. More narrowly, the concentration on technical procedures has meant that a sociological problem is defined by the techniques that can be employed. For example, a database with sound probability sampling, which permits the use of sophisticated techniques, is often prized for its own sake. *Instead of the research problem defining the methods to be employed, research techniques define the sociological problem to be addressed.* We welcome rigorous research, but technical procedures must not define and delimit the substantive and theoretical problems that sociologists examine.

The current methodological hegemony threatens the future of sociology as a viable scholarly enterprise. Aside from a few notable exceptions (e.g., Wallerstein, Bellah, and Wilson) contemporary American sociologists are not studying and contributing to the intellectual discourse about the most significant social, political, and moral issues confronting humankind. This situation is acknowledged by two recent past presidents of the ASA. According to Herbert Gans (1989:1), "our [sociologists'] ideas continue to be largely absent from the country's political thinking." Kai Erikson (1989:513), in reviewing Smelser's (1988) *Handbook of Sociology* (discussed at length below) notes that nothing is said in the volume about "Hiroshima and Nagasaki, the Holocaust, Vietnam, Bhopal or Chernobyl." Moreover, he continues, little is said "even about *categories* of events that have had such an impact on our times—wars, disasters, plagues. The index cites the nuclear family, for example, but not nuclear weapons."

Instead of the current crisis emerging from the fragmentation within sociology, I aver that the general failure to contribute to the major debates regarding the great intellectual, political, and moral issues on the societal and global scenes has led to the marginalization of the discipline. The diagnosis rests on the contention that the emphasis on techniques and methods is a key factor in sociology's marginalization, for research methods, as currently defined, have made sociology's contribution largely irrelevant to the major issues of contemporary social life. Consequently, I find a lack of intellectual excitement and a growing concern that "clearly something is wrong with sociology."

My critique (or negative appraisal) of the contemporary practices of American sociologists, as well as the overall direction of the discipline, is not an end in itself. On the contrary, my primary objective is to contribute to the rehabilitation of the classical sociological heritage of Marx, Weber, and Durkheim (and even Parsons to a degree). *Sociologists have, as these classical figures exemplify, a substantial theoretical and empirical contribution to make to the debates regarding the future course of societal and global developments.* Admittedly, the issues facing sociologists today are not those of the classical sociologists. But we must return to their concern with major social issues and adapt our research methods in order to examine the central theoretical and practical problems of the contemporary social world. Although we are committed to rigorous analysis, if sociology is to move forward, research techniques cannot set the intellectual agenda of the field.

Having laid out the general thrust of the argument, I document it in some detail. I proceed as follows:

1. I first demonstrate how sociologists have represented and evaluated the state of American sociology in the post-World War II era. I provide, in one sense, a brief history of the ways in which sociologists have viewed themselves and the discipline over nearly half a century.

Although sociologists generally have been resistant to the application of the sociology of knowledge to the discipline, they nonetheless have produced a sizable literature surveying the state of the field. These materials provide us with a background for evaluating how sociologists conceive of their discipline today.

I examine sociologists' self-evaluation of their discipline in terms of three rather loosely defined and overlapping periods. From 1945 to 1968, roughly at the height of American influence on the world scene, a number of handbooks summarizing and evaluating the discipline appeared. These volumes typically reflected a high degree of optimism concerning the progress of the field and the prospects for a science of society. The second period, roughly 1965 to 1975, was one of institutional crisis within the broader society, a crisis mirrored within sociology. The optimistic handbook tradition temporarily lapsed, and several critiques of the discipline were published. The most theoretically sophisticated of these was Gouldner's (1970) *The Coming Crisis of Western Sociology*. But, as I observe, the overall reaction of sociologists to Gouldner was one of deep hostility. The final period covers the years from 1975 to the present. As American society resumed some of its more routine character in the mid-1970s, sociologists began to express a renewed, but guarded, optimism about the discipline's progress and prospects. Still, there was a simultaneous concern with the threat of fragmentation and disarray within the field. This concern comes through clearly in Smelser's (1988) *Handbook of Sociology*, arguably the most discussed report on the state of sociology in the past quarter-century, and in reviewers' responses to it.

2. After documenting the shift by sociologists from heady optimism concerning the discipline's progress to a more cautious stance regarding its future, I analyze the basic assumptions underlying the use of technical research tools. I refer to these technical procedures, and especially the assumptions on which they rest, as the natural science model. This methodological paradigm dominates the discipline.

I purposely bypass the traditional positivist-humanist debate. Although I take note of significant differences within the natural science model—particularly between the proponents of the "hard version" and the "soft version" of the model—my goal is to spell out the basic presuppositions, or domain assumptions, on which mainstream sociology has been constructed.

3. Having reconceptualized the current state of the discipline in terms of the dominance of the natural science model, I critically analyze the model from a sociology of knowledge perspective. Here I demonstrate that the natural science model, although not without certain virtues, entails fundamental contradictions when applied to the study of the social world. The inherent logical flaws of the natural science model in studying human nature and social reality suggest that we must search for an alternative set of assumptions on which to build a sociology that can effectively come to terms with the over-riding empirical changes that dominate the present global landscape.

4. Finally, in view of the limitations of the natural science model, I outline two major features of an alternative sociology predicated on a different set of domain assumptions. First, I use this counterperspective as a means of eliciting and clarifying the major consequences of the natural science model for contemporary sociology. Second, I examine the implications of the alternative domain assumptions for a sociology that represents a counter to current mainstream efforts. The core features of this alternative are the explicit recognition that sociologists are influenced by the broader society and culture and, in turn, sociological activities contribute to shaping the nature of the social phenomena that are being studied. Although I am committed to a form of "objectivity," this cannot be achieved simply by perfecting the application of the natural science model.

A Historical Survey of Assessments of the State of Sociology

An analysis of the ways in which sociologists have perceived themselves and their discipline over the past half-century provides us with a social and historical context for our critique of the present state of the discipline. Here I am interested in delineating the broad shifts in the evaluations by sociologists of their own discipline; I make no pretense of exhaustive coverage of the literature on the field since World War II.

In the early history of American sociology, sociologists directed considerable attention to the field, but they focused mainly on its origins and general orientation. It was only after World War II that assessments of the state and direction of the field burgeoned. In the postwar period, some relatively distinct historical patterns emerged. Within the first two decades or so after the war, a "handbook" tradition favorably evaluating the field took hold. This was followed by a decade or so when assessments more critical of the field received greater attention. By the early 1980s, the trend toward more positive evaluations of the discipline reemerged, but these assessments differed substantially from those appearing in the two decades after World War II.

The Handbook Tradition (1945–1968)

Although some critiques of the field appeared before and immediately after World War II, the most representative form of disciplinary assessment in the first two decades or so of the postwar period was the handbook. A characteristic feature of this tradition was to have editors select contributors to survey, synthesize, and evaluate the major developments, issues, and problems in various subareas of the field. Among the first handbooks was a volume edited by Gurvitch and Moore (1945); followed by Gittler (1957); Merton, Broom, and Cottrell (1957); Roucek (1958); Lipset and Smelser (1961); Faris (1964); and Parsons (1968).

In general, these volumes expressed considerable excitement and optimism about the state of the discipline and its future prospects, becoming progressively more sanguine over the course of the period. Although all these volumes acknowledged various unresolved problems in the discipline, they typically evinced a belief that the obstacles could be overcome with more research and money—especially through greater funding for large-scale research by the federal government. The profession thus was portrayed in these sociological reports as making steady progress toward the status of a truly scientific discipline.

The great excitement and enthusiasm—approaching euphoria in some cases—of American sociologists in the post-World War II era corresponded broadly with great numerical growth in the discipline. This period also corresponded closely with increasing American political power and economic prosperity. In the main, sociologists' worldviews mirrored the optimism and satisfaction found in the broader society. To be sure, the period had its downside—McCarthyism, the Korean conflict, Sputnik—but, all in all, it was a time of great confidence and optimism. Sociologists could point to greatly increased public recognition. Riesman (1950) and Bell (1960), among others, provided conceptual frameworks (as well as supporting data) regarding American society that aided politicians, journalists, and the broader citizenry to make better sense of the social and cultural changes with which they were grappling. Also, sociologists were increasingly incorporated into the policy-making apparatus, particularly at the federal level as the welfare state expanded as a result of President Lyndon Johnson's Great Society programs. And, slowly but surely, sociologists began to acquire a relatively larger share of federal funding for research and training.

Even as the handbook tradition mirrored the enthusiastic optimism of the postwar period of the broader society, a few sociologists demurred from the disciplinary celebration. Before World War II, Lynd (1939) critically assessed developing trends within the discipline. And Sorokin (1956) and Mills (1959) launched critiques of the discipline at the height of its optimism. Others, such as those by Bramson (1961) and Stein and Vidich (1963), presaged the emergence of a much broader based critique of sociology in the late 1960s. By this time, the optimistic view of the broader society also had shifted considerably.

The Critical Interlude (1965–1975)

Certain challenges to the cultural values and social structure began to emerge in the late 1950s. The civil rights movement exposed fundamental weaknesses in the "democratic order." This movement served as one stimulus for the student protests of the 1960s, which, in turn, coalesced with the anti-Vietnam war protests. And then came the feminist attack against the patriarchal order. All in all, the conception of sustained social progress was eroded, and we witnessed a crisis of confidence in existing institutional arrangements, which was pushed even further by the Watergate debacle.

But countervailing trends in the 1960s also were under way. The neoconservative movement arose in part as a reaction to the welfare state, as defined by Johnson's Great Society, as well as to the civil rights, student, antiwar, and feminist movements. Neoconservatives called for constraints on the size and scope of the welfare state, thereby undermining support for sociology, which was being integrated increasingly into this apparatus (cf. Gouldner 1970).

Both the institutional crisis and the neoconservative reaction to it served as a brake on the "rising expectations" of the citizenry. Sociologists typically responded in two ways: with a more somber assessment of the field, or a critical analysis of the discipline. The latter receives emphasis herein. Admittedly, most of the critique originated on the periphery of the discipline, much of it from a new generation of sociologists entering the field in the late 1960s.

But even within the core of the discipline, some criticisms appeared. *The American Sociologist*, launched by the ASA in the early 1960s with the intent of furthering the professionalization process, came in the late 1960s to include reports on the discipline that raised questions—albeit mostly implicit and of rather limited range—about the current state of sociology. These were primarily empirical studies, adopting the prevailing methodology of the field in describing some of its characteristics in quantitative terms. In this respect, they more closely mirrored the discipline than constituted a thoroughgoing critique of it. Yet many of the articles suggested that the ideals espoused in the discipline diverged from actual practices. Only rarely, as in the case of an article by Martin Nicolaus (1969), did the journal publish explicit, fundamental critiques of American sociology in its academic and professional forms. These essays emphasized political and ideological presuppositions of the discipline, and many sociologists found the resultant charges highly offensive and unacceptable.

Some of the most critical commentaries on the state and nature of the discipline during this "crisis period" appeared in "little magazines"—a spontaneous set of publications emanating from various sociology departments, and often edited and produced by graduate students. A few of these journals, notably the *Insurgent Sociologist* (now *Critical Sociology*), have survived, thereby providing a continuing critique of American society and the state of sociology.

During the late 1960s and early 1970s, the effort to give self-conscious expression to a general sociology of sociology also was taking place. Considerable variation existed within this broad framework. The edited works by Tiryakian (1971) and Reynolds and Reynolds (1970) and the monographs by Friedrichs (1970) and Gouldner (1970) were the best known. Among these, the most sustained fundamental critique of the discipline explicitly informed by core sociological principles was Gouldner's (1970) *The Coming Crisis of Western Sociology*.

Within the sociological community, the appearance of an explicit sociology of sociology created a momentary, and ambivalent, stir. Friedrichs's (1970) *A Sociology of Sociology*, the least critical and controversial of the works aimed at an explicit sociological analysis of the field, received professional recognition in the form of an award from the ASA. Most of the others received little sustained attention. Only Gouldner's effort, directed at one aspect of the field, aroused disciplinary discussion over a sustained period. Yet the response to his book typically was negative, indeed hostile. The general character of the response is best illustrated by essays in the *American Journal of Sociology*. A review symposium of Gouldner's book appeared in the September 1971 issue, and a set of articles in July 1972 criticized his work. In addition, exchanges between Gouldner and his critics were published in 1973. Thus, the critique of *The Coming Crisis of Western Sociology* spanned almost two years in one of the three leading journals in American sociology.

Whether occasioned by benign neglect or fervent hostility, the sociology of sociology framework never influenced the discipline in any substantial sense. Gouldner's work won few adherents and has not been extended systematically. Such widely used survey texts on contemporary sociological theory as those by Turner (1991) and Wallace and Wolf (1991) ignore his contributions. Turner, for example, discusses such figures as Hechter, Emerson, and Cook, whose theories are derivative, while ignoring Gouldner's creative effort to formulate an alternative worldview within the sociology of knowledge tradition.

Contemporary Assessments of the Field

The demise of the more self-consciously critical sociology of sociology that emerged in the late 1960s paralleled the waning of the broader institutional crisis. By the mid-1970s, American society was less overtly contentious, and a more somber, back-to-business mood emerged. Conservative politics continued to make strides, culminating in Ronald Reagan's election in 1980. One of the major features of the conservative resurgence that propelled Reagan into the presidency was a sharp attack on the welfare state. This attack represented a challenge to the apparatus through which the discipline of sociology had gained increased status in the academic and broader governmental hierarchies. Even more specifically, the Reagan administration proposed severe reductions in governmental support for sociological research. Although the actual reductions were never as severe as those proposed, these political efforts signaled a threat to the scientific identity and status of sociology.

As these changes in American society unfolded, the self-understanding of the discipline also shifted. The assessments appearing during the 1980s revived the handbook tradition, albeit with certain differences from the earlier versions. Three such volumes—Short (1981), Borgatta and Cook (1988), and Smelser (1988)—constitute the most recent efforts to examine and report on the current state of sociology.

These three volumes, although differing in certain respects, represent a common approach to surveying and assessing the field. Each selectively surveys and comments on theoretical and methodological issues within several areas of contemporary sociology, with some attention to the future prospects and continuing problems in these areas. Each is presented as a relatively comprehensive representation of the state of contemporary sociology. These volumes reveal differences in their particular assessments of the field, but they collectively present a favorable overview of sociology's general direction, progress, and future prospects. But these volumes also reflect broader social developments in the 1980s. They give expression to a cautious optimism that sociology is on the right track but that there are problems to be addressed. Short's *The State of Sociology* (1981) bears closest resemblance to earlier handbooks. Although the euphoric celebration of the discipline of the earlier period is less in evidence, the volume still reads as a paean for sociology in the face of troubling conditions. It emphasizes the sustained accumulation of knowledge and great advances in sociological research. These developments have, according to the editor's and authors' reasoning, resulted from expanded and sophisticated databases. And the contributors promise continued progress if sociologists adopt formal theory and rigorous quantitative methods.

Borgatta and Cook, and the Smelser volume, published toward the end of the decade, are somewhat less sanguine than Short's account of the discipline. Although these volumes, too, present an overall positive assessment of the field, they direct greater attention to problematic issues confronting sociology. In Borgatta and Cook, several authors, for instance, suggest that the future of sociology requires a greater accommodation to applied sociology. In fact, Rossi (1990), an ex-president of the ASA, in reviewing the volume suggests that its contents provide evidence that "clearly something is wrong with sociology," for this collection demonstrates severe fragmentation within the discipline that has no "singular vision of the future" and no central concerns. This preoccupation with disciplinary fragmentation is given more explicit attention in the volume edited by Smelser.

Smelser's Handbook and Related Literature

Among the recent volumes, Smelser's *Handbook of Sociology* has received by far the greatest attention. In the official review journal of the ASA, *Contemporary Sociology* ("Symposium..." 1989), the Smelser *Handbook* has been accorded a distinction unequaled by any other treatise. A review symposium involving fourteen reviewers (including the two special editors) and covering thirty-nine double-column pages of text serves as an extraordinary validation of the work's perceived significance to the field. (Indeed, the symposium constitutes a "cultural event," to use Smelser's *mot* in his response to the critics of the volume.) Eight additional pages of *Contemporary Sociology* ("Commentary..." 1989) were allocated to Smelser's rejoinder and comments by others.

The *Handbook* in conjunction with the review symposium (and the subsequent commentaries) come as close to the "official" representation of the discipline as we are likely to possess for some years to come. Nonetheless, Smelser's collection, for all the widespread attention it received, represents a rather conventional extension of the handbook tradition. The contributors selectively survey what they regard as the main features of the field. Their analysis nearly always involves an overview of theoretical issues and research efforts existing in a subfield. Attention routinely is directed to recent accomplishments and to the direction in which the subfield is moving. Unresolved problems restricting further developments usually are given some attention. Overall, the chapters highlight selected aspects of a subfield, often glossing over highly contentious issues.

In the Introduction to the volume, Smelser assesses some of the general trends set forth in chapters of the *Handbook*. He draws particular attention to the proliferation of many specialized subfields. Differentiation of subject matter, perspectives, and methodological styles is, he concludes, the mark of the discipline. Smelser (1988:18) notes:

> Virtually every chapter in the book, . . . reveals . . . the "invasion" of
> all subfields of sociology by the different and competing perspec-
> tives and paradigms that characterizes the field as a whole. This
> makes for two effects: the increased diversity and richness of
> interpretative frameworks within each subfield, and a lesser degree

of consensus about what is the central organizing basis of knowledge generated in that subfield.

The reactions of the reviewers who made up the review symposium of the *Handbook* were, as might be expected, diverse. Still, the issue of disciplinary fragmentation emerged as a major theme. Nearly all reviewers expressed concern that the volume did not adequately and accurately reflect the extent of diversity in the field. Many reviewers were at least as concerned with what was omitted as with the treatment of what was included. In general, reviewers agreed with Smelser that a major identifying feature of contemporary sociology is the degree of differentiation (or fragmentation) it displays. The collective response of the reviewers suggests that the *Handbook of Sociology* would have been more adequately representative of "sociology as it stands" if additional topics and areas had been included.

Smelser, while noting the richness of disciplinary diversity, nevertheless expresses concern about consensus and codification as the field moves in the direction "of all periphery, no core." Although the editors of the review symposium, Craig Calhoun and Kenneth Land (1989), claim not to be unduly troubled with the field's diversity, they nonetheless contend that a more authoritative council—in effect, an "elite core" of sociologists—should determine the status of the field and how it should be represented. Specifically, they reason as follows (1989:475):

> If handbooks are to be canonical statements—as to some extent they must be—then it seems sociology would do well to pay attention to the editor's role. Revising or reaffirming a canon is too important and difficult a task for a single editor, or even two, chosen by a publisher. This is not simply a criticism of Smelser's efforts. On the contrary, part of the problem is precisely that sociology as a discipline does not have strong institutional settings for developing— and contesting—canonical representations of the field.

The growing concern with differentiation is not only reflected by the responses to the *Handbook*. This issue has received special attention in recent years by several well-known sociologists. Blalock, an ex-president of the ASA, has argued (1987) that the profession should standardize and require the use of methodological rigor within the discipline. He would in effect establish the validity of sound research procedures through the administrative apparatus of the professional association. Gibbs (1989) takes a somewhat different approach. He argues the need for a "core concept" around which the field can organize its theoretical and research efforts—and the core concept he favors is that of "social control."

My assessment of the current state of sociology differs from the perception represented in Smelser's *Handbook*, the reviewers' responses to that volume, as well as various sources evaluating the field. What is missing in this literature is any sense of sociology's marginalization within the broader intellectual community. In failing to perceive the discipline's most fundamental problem, sociologists have given scant attention to the possible source of the marginalization in the methodological hegemony that undergirds the diversity within the field. To the contrary, sociologists often reason that closer adherence to ever-more-technical scientific procedures—joined with more effective bureaucratic action—is the best way to deal with what is wrong in the discipline. In subsequent analysis, I argue that the preponderant reliance on the natural science model both derives from and contributes to the maintenance of the broader social structure in which sociology is located.

Aside from Smelser's brief comments, no author in the *Handbook* or reviewer in the symposium views the problematic conditions of the field as deriving from the institutional context in which sociology exists. Even Erikson, perhaps the most broadly reflective critic of the volume, shuns this kind of analysis. The expanding relationship between sociology and the state apparatus and the place of sociology in the changing nature of higher education in the United States are important contextual issues that are ignored. Consequently, questions regarding the implications for sociological inquiry of the discipline's integration into the broader institutional and organizational context on a societal and global level are not raised.

If we are to deal with the threat to sociology's intellectual viability, we must examine the linkage between features of the discipline and the historical conditions and structural forces of the broader society. Ironically, as indicated by the *Handbook* and the responses to it, sociologists are reluctant to examine their discipline in these terms.

A Reinterpretation of the State of Sociology

We suggested in the Introduction that contrary to the conventional understanding, evidence supports the conclusion that a new paradigm now dominates American sociology. This paradigm constitutes the methodological commonalities that underlie theoretical and substantive fragmentation—a "methodological hegemony" committed to uncovering natural and universal invariant relationships through an emphasis on quantitative techniques and procedures. Through the application of narrow, well-designed research studies, precision and replicability can, according to the current version, be attained. Such precision and replicability are possible though the quantification process.

Ironically, my views regarding methodological hegemony (as we have defined it) are supported by Smelser. Although Smelser, in his contribution to the *Handbook* and in his rebuttal to the critics of the volume, acknowledges the problems posed by fragmentation and increased specialization, he speaks also of a trend toward increased reliance of sociologists on the trappings of the natural science model. In discussing external influences on sociology, he notes pressures on the social and behavioral sciences pushing them in the direction of more sophisticated techniques and procedures as a means to maintain a low political profile and avoid controversy. Smelser (1988:15) states:

> The main response . . . is for spokesmen of the behavioral and social sciences to represent themselves as adhering to the model of positive science, as using *methodologically sound* techniques, and as, therefore, supportable on the grounds that they are legitimately scientific. This strategy emerges . . . as the one most likely to blunt criticism both within the donor agencies and on the part of other governmental officials. In the end . . . this response is a victory of the positive science emphasis. (Italics added.)

Smelser goes on to reason that the emphasis on technique and positive science dominates the discipline and in effect marginalizes the philosophical, moral, and social-problems traditions that have been the intellectual centerpiece of sociology. Smelser notes that major upheavals might reverse these trends, but in keeping with the thinking of his mentor, Talcott Parsons, Smelser seems to accept the inevitability of this "evolutionary process," and he appears to be unwilling to actively confront and redirect these trends.

The committed search for invariant relationships and the utilization of rigorous techniques and procedures as the dominant paradigm in contemporary American sociology have been pushed forward by a variety of sociologists. Certainly, the technical methodologists have been the most visible champions of this orientation. They include a somewhat diverse group that have differed among themselves as to the most appropriate logic and techniques to be employed in analyzing social data. They are, however, united in their call for technical rigor in the production of scientific knowledge. Among the more prominent of these sociologists during the post-World War II years have been Paul Lazarsfeld and his student, James Coleman, as well as Otis Dudley Duncan, Peter Blau, Hubert Blalock, Leo Goodman, Stanley Lieberson, and a number of sociologists who have been associated with William Sewell and the "Wisconsin School." The call for technical rigor has dominated *Sociological Methodology*, an official publication of the ASA. Moreover, most of the recent editors of the *American Sociological Review*—including Sheldon Stryker (1982 to 1986) and

William Form (1987 to 1989)—have been ardent advocates of the particular kind of methodological hegemony with which we are concerned.

While the aforementioned sociologists have focused their energies on refining techniques for collecting and analyzing data, they typically take for granted the underlying theoretical premises on which their scientific model rests. They have not detailed the domain assumptions (to appropriate Gouldner's terminology) or the basic presuppositions (to use the concept employed by Alexander). Some of these scholars are more adequate in analyzing the general procedures of the natural science model, but these are not seen in the context of the domain assumptions underlying the model.

Lieberson's (1985) *Making It Count* points out some of the issues I wish to address. His analysis constitutes a well-reasoned critique of the uncritical use of statistical analysis carried out by sociologists, but he fails to explicate the domain assumptions on which his commitment to statistical analysis rests. In order to understand the meanings and implications of the natural science model for the discipline of sociology, we must understand the basic procedures of the methodological paradigm, as well as the presuppositions that underlie them.

I am, to reiterate, employing the term, *natural science model*, to encompass the writings of more sociologists than the technical methodologists discussed above. The natural science model also occupies a central place in the work of a large number of sociological theorists who have been labeled (or have labeled themselves) as positivists. Yet commitment to the natural science model extends beyond the avowed positivists to theorists who appear to differ significantly from the positivist orientation. Yet the positivistically inclined theorists are the most visible and ardent proponents of the "hard" version of the natural science model. These include George Homans, James Coleman, Randall Collins, Jonathan Turner, and Jack Gibbs, among a host of others. At first glance, it might appear that such theorists would have carefully examined and explicated the domain assumptions underlying the techniques and research procedures that constitute the methodological paradigm of contemporary sociology. Although Homans (1987) and Gibbs (1972) have raised issues relevant to domain assumptions of the model, their efforts remain inadequate. They are intent primarily on justifying, in a rather abstract manner, the necessity of a version of the scientific method instead of specifying the presuppositions of the natural science model as they conceive it.

In addition to the "hard" version of the natural science model, there also is a "soft" version of this perspective. Although these theorists do not label themselves as positivists, their basic assumptions are essentially the same as those of the theorists mentioned above. Perhaps the most influential advocate of the "soft" version of the natural science model has been Robert K. Merton.[1] A sympathetic interpreter, Crothers (1987), describes Merton's perspective as a form of positivism. Merton's presuppositions are in keeping with sociologists identified with the positivist tradition. This comes to the fore in his work on the sociology of knowledge (1945b) and, in particular, his early advocacy of the logico-deductive method (1945a) (which has little or no relationship to the logic of his functional analysis).

Then we find sociologists such as Wallerstein, some of whose work we greatly admire. But, Wallerstein entertains a "split vision" of the sociological enterprise. On the one hand, he definitely grapples with grand problems and to some extent aligns himself with the emancipatory tradition of sociological theory. On the other hand, he and his colleagues (Hopkins and Wallerstein 1982) are committed to a belief in invariant laws of history as reflected in the Konratieff cycles.

A number of sociologists who ordinarily are associated with the humanist tradition are closer to the natural science model than often is recognized. Peter Berger (1986) is a case in point. In one of his more recent books, which is written in defense of capitalism, Berger concludes his analysis by listing fifty propositions that are cast in natural science model terms.

The overall goal of the proponents of the natural science model, as interpreted by sociologists, is to produce objective knowledge regarding the structure of a natural social world through the use of rigorous and precise technical procedures and methods. But this effort is predicated on domain assumptions about the nature of the social world. Commitment to technical procedures as the basis for objective knowledge presupposes the existence of a social world possessing certain properties objectively given in nature.

Central Domain Assumptions

I consider three *interrelated* presuppositions of this view of a science of society.

1. A structured social order. The most salient presupposition of the natural science model is that the social world possesses an order given in nature. This order exists in the form of systematically structured relationships between and among events and things of the social world. These structured relationships comprise regular, recurrent, and—ideally, at least—invariant associations as properties of nature. Structural relationships given in nature are expressible in terms of general scientific laws explaining the nature and necessity of naturally existing social relationships. These structured, ordered social relationships and the scientific laws that explain how the social world operates are what sociologists seek to discover through rigorous and precise research procedures.

Such sociologists as Homans and Merton differ in their degree of commitment to this principle and the manner in which they articulate the nature of these laws. Nonetheless, these sociologists presuppose the existence of social phenomena structured in a systematic manner. In turn, these ordered relationships are assumed to be discoverable as facts of nature.

Within the social sciences, the clearest illustration of the presupposition of a structured social world has been that of neoclassical economists regarding the laws of supply and demand. Many economists held to the proposition that the law of supply and demand was such that there should be no efforts to modify market forces. Such intervention would interfere with the laws of nature. Depressions were seen as the logical outcomes of natural laws and should be permitted to run their course, for these drove out inefficient entrepreneurs and left only the more efficient ones in the marketplace.

Although sociologists never have been able to point to this kind of natural law, they have attempted to do so. Michels's (1949) "iron law of oligarchy" illustrates this kind of effort. Despite the diversity within the discipline, the search for invariant relationships given in nature, even when stated in probabilistic terms, is the *raison d'être* for much of the effort in current sociological research.

2. Natural determination. A second domain assumption is that the social phenomena of the world stand in a naturally determined relationship to one another. The order of the social world is the product of some entities (forces) acting on other entities (objects) in regularly recurring ways. Many sociologists are hesitant to assign cause in the context of structured relationships. Since Hume's (1966) critique of cause as a nonobservable phenomenon, this concept has been the subject of extended debate within the physical and social sciences.[2] Yet sociologists who adhere to the natural science model, even those who eschew "causal language," presuppose a fixed and recurring relationship among phenomena that can be accounted for in terms of necessary and sufficient conditions. These sociologists assume that some conditions exist independently of and have consequences for other sets of conditions in ways that are not simply arbitrarily or theoretically established (allowing, of course, for feedback effects). Whenever sociologists speak of "the greater the X, the greater the Y"—such as the greater the occupational differentiation, the greater the suicide rate—they place themselves implicitly within the tradition of which we speak.

Within sociology, the search for invariant universal laws also entails assumptions about the nature of human agents. In naturally determined relationships, human agents are assumed to be objects of forces—external social forces or internal biological and/or psychological forces. As Larson (1981) has argued in justifying the need for greater governmental support of social science research, the common goal of all social science is to understand human behavior in terms of prior conditions. As I later note, much sociological research attempts to specify relationships between aspects of social structure or culture as external forces and human behavior, most often in an aggregate sense.

3. An independent, external social world. A third major set of assumptions undergirding the natural science model concerns the relation of the researcher to the social world under investigation. Proponents of the model presuppose that researchers can conduct their activities independently of the broader social and cultural processes in which they live and work and which they investigate. Adherents of this premise assume that properties of the social world are given in nature and exist independently of social agents' conceptions of them. As givens in nature, structured relationships can be discovered by independent investigators, as these relationships actually exist—as facts of nature.

Moreover, sociologists assume that if they can establish rigorous research procedures and techniques for collecting and analyzing data, they can sustain an independence of the social world they investigate. Researchers can thereby maintain value neutrality and attain objectivity in their research.

The more theoretically inclined proponents of the natural science model recognize that the beliefs and values of researchers may contaminate the research process. Lieberson, for example, acknowledges the possibility of bias in developing and evaluating causal principles. He writes (1985:178): "For reasons that are easily understood, researchers and theorists are influenced by their own experiences." But he concludes that "All we can do . . . is watch for biases in our tendencies" (1985:179). Because he does not perceive how the nature of the broader social order, particularly the role of bureaucratic organization in the contemporary world, impinges on the investigator and the research process, he does not regard this condition as a fundamental issue in research design.

Procedures and Practices of the Natural Science Model

The domain assumptions outlined above are the foundations for the increasing emphasis on rigorous and well-defined research procedures employed by sociologists in their efforts to establish objective knowledge of the social world. These include the quantification of data, the measurement of variables, and the use of a version of experimental design.

1. *Quantification of data.* Inasmuch as proponents of the natural science orientation assume an ordered and determined social world, it is hardly surprising that they call for a precise specification of structured relationships. This leads them to quantify the data regarding the social world. What this means is not altogether agreed on among social scientists. For example, there has been a fair amount of debate as to whether or not "ordinal data" are a form of quantification. But we can, for our purposes, put these internecine controversies aside, for advocates of the natural science model accept the principle that social data are quantifiable.

The acceptance of the principle of quantification rests on the premise that the structured relationships of the social world are composed of discrete and identifiable entities existing independently in nature. These discrete social entities are assumed to exist, as are the things in the physical world, as quantities. For example, Gibbs (1972) and Blalock (1969) speak of "properties" of the social world existing in amounts. As such, social phenomena can be measured, thereby making possible statistical analysis of the relationships between and among entities of the social world. Thus, the quantification of social data provides a sense of exactitude based on measurable entities.

Additionally, quantification of social data articulates with the use of survey research based on probability sampling in which discrete individuals are the units of analysis. When quantification is associated with traditional statistical analysis, the units of analysis not only are assumed to be discrete in nature but typically are regarded as equal to one another. It follows, therefore, that such data are additive: The whole is the sum of the parts. Probability sampling rests on these principles. In some circumstances, these premises match the data of the social world reasonably well. For example, data collected on age and sex of a population present no great difficulties. Also, in social orders where we find the idea that one person equals one vote, probability sampling predicated on assumptions of discreteness and equality does no violence to data associated with this principle. But in many other instances, assumptions relating to quantification do a serious disservice to the nature of the data (a point to which I return later).

2. *Measurement of variable association.* A second set of procedures of the natural science model closely interrelated with those involved in the quantification of social data is what Lieberson (1985) speaks of as the "control variable approach" or what Ragin (1987) refers to as the "variable-oriented approach" in social research. Although the variable approach manifests itself in a variety of formats and vocabularies, the basic concern in all these varieties is to establish the linkage between and among naturally occurring social entities conceived as variables. This feature is based on the premise that the phenomena of the social world vary and that variation in some phenomena are associated systematically with variation in others. Naturally occurring social relationships can be expressed in terms of independent and dependent variables. The role of the sociologist is to measure the effect of the variation in the independent variable on variation in the dependent variable. These relationships can be expressed in highly complex ways involving, for example, multiple independent variables, intervening variables, and various considerations of association and causality, but all these conceptions rest on the common premise that the social world is comprised naturally of measurable variables systematically associated with one another. William Sewell (1985), a former ASA president, has stated that 85 percent of all American sociologists engage in some form of variable research.

This disciplinary pattern is so pervasive that many younger sociologists trained in the 1970s and 1980s find it difficult (if not impossible) to reason about the social world in terms other than variable associations. Yet Ragin's (1987) *The Comparative Method* suggests that there are alternative orientations. Ragin, like Lieberson, is a well-informed practitioner of the natural science model who is aware of many of the difficulties and limitations of analyzing social phenomena in variable terms.

Ragin sets the case study off against the variable approach in sociological investigation and then seeks to meld these two approaches. He notes that the case study method can provide a more holistic orientation toward the study of social reality than is available in the variable-oriented approach. Yet Ragin is unclear about the meaning of this holistic orientation; he does not examine the logic underlying the relationships of the parts to the whole.

Ultimately, Ragin discusses the case approach because he wishes to modify and expand on the natural science model as it has been employed, for he recognizes that in comparative cross-cultural research it generally is impossible to study in depth more than just a few cases—particularly nations—at any one time. Ragin, who seeks to balance the case study and the variable approach, rests his defense of the case-study orientation on a version of the experimental design as undergirding the scientific method.

Before examining the experimental design as a basic procedure of the natural science model, one must consider still another aspect of the variable approach in sociology. There is a major division between sociologists who adhere to "induction" in contrast to the logicodeductive method.

Many sociologists, including Lieberson (1985), Sewell (1988), Skocpol (1984), and others, are committed to constructing theories through some form of inductive reasoning. They begin with data and use these data as a basis for developing propositions or theories. One cannot examine here the problems associated with the meaning of induction, including Popper's (1965) argument that the logic of "induction" does not exist. Suffice it to say that a number of sociologists—such as Homans (1982), Gibbs (1972), and Jonathan Turner (1991)—insist on the logico-deductive format in testing hypotheses or propositions. Formal theory construction calls for setting forth conditions and universal statements and deriving propositions that are testable. These sociologists are convinced that there must be a highly formalized linkage of theory to hypotheses. Still, whatever the differences between the inductivists and those advocating the logico-deductive orientation, both are committed to the variable orientation (and often to some form of experimental design).

3. *Use of the experimental design.* This procedure is viewed essentially as sorting out "causal" factors in social analysis. In some respects, one might contend that experimentation is even more fundamental than either the quantification process or the variable approach. One finds a group of scholars such as

Barrington Moore and Theda Skocpol—both of whom rely on qualitative data—depending heavily on the work of John Stuart Mill.

Yet ideally, experimentation is to be linked with quantitative procedures. About the only subfield where this is feasible (in any realistic manner) is social psychology. In point of fact, most sociologists work with data sets that are nonexperimental in nature. The social survey tradition, on which so many sociologists rely, falls into this category. Still, as Lieberson (1985:18ff) has reasoned, sociologists use a variety of statistical techniques such as "log linear analysis, path coefficients, multivariate regression techniques, demographic forms of standardization, and various cross-tabulation measures" as a means of approximating the experimental design. Lieberson observes (1985:19): I believe that most practitioners . . . would begrudgingly admit that such procedures are not quite the same as a true experiment. For the most part, however, such statistical manipulations would be seen as a "reasonable" approximation of the ideal—reasonable insofar as the plausible controls are taken into account. Lieberson goes on to raise questions about this approach to analyzing social data, but he does so within the framework of the natural science model.[3]

Countervailing Orientations

Although the natural science model has become the dominant orientation in contemporary American sociology, one can point to major figures in the field who, in the post World War II era, have advanced positions that are at odds with the natural science orientation. I single out Blumer and Gouldner for special attention. Both articulated telling criticisms of aspects of the natural science model. Yet neither did so in a systematic manner. What they did was to provide some of the building blocks on which we can construct an alternative conception of social science.

By singling out Blumer and Gouldner, another issue emerges. Both were committed to empirical analysis. Thus, it is possible to be highly critical of the natural science model and yet espouse empirical investigation of regularities within the social order. Still, these regularities do not necessarily involve invariant laws of nature.

Blumer's criticisms involve primarily a sustained objection to the procedures—and indirectly to the domain assumptions—of the natural science model. In keeping with the views of George Herbert Mead, Blumer argues that human agents are not, as the advocates of the natural science model would have it, discrete, isolated individuals. Instead, the concept of human beings is such that people are dependent on others for their definition of who they are. The notion of discrete individuals does violence to the nature of human nature. Blumer based his objections to public opinion research, as conventionally carried out, on his questioning of the premises on which the research rested.

Perhaps Blumer's most direct challenge to the natural science model was his critique of the variable concept in social research. He reasoned that variables are human constructions and are not part of any natural order. He raised a set of questions about the variable approach that authors of textbooks on research methods do not examine. In light of Blumer's relentless critique of some of the "sacred" premises of the procedures of the natural science model, it is little wonder that the symbolic interactionist tradition has been given short shrift within the discipline.

As for Gouldner, he did not systematically criticize the natural science model as such. In fact, one of the serious limitations of his *The Coming Crisis of Western Sociology* (1970) is his preoccupation with Parsons and his failure to deal with the dominant paradigm emerging within the discipline. The emphasis on rigorous technique as a means of creating a science of society had been under way for some time when he composed his well-known work.

Gouldner's critique of the natural science model concerns the relationship of sociologists to the world they study. Gouldner, like Mills, conceives of sociologists as active agents in either supporting or challenging the social order they investigate. Sociologists can never remove themselves from the social order they seek to describe and analyze. Although Gouldner sharply attacks symbolic interactionists such as Howard Becker for their stress on the adaptation of human agents to the social order and their consequent failure to recognize that sociologists can be active agents in the creation of a more humane world, Gouldner nevertheless has more in common with Mead and Blumer than he would have admitted. For, like Blumer, Gouldner perceives sociologists as interacting with the world they study. But, as suggested, he, unlike Blumer, was intent on changing the world, not merely accepting it as it is.

A Critique of the Natural Science Model

Although sociologists such as Blumer and Gouldner have questioned various dimensions of the use of the natural science model in sociology, my goal is to spell out more fully the serious limitations of the prevailing methodological paradigm—with its emphasis on refinement of procedures and, especially, techniques—in sociological inquiry.

I believe the critique of the natural science model must be anchored in sociological reasoning and not in the philosophy of science. Typically, philosophers of science (both of the natural and social sciences) have been inhospitable to a sociological perspective in the examination of science. Popper (1950), for example, has strongly objected to the sociology of knowledge orientation in general and its application to scientific inquiry in particular. Admittedly, Thomas Kuhn (1970), in his examination of the development of science, is more sympathetic to a sociology of knowledge orientation, but he has not advanced the kinds of criticisms I hope to set forth.

In fact, philosophers of science (and sociologists who have been influenced by this tradition) have devoted very little attention to the theoretical basis—the domain assumptions—of the natural science model, and in particular to the broader social context in which the natural science model, as practiced by social scientists, is embedded.

In order to examine critically the natural science model, I adopt one version of the sociology of knowledge perspective. This orientation is predicated on the premise that social activities are shaped by the social and cultural context in which they occur. Sociologists generally are ambivalent toward this point of view. They are, however, far more comfortable with the version of the sociology of knowledge put forward by Merton than that advanced by Gouldner. Merton (1945a) wrote an early article on the sociology of knowledge, and even now this essay remains a highly influential overview of this perspective. In addition, his theory and research on the sociology of science reflect his adept use of some of the principles undergirding the sociology of knowledge. Even in his sociological analysis of science, he has concentrated on social conditions affecting motivational patterns of scientists instead of focusing on structural conditions impinging on the processes and products of the natural science model. Similarly, he has been unwilling to turn the sociology of knowledge back on the discipline of sociology.

Gouldner, in contrast, turned his version of the sociology of knowledge back on the field itself in the form of a highly critical sociology of sociology. One could hypothesize that this was one major source (although not the sole source) of the hostile reaction toward him within the discipline.

One can illustrate aspects of the Merton orientation of the sociology of knowledge by examining certain informative works on statistical analysis published in the 1980s. I have already mentioned Lieberson's *Making It Count.* In this work he calls for a "social theory of data," which one would surmise must involve some use of the sociology of knowledge. In an even more explicit manner, Duncan (1984), in one of his last major publications, wrote about the history of quantification. He spoke of quantification as a social process, and he spent considerable space in detailing this argument. Duncan is essentially committed to the view that sociologists who analyze data collected by agencies over which they have no control face serious problems in carrying out scientific research. In effect, Duncan is concerned with the autonomy of the researcher vis-a-vis the data one seeks to analyze.

In keeping with Duncan's analysis, I also note Alonso and Starr's edited *The Politics of Numbers* (1987). In this volume, a variety of prominent sociologists grapple with the political construction of survey and census data, and with "official statistics" more generally. They accept the argument that quantification is a social process. I readily acknowledge the contributions to a sociology of knowledge analysis in the works of Lieberson, Duncan, and many of the contributors to the Alonso and Starr volume. I differ, however, in fundamental respects with these authors, for they have failed to confront the basic contradictions of the natural science model when applied to the social world.

The fundamental contradiction of the natural science model lies in sociologists' acceptance of a naturally ordered social world that is "causally" determined for the human agents they study but from whose laws of nature sociologists are exempt. This thesis is stated boldly, and thus one must elaborate on it at some length.

One defense by the adherents of the natural science model is that such problems can be met through the self-correcting mechanisms of science. Through rigorous procedures (including formalization of theory) and standardized techniques, we can generate research that can be replicated by other social scientists, thereby eliminating bias resulting from the experiences of individual researchers. And through standardization and replication of sociological investigations, we can uncover relationships that exist in nature independent of individual investigators. The routinized, rigorous application of technical procedures ensures that scientific sociology will become a reality.

That response, however, begs the question. If indeed quantification is a social process, and if we require a social theory of data, then we cannot eliminate the procedures and techniques that are employed from critical sociological scrutiny. Procedures and techniques, too, are socially produced. The question then arises: Why and how have these procedures and techniques come to have such a "sacred quality" that they are beyond sociological investigation? This situation is all the more problematic when we note that sociologists have produced a Code of Ethics that in effect sets rules as to how and under what circumstances these techniques can be employed. Moreover, Duncan's overall argument suggests that the procedures and techniques for generating quantifiable data are socially defined.

When social researchers claim a social autonomy for themselves, they create a dichotomized conception of human agents: those they study and themselves. They account for the activities of those they study in one way; they account for their own activities in different ways.

The advocates of the natural science model hold two divergent views of human agents: (1) the human agent as object, and 2) the social researchers who study them as subjects. The first have no basic control over their lives in that their activities are governed by natural social laws. But the sociologist can carry out activities unconstrained by the forces governing human nature and the social order. When viewed in these terms, the current methodological procedures are self-serving. They protect sociologists from having to confront the issues associated with the social conditions of their own activities.

This dichotomized conception of human agents must be questioned on both theoretical and empirical grounds. First, researchers indeed are affected by the social and cultural conditions in which they live and work. Second, considerable data lend credence that the researched can and do withhold data from researchers.

Earlier, it was noted that Smelser drew attention to the fact that sociologists have adopted rigorous procedures and techniques to avoid controversy and to maximize funding from the federal government. In other words, one of the social forces calling for stress on technical procedures is that in order to advance their own position in the social structure and to avoid social controversy sociologists have come increasingly to rely on technical procedures.

In addition to some rather transparent flaws in the assumptions and procedures of the natural science model, I am convinced that these assumptions and procedures are unduly restrictive of the sociological enterprise. They have led sociologists to avoid major social issues.

Alternative Sociological Assumptions and Arguments

Although the assumptions of the natural science model are useful in studying a limited range of social phenomena, they place serious strictures on the nature of empirical investigation of fundamental social and moral issues that confront humankind both on a societal and global scale. Consequently, one needs to be committed to proposing an alternative set of domain assumptions on which to base investigation and analysis of the social world, a form of social inquiry that both complements, and is independent of, the natural science model. Although I reject most of the basic presuppositions of the natural science model, I recognize that particular procedures associated with this orientation can be adapted for broader research purposes.

In formulating an alternative set of domain assumptions that undergird social inquiry, I eschew a commitment to historicism. This orientation perceives each social order, or even subset of persons within a social order, as "unique." In its more radical form, historicism is highly relativistic and leads one to avoid any search for commonalities underlying the human experience across cultures and over time. Although historicism, with its relativist foundations, often has been used to criticize the natural science model, one must avoid the solipsism associated with this orientation.

In articulating an alternative set of assumptions to the natural science model, I wish to take account of the social forces that shape human action. In one respect, I agree with the adherents of the natural science model who stress the constraints on human agents. But I part company with them in viewing how these social forces are constructed and how they can be changed and revised. I also differ sharply with social scientists who conceive of themselves as escaping (or being removed) from the social forces that shape the subjects of their investigation. Such an assumption flies in the face of empirical reality.

I now turn to articulating an alternative set of domain assumptions for conducting social inquiry:

1. Rather than assume that the existing social order derives from nature and reflects the fixed state of universal laws, I reason that the structural features of society are socially constituted. When I speak of the social construction (or social constitution) of the social order, I am not adopting the framework of, for example, Berger and Luckman (1966). They conceive of society essentially as being "reified" by human agents. But this leads Berger and Luckman and their followers to conceive of society or social organizations as epiphenomenal. The reality of the social order exists only as defined by human agents. For me, the constructed order (or organizational structure) is not reducible simply to human agents. Organizations are more than mere "reifications"; they have a reality somewhat apart from any human agent or set of human agents.

Society and organizations have an independence from human agents but cannot exist without them. One cannot add up the activities of human agents and thereby understand the organizational structure. Organizations provide resources for agents to attain social objectives, but they also exert powerful constraints on what human agents are able to accomplish. In effect, organizations both enable and constrain human activity (cf. Giddens 1984).

Above all, organizational structures are not a fixed natural order. Sociologists can discover and describe regularities within and among organizations. Yet these regularities may be rent by built-in contradictions (a concept foreign to the natural science model). Most important, human agents have reshaped the organizations of which they are a part, and they will do so in the future.

The major revisions that have taken place in eastern Europe and the former Soviet Union in the late 1980s and early 1990s were never anticipated by social scientists (including sociologists). Yet these occurred because of the collective activities of a variety of human agents working in concert with one another. And contrary to the reasoning of many social scientists, the outcome of the Persian Gulf War of 1991 did not determine the future of the Middle East. The future of the Middle East is still to be constituted as numerous "interest groups" participate in shaping social arrangements within this region.

Even bureaucratic organizations are socially constituted and thus can be reconstituted—at times by force, at times by more conventional means. The outcome of World War II led to a major reorganization of Nazi Germany and the division of East and West Europe. Now many of the resulting bureaucratic arrangements are being remade.

The tension between social structure and human agency is an empirical issue varying across time and space. At times, the constraints exercised by structural patterns over agents will be much greater than on other occasions. Differential power embedded in structural arrangements does exist and exerts varying constraints on participants in these relationships. But these arrangements are constructed, rather than products of nature; consequently, they can potentially be reconstituted in ways that significantly alter the structures of differential power. This alterative conception of the tension between agents and structures is predicated on an alternative conception of human nature.

2. Implied in the foregoing analysis is a conception of human nature that needs to be made explicit. My position differs from that advanced by social scientists who adhere to the economic-man model, to a Freudian conception of human nature, or the views of such behaviorists as Watson and, later, Skinner. In order to clarify a sociologically grounded conception of the nature of human agency, I build on, but revise considerably, the work of George Herbert Mead.

An essential feature of human agency is the "social mind." Most of the writings within the Meadian tradition have given primacy to the social self. But the social self, while an essential feature of human personality, is not as central or distinctive as the social mind. The very nature of the social self depends on the capacities of the mind, for instance, to take the roles of others and to reflect on how the definition of others comes to affect how one views oneself.

The primacy given to the social mind with respect to human nature has deep-seated implications for the social scientific enterprise. First and foremost, human agents are capable of "reflectivity"—of thinking about thinking. But the nature of thinking—its form and its content—is a product of human interaction. The nature of reasoning is not embedded in presocial properties. Even the scientific enterprise, including social scientific reasoning, is social in nature.

While the social mind is a product of interaction, human agents also have the capacity to reflect on the social world of which they are a product. Admittedly, agents often conform to structural constraints and to the expectations of others with whom they interact. Yet these agents are capable of critically distancing themselves from the social relationships in which they are embedded. They have the potential for reflecting on organizational arrangements and decoding the socially constructed nature of the arrangements to which they ordinarily conform. On this basis they may act to construct alternative organizational forms. For example, when Mahatma Gandhi helped to create, in a consciously creative manner, the passive resistance movement against British rule in India, he was able to mobilize a large-scale effort to remake a power structure that many persons deemed as immutable. Gandhi and his supporters ultimately brought about basic changes in the organizational structure within India and within the British Empire.

Although I reject, on theoretical and empirical grounds, the object status of human agents that underlies the natural science model, I do not accept the presupposition that agents are fully self-determining subjects. The social mind is a thoroughly social creation, and the organizational structures, or the interaction patterns that arise within these structures, shape the manner in which human agents reason. In this important respect, social constraints exist on human agents. Nonetheless, human agents are not limited to mere reproductions of social experience. Because of their social minds, human agents are capable of a complex memory system and therefore are able to reflect on their past experiences and bring reason to bear on the social forces that impinge on them. In the process they may blunt, modify, reshape, or reconstitute the social forces created by their predecessors.

The concept of the social mind, as it emerges within the context of social interaction, leads one to challenge another premise of the natural science model as interpreted by sociologists. I have mentioned that this model rests on the assumption that the units of analysis, typically individuals, exist as independent entities. The notion of probability samples that lies at the heart of statistical reasoning rests on this premise. But this assumption is unrealistic for many kinds of social inquiry.

Within this context, one notes also that the natural science model is predicated on the assumption that social scientists can add up these autonomous units to understand the whole, for example, formal organizations. (Typically these units are individuals, though they may be cities, nation-states, or other social units.) Yet inasmuch as individuals are characterized by social minds, they are not autonomous or independent units. Moreover, as noted earlier, the organizations that human beings create over time come to have a reality somewhat apart from human agents, though these organizations cannot exist without human agents. At the same time, this organizational reality is not a fixed order of nature but is subject to being reshaped by reflective social agents.

3. A third central domain assumption of this alternative form of social inquiry is that social researchers interact with, and are products of, their relationships with the subjects they study. Although researchers are able to achieve a particular kind of "objectivity," this conception of objectivity does not correspond with that held by the advocates of the natural science model within sociology. Insofar as objectivity can be achieved, the social researcher must be able to step back and critically examine the world that shapes him or her and in turn can be reshaped to some extent by the ongoing research process.

Earlier I examined the role of the researcher and criticized at some length the often unexamined premises of the natural science model as interpreted by sociologists—namely, that researchers are independent of the social world they study. I return to this issue when considering the problems associated with the validity of social knowledge.

Contemporary Sociology from the Alternative Perspective

One can now elaborate on the alternative domain assumptions as a means for enhancing social inquiry by examining some of the ongoing activities of sociologists in the United States. Sociologists carry out their theorizing and research in the context of large-scale bureaucratic structures and, in a variety of ways, their research serves to legitimate these bureaucratic arrangements. But, sociologists who adhere to the natural science model cannot, given their premises and research procedures, adequately investigate empirically the social organizations that both support and constrain them. In the process, they are unable critically to reflect on their activities and the knowledge they claim to be producing.

Sociologists have been hesitant, even resistant, to examine the discipline's growing incorporation into the nation-state apparatus and into the process of bureaucratic rationalization more generally. The natural science model calls for "value neutrality." But in practice this means that sociologists tacitly accept the values and beliefs as well as the goals of the bureaucratic structures that dominate the societal and global scene. In the name of objectivity, sociologists often serve the managerial sector of the powerful organizations in the United States. At the least, in their research they accept the social categories of, and the definition of the situation by, the powerful sectors of society and in effect do not consider the worldview of the disadvantaged. The natural science model, which assumes the existence of fixed and immutable laws of nature, calls on sociologists to conceive of existing social relationships as "legitimate."

I do not question the fact that research that takes goals of powerful state and corporate organizations as a given provides us with a body of knowledge that must be taken seriously. But such a social perspective does not provide us with support for the existence of natural social laws. We must not confuse the data that conform to the interests of corporate and governmental organizations with immutable social laws.

I can clarify my argument by analyzing the actual practices of sociologists in, for instance, the use of social surveys. In general the questions asked—or in more theoretical terms, the social categories employed by social researchers— often are imposed on diverse sectors of the population (e.g., the truly disavantaged) without permitting these respondents to restate the issues in their own terms. In social surveys, human agents often are viewed as "dependent units"—a premise I seriously question. Goyder (1987), in a full-scale monograph on nonrespondents, has observed that researchers typically treat respondents in highly behavioristic terms—as "objects." Social surveys often rest on the premise that one can reduce "biases" though a high degree of standardization and routinization of the interviewing process. But such reasoning can be questioned on empirical grounds.

At least two kinds of "nonrespondents" can be identified. One is the power elite, the other the truly disavantaged. Some members of the power elite may choose not to answer questionnaires because they view the questions as intrusive. The truly disavantaged often are difficult to reach, and even if they can be located, they may be suspicious of, and uncooperative with, persons who represent authority. The debate regarding the undercount in the 1990 U.S. census is likely to lead some sociologists to question survey data as a means for providing truly "objective" knowledge about U.S. society. Yet this debate has yet to be joined in an informed theoretical manner in the major journals that publish the findings of survey researchers.

In more theoretical terms, the natural science model, on which most survey research is based, articulates with a particular kind of knowledge system—one that is instrumentally important to the efficient operation of society as it is at present constituted. Even when the data are not employed directly in policy making, the data may serve to justify existing social arrangements. Consequently, far from discovering valid and objective scientific knowledge, sociologists carry out research that serves to support powerful organizations in modern society.

At every level of society, but particularly at the national level, administration depends heavily on information. In order to secure information needed for the efficient management of the social order, the state provides support for myriad information-producing organizations and activities. Accessibility to these funds has led many professional organizations, including the American Sociological Association, to relocate their headquarters in Washington, D.C., for the express purpose of greater lobbying access to federal funding sources. The status of the discipline has become dependent on this kind of support.

Perhaps the most prestigious agency for funding sociological research has been the National Science Foundation. It came into existence in order to advance the "national interest." As one looks back on the cold war, one finds that professional sociology was quite willing to accommodate to various administrative demands in order to enhance the federal funding of social research.

In the post-World War II era, most sociologists have come to accept the growth of large-scale organizations and the incorporation of sociologists into them as intrinsically necessary for building a science of society. In the process most sociologists have been unwilling to entertain the possibility that the organizational structures that have emerged are the sources of some of the major social and moral issues on the contemporary societal and global scene. The growth of the national security state, the emergence of life-threatening environmental issues, and the persistence of a truly disadvantaged social stratum are by-products of the bureaucratic organizational structures that support the privileged sector of modern society. As has been reasoned elsewhere, modern bureaucracy, with its emphasis on efficiency, has a built-in form of "social triage." This means that some sectors of the social order become expendable in order for the privileged sector to sustain its privileges.

Sociologists have yet to acknowledge that the great social issues of recent decades are intertwined with the nature of powerful organizational structures. For example, the Savings and Loan Association crisis in the United States, which many persons speak of as the greatest political and economic scandal in American history, emerged within the context of complex organizational structures in both the public and private spheres. A small, privileged elite profited enormously at the expense of the general public.

To understand such organizational patterns as reflected in the Savings and Loan situation, we are immediately confronted with a stark reality: The technical procedures advocated by the natural science builders are inadequate to the task. Yet the powerful grip of this orientation is so great that some sociologists (e.g., DiMaggio 1991) who claim to study organizations contend that there is no difference between such qualitative research as ethnographies and quantitative research based on social surveys.[4] I urge readers to review the statements by sociologists such as DiMaggio carefully and then draw out the implications of the existing strictures placed on studying major organizational issues and trends.

We cannot come to terms with the S&L scandal through the use of social surveys. This kind of research procedure cannot unravel the complex secrecy systems that were an integral part of the S&L crisis. To the extent that sociologists analyze this kind of organizational phenomenon, they must of necessity rely on court records, congressional hearings, journalistic accounts, and intensive interviews. Highly standardized research procedures will not plumb the intricacies of the multi-layered realities involved in this set of organizational activities.

I am not demeaning social surveys. They are useful but are of very limited value in studying the social processes associated with bureaucratic structures. In effect, by calling for the abandonment of the natural science model as it has been defined, one is more empirical than the empiricists.

To investigate adequately, for instance, the S&L phenomenon, one must of necessity interpret the intersection of human agency and organizational structures. One will find that human agents purposively created secrecy systems that they used as a basis for carrying out activities that furthered the narrowly defined goals of a privileged elite at the expense of a much larger public. For example, managers of S&L associations employed technical accounting procedures that sociologists must learn to decode. I clearly recognize the need in modern society for sociologists to understand quantitative data. In this instance, however, knowledge of accounting procedures would be more useful than a knowledge of traditional statistical techniques if organizational activities are to be understood.

The S&L phenomenon also highlights a central theoretical issue that is likely to confront modern society for decades to come. This is the relationship between regulatory practices of the state versus some form of "free market." When an adequate sociological analysis of the S&L situation is written, this will be a major starting point. Any theory of the market that does not take account of its place in the bureaucratic apparatus is doomed to failure. But these theoretical problems cannot be investigated if we continue to adhere to the narrow confines of the natural science model as it has been defined in recent decades.

That sociologists who adhere to the natural science model cannot study major bureaucratic and organizational relationships also means that these same sociologists are unable to examine the place of sociology within this context. I am calling on sociologists to investigate the structural context in which sociological activities such as research and teaching are carried out. By not doing so, sociologists are unable to gain a proper perspective on their own activities and their place in the broader social context. Without placing themselves within a broader organizational framework, sociologists never will be able to formulate a theory of data (called for by Lieberson 1985) or study the social processes that produce the quantitative data they rely on in their research (called for by Duncan 1984).

Sociology has been increasingly integrated into the bureaucratic rationalization process through the funding process that supports research that underwrites the structure into which sociologists have become integrated. This integration occurs on the national level, and as we move down into the university setting, we find that sociologists increasingly are being intertwined with the bureaucratic power arrangements on the societal and even global levels.

Within the university, sociology departments and research institutes are themselves becoming more bureaucratized. The fragmentation and differentiation so widely discussed with respect to Smelser's *Handbook of Sociology* are part and parcel of the bureaucratic process in modern society. And none of the reviewers of the Smelser volume saw fit to make this simple sociological linkage. Once this is done, then we can understand what is taking place within the discipline in light of broader social forces. Sociologists then can understand what is happening to them in sociological terms.

The hierarchy of authority, division of labor, and stress on efficiency affect the manner in which sociological research is carried out. They also affect the nature of sociological discourse within departments. These bureaucratic features also affect the nature of the promotion and merit system. Increasingly, universities evaluate sociologists on a yearly basis. Rewards are based on what one has accomplished for the year. Issues such as quality of research—and the nature and contribution to knowledge—lie outside the definition of the bureaucratic enterprise. But when sociologists are caught up in this practice, it also means that they no longer are addressing the major social issues that confront humankind. In its own way, this undercuts their legitimacy within the university and the society at large. The passive acceptance of organizational constraints may well be undermining the foundations of sociology itself. This should become somewhat clearer as I turn to issues concerning the validity of sociological knowledge.

An Alternative Sociology and the Sociology of Alternatives

Before turning our attention to the major implications of the argument and critique developed, we need to recapitulate the steps taken. We began with a critical evaluation of how sociologists are defining the present state of the discipline. The main concern today is with the fragmentation and specialization within sociology. My analysis has taken a sharply different tack. I have reasoned that underlying this fragmentation and specialization with respect to substantive and theoretical orientations is the rise of a "methodological hegemony," which rests on the premises of the natural science model and stresses standardized techniques and procedures as a basis for a scientific study of society. But this methodological hegemony has led sociologists into a cul-de-sac wherein strategic theoretical and social issues are shunted aside in favor of studying narrowly defined questions that are often marginally relevant to the major social trends of our times.

To counter the existing methodological hegemony, I have set forth an alternative set of assumptions as a foundation for social inquiry. Although assumptions cannot be tested empirically in any rigorous sense, the alternative assumptions I have outlined are more plausible empirically than those underlying the natural science model. Without broadening their database, sociologists cannot confront the problems associated with the large-scale organizations that dominate the contemporary scene.

Although sociologists must understand empirically the major social patterns and trends in this and the next century, they consciously must move beyond simply examining "what is." If we accept the fact that the social order has been constituted by human agents and is continually in the process of being reconstituted (in greater or lesser degrees) by them, then sociologists in their research will take sides (whether they admit it or not) regarding the present social order and its future. Today those who champion the natural science model charge those who consider alternatives as ideologues, never recognizing that in accepting "what is"—particularly as defined by members of the power structure—they are just as ideological as those they criticize. If we examine the work of social scientists in historical context, we find that they have woven political and moral positions into their theoretical and empirical analyses. Mommsen (1984) has documented this pattern with respect to Weber's sociology, and Lukes (1977) has demonstrated how Durkheim's empirical research fits with his moral and political commitments. Gouldner's (1970) critique of Parsons was founded on the charge that Parsons was an ardent intellectual advocate for and defender of the welfare state. At the time, Gouldner, as noted earlier, was severely castigated by his contemporaries. But with the benefit of historical perspective, we are likely to find that Gouldner, instead of being judged as irresponsible, will be perceived as a sophisticated (and rather moderate) critic of Parsons's theoretical and empirical orientation. Much of the critique lodged against Gouldner resulted from the fact that sociologists of the time defended themselves as having attained "value neutrality." Yet that judgment will not hold up as we look back at that era several decades later.

But let us consider the political and moral orientations of contemporary sociological analysis from a somewhat different vantage point. The natural science model builders use the social categories of the existing social order to analyze the social order. In general they accept the power structure's definition of existing society as the objective reality with which they must deal. But critics of American society, from Mills (1959) to Bellah (1986), implicitly have adopted a set of external standards by which to evaluate modern society. As Miller (1987) has reasoned: "The immorality of power was Mills' great theme." Miller also reveals how Mills employed, as a standard for his critique, a form of Jeffersonian democracy. In *Habits of the Heart*, Bellah (1986) and his colleagues have used the small community of the nineteenth century as their implicit standard for criticizing contemporary utilitarianism, which they see as tearing apart the social fabric of modern society.

Mills and Bellah stand apart on many issues; both, however, employ an image drawn from the past as a basis for evaluating the contemporary human condition. In doing so, they reflect a long-standing heritage in sociology. Liebersohn (1988), in his analysis of German sociology between 1870 and 1923, speaks of a utopian vision underlying an otherwise fatalistic orientation. Weber, Tonnies, Troelisch, and others were pessimistic regarding modernity, but hidden behind this "fatalism" was a kind of utopianism that perceived humankind overcoming the ills of modernity.

Here I wish to build more specifically on the writings of Mills and Bellah. Although I am sympathetic with their creative efforts, they err, in my judgment, in using the past as a standard, particularly a past not explicated in a straightforward manner. Both Mills's and Bellah's standard has a "dark side" that is conveniently ignored. Jeffersonian democracy, for all its virtues, was predicated on the voting power of the landed gentry, and it accepted slavery as a way of life. Small-town America, which Bellah idealizes, supported an exclusivity at odds with a multiethnic social order with which we must come to terms if we are to sustain human dignity in the modern world. The danger of using the past uncritically is to gloss over its starker side. Moreover, the past becomes a less than adequate standard for critically evaluating modern bureaucratic structures and the scientific technologies that support (and are supported by) them. To glamorize the past will not provide us with a sound basis for coming to terms with the social ills of the present and the future. We must look to creating more viable social arrangements (always keeping in mind that existing social structures are products of complex historical processes).

I wish to make more explicit the theoretical and methodological foundations of a critical perspective in sociology. This can be done by elaborating on Sjoberg and Cain's (1971) concept of "countersystem analysis."

The countersystem is constructed through negation of various facets of existing social arrangements and then elaborating a counter to what exists. The countersystem may be an idealized, theoretical construct or it may involve the essential elements of an existing social order. A theoretical countersystem and a more empirical version have their place in sociological analysis.

There are three distinct styles of countersystem analysis. First, as Mills and Bellah have tacitly recognized, an "external standard" can serve as a powerful tool for exposing both the premises and general empirical patterns of the social arrangements under investigation. One cannot readily perceive the nature of the normative order and the belief system if one attempts to understand it from within. Thus, Malinowski's (1922) description of *kula exchange* has provided generations of social scientists with an empirical basis for evaluating the exchange system associated with modern capitalism. The existence of kula exchange, for instance, raises questions regarding capitalistic exchange as inherent in the natural order of things.

Countersystem analysis as a means for advancing our empirical description and understanding of social phenomena is not part of the standard fare of research methods. Those who stress technical procedures and techniques (particularly quantitative tools) fail to perceive that in describing what is, sociologists need to step outside the social categories of the system of which they are a part. Lyng (1990) has provided us with an informative case study of this procedure. He takes holistic health as countersystem to the medical model. In so doing, he is able to delineate the essential features of the latter in ways not possible if one simply were to take the medical model and strive to analyze it in its own terms. Countersystem reasoning leads to an empirical grounding of sociological analysis, but in terms quite different from conventional wisdom.

A second style of countersystem analysis is the anticipation of alternative futures (Block 1990). The natural science builders in sociology typically have championed prediction as the standard for evaluating the validity of social theorizing. We have only to take stock of sociological inquiry and to observe the inadequacy of prediction as a justification for social inquiry. Often those who claim to predict future social arrangements take the social categories of the system they are investigating for granted and then assume that, given the stability of existing patterns, we should be able to predict what will occur. By now we have learned enough to know that major scientific innovations or social upheavals make meaningful social predictions a risky if not a fruitless venture. A far more realistic approach is to think in terms of a range of alternatives that is likely to occur. Through constructing countersystem orientations one can more readily perceive the range of possible alternative futures. We thereby also would avoid committing ourselves to the false premise that there exists a natural order over which human beings have no basic control. Had social scientists been thinking in terms of alternative futures, they might have anticipated (at least to some degree) the upheavals in eastern Europe and the former Soviet Union in the 1990s. These changes would have been much less surprising to social scientists.

The third style of countersystem analysis is to stimulate discussion and debate about the creation of more viable and moral social arrangements. If human agents can reshape (however modestly) the existing social organization of modern society, and if, as I consistently have argued, sociologists are part of the social process they investigate, then we must understand how sociological theory and research contribute to either sustaining or revising societal activities. In Gouldner's (1970:47) terms, "Every social theory facilitates the pursuit of some but not all courses of action, and thus encourages us to change or to accept the world as it is, to say yea or nay to it. In a way, every social theory is a discreet obituary or celebration for some social system." By taking the vantage point of a countersystem, we are able to gain a reasoned perspective on the role of sociological analysis and thereby attain a form of "objectivity" sorely lacking in the natural science model. One aspect of objectivity involves understanding the social consequences of social researchers' activities.

Countersystem analysis thus leads us to a conception of valid social knowledge that remains outside the purview of the natural science model. Adherents of this model would have us believe that valid knowledge results from the ability to replicate research findings through the use of standardized techniques and procedures, and thereby that one is able to predict the patterns within the natural order. So ingrained is this worldview among many sociologists that they fail to recognize that the concept of valid knowledge antedates the rise of the natural science model. Some proponents fail to grasp the multifaceted debate regarding validity and often equate validity with reliability—that is, if one has constructed standardized research tools, one can obtain valid knowledge.

Kenneth Prewitt (1980), an ex-president of the Social Science Research Council, has contributed to the enlargement of the notion of valid knowledge. He reasons, correctly in my view, that one consideration of the validity of social knowledge is its contribution to the "refinement of debate and a sharpening of intelligence upon which the collective management of human affairs depends" (1980:3). That is, validity can be judged in terms of the enhancement of discourse just as reasonably as by some technical standard. For Prewitt, Myrdal's (1944)

American Dilemma is exemplary of the kind of research that refined the nature of debate within U.S. society. Myrdal's ground-breaking research led to an extensive debate about the nature of the relationship of the white majority society to blacks, who had been so heavily discriminated against. The work of Bellah and his colleagues has served to sharpen the nature of debate between the ideals of "individualism" and self-interest and the ideals of the "community" and the concern for the public good.

Prewitt's argument is congruent with (albeit not the same as) that advanced by Habermas, who is deeply committed to the view that social theory should be judged in terms of its ability to advance human emancipation from repressive constraints. In keeping with Habermas's own standards, (1984, 1987) in *Theory of Communicative Action* he has probed deeply into the repressive nature of the bureaucratic rationalization process that has intruded into and undermined the "lifeworld"—a rather vague concept, which nonetheless refers to the ethical foundations of interpersonal relationships in modern society. If the deterioration of the lifeworld continues, so will the foundations of the ethical nature of human relationships.

Both Prewitt and Habermas thus have linked social theory and research with the advancement of the democratic process. The adherents of the natural science model have played down, or brushed aside, the meaning of social analysis for furthering the democratic process or, more generally, the quality of human existence.

Countersystem analysis is a conceptual tool that can be used in the advancement of the cause of the democratic ideal. It also is a tool for forging reasoned debate about alternative social structures or belief systems that will serve to overcome the ills that plague humankind as a result of the maldistribution of food supplies, the devastation of the environment as a result of toxic wastes, and the like.

In practice, political and moral debates and struggles regarding the nature of alternative structural arrangements have been an integral feature of the world landscape in recent decades. The neoconservatives, reflected by Reaganism, have sought to restructure the nature of the welfare state during the past several decades. On a much larger scale, the development of the European Community (EC) has been the result of a sustained effort to restructure the political and economic landscape of Europe. And the specific nature of this Community will take full shape in the context of a variety of political struggles in the decades ahead. The collapse of the Soviet Union has cast the debate about alternative futures into even more dramatic focus. Several countersystem proposals are implicitly on the table. Here is a situation for which adherents of the natural science model offer us no guidance for grasping the nature of future human events. Dismantling a highly centralized bureaucratic command economy has never before been attempted. And the alternative arrangements that must be put in place are not preordained. U.S. sociologists are at a loss, given the existing methodological hegemony, to address this grand empirical problem—the future of eastern Europe and the Republics of the former Soviet Union.

Some form of countersystem analysis will do much to rehabilitate sociology in that it will focus on the central organizational and value issues in the present world. Sociologists do not have all the answers. But the classical sociological tradition offers us some guidelines for producing the kind of theoretical analysis that is essential to the revitalization of sociology as a field that has something to say about issues that matter.

Several objections might be raised to countersystem analysis from Marx to Habermas, a group of critical theorists who have been hostile to any form of utopian reasoning. In part, this objection rests on the "idealistic" nature of utopian thought. In turn, conservative theorists from Edmund Burke to current neoclassical economists disclaim any association with utopian thought, when in fact Mises (1949, 1951) and Friedman (1962, 1980) have engaged in a form of this reasoning.

Perhaps the most sustained critique of utopian reasoning in recent decades was launched by Karl Popper. He strongly objected to the totalism associated with social theorists from Hegel to Marx. Popper (1950), in *Open Society and Its Enemies*, was responding to the consequences that resulted from fascism on the one hand and communism on the other. Yet Popper's solution rests on quicksand. He called for piecemeal planning instead of any form of utopian reasoning. A careful look at Popper's preconception reveals that his "alternative" is predicated on an economic-person model. I have already raised serious objections to the conception of agents as autonomous persons who are not shaped in the context of broader interaction patterns. Popper's argument would have human beings simply adapt to the broader social trends and forces of existing social patterns. And human agents would have little or no control over them. Moreover, his analysis is totally incapable of coming to terms with the revision of large-scale bureaucratic structures that now dominate the societal and global scenes. Popper did not grasp the implications of Weber's analysis of bureaucracy.

I, too, reject the reification of totalism. The imposition of some great planned design on human beings has been shown to have serious moral and political limitations. These past errors should not be repeated. But this does not mean that human beings (sociologists included) should revert to a fatalistic acceptance of ongoing social forces. An effort must be made to shape a more humane future.

To make effective use of countersystem reasoning, I integrate the theories of action advanced by Mead (1934) and Znaniecki (1952). Their conception of human action contrasts markedly with that of the neoclassical economists (one based on self-interest) as well as that formulated by Weber and Parsons. Parsons emphasized that members of a social order (or an organization) have a rather well defined end (or ends), and they select the most efficient means in order to attain their objective. But as Mead and Znaniecki observed, when human beings employ means to attain ends, the process itself leads to a redefinition of the ends. I return again to a recognition of an emergent social order that is being reconstructed.

If we apply the Mead/Znaniecki framework to countersystem analysis (however modestly), one concludes that countersystems are not to be reified by active human agents. Even if these are cast in ideal forms, they must be seen as the basis for discourse and debate, and thus they are subject to revision and change as human beings set about seeking to realize them. Moreover, the discourse about countersystems must be informed by moral considerations. This moral discourse, I argue, must be grounded in a theory of human rights. Without a well-worked-out set of guiding moral principles regarding alternative futures, we stand in serious danger of encouraging greater repression, rather than advancing the cause of human emancipation. One is committed to countersystem analysis because it is a basis for encouraging sociologists (as well as the broader citizenry) to consider reflectively alternative organizations and beliefs that might aid in improving the quality of life and human justice.

Conclusions

I delineated overlapping eras of American sociology since World War II. In a broad sense, each period reflects major political, economic, and cultural changes within the larger society. From 1945 to the mid to late 1960s, sociologists were euphoric about finally becoming a scientific discipline. With the critical inter-lude which was related, for example, to the highly contentious Vietnam war, serious questions emerged about sociology's role and status. Then, beginning in the mid-1970s, sociologists returned to "business as usual" but with less optimism regarding the progress of the field.

This brief historical overview sets the stage for an evaluation of the discipline in the 1990s. Nowadays, sociologists' major source of concern is with the fragmentation and differentiation of the discipline into numerous empirical subspecialties and the rise of a multitude of theoretical voices. But my evaluation of the present state of affairs is at odds with conventional wisdom. Underlying the fragmentation and differentiation is a "methodological hegemony" based on an adherence to the natural science model. This has led sociologists to stress rigorous, standardized research based on quantitative data. Yet this trend has led sociologists to avoid the central social and moral issues facing humankind.

I have delineated the presuppositions of the natural science model and have outlined the research procedures associated with these domain assumptions. This analysis has led to the conclusion that this model, when applied to the social world, has fundamental flaws.

One serious flaw ensues from a keystone assumption that can be challenged both theoretically and empirically. Proponents of the natural science model are firmly committed to the existence of an objective social world governed by universal social laws. Evidence abounds to the contrary that human agents constitute and reconstitute the structure of the social world.

I agree that the constituted structures comprise a reality that influences human action in a variety of ways. Yet sociologists forgo the logic of their own reasoning through their contention that their own scientific activities are exempt from these structural influences. They have been unwilling to examine how social trends and social forces shape the nature of sociology, including theoretical formulation, data collection and analysis, and the knowledge claims produced through the application of the natural science model. If sociologists recognize that they are part of the social process they study, they will of necessity reevaluate the natural science model and its claim to "objectivity" and to the discovery of invariant laws of nature.

The natural science model has led sociologists to study problems that are amenable to standardized, quantifiable data. This means, first, that many great social issues relating to powerful organizations, for instance, fall outside the purview of social research. Organizational domination and the rise of secrecy systems cannot be examined if one assumes that the units of analysis are "autonomous" and that the whole is simply the aggregation of the sum of the parts. Without a sounder theory of large-scale bureaucratic structures, sociologists cannot come to terms with their place within a society—and with the fragmentation and differentiation of the discipline with which they are concerned.

Second, the natural science model also means that sociologists often examine social order by employing social categories of the order they investigate. This is typical of research carried out by the U.S. Census Bureau. But this is a form of "historicism" that then is passed off as leading to the discovery of invariant laws of nature.

Third, the natural science model cannot formulate a social theory that Lieberson rightly regards as essential to advancing our interpretation of the data employed in social research. How can we interpret data when we do not in effect understand how and why it is generated?

I have set forth an alternative set of assumptions on which to construct a more adequate form of social inquiry. In doing so, I wish to return to strategic aspects of the classical sociological heritage. Major theoretical and empirical issues should dictate the methods employed. The methods and techniques should not dictate the selection of the problem.

By incorporating a broader range of empirical data than now is admissable, one becomes more empirical than the so-called empiricists. But I also argue for an alternative kind of sociology that calls for the examination of alternative futures. I advocate a form of countersystem reasoning for several reasons. By utilizing social categories other than those of the system being studied, one can provide a fuller empirical understanding of the social order being investigated.

I also believe it is essential that we move away from the dead-end street of seeking to predict human endeavors and seek instead to anticipate a range of alternative futures. Then, too, in keeping with an alternative set of presuppositions, sociologists need to engage in examination of more viable alternative futures. The nature of future social arrangements is part and parcel of the major debates going on worldwide. For sociologists to remove themselves from this ongoing discourse is to abdicate a central role for the discipline. One has only to point to the likes of Mills and Bellah to perceive that a few sociologists have done what I advocate. Yet I propose to restructure the manner in which the study of alternatives is conducted. The intention is not to replace public opinion surveys and analyzes of census data but to recognize that these are but one small part of a much larger puzzle with which sociologists must grapple if they are to sustain sociology's legitimacy as a teaching and intellectual endeavor.

Notes

1. Linking Merton with the natural science model, and implicitly with the positivist tradition, in sociology runs against prevailing perceptions of Merton's position within the field. Merton has typically been identified as one of the most prominent theorists within the functionalist orientation, a theoretical position generally assumed to be at odds with positivism. Yet Merton has argued, in essays dating back at least to 1945, for formal theory construction within sociology. His version of formal theory emphasizes the precise specification of relationships among variables, the logical derivation of propositions, and the testing of propositions using quantified data. Crothers (1987:53ff) contends that Merton does not differentiate between the natural and social sciences except in terms of their different stages of historical development. Jasso (1988), arguing for a revitalization of theoretical construction and analysis that equates theory with postulates and predictions, has singled out Merton (along with Milton Friedman and George Homans) as a major expositor of social scientific method based on the natural science model.

2. The issue of causality has a long and convoluted history in philosophical debate. These debates have been carried over to the social sciences. Considerable attention to causation surfaced within sociology during the late 1960s and early 1970s, particularly in a spate of books championing various forms of formal theory construction. Although Blalock (1969) and Gibbs 1972), among many others, debated the use of causal language and the terminology of covariation in the construction of formal theory statements, it is apparent that their basic assumptions about the nature of the social world are similar. More recent proponents of theoretical formalization, such as Jasso (1988), express few reservations about causal language or assumptions of natural social causality.

Today, the issue is most likely to occur in the form of admonitions to be properly cautious and tentative with respect to claims about cause and effect, not about the issue of cause itself (Glenn 1989; Lieberson 1991). For an informative discussion of some of the issues concerning causality that could profitably be examined by sociologists, see John Hicks (1979) *Causality in Economics*.

3. In his 1991 Presidential Address, Lieberson (1992) continues to soften some aspects of the utilization of the natural science model within sociology. He argues specifically, for example, against a deterministic perspective on the social world. But in proposing to substitute a probabilistic epistemology for a deterministic one, he is essentially accommodating to the reality that sociological research rarely accounts for all the variance. His argument for an enlarged interpretation of evidence does not fundamentally alter what is to be accepted as evidence or how this evidence is to be obtained. Despite his reservations, he remains much closer to the natural science model than to any genuine alternative, as his terse comments on Bellah et al. (1985) clearly indicate.

4. In the context of discussing data appropriate to micro-macro linkages, DiMaggio (1991:83) suggests that differences in the data are generated at each level: "A satisfactory approach to articulating micro and macro levels of analysis requires simultaneous attention to both cultural and relational aspects of role-governed behavior. But cultural aspects (i.e., those institutionalized in cognition) are intrinsically qualitative, pushing researchers toward taxonomic specificity, whereas concrete social relations require mathematical reduction involving high levels of abstraction.

He subsequently reasons, however, that there is no fundamental difference between quantitative and qualitative analysis, except in the sense of the form of expression. DiMaggio (1991:94) states: "Qualitative is used in two senses in social science writing: in opposition to quantitative (e.g., ethnography versus survey analysis) and in opposition to formal (discursively specific as distinct from formal and abstract). Because social scientists operate in a cultural tradition that includes an untheorized binary opposition between 'hard' and 'soft,' the two senses are often conflated, but they should not be. I use qualitative only in the second sense. There is no reason that measurement of scripts, premises, and cognitive maps cannot be as precise and as quantitative as measurement of social relations; but there is good reason, as Nadel argues, that the former is unlikely to be as abstract." Captured and captivated by the natural science model, he thinks only in terms of "hard" and "soft" versions of this model rather than in terms of categorical alternatives to it, alternatives growing out of fundamentally different domain assumptions about the nature of the social world.

References

Alonso, William P., and Paul Starr, eds. 1987. *The Politics of Numbers.* New York: Russell Sage Foundation.

Bell, Daniel. 1960. *The End of Ideology: On the Exhaustion of Political Ideas in the Fifties.* Glencoe, Ill.: Free Press.

Bellah, Robert N., Richard Madsen, William M. Sullivan, Ann Swidler, and Stephen M. Tipton. 1986. *Habits of the Heart: Individualism and Commitment in American Life.* New York: Harper & Row.

Berger, Joseph. 1989. "Sociology's Long Decade in the Wilderness." *New York Times,* May 28, 6E.

Berger, Peter L. 1986. *The Capitalist Revolution.* New York: Basic Books.

Berger, Peter L., and Thomas Luckmann. 1966. *The Social Construction of Reality: A Treatise in the Sociology of Knowledge.* Garden City, NY: Doubleday.

Blalock, Hubert. 1969. *Theory Construction.* Englewood Cliffs, N.J.: Prentice-Hall.

———. 1987. "Providing Tough Intellectual Challenges: The Issue of Quality Training." *The American Sociologist* 18:19–23.

Block, Fred. 1990. *Postindustrial Possibilities.* Berkeley: University of California Press.

Bloom, Allan. 1987. *The Closing of the American Mind.* New York: Simon and Schuster.

Blumer, Herbert 1969. *Symbolic Interactionism: Perspective and Method.* Englewood Cliffs, N.J.: Prentice-Hall.

Borgatta, Edgar F., and Karen S. Cook, eds. 1988. *The Future of Sociology.* Beverly Hills: Sage.

Bottomore, Thomas, S. Nowak, and M. Sokolowska, eds. 1982. *Sociology: The State of the Art.* Beverly Hills: Sage.

Bramson, Leon 1961. *The Political Context of Sociology.* Princeton: Princeton University Press.

Calhoun, Craig J., and Kenneth C. Land. 1989. "Editors' Introduction," *Contemporary Sociology* 18:475–77.

"Commentary: Exchanges on the *Handbook* Symposium." 1989. *Contemporary Sociology* 18:851–59.

Crothers, Charles. 1987. *Robert K. Merton.* London: Tavistock.

DiMaggio, Paul. 1991. "The Micro-Macro Dilemma in Organizational Research: Implications of Role-System Theory." Pp. 76–96 in J. Huber, ed. *Macro-Micro Linkages in Sociology.* Newbury Park, CA: Sage.

Duncan, Otis D. 1984. *Notes on Social Measurement: Historical and Critical.* New York: Russell Sage Foundation.

Erikson, Kai. 1989. "Drawing Boundaries." *Contemporary Sociology* 18:511–13.

Eulau, Heinz., ed. 1989. *Crossroads of Social Science.* New York: Agathon Press.

Faris, R.E.L., ed. 1964. *Handbook of Modern Sociology.* Chicago: Rand McNally.

Friedman, Milton. 1962. *Capitalism and Freedom.* Chicago: University of Chicago Press.

Friedman, Milton, and Rose Friedman. 1980. *Freedom to Choose: A Personal Statement.* New York: Harcourt Brace Jovanovich.

Friedrichs, Robert W. 1970. *A Sociology of Sociology.* New York: Free Press.

Gans, Herbert J. 1989. "Sociology in America: The Discipline and the Public." *American Sociological Review* 54:1–16.

———., ed. 1990. *Sociology In America.* Newbury Park, CA: Sage.

Gibbs, Jack P. 1972. *Sociological Theory Construction.* Hinsdale, Ill: Dryden Press.

———. 1989. *Control: Sociology's Central Notion.* Urbana: University of Illinois Press.

Giddens, Anthony. 1984. *The Constitution of Society.* Berkeley: University of California Press.

Gittler, A.W., ed. 1957. *Review of Sociology: Analysis of a Decade.* New York: Wiley.

Gouldner, Alvin W. 1970. *The Coming Crisis of Western Sociology.* New York: Basic Books.

Goyder, John. 1987. *The Silent Majority: Nonresponders on Sample Surveys*. Boulder, CO: Westview Press.

Gurvitch, Georges, and Wilbert E. Moore, eds. 1945. *Twentieth Century Sociology*. New York: Philosophical Library.

Habermas, Jürgen. 1984. *The Theory of Communicative Action: Reason and the Rationalization of Society*. Vol. I. Boston: Beacon Press.

———. 1987. *The Theory of Communicative Action: Lifeworld and System: A Critique of Functionalist Reason*. Vol. II. Boston: Beacon Press.

Hicks, John. 1979. *Causality in Economics*. New York: Basic Books.

Homans, George C. 1982. "The Present State of Sociological Theory." *Sociological Quarterly* 23:285–99.

———. 1987. *Certainties and Doubts: Collected Papers, 1962–1985*. New Brunswick, NJ: Transaction Books.

Hopkins, Terence, and Immanuel Wallerstein. 1982. *World Systems Analysis: Theory and Method*. Beverly Hills: Sage.

Hume, David. 1966. *Enquiries Concerning Human Understanding and the Principles of Morals*. Oxford: Clarendon Press (orig. pub. 1748).

Jasso, Guillermina. 1988. "Principles of Theoretical Analysis." *Sociological Theory* 6:1–20.

Kuhn, Thomas S. 1970. *The Structure of Scientific Revolutions*. Rev. ed. Chicago: University of Chicago Press.

Larsen, Otto. 1981. "Need For Continuing Support for Social Sciences." *Footnotes* 9(March):1.

Libersohn, Harry. 1988. *Fate and Utopia in German Sociology, 1870–1923*. Cambridge: MIT.

Lieberson, Stanley 1985. *Making It Count: The Improvement of Social Research And Theory*. Berkeley: University of California Press.

———. 1992. "Einstein, Renoir, and Greeley: Some Thoughts about Evidence in Sociology." *American Sociological Review* 57:1–15.

Lipset, Seymour M., and Neil Smelser, eds. 1961. *Sociology: The Progress of a Decade*. Englewood Cliffs, NJ: Prentice-Hall.

Lukes, Steven. 1977. *Essays in Social Theory*. London: Macmillan.

Lynd, Robert S. 1939. *Knowledge for What? The Place of Social Science in American Culture*. New York: Grove Press.

Lyng, Stephen. 1990. *Holistic Health and BioMedical Medicine*. Albany: State University of New York Press.

Malinowski, Bronislaw. 1922. *Argonauts of the Western Pacific*. New York: Dutton.

Mead, George H. 1934. *Mind, Self and Society*. Chicago: University of Chicago Press.

Merton, Robert K. 1945a. "Sociology of Knowledge." Pp. 366–405 in George Gurvitch and Wilbert E. Moore, eds. *Twentieth Century Sociology*. New York: Philosophical Library.

———. 1945b. "Sociological Theory." *American Journal of Sociology* 50:462–73.

Merton, Robert K., Leonard Broom, and Leonard S. Cottrell, Jr., eds. 1959. *Sociology Today: Problems and Prospects*. New York: Basic Books.

Michels, Robert. 1949. *Political Parties*. New York: Free Press.

Miller, James. 1987. *Democracy in the Streets: From Port Huron to the Siege of Chicago*. New York: Simon and Schuster.

Mills, C. Wright 1959. *The Sociological Imagination*. New York: Grove Press.

Mises, Ludvig von. 1949. *Human Action: A Treatise on Economics*. New Haven: Yale University Press.

Mommsen, Wolfgang J. 1984. *Max Weber and German Politics 1890–1920*. Chicago: University Chicago Press.

Myrdal, Gunnar, with Richard Sterner and Arnold Rose. 1962. *An American Dilemma: The Negro Problem and Modern Democracy*. New York: Harper & Row (orig. pub. 1944).

Nicolaus, Martin. 1969. "Remarks at the ASA Convention." *The American Sociologist* 4:154–56.
Parsons, Talcott., ed. 1968. *American Sociology: Perspectives, Problems, Methods*. New York: Basic Books.
Popper, Karl R. 1950. *The Open Society and Its Enemies*. Rev. ed. Princeton: Princeton University Press.
———. 1965. *The Logic of Scientific Discovery*. New York: Harper & Row.
Prewitt, Kenneth, Frederick Mosteller, and Herbert Simon. 1980. "Testimony at National Science Foundation Hearings." *Items* 34:1–7.
Ragin, Charles C. 1987. *The Comparative Method: Moving Beyond Qualitative and Quantitative Strategies*. Los Angeles: University of California Press.
Reynolds, Larry T., and Janice M. Reynolds, eds. 1970. *The Sociology of Sociology*. New York: McKay.
Riesman, David (with Nathan Glazer and Reuel Denney). 1950. *The Lonely Crowd: A Study of the Changing American Character*. Garden City, NY: Doubleday.
Ross, Dorothy. 1991. *The Origins of American Social Science*. New York: Cambridge University Press.
Rossi, Peter H. 1990. "Moving Forward?" *Contemporary Sociology* 19:623–24.
Roucek, Joseph., ed. 1958. *Contemporary Sociology*. New York: Philosophical Library.
Sewell, William H. 1985. "Getting On-Line." *New York Times*. April 28, Sec. 4, 7.
Short, James F., ed. 1981. *The State of Sociology: Problems and Prospects*. Beverly Hills: Sage.
Sjoberg, Gideon and Leonard D. Cain. 1971. "Negative Values, Counter System Models, and the Analysis of Social Systems." Pp. 212–29 in Herman Turk and Richard Simpson, eds. *Institutions And Social Exchange: The Sociologies of Talcott Parsons and George C. Homans*. Indianapolis: Bobbs-Merrill.
Skocpol, Theda., ed. 1984. *Vision and Method in Historical Sociology*. New York: Cambridge University Press.
Smelser, Neil J., ed. 1988. *Handbook of Sociology*. Newbury Park, CA: Sage.
Sorokin, Pitirim 1956. *Fads and Foibles in Modern Sociology and Related Sciences*. Chicago: Regnery.
Stein, Maurice, and Arthur Vidich, eds. 1963. *Sociology on Trial*. Englewood Cliffs, NJ: Prentice-Hall.
"Symposium: Smelser's *Handbook*: An Assessment." 1989. *Contemporary Sociology* 18:475–513.
Tiryakian, Edward A., ed. 1971. *The Phenomenon of Sociology: A Reader in the Sociology of Sociology*. New York: Appleton-Century-Crofts.
Turner, Jonathan H. 1991. *The Structure of Sociological Theory*. Belmont, CA: Wadsworth.
Wallace, Ruth A., and Alison Wolf. 1991. *Contemporary Sociological Theory: Continuing the Classical Tradition*. Englewood Cliffs, NJ: Prentice-Hall.
Wallace, Walter L. 1983. *Principles of Scientific Sociology*. New York: Aldine. Znaniecki, Florian. 1952. *The Cultural Sciences*. Urbana: University of Illinois Press.

| Chapter | **2** | THE BUREAUCRATIZATION OF SOCIOLOGY: ITS IMPACT ON THEORY AND RESEARCH |

Gideon Sjoberg and Ted R. Vaughan

The "bureaucratization" of U.S. society, as well as of the broader global setting, has had a profound impact on the discipline of sociology. Especially since World War II, the bureaucratization process has affected the manner in which sociologists carry out their research, policy analysis, and teaching activities.

Sociologists, so our reasoning goes, hold a relatively tenuous position in the bureaucratic structures of the United States (and in the global context). This has led them to seek legitimacy through increased reliance on techniques and methods at the expense of theoretical analysis and ideas. But the emphasis on techniques and methods seems destined to undermine the foundations of sociological inquiry.

No one, to our knowledge, has grappled directly with the issue of how bureaucratic arrangements have molded the sociological enterprise. Turner and Turner (1990), writing on sociology as *The Impossible Science*, treat the discipline as if it has developed in relative isolation from powerful organizational forces. Although they are aware of certain influences of large-scale organizations on American sociology, they simply fail to comprehend the far-reaching implications of these structures in shaping the nature of the discipline. Among major critics of sociology, only Mills (1959) seems to have anticipated some of the central issues relating to the creation and production of social knowledge within a bureaucratic environment—on the departmental, university, disciplinary, societal, and global levels.

Herein we consider how the bureaucratic process has shaped the social context in which sociologists function, and how, in turn, sociologists have responded to the organizational structures in which they are embedded. We thereby strive to clarify the meaning of Weber's "iron cage" for the construction of contemporary sociological knowledge. Weber employed this concept in largely metaphorical terms, and sociologists have not assessed how bureaucratic structures shape the creation of their own body of knowledge. In carrying out our task, we are studiedly critical of "mainstream sociology" in the United States,

54

particularly the "methodological hegemony" that dominates large sectors of the sociological discipline today.

We first discuss our orientation toward bureaucracy, including the rationalization process. We build on, yet modify in marked ways, Weber's formulation as well as those of scholars who have followed in his footsteps. Thus, we contrast our effort with that of a contemporary figure such as Jürgen Habermas, who, using Weber as a point of departure, has critically evaluated the rationalization process.

After outlining our theoretical framework, we briefly discuss the growth of bureaucratic structures on the global and societal levels. We then delineate the manner in which the discipline of sociology, especially that anchored in universities, is positioned vis-à-vis the corporate-governmental apparatus in the broader society and the global bureaucratic system. Concomitantly we analyze how adoption of the natural science model by sociologists has served to integrate them into the ongoing bureaucratic apparatus.

Our analysis is predicated on a particular sociology-of-knowledge perspective. On the one hand, we reject the relativism within which many sociologists of knowledge become encased; on the other, we reject the principle that sociologists can isolate, in any meaningful way, natural social laws. We are strongly committed to empirical investigations. Our goal is to craft a sociology that not only supplements the natural science model but also has an integrity of its own (Sjoberg et al. 1991). In the words of the natural science model, we find that sociologists are limited to analyzing "necessary," rather than "sufficient," conditions. Nevertheless, sociologists can play a constructive role in describing and interpreting what is. In turn, their theory and research can either support what exists or assist in the construction of "alternative futures."

Our view of the sociology of knowledge relies heavily on George Herbert Mead's conception of the "social mind." As such, we recognize that knowledge emerges in the context of human interaction. How one thinks and what one thinks about is a social creation. Consequently, sociologists are part and parcel of the social order they investigate. Yet they can attain a degree of "objectivity"—not through technical and standardized research procedures but through some form of "countersystem analysis" (Sjoberg and Cain 1971). We can never escape our cultural or organizational setting in any ultimate sense, as Kant, Popper, and other philosophers who adhere to the notion of "rational thought" as independent of social interaction would have us believe. Yet we need not be total prisoners of our time. One means of coping with this complex methodological problem is to recognize that we should not only study what is but also create social alternatives—countersystems—that not only become standards for evaluating what is but also serve as the basis for creating new kinds of social arrangements. To employ the social categories of one's own social order to evaluate that same social order means that one is a captive of the existing system. Ironically, sociologists have produced a considerable body of literature on how knowledge is shaped in, for instance, the natural sciences, but with rather rare exceptions they have been unwilling to turn their theoretical analysis back on themselves.

The Nature of Bureaucracy: Selected Theoretical Considerations

Inasmuch as our objective is to understand the sociological enterprise within a bureaucratic context, both societally and globally, we must sketch out our theoretical orientation for interpreting bureaucracy. Galbraith (1983) had it right when he spoke of our living in an "age of organizations." In order to comprehend the nature of these bureaucratic structures we begin, as do most students of bureaucracy, with Max Weber's classic formulation.

Social Characteristics

The bureaucratic system displays several essential features: hierarchy of authority, specialization or division of labor (within and among organizations), and an emphasis on efficiency, or what some theorists would term "formal rationality." Other facets of bureaucracy, such as emphasis on the office rather than the person, could be delineated. Still it is hierarchy, specialization, and formal rationality that command our attention. The interplay among these phenomena leads to the standardization and routinization of a wide array of social activities in modern society and on the global scene—the "rationalization process."

The concept of "rationalization" has been employed in a variety of ways (Held 1980:65-70). For example, one group of scholars equates it with formal rationality, another more broadly with the cultural consequences of bureaucratization. Habermas (1984, 1987a), in his wide-ranging critique of the rationalization process, employs this concept in the last-mentioned manner. While we are sympathetic with his worldview, Habermas's analysis is flawed in that he slights the structural features of bureaucratic arrangements. For us, the rationalization process is furthered by the structural (or organizational) relationships as well as by the cultural system associated with bureaucracy.

As for hierarchy, it existed before modern bureaucracy. Nevertheless, the hierarchy of authority that characterizes present-day bureaucracy serves to integrate and provide direction (through the use of formal rationality) for the activities of persons who carry out highly technical tasks on a variety of levels within the system.

The members of the managerial sector claim the right to construct, and to speak for, the "needs" or "requirements" of the system as a whole. To further formal efficiency and enhance their own power, they seek to de-skill and thereby standardize and routinize the activities of sizable sectors of the labor force, but they are also confronted with a burgeoning of technical experts in the lower reaches of the hierarchy. The role of these experts requires special attention.

Nowhere is the specialization of knowledge more dramatically highlighted than in large-scale universities. A comparison of university course catalogues between 1940 and 1990 brings to light the enormous specialization in courses (and knowledge) that both reflects and fosters specialization in the organizational field within which universities are encased.

Modern bureaucratic structures have served, although in diverse ways, the cause of both capitalism and communism. It is the genius of Weber that he recognized that modern capitalism operates within large-scale bureaucratic structures (though he never clearly spelled out the implications of his general observations). The classical and neoclassical economists' conception of economic activity is grossly outmoded because of their failure to acknowledge that "the market" functions within a bureaucratic context. Many modern-day proponents of neoclassical economics are hostile to governmental structures though these have served to create the social and legal climate in which capitalism has flourished. Moreover, these economists are unwilling to face the fact that the market is both constrained and advanced by bureaucratic corporate structures legitimized by the legal system.

The place of hierarchy, expertise, and formal rationality is cast in bold relief when we compare the "capitalist" and "communist" systems, particularly as a result of the massive upheavals in the former Soviet bloc in the late 1980s and early 1990s. In both the capitalist and the traditional communist systems, attention has been given to "efficiency." In both an effort has been made to stimulate efficiency through administrative control. Taylorism was invented as a managerial tool to generate efficiency in the West, and it was adopted, in part at least, by the command economy in the former Soviet Union (Beissinger 1988). What has set the capitalist system apart from the communist one is that the market, in theory, if not always in practice, has been a means for the efficient allocation of "resources." Thus, capitalism has relied on both managerial and market mechanisms to promote efficiency.

Human Agency and Bureaucracy

To clarify the nature of bureaucracy we must come to terms with human agency. Although Weber reasoned that sociology must begin with the study of human actors, he did not follow through on his own premise in detailing the nature of bureaucracy. In his writings on bureaucracy the actor disappeared from consideration. Now we must reintegrate human agency into any analysis of bureaucracy, especially if we are to understand how sociologists intersect with the organizational structures in which they live and work.

The relationship of human agents to organizations leads us to confront the micro/macro debate that dominated much sociological theorizing in the 1980s, though the roots of this debate can be traced back to Durkheim, Marx, and Weber. One school of thought rids sociological analysis of human agents (e.g., Mayhew 1980) and would concentrate solely on social structure. A second group of sociologists (Collins 1981) contends that one can in effect add up the activities of individual actors and acquire knowledge of organizations. This version of neoclassical economics cast in sociological terms has come to gain a considerable following in recent decades (Opp 1985). A third perspective, articulated by Blau (1987), holds that sociologists are destined to analyze the micro and macro levels separately from each other.

A fourth school of thought stresses the interplay between human agency and organizations. Giddens (1984), in *The Constitution of Society*, has championed this orientation. We, too, adhere to it, but our version differs from that advanced by Giddens (Vaughan and Sjoberg 1984).

Sociologists cannot come to terms with bureaucratic organizations without taking account of both human agency and organizations and the complex interplay between the two. We cannot simply add up human agents and hope to understand bureaucratic structures. Thus, organizations are something more than the sum of "individual agents," though organizations cannot exist without the latter. Moreover, the power of organizational structures is greater than any small subset of individuals, though the collective action of human agents may lead to revisions of bureaucratic structures (as witness the changes in eastern Europe in the late 1980s and 1990s). In effect, a dialectical tension exists between bureaucratic structures and human agents.

The role of the human agent within the bureaucratic setting deserves special attention. As alluded to earlier, we place the "social mind"—not the "social self"—at the center of human agency. The concept of the mind was dropped from social theory in general in about 1920, only to be resurrected in the 1980s not only by some sociologists but also by cognitive psychologists.

Our version of the mind is characterized by its social nature, particularly its reflectivity. We anchor our theorizing in Mead (1934) and to some degree Dewey, who wrote of the importance of intelligence. Human agents are able to think about thinking. But how they reflect about their social world is grounded in the social process. The logical modes of reasoning persons employ, their domain assumptions, and their social memory are shaped by human interaction. We do not underestimate the role of habit or how organizational structures constrain reflectivity. But as social scientists have been rudely reminded on more than one occasion, efforts to repress reflectivity have their limits, even in totalitarian orders. Bureaucratic structures are characterized by a variety of contradictions—between hierarchy and specialization and between a top-down and a bottom-up view of social reality—and human agents reflect on these, even in the face of sustained organizational repression.

The social mind permits human agents to respond in a proactive manner and thereby to cope with and at times remake the bureaucratic structures that mold their thought processes in the first instance. In the modern world large-scale organizations are central for understanding the production of social knowledge. The manner in which a person's thinking is formed is associated with one's position in the bureaucratic structure. For example, persons in power are less constrained by the rules than those with limited or no power. The powerful also have a special interest in sustaining their privilege, and thus their reflectivity is constrained by their commitment to "system maintenance." As we move down the bureaucratic hierarchy, we find that occupants of the lower positions—those involving less power but often demanding specialized knowledge—are severely limited in their activities by myriad rules or regulations. Within this framework, members of the managerial sector create secrecy systems in order to preserve a monopoly over knowledge of how decisions are made. They reinforce their control by delegating blame to lower-status personnel, albeit under the guise of responsibility. In turn, human agents in lower-level positions react by creating secrecy systems to protect themselves against undue manipulation by those in power (cf. Williams et al. 1983).

In addition to the secrecy arrangements that the privileged and the less privileged construct, organizations often demand secrecy of all their employees as they compete with other systems in a hostile environment. For example, corporations seek special economic and political advantages through hiding information from their opponents. Secrecy systems, one must remember, often result from the studied responses of human agents.

Our brief overview of bureaucracy has stressed the need for coming to terms with the activities of human agents in order to comprehend organizational activities. Agents reflect on, create, utilize, and respond to organizational domination as they advance their own agenda as well as the goals of the organization. Consequently, we must view sociologists as we do other human agents, for their actions may reinforce or modify or remake organizational environments in which they carry out their teaching and research. Still, we must be constantly aware of the constraints imposed on human agents, including sociologists, by the bureaucratic imperative.

The Organizational Context of the University in Societal and Global Settings

We return to one of our central themes: We cannot come to terms with the position of sociology in academia without locating it within the existing bureaucratic arrangements on both the societal and global scenes. Herein we outline some of the major configurations that have evolved since World War II, particularly sociology's integration, most often in a loosely coupled manner, into powerful organizational structures.

The Societal Level

Sociology in the United States prior to World War II was a discipline characterized by small-scale research projects carried out within the qualitative tradition. Although the Chicago School profited from foundation support in the 1920s, empirical research at this university was largely carried out by individuals. And although Howard Odum built a research institute at the University of North Carolina, it had a regional focus. Admittedly, some sociologists received federal funding for their research efforts; yet, with some exceptions (e.g., Converse 1987), their projects generally were carried out by individual researchers with minimal support structures.

World War II marked a major transition period for higher education, and the resultant changes deeply affected sociology. In order to understand the contemporary sociological enterprise, we first must take account of the historical changes in the society and their impact on university life.

Sociology has been anchored primarily in departments in the university setting. But to understand sociology's status we must examine its position in what Clark Kerr (1963) speaks of as the multiversity as well as less powerful educational institutions. The data support the assertion that the university bureaucracy has proliferated greatly since World War II (Grassmuck 1991:A22). One rationale for this expansion rests on the need to integrate the internal activities of the university; another, more compelling reason is to integrate the internal operations with powerful societal (even global) organizations, governmental and corporate, with which the university has become so intimately involved. In addition, this administrative apparatus has come to have a life of its own.

Within the university two major power centers can be isolated. One is related to the natural sciences, including the applied areas of engineering and medicine. The second is founded on the business-law complex. The natural sciences (and related enterprises) have been intertwined with the governmental apparatus and increasingly with the corporate sector. One major feature of World War II was the heightened role of the natural sciences in building military power. University scientists, directly or indirectly, played a decisive role in the Manhattan Project, which culminated in the construction of the atomic bomb. This set the stage for a new relationship between the natural sciences and government and corporate bureaucracies.

After World War II, several interrelated social forces propelled the growth of scientific activity. One was the direct financial support for scientific research by the federal government. If we rely on Bruce L.R. Smith's (1990) work as a guide to scientific policy in the United States, a number of patterns can be highlighted. One is the underwriting of scientific activity by the military establishment. Military planners recognized that modern technology is founded on scientific advances and that therefore military superiority ultimately rests on innovations in the natural sciences. Thus, while the establishment of the National Science Foundation was being debated, major funding was already under way (Smith 1990:48–49):

> The Office of Naval Research, created by statute on August 3, 1946, took the lead in funding basic research in the universities on a wide variety of subjects related to naval missions. The ONR had an unexpended $40 million appropriation left from wartime construction funds, an initial budget, a strong staff built up for its wartime predecessor office, and excellent leadership . . . It quickly moved to support investigators in universities across the country and to institutionalize in the navy a program of support for basic research. The other services followed suit and established similar offices, most of whose funds were also devoted to basic research in the universities.
>
> The Atomic Energy Commission, also created in 1946, supported basic research as well. In particular, it administered programs in high-energy physics and later in fusion energy at large facilities. Most of the AEC budget, as with those of other mission agencies, funded development and production, and the commission operated or supported an extensive network of national laboratories (some affiliated with universities or university consortia, some not) . . . Moreover, it was considered impractical to transfer the support for basic research in universities undertaken by the AEC, the National Institutes of Health, and the Defense Department and to disrupt the ties that had developed.

Although the National Science Foundation came into being in 1950 and often is perceived as a major force for advancing basic research in universities, a far broader array of agencies of the U.S. government, particularly those with an interest in national security, were, as a by-product of the Cold War, essential to the funding of research in the natural sciences in universities.

The Soviet Union's advances in space technology, reflected in the launching of Sputnik in 1957, served to justify increased spending for research in the United States. In 1963, 93 percent of all federal research and development funds came from the Department of Defense, the Atomic Energy Commission, and the National Aeronautics and Space Administration (NASA) (Smith 1990:50). Although NASA is ostensibly a civilian agency, it was created in response to Sputnik and has been closely associated with military activities.

The funding of the natural sciences had a profound impact on research universities as well as lesser-status institutions. Although this pattern began to emerge during World War II, it flowered in the postwar years. By way of illustration we call attention to the structural basis of the nation's two major nuclear weapons research laboratories. One is the Lawrence Livermore Laboratory in California; the other is the Los Alamos National Laboratory in New Mexico. Both have been managed for the Department of Energy by the University of California. That the most prestigious state university in the United States has been a cornerstone of the nuclear weapons industry, and how in turn this arrangement has had an impact on higher education in the United States, has yet to be critically evaluated (Dickson 1988:134–37).

While some basic research relating to national security and funded by federal agencies has had a direct impact on the organizational structures of universities, in other instances the effect has been more indirect. The informative case study *The Space Telescope: A Study of NASA, Science, Technology, and Politics* by the historian Robert W. Smith (1989) documents the political activities of natural scientists in advancing the cause of Big Science. Scientists furthered their research agenda by acting as skilled bureaucratic politicians.

The Space Telescope was twenty-five years in the making; ten years were devoted to its actual construction. NASA played a powerful role in this effort. At the same time astronomers, who were based primarily in universities, were deeply involved in constructing a coalition that was able to convince the legislative and executive branches that the telescope was workable and scientifically essential and therefore that the expenditure of huge amounts of federal monies was justified. The astronomers became the prototypes of the scientific entrepreneur (Smith 1989:387): "It would . . . be a mistake to think that the astronomers acted in isolation; rather, they joined with managers and professional lobbyists employed by the contractors, as well as anybody else who could help, in a loosely coordinated coalition, one that also had strong NASA links." Although Smith speaks of a loose coalition of astronomers, he also recognizes that a number of them were immersed "in the highly ordered and hierarchical world of the Space Telescope" (1989:379), and they had to cope with considerable strife and tension, the hallmark of bureaucratic politics.

In the case of the Space Telescope, technical scientific decisions relating to its construction were shaped by political, especially bureaucratic, constraints. In the world of Big Science, the peer-review, or merit-review, system often is subjugated to the political process—a fact given all too little attention by sociologists who work within Merton's framework of the sociology of science.

Merton (1973) created the sociology of science as a "safe topic" by failing to examine the scientific enterprise within the context of highly charged bureaucratic politics, including its place in the Cold War.

The data on science and technology in the post World War II era bring other issues to light. Scientific activity has thrived because it has been an essential tool in the maintenance of state power. Science and technology have been the handmaidens of U.S. political, military, economic, and cultural dominance on the world scene. From the perspective of the early 1990s, we can observe just how little attention sociologists have given the role of the Cold War in shaping scientific (including sociological) activities. The preoccupation with the former Soviet Union, and the resultant East/West conflict, glossed over the role that, for instance, science played in advancing and maintaining U.S. control on a worldwide basis. The journalist Sheehan (1988:43), whose *A Bright Shining Lie* became a best seller, observes that in the early 1960s, "America had built the largest empire in history . . . The United States had 850,000 military men and civilian officials serving overseas in 106 countries" (cf. Gerson and Birchard 1991). The implications of this phenomenon have been studiously avoided by most sociologists. That the expansion of this empire has been facilitated by the science and technology developed within and outside the university is a reality of the twentieth century.

Still, the interrelationships of the university, particularly the natural science wing, with powerful bureaucratic structures are becoming more, not less, complex. A special issue of *Academe*, titled "The Entrepreneurial University" (1990), aptly captures the organizational changes that are now under way. A number of universities are becoming embedded, particularly through the biomedical sector, into the corporate apparatus, with a resultant emphasis on profit making. If this pattern continues to escalate, even more dramatic revisions are in store for higher education—and sociology.

At this point we must sharpen the focus of our argument. In 1963 Clark Kerr (1963:20) spoke of the modern multiversity as "a mechanism held together by administrative rules and powered by money." In view of the trends during the past three decades, we can reformulate his thesis. Major universities are increasingly dominated by an administrative (or managerial) elite and powered by money. Research institutes, as well as new forms of corporate ventures, are the organizational vehicles for funneling external funds into the coffers of the natural science wing of the university.[1]

Yet the natural science complex is but one of two power centers of the modern university. The second is that associated with business and law schools. Although in recent years the corporate sector has become increasingly involved in funding scientific research (cf. Dickson 1988), the scientific sector after World War II owed its primary support to government largesse. The business/law school sector owed its primary allegiance to the corporate sector. Nor should we underestimate the growth and power of this segment of the university. Business schools have been among the fastest-growing divisions of universities in the United States since World War II (Locke 1989).

While we need not dwell on the business school's integration into, and sponsorship by, the corporate sector, we should be attentive to the fact that the faculties of modern business schools have justified their existence by appealing to the natural science model. Scientific management, in its various forms, is the basis of a large segment of the business school curriculum.

Law schools have always produced students for the legal system, which has been an arm of the state. Increasingly, however, these schools also are integrated into large-scale corporate structures that dominate the societal and global spheres. Large law firms themselves are bureaucratic enterprises. The controversy at the Harvard Law School in the early 1990s is symptomatic of what has transpired in recent decades. The intense debate brought to light the concern of a segment of the faculty that contends that law schools increasingly are becoming the training ground for the corporate managerial class (Emerson 1990).

Overall, then, the power blocs within the university, with which the social sciences (and humanities) must contend, are integrated into, and supported, often in a lucrative manner, by powerful bureaucratic structures within the broader society.

The Global Scene

But viewing the power structure within the university and its linkage to the national (or societal) setting is much too limited a perspective. Reich (1991), among others, has made us aware of the interlocking networks of the global economy. Nonetheless, he fails to confront the organizational domination that has accompanied worldwide bureaucratization (Teichova 1986). We here consider, in more or less descending order of their social power, the transnational organizations that serve the interests of finance capital, science and technology, mass communication, and the production of manufactured goods. Although the organizations associated with each of these realms are intertwined in a variety of ways, they are distinguishable in "ideal type" terms.

Any consideration of multinational organizations leads us to confront their complex relationships to nation-states. Although any systematic analysis of this problem area is well beyond our objective, we surely do not dismiss the nation-state system and its military power, notably that of the United States. Although multinational organizations are often underwritten by the organizational structure of the nation-states, these multinational systems, especially those based in the United States, Japan, and various European nations, have considerable autonomy in governing their own affairs (Wachtel 1990; Kennedy 1988). In part they owe their existence to what Weber perceived as their "technical efficiency." But that is not the whole story. These organizations, following Galbraith's (1991) logic, have a life of their own as their managers pursue a form of self-aggrandizement.

We can consider only some of the general contours of the growing domination of world bureaucratic organizations. Yet these are, directly or indirectly, shaping the nature of the sociological enterprise, not just in the powerful industrial nations but especially in the less developed ones.

Our conceptualization places us at odds with world system analysis (Shannon 1989) as well as with the modernization perspective (Sutton 1990). Both schools of thought have skirted, even avoided, analyzing the global bureaucratic structures that have come to shape the economic, political, and cultural landscape in recent decades. The champions of both schools have failed to reformulate and adapt the Weberian orientation to the social realities of the twentieth and the coming century.

The most powerful transnational organizations in today's world are those associated with finance capital. Hilferding (1981; orig. 1910), the Austrian neo-Marxist, writing in the early part of this century, was decades ahead of his time in recognizing the emerging ascendancy of finance capital. In addition to banking enterprises (and related financial institutions) in the United States, Japan, and western Europe (which often are supported by the policies of nation-states), the World Bank and the International Monetary Fund mold, in multifaceted ways, the economic destiny of people throughout the world. Thus, when Poland broke "free" of Soviet domination, it was subjected to economic control by major lending agencies in the West, including the IMF. Poland, in order to modernize and upgrade its economic system, requires capital, and the lenders of capital impose a variety of social conditions as a requirement for obtaining loans. The current "ideology" calls not only for Poland but also for other East European nations to adopt a laissez-faire economic system that, ironically, is not adhered to in any fundamental sense by the powerful industrial nations that impose the aforementioned conditions on the lenders.

If we turn to the nations of Latin America, we find that they have become captives of international debt and powerful banking interests, especially those located in the United States. At the same time, a number of leaders of the nations that made up the former Soviet Union, in their efforts to reform a command economy, have been cognizant of the need for finance capital from international lending agencies and advanced industrial countries. Slowly but surely, the structure of international finance capital will reshape the curriculum of business and law schools, and we are likely to have a "trickle down" effect into sociology.

A second strategic element of the global bureaucratic system is the organizational structures whose agents develop, disseminate, and apply scientific knowledge. Here the social sciences, apart from some elements of economics and political science (e.g., Murray 1991), occupy a marginal role, being oriented primarily to nation-states. Universities and research institutes lie at the core of these emerging organizational structures. Yet corporations also have research and development arms that often function in concert with various research arms of the university. Although the organizational structures supporting the scientific/technological complex are "loosely coupled," they have emerged as a power constellation to be reckoned with.

Nowadays, research institutions are the foundation of political (including military) power in modern industrial societies. They also undergird the political and economic controls of transnational organizations. Dickson's (1988:165) observations are pertinent to our analysis: "Science has also taken on a new political significance in international relations. A relative decline in the more overt forms of military and economic power of major industrial nations has led them increasingly to use their hegemony in science and technology to fight for positions in the international system."

Modern military power rests on scientific/technological advances (though countervailing forces, as evident in Vietnam, set limits on crass reliance on modern technology). Moreover, scientific/technological innovation is the motor of modern industrialization. The breakthroughs that have resulted from new computer technology have led to a restructuring of the manufacturing sector. And it seems likely that genetic engineering will have wide-ranging effects on many dimensions of modern life.

Although the powerful universities and research institutes are based in modern industrial nations, their linkages are global in nature and are becoming increasingly more so. Science at its core requires some form of transnational communication.

There are numerous ramifications of the scientific and technological complex. The rise of Silicon Valley is one expression of the linkage of corporate activities to the scientific/technological complex of universities. It is no mere accident that this region emerged under the spires of Stanford University and the University of California at Berkeley. If we look at the situation in global terms, the European Community is destined to stimulate increased internationalization of scientific activity as organizational linkages across once-sacred national boundaries become commonplace.

In a different sense, the former Soviet Union failed to sustain a competitive power base within the world scientific/technological complex. It suffered a relative loss of military power, and its productive capacity suffered in comparison to the United States, western Europe, and Japan. The command economy, which functions within a highly bureaucratized society, has stifled scientific and technological innovation, and the resulting isolation of the former Soviet Union from the world's scientific/technological system has spurred many of the efforts to reform this social order (e.g., Schweitzer 1988).

Perhaps the most dramatic feature of the new world scientific/technological organizational structure is that it is driving an ever greater wedge between the powerful industrial nations and the less developed ones.[2] The former profit from the brain drain from the latter. Moreover, the enormous resources (both in human and in finance capital terms) needed to sustain and expand a scientific/technological complex lead the less developed nations to fall increasingly farther behind the dominant industrial powers that house scientific/technological facilities. The cost of building and sustaining scientific laboratories and maintaining research libraries—to mention only some aspects of the scientific infrastructure—places most African nations, for instance, in a totally disadvantageous position. Here we have an instance of stark dependency. But understanding this situation requires knowledge about the organizational structure of the modern scientific/technological complex.

A third bureaucratic complex that has come to dominate the world system is associated with the mass communication (especially the mass media) network. Bagdikian (1990:239) states: "Instead of control by governments, public opinion is increasingly controlled by a small number of private corporations." He (1990:240) then contends that these global giants

> move internationally without even the mild antitrust restraints of their home countries . . .
>
> Their names are seen in headlines as actors in a financial competition that is now entered only by mammoth corporate organizations, backed by the largest multinational banks and their politically compatible national regimes. They already command international audiences larger than any political leader in history.

The transnational organizational structure of the mass media has manifold social consequences. The managers of these corporations are able to exert formal and informal social controls on those who would challenge the existing social arrangements with which the former are aligned. These mass media conglomerates have the wherewithal to suppress social and political dissent that might challenge the foundations on which the managerial sector rests. Not that fractures are absent among and within organizations. Nonetheless, the domination of these new organizational structures significantly affect the nature of public discourse (including sociological debate). This phenomenon must be interpreted sociologically if we are to come to terms with what is occurring before our very eyes. Although new technologies may in part counteract these patterns, we have reason to be concerned with the suppression of alternative minority standpoints.

The mass media bureaucracies also are advancing the cause of "consumerism" on a global basis. The diffusion of blue jeans and rock music is merely symptomatic of a social process that only recently has captured the attention of social scientists. The ability of transnational organizations to shape consumer tastes has led vast numbers of people to emulate the lifestyles of peoples in powerful industrial nations. The new social expectations regarding quality of life, as defined by consumerism, are drawing persons in developing nations into the orbit of consumer capitalism.

The fourth bureaucratic organizational system concerns the production of goods. Most sociologists who conduct research on transnational economic arrangements have focused on this particular phenomenon. Special attention has been given to, for instance, the transfer of manufacturing jobs from the United States to less developed nations. Although this trend is taking a severe toll on sizable elements of the U.S. populace, the manufacturing sector is nonetheless subject to control by organizations associated with finance capital, the scientific/ technological complex, and the mass media, and these have their base in advanced industrial nations, not in the poverty-stricken regions of the world. Any understanding of the broader global bureaucratic system must consider the manufacturing system within the framework of more powerful organizational arrangements.

But why analyze the emerging world bureaucratic systems in our effort to understand contemporary U.S. sociology? Several tentative conclusions come to mind. These global transnational organizations enjoy a semiautonomy with respect to nation-states (cf. Kennedy 1988). Concomitantly, major research universities are being integrated into, and supported by, transnational structures. This is especially true for the science, engineering, and business school/law school complexes. Although there is a growing international set of linkages among sociologists, they play only a marginal role in the power structures that have come into existence in the world system. Still the discipline, especially as expressed by its dominant research mold, is highly integrated into nation-state structures. Nonetheless, sociologists must come to understand these global organizational structures, for they shape social policies in the manufacturing arena, in race and ethnic relations, and in a host of other realms on the national scene. Most significant, for our purposes, these global structures are typically not amenable to research via the natural science model with its stress on highly standardized quantitative procedures. We return to these and other related themes as our argument unfolds.

The Position of Sociology in the Bureaucratic Context

The social sciences have played a secondary role, at least in the post World War II years, with respect to the major power centers in the modern university: the natural science and the business/law school complexes aligned with, or integrated into, rather well-defined power blocs of the nation-state. But just where do the social sciences fit? Economics, political science, and history have been the core social sciences, and each of these has had a "natural constituency" with respect to power arrangements in the broader social order. In the next tier, we find psychology, and, after that, sociology and anthropology occupy a disadvantaged position among the social sciences in the university setting. Geography may be in the most precarious position of all.

The Social Sciences (Other Than Sociology)

As for the core sector of social science, economists have for several centuries helped to shape, or to rationalize, the policy of nation-states in the West. We can trace this pattern from Adam Smith to Ricardo to the modern era. During the nineteenth century, economics reinforced its position by taking over a number of the trappings of the natural science model. Political economists such as John Stuart Mill introduced the experimental design into social inquiry, and William Jevons advanced the cause of mathematical model building that has given economics an aura of scientific respectability. In the United States the formal institutionalization of economics into the power arrangements of the state was attained with the establishment of the Council of Economic Advisers in 1946. Economics alone among the social sciences commands a Nobel prize: "Its formal mode of argument, mathematical apparatus . . . and rigorous logic have made it the model for the 'softer' social sciences" (Heilbroner 1991:457).

Both governmental and corporate leaders nowadays look to economists for analysis and interpretation of a vast body of quantitative data. The very nature of business activity is such as to emphasize quantification. Moreover, the state not only is engaged in taxation but also in managing the "free market" economy. In the process the state apparatus collects a vast amount of data regarding a variety of economic activities. Political decision makers rely on economists to help in the construction and justification of administrative decisions associated with the regulation of the "free market." Although economists no longer speak of "fine tuning" as they did in the 1960s, they nonetheless play influential roles in shaping the nature of the modern political economy. Moreover, they are widely cited and discussed in (and even contribute to) the *Wall Street Journal*, *Business Week*, *Fortune*, and the like. This means that they have a well-defined, though controversial, role in molding the nature of state and corporate policies.

Political scientists are almost by definition an integral part of the administrative power of the state. Although the discipline is plagued with sharp internal divisions (cf. Almond 1990), it nonetheless is interwoven with national, state, and local power apparatuses. Insofar as public administration can be seen as a wing of political science, the discipline becomes a rather direct training ground for the personnel who staff government agencies.

The role of political scientists in the state structure is multifaceted in nature. For example, the post-World War II period saw the rise of a host of research institutes that focus on foreign studies—e.g., Soviet studies, Latin American studies, East Asian studies. Political scientists (as well as historians) have played strategic roles in these programs. In this manner they have linked the discipline into the global hegemony associated with the dominance of U.S. military might after World War II. Political scientists have been called on to assist national decision makers in understanding the political institutions and cultures of other nations as the United States has sought to sustain its military and political dominance on a worldwide basis. Moreover, a number of American political scientists have worked closely with various governmental structures in developing nations in particular.

Some scholars might quarrel with where to place history, but we have located it among the social sciences. Although historians are not as prominent as they once were in defining the social and political culture of a nation, their place remains relatively secure. Historical writings, when examined from a sociology-of-knowledge perspective, are an essential feature for sustaining the legitimation of major organizations and power blocs in the modern world. The intense struggles over how history should be written bear witness to the premium placed by those in power positions (or those seeking to attain greater influence) on constructing history so as to defend their legitimacy.

Within the U.S. during the past several decades, ethnic minorities and women have fought a persistent battle to rewrite U.S. history and to demonstrate how African Americans, Mexican Americans, and women have helped shape the course of U.S. history. This particular effort to rewrite "official history" resulted from movements by ethnic minorities and women to gain greater equality within the social and political spheres. Yet these political gains require a historical legitimacy that can be achieved only through a reconstruction of the "social memory" of those who traditionally were ignored in the creation of American history.

The efforts at historical revisionism are cast into broader relief as one looks at the contemporary debates about Eurocentric history. Such activity involves a conscious effort to rewrite the past in order either to support older European and U.S. power arrangements or to undermine them. These intense intellectual quarrels about the historical record have direct relevance for the legitimacy of present-day power relations on a global basis.

As we turn from the core disciplines of the social sciences to psychology, we discover that it has legitimated itself through a close relationship to one wing of the biological sciences as well as by a formal linkage with the administrative power of the state. Intelligence testing became an essential element of psychology early in this century under the leadership of, for instance, Goddard and Terman. "Scientific psychology" received a major boost during World War I when Yerkes was able to test vast numbers of persons in the military. Subsequent publication of these findings fueled interest in testing, and it was later to become institutionalized as part and parcel of the educational system.

In a different vein, industrial psychology has forged a link between this discipline and the corporate sector. Moreover, the growth of clinical psychology has been "spurred in large measure by expansion of government support for mental-health services" (Raymond 1991:A10). One group of clinicians has aided the privileged middle class in accommodating to the tensions and conflicts associated with modernity. Another has been employed to rationalize the labeling of the economically underprivileged and mentally unstable and thus to keep the maladapted in their place. Admittedly, psychology today is deeply divided between those who wish to identify formally with the natural sciences and the "clinical practitioners" (though both groups seem to need one another).[3]

Sociology

Our highly adumbrated overview of the other social sciences has been a prelude for interpreting sociology's position in the broader social setting. As we look at the other social sciences—notably economics, political science, history, and psychology—we see that each has been involved in shaping or justifying the administrative policies of the state (and, in varying degrees, of the corporate sector as well).

Sociology's position has been, and continues to be, relatively insecure within the bureaucratic structure of the larger society (to say nothing of the global level). Sociology was a latecomer on the social science scene. The Chicago School, which dominated pre-World War II sociology, grounded its legitimacy in providing an understanding of new immigrant groups and marginal or deviant groups within the rapidly changing urban environment. Although individual sociologists were linked to the state apparatus, the discipline as a whole, except for rural sociology, had few, if any, direct ties with state and corporate structures before World War II.

During and after the war, several trends emerged in the discipline. Two deserve special mention. One group of sociologists focused on major societal and cultural issues. During the 1950s and early 1960s, sociologists such as Daniel Bell, David Riesman, and C. Wright Mills contributed to the political and social discourse about the nature of American society. During this era, sociology in the U.S. achieved a measure of public attention unmatched in its history.

Parsons was, in a real sense, part of this phenomenon. As the most influential American sociological theorist in this century, he was, as Gouldner (1970) rightly contends, a central interpreter and rationalizer of the welfare state (and the American dream). Parsons's theorizing helped to shape a major epoch in U.S. history.

What Gouldner (1970) missed in *The Coming Crisis of Western Sociology* was another overriding trend—the emerging dominance of the natural science model in sociology. The increased reliance on quantitative methods, with a stress on standardization and replication, and their linkage to the welfare state (as well as the corporate apparatus) escaped Gouldner's sociological eye.

As sociologists adopted quantitative methods, a distinct movement occurred, notably in research universities, away from individual scholarly endeavor to organized research activities. Many sociologists have attempted to emulate the organized research efforts of their colleagues in the natural sciences. The sharpest break in sociological practice resulted from increased reliance on survey research. Jean Converse (1987) provides us with a highly useful history of this trend, and, although our analysis differs from hers, we rely rather heavily on her account.

Converse documents how the survey approach was advanced by Stouffer's *The American Soldier* during World War II. This large-scale enterprise legitimized this kind of research as useful to the state apparatus. Actually this research was not the only sociological inquiry to come out of the war. A number of sociologists, who later were to become national leaders, were trained in bureaucratized research during their stint with the armed forces.

Converse also provides us with much-needed details on the growth of the Bureau of Social Research at Columbia, the National Opinion Research Center (NORC) at Chicago, and the Institute for Social Research (ISR) at the University of Michigan. The Bureau of Social Research, which had its origins in market research, is the single most striking break with the early Chicago School style of research (Coleman 1990:619-20). The bureau was built around Paul Lazarsfeld, an entrepreneurial sociologist par excellence. It was funded by foundations and corporations largely committed to research relating to the mass media. This was a research organization that could draw on support from corporations housed in New York, the media capital of America.

Although Lazarsfeld was the bureau's master builder, he was greatly aided and abetted in his efforts by his friend and colleague Robert K. Merton. While Parsons was constructing grand theories at Harvard, Columbia was training a cadre of sociologists such as James Coleman, Peter Rossi, and Charles Glock, many of whom took the lead in institutionalizing research centers in other universities. Merton's role in the bureau is instructive. After his association with the bureau's activities, he appears to have been far more influenced by Lazarsfeld than vice versa. While Merton's own sociological imagination suffered from this collaboration, he nonetheless became a strategic bridge between empirical research and Parsonian functionalism, the dominant theoretical paradigm of that era.

The National Opinion Research Center, which moved from the University of Denver to the University of Chicago in 1947, was in part built by some of Lazarsfeld's students. Rossi, for instance, was for some years its director. Yet the NORC has been more interdisciplinary than the Bureau of Social Research and never was as central to sociology at Chicago as the bureau was to sociology at Columbia.

The Survey Research Center at the University of Michigan also deserves special mention. The center combined, as the larger partner, with the Institute of Social Research in 1949. Unlike the Bureau of Social Research and the NORC, the links of the SRC/ISR seem to have been more with the government than with the corporate sector, for Likert brought the ISR from Washington and cultivated considerable ties with the federal agencies that funded social research.

In the case of the SRC/ISR, the members of the sociology department at Michigan have been only one part of this enterprise. But, the spillover of its presence on the sociological program has been considerable. Converse (1987:346) writes:

> SRC/ISR also had a close relationship with the university's Detroit Area Study (DAS), a graduate practicum in survey research which was established in 1951 by sociologist Ronald Freedman, founding director. DAS was a two-semester course that conducted an annual survey in the Detroit metropolitan area. It was similar to and perhaps molded on the ORC-NORC Denver Community survey. Initially, DAS was supported by a grant from the Ford Foundation, and funds were administered through SRC and an interdisciplinary committee. In 1958, the university assumed full support for DAS and channeled funds through the sociology department.

Viewed in this light, the SRC came to shape the nature of the sociology program at Michigan in keeping with the ever rising dominance of survey research in the 1950s.

The Bureau of Social Research, the NORC, and the SRC have been major vehicles for advancing sociological research, and they have spawned a variety of smaller enterprises at universities in American society. At the same time, survey research centers are only a small part of the efforts to integrate sociology into the bureaucratic structure of the university and to institutionalize relatively large-scale research efforts. Another constellation of research activities has been spawned by the population centers that emerged at universities in the 1950s and afterward. These have been powerful organizational bases for sociologists in such universities as Wisconsin, Michigan, Texas, North Carolina, and Pennsylvania, to mention only some. These have been heavily funded by the federal government and have relied on data collected by the decennial census as well as the numerous other surveys carried out by the U.S. Bureau of the Census.

In addition, sociologists have been the creators of a variety of other centers and institutes or they have been intimately involved with them. These include urban institutes, criminal justice programs, and gerontology or aging centers, as well as specialized programs such as those relating to science and drug abuse. Our intention is not to catalogue the growth of these centers or institutes but to take account of the theoretical and methodological implications of this organizational phenomenon for the discipline. These organizational structures have encouraged the emulation of the natural science model by sociologists.

To clarify our argument, we single out two divergent programs as case studies of organized research and the development of the modern sociological enterprise. The most important has been at the University of Wisconsin at Madison, but that at Georgia illustrates how less powerful institutions have carved out special niches for themselves.

The Department of Sociology at the University of Wisconsin is especially instructive. In the early 1980s this department was ranked No. 1 in the Jones-Lindzey prestige rankings. Its faculty is perhaps the largest of any department in the United States, and the department exerted a major influence on the course of the discipline during the past two decades.

What characterizes this department and how did it achieve its present status? If one looks closely at its program, it is rather diverse. Yet many of its central figures have been closely linked to Rural Sociology, the Population Center, or the Institute on Poverty. The latter is a striking illustration of the impact of the Great Society on the social sciences, sociology in particular (cf. Haveman 1987:43-46).

Our view of the Wisconsin department is in general supported by a careful reading of Sewell's (1988) brief autobiography. Sewell, like Lazarsfeld, has been a major academic entrepreneur (though his sociological contributions are less imaginative). Sewell was heavily influenced by his experience in rural sociology—first at Oklahoma A&M University (now Oklahoma State University) and later at the University of Wisconsin at Madison. At Oklahoma A&M he held half-time appointments in rural sociology and sociology, and when he moved to Wisconsin this arrangement continued. He also served a stint in the navy, and after the war was involved with a large-scale survey on the impact of bombing on Japan. He had thereby forged ties with the Washington bureaucracy that were to stand him in good stead.

Sewell relied on the rural sociology model in constructing the Wisconsin department. Although he was more innovative than most rural sociologists, his vision was severely constrained by that heritage. From his research on the socioeconomic status scale at Oklahoma A&M to the research on educational and occupational aspirations and achievement at Wisconsin, his sociology has been Middle America to the core. His research efforts have been justified, both theoretically and empirically, by that particular worldview.

Our second case is Paul Roman at the University of Georgia. He has promoted a large-scale research effort on "employee assistance programs" in the workplace. His efforts are captured in a trade journal; his photo appears on the cover, and an article titled "A Research Empire for Roman" (Read 1988:32) lauds his contributions. He has advanced sociological research based on federal funding, and he is perhaps the leading sociological practitioner in this area of specialization. What he does, he does about as well as did Sewell, though Roman's agenda is more narrowly circumscribed.

Our consideration of the growth of research institutes and large-scale sociological research is not an end in itself; the theoretical implications are what command our attention. The movement away from research carried out by individual scholars to organized research staffs has called for funding on a scale that was far greater than in the past. Although private foundations have continued to provide support for sociological research, sociologists have turned increasingly to the federal government for financial assistance. It is the matter of federal funding on which we next focus.

The Natural Science Model, Research Procedures, and the Bureaucratization Process

Having located the changing nature of the sociological enterprise in the United States in the context of the bureaucratic structures of the university and the broader social order after World War II, we now describe the political actions targeted toward achieving financial support for organized sociological research and the resulting dominance of the natural science model.

We consider several interrelated questions: How is the natural science model, and the research procedures associated with it, interlaced with the bureaucratization process? How, in turn, does this pattern lead sociologists to focus on certain kinds of empirical data and ignore others? What is the sociologist's role in legitimizing the bureaucratic structures that support social research in the first instance?

The interconnection between the natural science model and bureaucratization is not well articulated by sociologists. The principles associated with bureaucracy and those related to the natural science model have been grounded historically in overlapping intellectual and practical traditions. The "scientific revolution" was not intrinsically associated with the formation of modern bureaucratic systems. Nevertheless, bureaucracy has been intertwined with the development of the scientific method, in particular with the products of science.

Scientific advances have made it feasible to construct large-scale bureaucratic organizations, and these serve to integrate the various modes of specialization that typify so many realms of modern life. In addition, the scientific method can be conceived of as furthering formal, rather than substantive, rationality.

Earlier we took account of the prestige and power of the natural science and technological complex with respect to the bureaucratization process. We now look more closely at how this arrangement has affected the funding of sociological research. To do so, we must consider the nature of the natural science model as it has been articulated by sociologists (or social scientists more generally).

The Premises of the Natural Science Model

Vaughan (in this volume) and Sjoberg et al. (1991) have articulated the premises, as well as research procedures, of the natural science model. Here we highlight some features of this model as these bear on our succeeding discussion.

A number of differences among proponents of the natural science model can be cited. For instance, some advocate the logico-deductive orientation, whereas others are committed to inductive procedures. While granting that these differences generate intense debates, the adherents of this model nonetheless agree that a social order exists "out there" quite apart from the observer (or social scientist). This social order is characterized by well-defined regularities, and these can be discovered through the application of rigorous research procedures such as those associated with experimentation and quantification.

In order to employ rigorous, standardized research procedures in collecting and analyzing data, the scientific sociologist must reduce the social order to basic elements, notably "variables." In practice, "individuals" are the primary unit of analysis, although sociologists also can treat organizations (e.g., firms) or nation-states as if they were autonomous, individual units. Inasmuch as these entities are "discrete," probability sampling is feasible, and ultimately the "whole" (such as a large-scale organization) is defined by aggregating the parts.

Adherents of this model also assume that carefully designed investigations of narrowly defined problems will provide the "bricks of knowledge" that can be employed to construct a larger scientific edifice. But they have not drafted a blueprint for constructing the knowledge complex they envisage. This is particularly true for the "inductivist" wing.

The champions of this model typically do not admit that basic contradictions may exist within the social order. Moreover, they typically take appearances for granted. They generally are willing to work within the confines of "officially defined" reality.

Another guiding premise of the natural science model is that "value neutrality" and "objectivity" can be attained. Sociologists as scientists can bracket their political and moral sensibilities as citizens in their quest for social regularities that inhere in a natural order. Here the Weberian and Parsonian tradition converges with the positivist stance as articulated by the Vienna Circle.

The Linkage of the Natural Science Model and the Bureaucratic Process

That the research procedures of the natural science model, notably quantification, and bureaucracy are mutually supportive of each other can be documented from several vantage points. In the postwar years, government funding for social research, along with the rise of research institutes and centers within and outside the university, was based on an appeal to the natural science model.

Government funding did not come automatically to the social sciences in the postwar era. Although financial support for the social sciences is still only a meager part of the funding for the sciences, monies nonetheless have become available to a large body of sociologists from a variety of funding agencies. For example, John Clausen had a hand in advancing sociological research at the National Institute of Mental Health just after the war (Sewell 1988:130).

The political struggle to incorporate social science, including sociological, research into the NSF is especially instructive. Riecken (1986), who acted as an internal advocate for funding social science in the NSF, has provided us with essential details about this process. He documents how social scientists staked out their claim against the opposition to the funding of social research by various interest groups, including natural scientists. They did so by a commitment to positivism. Also, in the 1950s, a conscious effort was made to avoid highly controversial topics.

We must remember the social climate of that era. A number of the opponents of sociology equated it with socialism or social reform. The lack of rigor and objectivity led conservatives, especially that brand fueled by McCarthyism, to view social science as a subversive activity. Thus, the recourse to social research that is "methodologically rigorous, objective, verifiable, and generalizable" (Riecken 1986:215). Riecken (1986:219) next inserts an informative set of observations:

> *It cannot be said too plainly or bluntly: the growth of support for social science at NSF was not the direct result of social scientific accomplishments as such, much as we might wish it otherwise.* It was the result of strong external support for the program on the part of respected advisers, a rising budget that prevented NSF expansion from being a zero-sum game, a degree of skill at administrative politics within the agency, and the fact that, in the first decade or so,

grantees committed no serious gaffes or egregious offenses to the conventional morality or established values of those who controlled authorization and budget. (italics added)

Riecken points to, though it is not his task to investigate, the aura surrounding the natural sciences in the 1950s and 1960s. This was when sociology was gaining support for federal funding. Social scientists had achieved sufficient stature so they could claim that, by employing the methods of natural sciences, they, too, could advance the public good or "national interest" (cf. Klausner and Lidz 1986).

The conscious effort to utilize the natural science model continued into the 1970s. The first-named author's experience as a member of the NSF's Advisory Panel for Sociology in the mid-1970s provides limited insight into the ongoing pattern of emulation. One person was rather explicit that a particular request for funding of a large-scale research project in demography was an effort to demonstrate to the power brokers at NSF that sociology required "Big Science" funding. Although the project was small compared to those in the natural sciences, the sociologists set out to justify funding for a project that would be socially meaningful and that involved making use of quantifiable data on a rather grand scale.

The NSF's support for sociology was, it would appear, furthered by funding practices in other agencies. Also, from the 1930s through the 1960s, a shift occurred in the belief system in U.S. society. In the 1930s and 1940s numerous politicians were deeply suspicious of pollsters (cf. Converse 1987:207-11), but by the late 1960s public opinion surveys had become an instrument that adroit politicians would employ to advance their political careers and agendas.

By the time the programs of the Great Society were enacted into law in the 1960s, survey research had become institutionalized in the United States. Funds began to flow to social scientists in order to conduct evaluation research—a growth industry during the 1970s. It is not feasible to evaluate government programs via the "market mechanism." Another mode for judging the efficiency (or effectiveness) of new government initiatives had to be developed. Thus, a variety of sociologists have been funded for research relating to the evaluation of social programs.

Admittedly, psychologists began employing standardized testing as a tool for evaluating mass education many years earlier. Conventional wisdom has it that students can be routed into proper educational channels through standardized or "universalistic" criteria that are scientific in nature. Any challenge to the biases of these tests has typically been met with the counterargument that the tests are standardized and reflect basic social reality. What the proponents of these tests do not tell us is that the instruments are standardized from a top-down perspective—from the orientation of those who have been successful in the system. They conveniently ignore the fact that the measurement of "intelligence" is interpreted within the framework of a hierarchical, bureaucratic order.

But to return to our thesis concerning the funding of sociological research. Sociologists, after the early battles were won, gained a measure of social and political legitimacy as their research procedures were perceived as having practical application within large-scale organizational settings.

The natural science model is interlaced with the bureaucratic apparatus in another significant respect. As suggested earlier, adherence to the claim of "value neutrality" or "objectivity" means that scientific sociology poses no intrinsic challenge to existing hierarchical arrangements. The power of the natural science model as a vehicle for providing researchers with scientific respectability is nowhere more clearly demonstrated than in the actions of Marxist sociologists in the 1970s and 1980s. Attewell (1984), in his review of political economists, spoke glowingly of the increased acceptance of Marxism by mainstream social scientists because Marxist scholars have demonstrated that they can employ rigorous statistical techniques in their analysis. Erik Olin Wright (1985) claims to have carried out a Marxist sociological survey. But his contributions are built on the research procedures of the "Wisconsin model" developed by Sewell and his associates. After all, Wright is unable to analyze, in any effective manner, either the truly powerful or the truly disadvantaged. Significant sectors of both groups, for different reasons, do not respond to national social surveys.

The Domination and Contributions of the Natural Science Model

We need to specify more fully the consequences of the efforts by sociologists to gain access to federal funding sources. This process has escalated the domination by the natural science model in contemporary sociology.

The postwar trends are, in a sense, an extrapolation of long-standing historical conditions. Ross (1991) has recorded in detail the appeal to the scientific model by social scientists in the early decades of this century. Therefore, the evolution of the quantification process should occasion, with the benefit of hindsight, no surprise. The hegemony of the natural science model is reflected in the nature of journal articles published during the past few decades. Hanneman (cf. Turner 1989) has examined the articles published in the *American Journal of Sociology*, and Wilner (1985) has done the same for the *American Sociological Review*. The shift to the "variable approach" and concomitant reliance on statistical techniques are now the order of the day. This pattern has been accompanied by a heightened emphasis on statistical training in graduate education (Schwirian and McDonagh 1991). Although selected countertrends can be singled out, priority continues to be given to statistical techniques, and theory is downplayed. This has resulted in a disjuncture between theory and methods or techniques (e.g., Turner 1989). In many articles theory is tacked on, more or less as an afterthought. What we have is increased specialization regarding substantive areas, but within this diversity is found a dominant methodological paradigm, one based on quantitative techniques and methods. We are cognizant of the internecine warfare among adherents of quantification. But these debates pale into insignificance when we observe the hostility of many of these sociologists to wide-ranging theoretical ideas employed to interpret qualitative data. Moreover, the natural science model is highly entrenched in such well-established specialties as criminology, demography, rural sociology, the family, and social psychology.[4]

Although we are studiedly critical of the natural science model, we recognize its substantial contribution—within a well-circumscribed framework —to the formation and maintenance of modern social orders. Quantified data, as reflected in accounting practices, are the basis for many decisions in both corporate and governmental sectors. The relentless preoccupation with profit and loss in the corporate sector, and with spending and deficits in the governmental sphere, heightens public awareness of the all-pervasive role that numerical data play in people's daily activities in modern social orders.

Social surveys, the staple of contemporary empirical sociology, fit into this overall commitment to quantification. Members of the executive and legislative branches of the federal and state governments often rely on survey data for making a number of decisions. The surveys conducted by private and academic organizations as well as by the Bureau of the Census provide us with practical knowledge of one slice of modern society that it would be foolhardy to ignore. Nonetheless, the manner in which quantitative data are collected—namely the kinds of questions asked and how these questions are asked—serve to legitimate the activities of the organizations that underwrite the research in the first instance.

Hierarchical Arrangements, the Reward Structure, and the Education Process

We have looked, however hurriedly, at the position of sociology on the societal and global scene and on how sociologists in recent decades have sought to establish themselves as worthy of federal funding. We now consider the implications of these patterns for social life on the departmental level. Here we enter the realm of the "sacred." How the bureaucratic (or rationalization) process has had an impact on the nature of the educational process and reward structure within departments is a "black box" with respect to sociological investigation. We glean some relevant data by reading the autobiographical accounts, for example, of Homans (1984) and those sociologists represented in Berger (1990) and Riley (1988).[5] Such works as that by Martindale (1976) are of some interest. We also have relied on *Footnotes, The American Sociologist,* and *Teaching Sociology,* among other publications. Moreover, we have made a special point of discussing the normative arrangements we analyze with numerous colleagues from a wide variety of universities and colleges during the past thirty years, and especially during the past seven or eight years. We focus on the mainstream, but acknowledge countervailing currents.

What is transpiring in sociology departments is not unique. Although Hackett (1990) emphasizes cultural systems (whereas we focus on social structure), his observations regarding departments in the natural sciences sustain our contention that the bureaucratization process permeates university life in a manner not yet explicated.

The Hierarchical System

We begin with a recognition of the hierarchical nature (in a loose sense) of universities and departments in America. The research universities that grant doctorates command the key influence and power.[6] Even within this group, we find a *keen sensitivity* to one's own department's position in the "pecking order." The status of sociology departments has been a focus of numerous publications. The second-named author wrote one of the earliest works on this topic (Knudsen and Vaughan 1969). Departmental status is a common topic of conversation among sociologists.

The powerful departments are able to attract the well-published scholars and high-quality graduate students; to gain monies from state, foundation, and corporate sources; and to control—though this assertion is hotly contested by members of the power elite—the strategic publication outlets, especially the major journals. The University of Chicago's sponsorship of the *American Journal of Sociology* and the University of North Carolina's links to *Social Forces* have bestowed special advantages on these departments. Their faculties and graduate students have profited greatly from this relationship.

The research universities are most readily able to generate monies from funding agencies for graduate programs, which are expensive to underwrite. At the same time, graduate students in these universities are the source of highly reliable cheap labor, which assists professors in escaping the most burdensome chores associated with undergraduate teaching and social research.

The hierarchy of universities and departments has been institutionalized in state-supported systems. This is based on the premise that research universities are the engines for technological and economic development. In California the university system has a major advantage over the state system, and even within the former, the campuses of Berkeley and Los Angeles command special privileges. In Wisconsin the University at Madison is the flagship institution, that at Milwaukee a distant second, and other campuses occupy lesser positions of power. Although private schools represent a special case, the institutionalization of hierarchical control within and among states is well established. The salary structures typically reflect the power arrangements. The highest-paid sociologists typically are found at the powerful research universities.

Employment Patterns and the Reward System

Some decades ago, Caplow and McGee (1958) provided data relating to how the elite universities feed on one another. This results from the powerful networks among members of departments (sociology included) at these institutions. Also, persons who secure their doctorates from powerful elite institutions have the proper sponsorship to make it in a publish-or-perish system. One's sponsors can assist younger scholars in breaking into major journals, in publishing in highly visible anthologies, and in having their monographs appear under the imprimatur of "high-status" publishers. On a number of occasions we have heard editors say: "Supply us with the names of sociologists (or other social scientists) at prestige universities, and their positive reviews will facilitate publication of the book." Although exceptions to these patterns exist, they cast the basic norms into broad relief.

Moreover, if departments employ persons from prestigious institutions who are in high demand, they can more readily justify their hiring practices with their own administrations. This pattern enhances the legitimacy of the department in the eyes of the local administration.

But our primary emphasis is not on the employment of newly minted doctorates but on the changing reward structure in departments. These fundamental revisions have reflected the broader social forces outlined earlier.

Social status, as measured in monetary terms, depends on one's publication record, one's administrative success and political acumen either within the university or in the professional apparatus, one's grantsmanship, and one's marketability. Although the reward system in sociology departments is off-limits with respect to scholarly analysis, some of the more overt changes deserve to be mentioned.

In ideal terms, the quality of a sociologist's publications should be ranked foremost. The likes of Charles Tilly, William Julius Wilson, Neil Smelser, and Seymour Martin Lipset are, we assume, well rewarded. But once one drops below their level of scholarship, all manner of controversy (and inconsistency) can be discerned. Many sociologists are well known within limited sociometric circles in the discipline, but they are unknown, or are viewed with disdain, outside their narrow areas of expertise.

Although not analyzed in print, the aforementioned patterns are rather well understood. What commands our attention here are selected patterns that have emerged in recent decades. One is the growth of the superprofessor. Some of them remain highly independent scholars. But a significant set of superprofessors are academic entrepreneurs, master grantsmen or grantswomen. Administrators are deeply intent on building or sustaining a faculty with national prestige. This greatly assists the university in securing funds from public or private sources. Superprofessors also attract highly qualified graduate students who are the lifeblood of research universities. These superprofessors often are removed from undergraduate and even at times graduate teaching.

More and more, superprofessors are academic entrepreneurs who are able to attract funds from the federal (or state) government, from foundations, or from the corporate sector. Glenn (1991:445), in a brief essay on graduate education in sociology, concludes:

> Perhaps the most pernicious change in the past two or three decades has been the tendency for grant-getting to become an end in itself rather than merely a means to doing important research. In many if not most departments, a sociologist will be more highly rewarded for doing research that costs $400 thousand than for equally important work that costs only $40 thousand—a perverse negation of the norm of efficiency. More than a few departments now openly and explicitly base hiring, promotions, and salary increases on grantsmanship, giving that criterion at least equal standing with quality and quantity of publications.

This situation, viewed in theoretical terms, results from the growing dominance of the administrative sector of the university and the logic of the administrative reward structure.

Administrators reason somewhat as follows: They justify their own efforts in terms of "system maintenance," especially in raising monies. Consequently, administrators give primacy to academic entrepreneurs—sociologists involved in local administrative activity but especially those who secure large grants from outside sources (primarily the federal government).

Unquestionably an administrative infrastructure is necessary to support a modern university. The danger to scholarly endeavor lies in administration as an end in itself.[7] The sociologist as a grantsperson brings in much-needed outside funding; the resulting overhead underwrites the administrative apparatus, which continues to expand.[8] In addition, academic entrepreneurs often have direct access to high-level administrators, and because of the primacy of money, they are rewarded directly for their efforts. Consequently, we find a number of sociologists in diverse universities in the United States who have made limited contributions to sociological scholarship but are handsomely rewarded financially by local administrators because of their fund-raising abilities. These sociologists have cultivated connections with particular funding agencies, and these social bonds are reinforced by members of a sociometric circle who evaluate one another's proposals.

Grantsmanship in sociology is closely interwoven with commitment to the natural science model. Access to strategic data sets and the application of sophisticated quantitative techniques greatly assist the researcher in attaining funds for research. By relying on established data sets, the researcher can anticipate, in general terms, the results of the findings. These are defined by the nature of the questions included in the survey. This situation greatly reduces the risks of failure, and the funding agency generally can be assured that numerous publications will result from the project.

If one has access to a data set (ideally a national survey), graduate students and a staff of technical experts (such as those with the requisite computer skills) can be put to good use. These persons can construct the tables and compose the rough drafts and then coauthor articles with the project director. The process is greatly facilitated by the fact that the research topics are narrowly circumscribed and the techniques are, within narrow boundaries, standardized. The resulting publications typically are not ground breaking. Instead, researchers work within well-defined paradigms, and the publications are perceived as making modest incremental advances to social scientific knowledge. Given this framework, the sheer number of publications takes on added significance as a status maker.

The reliance on one's staff to carry out everyday chores frees principal investigators to expend their efforts in, for instance, writing future grant requests. Once a grant is funded, it becomes necessary to secure another one. Unless this procedure is followed, the infrastructure on which this kind of research effort is founded can hardly be maintained.

The Impact on the Intellectual Process

The educational ramifications of the adoption of the natural science model, with its emphasis on techniques applied to ever narrower realms of specialization, have been far-reaching. Although countertrends exist, the fact that graduate students often are expected to carry out specialized research as part of their graduate education provides added impetus to a preoccupation with quantitative techniques and methods. There seems little doubt that statistical virtuosity has received increased priority in contemporary graduate education (cf. Schwirian and McDonagh 1991). Theoretical ideas, as these relate to large-scale substantive problems, are visibly downgraded (cf. Blalock 1985).[9]

The natural science model also has given rise to an emphasis on the quantity of publications among the faculty. To be sure, leading figures in sociology such as Parsons and Homans were highly prolific. Nevertheless, sociologists like Blumer and Garfinkel have left an indelible mark on the discipline with a few strategic publications. Yet concern with the quality of one's contribution to sociological knowledge is on the decline. The criterion of quality becomes increasingly difficult to invoke when the emphasis is on articles that supposedly lead to small incremental advances in social knowledge within a narrowly defined substantive area.

The quantity of publications typically has come to replace quality as a primary means of evaluating colleagues. In many departments we find yearly evaluations. This gives primacy to short-range projects and to the publication of items on an annual basis. Also, colleagues are in a bind when called on, year after year, to rank-order colleagues who work in widely divergent subspecialties. Counting articles in refereed journals serves as a convenient political escape from a highly divisive process that pits colleague against colleague. (The concept "refereed journal" glosses over numerous political and intellectual issues that await critical examination.) Another quantitative criterion employed is the Citation Index. But this does not inform us whether a citation relates to a core idea or whether it is mere "window dressing." Overall, the "rationalization" of evaluation reinforces the natural science mode of publication: numerous short research reports (often coauthored) on highly specialized topics.

The quantification of quality can be illustrated by a stark case that came to our attention. A rather well-known sociologist took out a ruler and measured the number of inches in the Citation Index of the persons being considered for promotion and made his judgment accordingly. While perhaps extreme, this action provides a glimpse into the mind-set that has emerged in contemporary sociological departments regarding the primacy of quantity of publications. Under these circumstances, most sociologists are discouraged from working on large-scale problems for which there is no immediate payoff.

Other consequences of recent trends can be delineated. One of the most striking phenomena in the past decade or so is the fact that the emphasis on grantsmanship and quantity of publications is being emulated by sociologists at colleges and universities whose primary mission has been teaching, not research. The faculty at these schools is under increased pressure to secure external funding. In addition, faculty members are expected to produce a certain number of publications in refereed journals before they can receive tenure and promotion. Although social research, if properly carried out, can enhance teaching, this emulation of the patterns adopted by the research universities is leading to "goal displacement" and the consequent destruction of the teaching process. Yet the indoctrination process begins in graduate school. Younger faculty members are trained to be specialized researchers. Often they are not expected to gain satisfaction in teaching as a calling. An undergraduate college teacher becomes a second-class citizen in the status system of the discipline.

The Limitations of the Natural Science Model

We have provided background data on sociology's place in the bureaucratic structure on the societal and global scenes and have outlined the manner in which the natural science model has become institutionalized within sociology. Although we openly acknowledge the contribution of this model to a facet of social inquiry, the hegemony of this model poses serious threats to the foundations of sociological inquiry. Now that the natural science orientation has achieved ascendancy, we can more readily observe its serious shortcomings.

Our diagnosis regarding a crisis in the discipline requires justification. Our argument proceeds on two interrelated fronts. First, we reason that an emphasis on techniques and methods, shorn of broader sociological theory and ideas, cannot sustain sociology's legitimacy in competing disciplines. This first claim is intimately related to our second one: that the limitations of the natural science model are such that it cannot address the overriding social and moral issues that confront humankind. In order to sustain a democratic social order, these large-scale problem areas demand serious scholarly analysis.

Undermining the Sociological Heritage

The emphasis on techniques and methods is eroding the sociological heritage. Sociology, as defined by the classical sociological heritage of Durkheim, Weber, Marx, and even Parsons, emphasized theoretical ideas and adopted research procedures in order to advance their understanding of the problem areas being investigated. The primary goal of these scholars was to explain the meaning of the changes that resulted from the great transformation from a preindustrial to an industrial (or capitalist) social order. The structural and cultural changes associated with modernity posed severe problems that never have been fully resolved. Yet the classical sociologists provided a framework for making sense of the manner in which persons ordered their lives as a result of this great transformation.

The grave social issues that confront contemporary humankind are of a different order from those faced by the classical sociologists. Nuclear and biological warfare, the economic plight of most Third World people, racial and ethnic conflicts, the destruction of the environment, and the emergence of a global bureaucratic order are among the social phenomena that demand socio-logical investigation. Yet the natural science model fails miserably in coping with these social and moral issues (cf. Erikson 1984; Kurtz forthcoming).[10]

In view of this situation, the sociological enterprise is being undermined in concrete ways.[11] If sociologists continue to justify their existence in large measure by using technical quantitative procedures, then the discipline will lose its raison d'etre. The methods and techniques can readily be borrowed by other disciplines. Coleman (1990) implies the research procedures developed by the Bureau of Social Research at Columbia were taken over by marketing firms outside academia. Babbie's widely used textbook on research methods now has been modified to meet the needs of the social work profession (Rubin and Babbie 1989). There is absolutely no reason why the techniques on which most contemporary sociologists pride themselves will not be borrowed en masse by other disciplines or professional schools. What, then, is the justification for sociology's existence? Ultimately sociology must rest its position in society on the ability to advance theoretical principles that will help to clarify societal, as well as cross-societal, problem areas.

One consequence of the overreliance on sophisticated techniques and procedures is that sociology will be less and less able to justify its position in the core teaching curriculum. Among the major consumers of sociology have been students. But if techniques and procedures are borrowed by other fields, and sociology continues to downplay theoretical ideas as a basis for clarifying modern social issues, then the discipline will have little if anything to offer one of its primary constituencies—students.

The demise of sociology at Washington University in St. Louis during the 1980s is a danger sign we can ill afford to ignore. Although the controversies associated with the department provided a convenient weapon for the administration's actions, the fact that the sociology department was excised by a major private university suggests that the discipline is by no means secure in the U.S. academic setting. Selected case studies that have come to our attention indicate that sociology has been in an embattled position in institutions in which the discipline once had a secure stronghold.

Our reasoning leads us to another facet of sociology's current crisis. Although the natural science model has made sociological skills useful for governmental and private organizations, what will happen when existing research techniques are taken over by schools of social work, schools of public affairs, and so on? Contemporary sociology also must justify itself by addressing a con-stituency outside its own confines, both within and outside academia. Robert Bellah, Alan Wolfe, William Julius Wilson, and Immanuel Wallerstein have demonstrated that sociology can contribute to the advancement of democratic discourse on a grand scale. Bellah et al. (1985) and Wolfe (1989) have done so with respect to the meaning of life, Wilson (1987) with respect to the truly disadvantaged, and Wallerstein (1983; 1987) with respect to the world system. But they are exceptions. Moreover, in each instance, these scholars have emphasized theoretical ideas and have adapted research data in order to advance our understanding of empirical phenomena. Such is impossible to accomplish if one strictly adheres to the natural science model, with its emphasis on techniques and standardization. The limitations of the natural science model for sociological inquiry are real.

Specifying the Limitations of the Model

Up to now, we have in general taken the limitations of the natural science model for granted. Yet documentation for our assertion is in order. Here we merely highlight some of the more transparent failings of this orientation. We concentrate first on an internal critique of the weaknesses of this model and then we consider why fundamental sociological problems will be ignored if this model continues to hold sway.

1. *The internal critique.* Inasmuch as the proponents of the natural science model have been committed to the quantification of social data, we here single out some of the contradictions that emerge from this effort. We begin with the innovative work of Otis Dudley Duncan (1984) who, in the post World War II era, stands as an exemplar of the employment of quantitative analysis in the discipline.

In one of his last works, Duncan approached quantification (or, more specifically, measurement) as a sympathetic critic. He began with the premise, with which we agree, that measurement is a social process. The quantification of data, from its inception in early civilized societies, has been a human construction. Duncan (1984:221) concludes that "this may be the best assurance we can have that there is ultimately something valid about our enterprise. But it may also be the key to our most serious difficulties in carrying that enterprise through to a *truly scientific level of achievement*" (italics added). That sociologists employ data collected for administrative, rather than scientific, purposes leads to serious methodological problems.

Duncan's case is supported by the recent work of the economist Eisner (1989:1), who, in his presidential address to the American Economic Association, stated that "econometricians, theorists, and economic analysts of all stripes have lost essential communication with the compilers and synthesizers of their data." In matters of income, employment, prices, and consumption, "many of us have literally not known what we are talking about" (1989:3).

Eisner's reasoning is given credence by the contributors to the edited work of Alonso and Starr, *The Politics Of Numbers* (1987). As the title suggests, political decisions greatly affect the manner in which numbers are collected and employed.

But to return to Duncan's analysis, he is correct in conceiving of measurement as a social process. Duncan (1984:238) goes so far as to state that "what will be measured will be what the society wants or allows to be measured." Nonetheless, Duncan falls far short of drawing out the implications of his implicit sociology-of-knowledge perspective. He clings to a "natural science model" ideal that is unrealistic. For example, he (1984:222) speaks of the power of demographic models in studying "groups, organizations, social relationships, and the like, and not necessarily human individuals." Thus, although Duncan contends that measurement is a social process, he purports to understand demographic processes without taking account of human agents who answer the questionnaires on which the demographic data are based. We commend Duncan for clarifying some of the weaknesses of measurement as employed by sociologists. Nonetheless, he still adheres to the presupposition that sociologists can live in a world apart from their respondents and the social order they investigate. Ultimately Duncan is incapable of interpreting the fundamental relationships of measurement and the bureaucratic process in modern society.

Other serious flaws in the natural science model come to light in a recent book by Fligstein, *The Transformation Of Corporate Control* (1990). We single out this research effort because of its likely influence on the field of organizations. But its impact will result not from analysis of quantitative data but from his theoretical contribution. Fligstein includes an Appendix, "The Data Base," in which he discusses the data employed in his analysis. That he fails to consider the weaknesses associated with the construction of these data need not delay us here. Of far greater import is the fact that Fligstein, in his Appendix, neglects to formally acknowledge another primary data base on which he relied. In Chapter 7, "The Finance Conception of Control," he cites numerous quotations by executives, as reported in *Vital Speeches, Business Week,* and the like. These data are used to support Fligstein's (1990:226) contention that "The sales and marketing conception of control came to dominate the largest firms after World War II . . . The finance conception of control stressed the use of financial tools to evaluate produce lines and divisions."

What makes these qualitative data (which are not analyzed systematically) so striking is that they serve as the foundation for Fligstein's innovative theoretical contribution on "The Social Construction of Efficiency" (1990:chap. 9). Consequently, Fligstein relies on highly qualitative data to interpret his apparently "rigorous" quantitative evidence.

Fligstein is not unique among adherents of the natural science model in relying heavily on qualitative data for his theoretical analysis. Sewell and his associates drew on their autobiographical backgrounds (and the belief and value system of their era) when interpreting data on status attainment in Wisconsin (cf.

Knottnerus 1987). Sewell's claim to objectivity carries with it the heavy baggage of mid-American ethnocentrism (cf. Sewell 1988), which then is glossed over by the use of technical statistical techniques. He apparently was seeking to establish scientific generalizations that held well beyond the groups he studied. But his premise is a highly dubious one.

2. *The external critique.* The limitations of the natural science model become more dramatic when we consider the social phenomena its adherents are thereby unable to address. We have discussed some of these matters elsewhere (Sjoberg et al. 1991); here, however, we build on and extend our analysis in a somewhat different manner. Even so, we limit our attention to three main topics, and single out only selected realms for special attention. The first, and the most significant, relates to bureaucracy or large-scale organizations; another to "historical revisionism"; and the third to the natural science model's inability to come to terms with the future.

Inasmuch as "reductionism" or "methodological individualism" inheres in the natural science model, its proponents necessarily have avoided numerous social issues regarding the nature and impact of large-scale organizations. Galbraith (1991:136), an economist who is controversial but not radical, has written:

> Great organization is a commonplace in our time. The myth that it serves social purpose is deep in our faith in our scholarly instruction...
>
> The military-industrial bureaucracy, the extreme case, serves extensively its own ends... Democracy, like the market, is then the covering facade behind which it pursues its own interest.

He further reasons:

> The pursuit by great organization of its own interest should now be central in our research, writing and instruction. If it is not, we are cooperating in a major and economically, socially and politically damaging exercise in concealment. Of this as scholars we must not be guilty.

Most sociologists in recent decades have failed dismally to grasp the manner in which organizations function and how they impact the lives of human beings in the everyday world. If we recall our earlier discussion regarding the growth of world bureaucratic organizations, we find that race and ethnic relations, local economic growth, and so on must be viewed in this larger context. Although some sociologists (e.g., Featherstone 1990) are grappling with the concept of a "global culture," sociologists who are analyzing the structure of transnational organizations are few indeed (cf. Kennedy 1988).

A commitment to the natural science model makes investigation of large-scale organizations, whether societal or global, well-nigh impossible.[12] One can not rely on standardized research procedures, for example social surveys, to gather data on the most salient features of these organizational structures. For one thing, we cannot add up the attitudes or characteristics of the individual members of the organizations and hope to understand the whole. Moreover, both state and corporate structures collect data and release them to the public in a selective manner. Much information is hidden from public scrutiny because of legal constraints imposed on the dissemination of information. And the data that are made public—such as those reported to the U.S. Securities and Exchange Commission—are products of competing interest groups in the nation-state in question. If we turn to transnational bureaucratic organizations, which enjoy a semiautonomy from nation-states (or have their headquarters in nations that require only limited reporting), the data regarding their operations often must be pieced together from fragmentary data.

As our analysis unfolds, we confront an issue with wide-ranging methodological implications: the role of "secrecy systems" in both private and public organizations. (We must not confuse secrecy systems with the formal/informal distinction. Secrecy may be formal, or it may be informal.) The secrecy systems of powerful bureaucracies are studiously avoided by mainstream organizational theorists and researchers (e.g., Morgan 1986; Perrow 1986). Stinchcombe (1990), in his *Information And Organizations* (a work praised by the renowned economic historian Chandler [1991]), has seen fit to analyze information systems within organizations without taking secrecy systems into account. Stinchcombe would have us believe that the flow of information within the FBI, the Federal Reserve Board (Grieder 1987) and large-scale corporate structures is not channeled by the secrecy systems that inhere in these organizations. This is out of keeping with empirical reality.

No contemporary theorists—even Mills and Gouldner, to say nothing of Parsons, Homans, and Blumer—have seriously analyzed bureaucratic secrecy systems. A few sociologists, such as Georg Simmel and more recently Erving Goffman, have dealt with the matter of secrecy, but they have done so in ways that are only indirectly useful for interpreting bureaucratic power arrangements. When we turn to the writings of methodologists (or, more narrowly, sociologists who write on research methods) the picture appears even more grim. No prominent sociologist writing on methodology or research methods has given this topic serious sustained consideration. Admittedly, secrecy systems are interwoven with the problem of the need for "technical experts" and the issue of "special interests," as sociologists grapple with understanding the process of how powerful bureaucratic organizations such as those associated with the national security state come into existence, how they are maintained, and how they might come to be dismantled.

Some may contend that we are overstating the role of secrecy in modern society. But the empirical data strongly support our position. Totalitarian orders such as Hitler's Germany and Stalin's Soviet Union were predicated on the systematic use of secrecy in order to build and maintain power arrangements. We can also point to the resistance to change in China: The Tiananmen Square massacre is but a facet of a much larger problem confronting leaders who must grapple with the secret arrangements that are part of the Maoist organizational legacy.

While the situation is not as dire, the secrecy systems of large-scale organizations, both in the public and the private spheres, have for decades threatened the effective functioning of a democratic order in America. Many social scientists have perceived Watergate as an aberration, but then in the 1980s the Iran-contra scandal came to light. Its full implications with respect to undermining democratic principles have yet to be grasped. If we look back on U.S. history some decades ago, we find that secrecy systems made it feasible to have the Japanese on the West Coast sent to "concentration camps" (cf. Irons 1983), and we continue to learn how the secrecy systems after World War II kept vast amounts of vital information from the citizenry. For example, only recently has it come to light that the U.S. government suppressed data regarding the use of biological warfare by the Japanese in China (e.g., Williams and Wallace 1989). Also, we have learned that the damaging effects of toxic wastes were known to government agencies years before they were made public. We finally have reports in the mainstream press that describe how the military/industrial complex, during the post World War II era, contaminated the environment on a massive scale (e.g., Schneider 1991).[13] Also, we have become aware of the enormous environmental damage in Eastern Europe and the former Soviet Union. So, too, the repression of intellectual dissent by the state and corporate apparatus in the United States has been more widespread than sociologists have been willing to acknowledge in their theory and research (cf. Diamond 1992).

As to the private sector, corporations have never been forthcoming with data regarding their internal operations. There is a long history of corporate cover-ups regarding flawed products or financial machinations that ultimately undermined the companies involved. As we turn to the international scene and contemplate research on the global bureaucratic arrangements discussed earlier, it becomes clear that the use of standardized research procedures presented in methods textbooks is largely irrelevant.

Corporations, in order to sustain special advantages over their competitors, are highly unlikely to reveal data that can be employed by potential competitors. Thus, "official histories" about corporations, although they are not to be dismissed, conveniently construct reality to cast these corporations in a positive light. For example, when reading between the lines of a history of one of the largest international banking enterprises in the world—the Hong Kong and

Shanghai Banking Corporation (King 1991)—one comes away with the distinct impression that far more transpired than was actually recorded. For instance, one looks in vain for more data on the "precarious relationship" between this bank and the People's Republic of China under Mao. In general, financial corporations are particularly secretive. Thus, when Wachtel wrote *The Money Mandarins* (1990), a study of international finance capital, he had to rely on data that most sociologists ignore: "The best source of information has been economic and financial journalists who have produced a rich body of factual and analytical material on the world economy" (1990:xvii-xviii).

The aforementioned issues need to be cast in more general theoretical terms. If sociologists are unwilling to study the interaction between human agents and the organizational structures within which agents carry out their activities, we cannot advance our theoretical analysis of power relationships founded on hidden arrangements. The data strongly support the assertion that human agents interpret and manipulate organizational rules in order to further their own social power. It is not accidental that sociologists such as Coleman (1990), who would have sociology adopt a form of the economic man model, are unable and unwilling to confront the role of secrecy systems within large-scale organizations. He exemplifies a genre of sociologists who, because of their theoretical presuppositions, find themselves unable to explicate the interplay between human agents and their organizational settings.

Our reasoning leads us to one of the most serious problems facing sociology today: the nature of the "market." Earlier we contended that Weber perceived the market system as functioning within bureaucratic organizations. As a result of the social upheavals that have occurred during the present century, sociologists, if they follow Weber's analysis, stand in an unusual position to contribute to social knowledge and public discourse regarding the nature of political economy. But they will be unable to do so if they analyze capitalism, as has been the vogue in sociology during the past few decades, as though it were independent of organizational contexts.

As a result of the social earthquake in the former Soviet bloc, we have learned that the command economy—or the control of economic decisions through bureaucratic directives—when carried to an extreme, is self-defeating. Yet the Reagan era of the 1980s, a period when deregulation of the market was idealized and greed was deemed a virtue, underlines the long-understood limitations of a laissez-faire economy (e.g., Kuttner 1991; Simon and Thompson 1991). The crisis on Wall Street as a result of overreliance on junk bonds, as well as the Savings and Loan debacle, is symptomatic of the stark failure of the laissez-faire model, especially when market activities are embedded in organizational settings wherein secrecy systems are rife.

As clearly as anyone we know, Littrell (1989) has demonstrated the highly complex nature of the market within the U.S. health system. Of necessity his research procedures do not conform to those advocated by proponents of the natural science model. Essentially, Littrell has been able to document empirically how the demand for medical technology is created through, for instance, studied manipulation of accounting procedures. Just what the meaning of the market is becomes more problematic when we look at the defense establishment. The development and procurement of weapons systems have never been subject to the law of supply and demand.

In view of the emerging global bureaucratic structures as well as the varied economic activities in, for example, the United States, Japan (e.g., Kreinen 1988; Okimoto 1989), western Europe, and the former Soviet bloc, sociologists must give priority to rethinking the nature of the market. They are likely to make their most salient contributions if they break with mainstream economic thinking.

In coming to terms with the market within the framework of powerful bureaucratic organizations, sociologists will need to consider how economic activities can (and should) be regulated. Inasmuch as the market is not "self-correcting," how will it be possible to sustain the social accountability in economic activities required to maintain a reasonable quality of life? Here we must be mindful of the fact that most capitalists have favored a selected, and limited, set of regulations in order to provide a modicum of stability and trust in which to carry out their activities.

We thus return to our thesis: No adequate theory of the market is possible without further advances in our understanding, both theoretical and empirical, of bureaucratic organizations. The challenge to sociology is a formidable one. Yet this challenge can be met if the natural science model, as now practiced, gives way to sociology predicated on the classical heritage wherein ideas dictate the methods and procedures for organizing and interpreting data, and not vice versa.

The necessity to rely on alternative methods and procedures in social research becomes apparent if we are attentive to the invaluable data that come to light as a result of "social ruptures" in the activities of large-scale organizations. The study of powerful transnational bureaucratic systems associated with finance capital is ordinarily closed to social scientists. Therefore, we come to rely on what we can learn from, for example, the Japanese stock scandals of 1991 (e.g., Curran 1991; "Hidden Japan" 1991), as well as the scandals that have riddled financial institutions in the United States in the 1980s and 1990s (e.g., Faltmayer 1991).[14] We have already mentioned the crises linked to the sale of junk bonds and the Savings and Loan debacle. Other "dirty linen" has been aired as a result of the manipulation of bids on U.S. Treasury notes by Salomon Brothers ("The Salomon Shocker" 1991). To these ruptures we must add the international crisis surrounding the Bank of Credit and Commerce International. This case seems destined to reveal much about the nature of decision making by international financial organizations (e.g., Banquet 1991; Lohr 1991; Furman 1991).

But the social ruptures surrounding financial institutions are not the only ones that call for careful research and theoretical analysis. We have much to learn about the international power of the U.S. nation-state in recent decades if we analyze the data that became public as a result of the overthrow of Ferdinand Marcos in the Philippines during the 1980s. But it is not only crises on a macro level that await careful investigation but also those associated with ruptures that occur on the community level as corporations and local police intrude into the lives of citizens (cf. Safire 1991). If we are to examine the social phenomena mentioned here, the case-study approach is indispensable.

Moreover, we continue to identify the manifold ramifications for social theory and research of schisms in the former Soviet bloc in the late 1980s and early 1990s. How does one revise the organizational structure of a command economy? How will the racial and ethnic conflicts that emerged as a result of shifts in the control of state power during the 1990s lead sociologists to reformulate their theoretical understanding of this highly charged social realm? These are only some of the more glaring issues that are sure to demand a rewriting of the conventional wisdom of American sociologists in the post World War II era.

In a larger sense, we must recognize that the power base of sociologists in academic settings does not generally permit researchers to study firsthand many social activities, particularly those associated with the "hidden side" of bureaucracies and those activities of individuals that typically are hidden from powerful organizations (e.g., Sjoberg and Miller 1973; Sjoberg 1976). But we can make use of court records, legislative hearings, newspaper accounts, autobiographies, and the like in an imaginative manner in order to expand our theoretical knowledge about the nature of bureaucratic organizations—their impact on the lives of people who depend on, and are often manipulated by, managers of these structures.[15]

In addition to the limitations of the natural science model for studying powerful organizations, we perceive how adherents of this model are unable to face up to "historical revisionism." During the Mikhail Gorbachev era in the former Soviet Union, the history of Stalin's rule was extensively rewritten (Davies 1989). The history of that sector of the globe will undergo further drastic reinterpretations as additional data come to light.[16] And scholars in the new nations being formed out of the former Soviet Union will proceed to reconstruct versions of the social and political events of the twentieth century. So too, the history of China is being reconstituted with the demise of Maoism (e.g., Schwarcz 1992).

We need not limit ourselves to the Communist orbit. During the 1980s, a heated controversy erupted among German intellectuals regarding the meaning of the Nazi past (Maier 1988), and one of the most contentious struggles among contemporary U.S. historians occurred with respect to the Nazis' rise to power (e.g., see the bitter exchange in Feldman 1984 and Abraham 1984).[17]

The past several decades have also evinced an intense struggle regarding Eurocentrism in Western history. Bernal's (1987, 1991) widely debated magnum opus, *Black Athena*, is but one manifestation of the effort to reevaluate the historical record as Europe's traditional political and cultural dominance has been challenged from within and without. This revisionist movement is reinforced by newly discovered data, some of which was available but, until recently, ignored.

But what are some of the implications for sociology of the challenge to Eurocentric history? We learn that the evaluation of historical facts is not as fixed as many sociologists assume. A significant amount of historical reinterpretation has resulted from shifting power relationships on a societal and on a transnational basis.

If we place the sociological enterprise within a larger historical and cross-cultural context, we can readily surmise that future sociologists and historians who examine contemporary sociological research will view it in a fashion that the champions of the natural science model fail to contemplate. They proceed as if their research will withstand historical reinterpretation. But such reflects a failure to recognize that one's own work is part of an ongoing historical process.

Unfortunately, historical sociologists such as Tilly (1982, 1984) and Skocpol (1984) have studiously avoided the methodological problems that inhere in the ongoing rewriting of the historical record. Their reluctance to confront this issue rests in part on the prevailing presupposition, which is predicated on the natural science model, that a social world exists apart from the observer and that that realm, studied properly, will result in an understanding of the laws of nature. Nonetheless, as historical reinterpretation of political and cultural patterns in the United States and abroad, as well as of past sociological activities, continues apace, one must acknowledge the failure of sociologists in general, and historical sociologists in particular, to address a widespread empirical pattern.

We can point to countless shifts in the interpretation of both current and past events. For instance, Minter (1986:355), in his *King Solomon's Mines Revisited*, contends that

> the historiography of southern Africa shows a succession of scholarly paradigms that have strong parallels, if not exact correlations, to the history in which the scholars themselves are embedded.

We elaborate on our perspective by considering a likely reinterpretation of sociological research as conducted since World War II. Sociology will be perceived, we hypothesize, by future sociologists and historians as having been heavily shaped by the organizational structure and cultural system associated with the struggle for ascendancy between the Soviet Union and the United States—that is, the Cold War. The caution displayed by the managers in the NSF in securing funding for social science research during the 1950s is symptomatic of the constraints that were endemic to the Cold War era. American sociologists have often shunned highly controversial topics. For example, they have discussed intellectual repression in totalitarian orders, but they have given this process in the United States almost no attention.

Compelling reinterpretations likely will come to the fore when U.S. political and economic power (the latter in particular) is more fully challenged by the European Community and Japan. To this, we can add further unanticipated restiveness by people in Third World nations.

George Herbert Mead (1938) recognized that the past comes to be reconstituted as a result of events in the present. What he failed to consider is the impact of a restructured set of power relationships on historical revisionism. How the dominant sociological paradigm of the past several decades will be interpreted will thus depend on future power constellations as well as shifting cultural and ideological orientations. That these will occur is a safe "prediction"; how they will occur is far more problematic. But the end result will be a struggle for the "social memory" regarding the nature of current sociological investigation, and existing data (especially on the demise of the Cold War) suggest that many future social historians will not perceive contemporary sociology as a "scientific enterprise"; instead, they will regard most research as supportive of the dominant organizational and cultural activities of the post World War II era.

Still further clarifications are in order. Although historical revisionism is an ongoing process, we do not thereby assume that relativism regarding possible reinterpretations reigns supreme. World War II did occur, the Cold War was a reality, and so on. A reevaluation of the nature and impact of the Cold War will result not only because of new power relationships but because new information from currently sealed archival materials will become available for public scrutiny. Even so, limits on how these past activities are reconstituted do exist. It is understanding the nature of the reinterpretation process—within broad limits—that makes this methodological problem such a formidable one. Nonetheless, if sociologists come to recognize that their activities are part of ongoing historical activities, they are more likely to step back and reflect on the potential limitations of their current research efforts.

Our analysis of the past leads us to the third problem area wherein strictures on the natural science model are cast into bold relief: understanding the future. Adherents of standardized research procedures often contend that "prediction" is the ultimate basis for validating social scientific knowledge (Gibbs 1990). Yet these sociologists can point to few successful attempts at predicting the course of future social events. If prediction becomes the justification for social science knowledge, then the failure of social scientific activity seems assured.

Sociologists stand in dire need of a more realistic means of coping with the "future." We are convinced that the examination of possible alternative futures, through countersystem analysis, is a far more adequate approach (Sjoberg and Cain 1971). Sociologists will be on firmer footing if they strive to anticipate future social and cultural arrangements rather than if they attempt to predict them.

In view of the enormity of unanticipated changes on the global scene during the past few decades—the starkest among them being the breakup of communist regimes in eastern Europe and the internal changes in the former Soviet Union during the late 1980s and early 1990s—sociologists must begin to contemplate the possible future by outlining alternative scenarios. This is not a call for sociology as science fiction. Instead, we require careful theoretical analysis of possible alternatives, based on some empirical grounding. This kind of effort to anticipate the future is far more likely to succeed than is reliance on prediction, and it would have the added advantage of calling attention to the fact that what exists cannot necessarily be projected, in a simplistic manner, onto the future. Scientific innovations, a remaking of power relationships, and a variety of social movements have demonstrated that the future is not a fact. Moreover, sociologists have a role to play in constructing more viable social arrangements.

In sum, then, we have outlined three limitations of the natural science model: those relating to the investigation of large-scale organizations, historical revisionism, and the nature of the future. Other strictures on social inquiry imposed by the natural science model could be elaborated on, not the least of which is the failure to deal with moral issues. Nevertheless, our analysis should suffice to underline the need to legitimize an alternative kind of sociological investigation.

Conclusions and Implications

Our thesis has been that the bureaucratization process has *fostered* the development of the natural science model in sociology, and this model has in turn served the interests of existing bureaucratic structures. Yet the natural science model, founded as it is on "methodological individualism," can investigate only a limited facet of the social context of which it is a part. The most significant features of bureaucratic organizations—for instance, the powerful secrecy systems—are beyond the reach of investigation by sociologists who emphasize the natural science model, with its stress on standardized techniques and procedures, and who downplay theoretical analysis. *If our reasoning stands up to scrutiny, we are led to conclude that numerous sociologists in the United States have entered Weber's iron cage.* They are incapable of analyzing, on theoretical and empirical grounds, many essential features of the social setting in which social knowledge is produced.

Gouldner, in *The Coming Crisis of Western Sociology* (1970), diagnosed the crisis of the discipline as resulting from the theorizing of Parsons, and the latter's justification of and failure to perceive the weaknesses in the welfare state. Our diagnosis of the discipline, two decades after Gouldner's treatise, is decidedly different. Contemporary sociology's ills result from an over-reliance on the natural science model as defined by methods and techniques, which should not become ends in themselves. Instead they are tools to advance the cause of broader intellectual endeavors.

Sociology's current emphasis on the "variable approach" has resulted from changes during the post World War II era within the university, the society, and the global setting. During this period two power nodes have emerged within the university: the natural science and the law school-business school complexes. Both are integrated into the powerful societal organizations as well as the emerging global organizational structures.

Within this organizational setting the social sciences have occupied a secondary role, and among the social sciences sociology occupies a less-than-favored position. In an effort to acquire legitimacy within the societal framework, sociology has attempted to serve the interests of vital organizations, particularly certain governmental structures. To justify its efforts, it adopted the natural science model that, when translated into everyday practice, has resulted in an overreliance on techniques and methods. This strategy has meant that many sociologists have become dependent on the "data sets" generated by the organizational structures of U.S. society. American sociology has been, contrary to its avid supporters, largely ethnocentric in nature.

We have taken care to observe that the natural science model has made distinctive and not-to-be-denied contributions to understanding modern society. However, these advances have been achieved within a narrow framework, for most contemporary sociologists define the great social and moral issues of our time as lying outside the scope of social inquiry.

The dangers posed by the hegemony of the natural science model are seriously undermining the social and intellectual foundations of the discipline. *Sociology, by defining itself in terms of its techniques and methods, is now placed in a highly vulnerable situation.* These techniques and methods can readily be appropriated by, or absorbed into, the ongoing activities of business schools, schools of communication, schools of social work, and schools of public affairs. Each of these academic enterprises has powerful constituencies outside the university for which sociology has no counterpart. Sociology cannot compete with them for resources. Thus, if contemporary trends in the discipline are not reversed to some degree, sociology increasingly stands to lose its legitimacy within the academic setting.

Closing down the department at Washington University in St. Louis and the resultant publicity from a projected downsizing of sociology at Yale are the most

visible signs of the serious difficulties that confront the discipline (Levine 1992).
Yet a common response by many sociologists to the current situation is: "Do
more of the same, but do it better." In effect, sociologists should stick to their
knitting.[18] We strongly agree with the principle that sociologists need to pay
special attention to students as well as sustain a power base within their
universities. Nonetheless, narrow administrative solutions are no substitute for
a reconstitution of the discipline in broader intellectual terms.

Theoretical ideas must again play a central role in interpreting the major
empirical issues that plague humankind. *Sociology can (and must) contribute
substantially to understanding global bureaucratic structures—those discussed
earlier in this essay.* Microprocesses, such as those relating to the family or the
repression of political dissent, can be grasped effectively only if they are set
within a larger structural framework. Although Habermas (1984, 1987a) theo-
rizes about the impact of the rationalization process on "the lifeworld," his
analysis remains so abstract that the nature of specific empirical issues eludes us.

The methodological individualism of the natural science model means that
sociologists are "disconnected" from, or can investigate only tangentially,
contemporary power centers. Nonetheless, if sociologists are to address the
grave issues that confront the new nations of the former Soviet bloc or poverty
and destruction of the environment in the economically and politically disadvantaged nations in the world, research on the activities of global organizations
must be given priority. We restate our argument in somewhat different terms: If
sociologists are to be more than "staff members" with respect to middle-level
managers of bureaucratic organizations within U.S. society, they must examine
the nature and consequences of powerful bureaucratic structures as well as the
values and goals that are shaping the future of humankind.[19]

Within our countersystem framework, theoretical ideas play a central role in
the interpretation of empirical issues. Sociologists, if we use the works of
Durkheim and Weber as a guide, can analyze societal patterns in broad,
"holistic" terms, and the advances in understanding human nature achieved by
the philosopher/sociologist Mead resulted from placing individuals within the
ongoing process of interacting human agents. Linking theoretical ideas to some
of the substantive issues enumerated here will be difficult for other social
scientists to replicate and almost impossible for scholars anchored in professional
schools to carry out. Yet to advance the agenda we are advocating means that
sociologists will be unable to rely simply on standardized data sets collected by
present-day administrative units. We are called on to piece together a much wider
range of evidence, data that do not receive the "time of day" from most
sociologists who write on research methods.

But the question arises: How is a reconstituted sociology to be justified in the
contemporary world, dominated as it is by powerful bureaucratic structures? A
major rationale for an idea-based sociology, which focuses on the empirical

issues of the late twentieth and early twenty-first centuries, rests on a recognition that sociology can play a strategic role in maintaining and expanding on democratic principles. Admittedly the concept of democracy is highly contested. But in the face of much criticism, it remains a viable ideal. Ironically, recent administrations in the United States have championed democratic practices for other societies but often have devoted little or no sustained effort to furthering the democratic process within the American social order.

If we look back on the works of Dewey and Mead, as well as the current theorizing of the critical theorist Habermas, with his emphasis on communicative reasoning, we recognize the long-standing historical importance of sustaining, and enlarging on, the democratic process. The problem of how to enhance democracy is all the more pressing in a societal and global setting dominated by powerful large-scale organizations. That sociologists must seriously examine the nature and input of these powerful organizations is in line with our commitment to elaborating how democracy can become more effective. It is not feasible to follow the path of C. Wright Mills, who idealized the "Jeffersonian model." Modern industrial society cannot be sustained in the context of a rural-based economy. The past is not as idyllic as many scholars would have us believe.

We must look forward to theory and research that help restructure organizations as well as make them more accountable to a broader public (even a global) "good." Within this situation sociologists must pay ever greater attention to the increasing race and ethnic tensions that are part of the world scene. But instead of seeking to resolve these by underwriting bureaucratic rationalization through standardized research methods, sociologists are in a position to assist, through theoretically informed analysis, the mutual understanding of race and ethnic minorities on a societal and global scale.

We live under no illusions that our alternative, or countersystem, can be attained. Resistance is built into the university—and even into departmental structures. But we should undertake a serious effort to reconstitute sociology's claim to advancing the cause of public discourse. In the process, sociologists may find surprising allies even among some members of governmental organizations who have become aware of the failings of the structures within which they work. If sociologists recognize that the natural science model can be only one facet of their enterprise, they can reclaim a fundamental role in the university and college curriculum and thus reinforce links with one core constituency: students. In addition, sociological theory and research that establish the discipline's claim to a fundamental understanding of societal and global issues will revitalize the field. Fortunately, the heritage of which we speak is being kept alive by sociologists such as Bellah, Wolfe, Wilson, and Wallerstein.

At this point, there are social scientists who will contend that we have ignored the attacks against "positivism" by the postmodernists. Yet the impact of postmodernism on research procedures in sociology has been minimal. More pointedly, the postmodernists, we are convinced, have not faced up to the issues relating to bureaucratization (and rationalization) as well as to the racial and ethnic divisions in the modern world.

A sustained sociological critique of postmodernism is beyond our general objective. We share Habermas's (1987b) disquiet with postmodernism. At the same time, we would push forward a critique in still other directions. Wolin (1990), an eminent political theorist, has outlined one line of reasoning that is congruent with our thinking. He (1990:27-28) perceives postmodernism as playing into the hands of a "managed democracy."

> By managed democracy I do not mean that people are puppets manipulated by Washington, Wall Street, or Nashville. It is more disturbing than that. Managed democracy is a created world of images, sounds, and scenarios that makes only occasional contact with the everyday reality of most people. The rest of the time that world floats in dissociation, a realm wherein reference has been suspended . . .
>
> In the self-defined age of information and communication, where knowledge is said to be power, and new knowledge more power, managed democracies do need intellectuals who are adept with words and images, who realize that words are more important than beliefs.

Wolin (1990:29) continues his onslaught by contending that "technicians of culture are as necessary as legal, managerial, and scientific technicians."

The postmodernists are trapped by their relativistic worldview and their commitment to a version of the "new individualism." They fail to grasp the fact that they only reinforce the power of large-scale organizations by their intellectual disengagement from, and tacit support of, these entities.

We must look elsewhere than to the postmodernists for a reconstitution of sociology. We have mentioned the countervailing trends within sociology as exemplified by Bellah, Wilson, Wolfe, and Wallerstein. We must expand on their efforts and strike out boldly in new directions. Moreover, the social ruptures destined to arise in the future should be used to challenge the current methodological hegemony that has kept mainstream sociology from addressing the great problems of our age. Certainly we must look forward to taking advantage of changes on the global scene. The impact of European sociologists, particularly as the European Community wields increased economic and political power, is likely to grow. While one sector of European sociology has adopted the natural science model, other sectors are opening up new avenues that are worthy of pursuit. Also, we can expect new challenges in the years ahead from segments of the social science community in the Third World. Some of these scholars are likely to become disenchanted with the solutions offered by mainstream U.S. sociology to the pressing difficulties faced by their societies. We must be prepared to take advantage of historical opportunities to forge a sociology that, empirically and theoretically, not only supplements the natural science model but also has an integrity of its own in addressing the challenges encountered by humankind on so many fronts.

Acknowledgements

*We gratefully acknowledge the ideas provided by Boyd Littrell in his many conversations with the first-named author over the past two decades. In particular, we have been influenced by his views regarding the role of democracy as a basis for legitimating sociological inquiry.

Notes

1. One could trace the intellectual roots of some of our ideas to those of Veblen (1954). Still, Veblen did not grasp the issues relating to bureaucratic organizations with which we are preoccupied.

2. There is a wealth of literature on developing and newly industrialized nations and the university system, including the scientific enterprise itself. We would not pretend to cite the massive literature that exists. We have consulted a rather wide range of writings, Altbach et al. (1989), Vessuri (1986), and Morna (1991). Also see some of the articles in "Universities under Siege" (1990).

3. For clues regarding the bruising political battles within the American Psychological Association in the late 1980s see, for example, "Five-Year Report of the Policy and Planning Board, 1990: Five Years of Turbulence, Change and Growth within APA" (1991).

4. If we single out particular specialties in sociology for scrutiny, our criticisms become more pointed. For example, Jencks (1987:41), in evaluating our knowledge about cross-cultural patterns with respect to crime, states: "We are not, I think, any closer to understanding why cultures differ from one another, or why they change over time, than we were thirty years ago. Worse yet, young social scientists are seldom interested in such questions. Most of them prefer mathematical games, which are absorbing and fun to play but have almost no chance of telling us anything useful about anything. Without a clear understanding of why Europeans and Japanese respect one another's person and property more than Americans do, it is hard to see what practical benefits we can reap from simply knowing that culture and history are important."

Next we turn to the field of rural sociology. Falk, who must be viewed as an insider, coauthored with Zhao (1989) an essay that evaluates the articles that appeared in *Rural Sociology* between 1976 and 1985. They conclude that the articles generally are atheoretical and data driven (Falk and Zhao 1989:597):

> Theory found in the opening pages is typically abandoned at the paper's conclusion. In fact, in many cases the concluding section could be written completely independent of any theory mentioned at the paper's outset.

What more damning evaluation could be drawn? But then, rural sociology differs very little, in our view, from such subspecialities as "the family." The main difference is that the latter includes more monographs of wide-ranging theoretical and practical significance.

Although a few of the monographs on the family are first-rate, many brief research reports, which are cast in the natural science mode, deserve critical analysis. For example, Sara S. McLanahan (1990), a widely published and highly respected sociologist in the study of the American family, has written a chapter "The Two Faces Of Divorce: Women's and Children's Interests," in the presidential series of the ASA edited by Joan Huber. McLanahan (1990:202) proceeds as follows: "What are the policy implications of this research? Should the government outlaw divorce for couples with children? Should it make divorce more difficult by changing the tax code? To answer these questions the costs and benefits of such an action must be evaluated from society's as well as the individual's point of view. With respect to costs, outlawing divorce would impose major restrictions on individual freedom and expose women and children who live in abusive situations to considerable harm. . . . With respect to benefits, the answer is less clear. Until the selectivity issue is resolved, we cannot be sure how much of the negative impact of family disruption is due to divorce per se. Moreover, the magnitude of the effect of divorce on society as a whole is not always large. Outlawing divorce would raise the national high school graduation rate from about 86% to 88%, assuming no selectivity into divorce. It would reduce the risk of a premarital birth among young black women from about 45% to 39%."

McLanahan adds a footnote observing that the "estimate" for high school completion and the estimate for premarital birth are based on other research she has authored or coauthored. "Both sets of estimates assume that all of the negative impact of family disruption is due to the disruption itself as opposed to preexisting characteristics of parents" (1990:204-5).

What is one to make of this reasoning? We discern a "reification" of quantitative data; they come to have a life of their own. Although the author qualifies her generalizations to a modest degree, we must face up to the unstated assumptions that are not explicated. Would the patterns she discusses hold if the United States experienced a major depression? Or what would occur if large-scale governmental programs were instituted for disadvantaged persons? McLanahan assumes a stability regarding the value system and organizational structure that is unwarranted in an era of rapid change. Moreover, the ethics of utilitarianism that undergird cost-benefit analysis are apparently not understood.

We are talking about top-of-the line work in the quantitative study of the American family. Unfortunately, adherence to the natural science model results in fundamental theoretical issues being taken for granted or pushed aside.

Overall, we end on the note on which we began this discussion. If we evaluate a number of the traditional specialties in U.S. sociology, we find that many of the leading practitioners rely too heavily on "official data categories" of governmental agencies and stress technical virtuosity at the expense of sustained theoretical analysis.

5. See also selected articles in Sjoberg (1989).

6. Within this essay we are unable to analyze the structure of the American Sociological Association. This association is best known for its sponsorship of national meetings and a variety of publications that facilitate communication among sociologists. It also serves as a lobbying arm for sociologists with the federal government and as a vehicle for promoting sociological activities on the national (and to some degree global) level. Although somewhat loosely structured, the association is becoming increasingly bureaucratized. In the process, the ASA is a vehicle for sustaining the power of sociologists at "elite" institutions. For example, the variety and kinds of papers presented at national meetings are pluralistic, but our tentative observations suggest that the formal publications sponsored by the ASA typically screen out the more "heterodox ideas" presented at the annual meetings. A careful analysis of the organizational structure of the ASA would prove highly informative.

7. Kerr's (1989) observations about the university, a quarter of a century after he composed his justly famous work on the multiversity, are instructive. We agree with, for instance, his description of the decline of university citizenship. This pattern has seeped down to the departmental level, with a consequent rise of power by a more centralized administrative structure. While we must not idealize the past, it is nonetheless apparent that Kerr does not analyze the impact of the administrative sector on the process he has isolated. His myopia is perhaps understandable. He was an early leader in building this administrative apparatus while president of the University of California at Berkeley, and he also seems to have rewarded the academic entrepreneurs who built the scientific laboratories (including those related to the defense establishment) that channeled funds into that distinguished university.

8. The growth of the administrative apparatus at the University of Texas system is revealed in a newspaper account based on the open-records law. The

formal budget does not contain the "perks" available to high-level administrative officials (e.g., Ratcliffe 1991). If one reads the *Chronicle of Higher Education*, we find this pattern replicated in many other U.S. universities.

9. Blalock (1985:247), a leading exponent of the natural science model, has written: "One of the most serious problems . . . is the apparent fact that theoretical training usually has no immediate impact on one's publication record. The kinds of theoretical issues that I believe need to be tackled usually require a considerable period of mulling over, formulating and reformulating, and quite a risk from the standpoint of one's output of publications. It is much easier to become a member of a team, produce a couple of joint articles, and then to continue this pattern of research production."

He goes on to state: "Although it is an exaggeration to claim that almost any publication will do, the disagreement within our discipline regarding just what is good and poor sociology exacerbates the tendency to count all publications as nearly equal."

10. Kurtz (forthcoming) has provided us with specification of one aspect of Erikson's argument. Kurtz offers detailed data on how war and peace studies have fared in sociology. They have not been central to disciplinary activities; peace studies, in fact, have been marginalized. Kurtz's essay serves to document our contention that the natural science model has undermined research on major social issues in sociology.

11. Many features of the bureaucratization of sociology should be considered in a book-length monograph. The impact of publishing on the discipline is a much-neglected topic. Here we must look closely at what is happening, for example, to library purchases. The natural sciences have been constructed to a high degree on disseminating information through journals. But the cost of these has skyrocketed in recent years and has resulted in what has been termed "the serials doomsday machine." One scientific journal is listed as costing $7000 per year, another as having risen 109 percent in cost between 1986 and 1989 (Okerson and Stubbs 1991:36).

What might these changes mean for sociology? The cost of serials, especially in the natural sciences, apparently is leading to a decline in the purchase of monographs, including those in sociology. Moreover, this pattern will mean that "marginal" publications—those most likely to contain dissenting views—will be less able to gain a place in libraries and thus be passed on to future generations. The effect of the library purchasing system on the support and the dissemination of knowledge is worthy of serious attention by sociologists intent on sustaining dissent within the discipline as well as on the societal and global scene.

As library purchases of monographs decline, publishers are looking more and more for mass-market items. Works that go against the grain are less likely to be published, and their authors will have greater difficulty attaining tenure and promotion. The position of the "renegades" is already a tenuous one. What of their future in view of some of the aforementioned considerations?

12. In some instances, the commitment to "methodological hegemony" and the summary dismissal of major social issues relating to bureaucracy are somewhat roundabout. Gibbs is a case in point. He is so devoted to formal theory construction and to the standardization of procedures in order to achieve predictive power that he dismisses Giddens and Habermas out of hand. According to Gibbs (1989:x-xi), "the discursiveness of Giddens' (1984) recent structuration theory is perhaps unprecedented; and the willingness of sociologists to take Habermas' (1984) theory of communicative action seriously indicates an unlimited tolerance of discursiveness." Gibbs's commitment to methodological individualism (which is not as explicit as it should be) in part leads to his refusal to acknowledge the social control being analyzed by Habermas's theory of bureaucratic rationalization. And that by a person who would make control sociology's central concept! Moreover, Gibbs spends about 461 pages justifying formal theory construction in discursive and turgid prose. Thus, *empirically*, he relies on the very theory he attacks so derisively.

13. For purposes of emphasis, we observe that the military-industrial complex has been able to destroy the environment at home and abroad on a massive scale largely because of a formal secrecy system that was justified by the national security state.

14. A sociological analysis of the financial scandals in Japan and in the United States would be informative from a number of standpoints. The reports by various financial writers suggest that these events cast light on the organizational structure of world finance capital. The scandals in Japan affect financial institutions in the United States, for the latter cannot invest in the market as "equals," given existing rules and regulations (also see articles in *Far Eastern Economic Review* [1991] for another perspective on this scandal). Moreover, the recent fixing of bids on U.S. Treasury notes by Salomon Brothers may well have affected the interest rate structure in Europe (e.g., Stern and Jereski 1991). Thus, through these scandals we acquire an understanding of the intricate web of arrangements of international financial institutions, as well as an understanding of the relationship of the world financial structure to various nation-states. Also, as noted in the text, various elements of the corporate community appear to recognize the necessity for adherence to "relatively fair and stable contractual relationships" if the bureaucratic arrangements relating to finance capital are to maintain long-term legitimacy on the world scene.

15. The necessity to rely on documentary data in studying powerful financial institutions is supported by Glasberg's (1989:200) observations. She relied on case studies in her research on the effects of the social control of banks on corporations and the state: "I would have liked to interview the key actors involved in each of the cases. Indeed, I repeatedly wrote to and called several of

the corporate actors in an attempt to interview them, either in person or by telephone. Each attempt met the same response: they were not interested . . . Hence my research depended on governmental and archival documents, business press information, and interviews with business analysts and lawyers.

"Although the method I used is time-consuming and tedious, it is also most rewarding. It can produce clear details of relations and processes that remain hidden in statistical analysis."

16.News accounts (Schmidt 1992) indicate that a British firm has gained publication rights to secret documents of the Communist Party's archives in Moscow. The first set of materials to be released will include more than 300,000 documents. As a result of this information, a number of long-cherished generalizations about the party and its leadership are likely to be discarded.

17. Herein we are unable to explore the many methodological ramifications of the Feldman/Abraham debate. Readers should not only study the articles that are cited but also should consult the full debate in *Central European History* (1984), as well as the replies and counterreplies. They should also examine the other writings about this debate.

Abraham committed some egregious errors in his original historical research on the role of the business leaders in the rise of Nazis to power in Germany. This debate also reflects sharply differing domain assumptions regarding historical evidence and, if this debate is placed in proper perspective, reveals a great deal about a "nasty side" of academic life—in this instance relating to the American historical profession. These kinds of data do not often find their way into print.

18.Many of the proposed solutions to the current predicament within sociology can be found in *Footnotes* and in the newsletters of the sections of the ASA or the regional or other sociological societies. For example, Land's (1991) first important piece of advice for averting the abolition of sociology departments was for sociologists to stick to their knitting. Falk (1992) likens a sociology department to a business. He speaks of sociology seeking a niche in the marketplace and of sociology as a commodity in the stock market. Administrators are investors who seek a return on their investment and sociology must respond accordingly. The themes of Land and Falk are typical of those articulated by many sociologists.

19. Ideas do have consequences, even when their impact is indirect. Within the field of economics, it is not the narrow technical works that have shaped the course of economic discourse. Heilbroner (1990) speaks of economists with "vision" as having made a difference. His views are supported by Waligorski's (1990) analysis of the political and moral theory of conservative economists. Waligorski's (1990:185) data support the contention that "conservative economic theory is also a normative political theory that has serious implications for widely accepted ideas, values, and policies."

References

Abraham, David. 1984. " A Reply to Gerald Feldman." *Central European History.* 27:179–244.

Almond, Gabriel. 1990. *A Discipline Divided.* Newbury Park: Sage.

Alonso, William, and Paul Starr, eds. 1987. *The Politics of Numbers.* New York: Russell Sage Foundation.

Altbach, Philip G., Charles H. Davis, Thomas O. Eisemon, S. Gopinathon, H. Steve Hsieh, Sungho Lee, Pang Eng Fong and Jasbir Sarjit Singh. 1989. *Scientific Development and Higher Education.* New York: Praeger.

Attewell, Paul A. 1984. *Radical Political Economy Since the Sixties.* New Brunswick: Rutgers University Press.

Bagdikian, Ben H. 1990. *The Media Monopoly.* 3rd ed. Boston: Beacon Press.

Baquet, Dean. 1991. "Handling of the B.C.C.I. Case Arouses Deep Suspicions." *New York Times,* September 6 A1, C1.

Beissenger, Mark R. 1988. *Scientific Management, Social Discipline, and Soviet Power.* Cambridge: Harvard University Press.

Bellah, Robert N., Richard Madsen, William H. Sullivan, Ann Swindler, and Steven M. Tipton. 1985. *Habits of the Heart.* Berkeley: University of California Press.

Berger, Bennett M., ed. 1990. *Authors of Their Own Lives.* Berkeley: University of California Press.

Bernal, Martin. 1987. *Black Athena: The Afroasiatic Roots of Classical Civilization: The Fabrication of Ancient Greece 1785–1985.* Vol. I. New Brunswick: Rutgers University Press.

———. 1991. *Black Athena: The Afroasiatic Roots of Classical Civilization: The Archeological and Documentary Evidence.* Vol. II. New Brunswick: Rutgers University Press.

Blalock, Hubert M., Jr. 1985. "Quality Graduate Training: A Time for Critical Appraisals." Pp. 239–57 in Frederick L. Campbell, Hubert M. Blalock, Jr., and Reece McGee, eds. *Teaching Sociology.* Chicago: Nelson-Hall.

Blau, Peter M. 1987. "Microprocesses and Macroprocesses." Pp. 83–100 in Karen Cook, ed. *Social Exchange Theory.* Newbury Park: Sage.

Caplow, Theodore, and Reece J. McGee. 1958. *The Academic Marketplace.* New York: Basic Books.

Chandler, Alfred D. 1991. "History and Organizational Sociology." *Contemporary Sociology* 20:340–42.

Coleman, James S. 1990. *The Foundations of Social Theory.* Cambridge: Harvard University Press.

Collins, Randall. 1981. "On the Micro-Foundations of Macro-Sociology." *American Journal of Sociology* 86:984–1014.

Converse, Jean. 1987. *Survey Research in the United States.* Berkeley: University of California Press.

Curran, John J. 1991. "What's Wrong with Tokyo's Market." *Fortune* 124(September):75–80.

Davies, R.W. 1989. *Soviet History In the Gorbachev Revolution.* Bloomington: Indiana University Press.

Diamond, Sigmund. 1992. *Compromised Campus: The Collaboration of Universities with the Intelligence Community, 1945–1955.* New York: Oxford University Press.

Dickson, David. 1988. *The New Politics of Science.* Chicago: University of Chicago Press.

Duncan, Otis Dudley. 1984. *Notes on Social Measurement: Historical and Critical.* New York: Russell Sage Foundation.

Eisner, Robert. 1989. "Divergences of Measurement and Theory and Some Implications for Economic Policy." *American Economic Review.* 79:1–13.

Emerson, Ken. 1990. "When Legal Titans Clash." *New York Times Magazine.* April 22, 26, 28, 53, 63, 66–9.

"The Entrepreneurial University." Special Issue. 1990. *Academe* 76:9–26.

Erikson, Kai. 1984. "Sociology and Contemporary Events." Pp. 303–10 in Walter W. Powell and Richard Robbins, eds. *Conflict and Consensus: A Festschrift in Honor of Lewis A. Coser.* New York: Free Press.
Falk, William W. 1991. "Strengthening Sociology's Relation in the University." *Footnotes* 19(December):1, 4.
Falk, William W., and Shanyang Zhao. 1989. "Paradigms, Theories and Methods in Contemporary Rural Sociology: A Partial Replication and Extension." *Rural Sociology* 54:587–600.
Faltermayer, Edmund. 1991. "The Deal Decade: Verdict on the '80s." *Fortune* 124(August 26):58–69.
Featherstone, Mike., ed. 1990. *Global Culture: Nationalism, Globalization and Modernity.* Newbury Park: Sage.
Feldman, Gerald D. 1984. "A Collapse in Weimar Scholarship." *Central European History* 27:159–77.
Fligstein, Neil. 1990. *The Transformation of Corporate Control.* Cambridge: Harvard University Press.
"Five-Year Report of the Policy and Planning Board 1990: Five Years of Turbulence, Change, and Growth within APA." 1991. *American Psychologist* 46:678–788.
Furman, Craig. 1991. "Backward Slide: BCCI Debacle Leaves an African Country All the More Troubled." *Wall Street Journal.* August 6, 1, A8.
Galbraith, John K. 1983. *The Anatomy of Power.* Boston: Houghton Mifflin.
———. 1991. "The Sting of Truth." *Scientific American* 264 (May):136.
Gerson, Joseph, and Bruce Birchard. 1991. *The Sun Never Sets . . .* Boston: South End Press.
Gibbs, Jack P. 1989. *Control: Sociology's Central Notion.* Urbana: University of Illinois Press.
———. 1990. "The Notion of a Theory in Sociology." *National Journal of Sociology* 4:129–58.
Giddens, Anthony. 1984. *The Constitution of Society.* Berkeley: University of California Press.
Glasberg, Danita Silfen. 1989. *The Power of Collective Purse Strings.* Berkeley: University of California Press.
Glenn, Norval D. 1991. "Some Troublesome Trends and Persisting Weaknesses in Sociology Graduate Education." *Teaching Sociology* 19:445–6.
Gouldner, Alvin W. 1970. *The Coming Crisis of Western Sociology.* New York: Basic Books.
Grassmuck, Karen. 1991. "Throughout the 80's Colleges Hired More Non-Teaching Staff Than Other Employees." *Chronicle of Higher Education* 37(August 14):A22.
Greider, William. 1987. *The Secrets of the Temple: How the Federal Reserve Runs the Country.* New York: Simon and Schuster.
Habermas, Jürgen. 1984. *The Theory of Communicative Action: Reason and the Rationalization of Society.* Vol. 1. Boston: Beacon Press.
———. 1987a. *The Theory of Communicative Action: Lifeworld and System: A Critique of Functionalist Reason.* Vol. II. Boston: Beacon Press.
———. 1987b. *The Philosophical Discourse of Modernity.* Cambridge: MIT Press.
Hackett, Edward. 1990. "Science as a Vocation in the 1990s: The Changing Organizational Culture of Academic Science." *Journal of Higher Education* 61:241–79.
Haveman, Robert H. 1987. *Poverty Policy and Policy Research: The Great Society and the Social Sciences.* Madison: University of Wisconsin Press.
Heilbroner, Robert. 1990. "Analysis and Vision in the History of Modern Economic Thought." *Journal Of Economic Literature* 28:1097–1114.
———. 1991. "Economics as Universal Science." *Social Research* 58:457–74.
Held, David. 1980. *An Introduction to Critical Theory.* Berkeley: University of California Press.
"Hidden Japan." 1991. *Business Week,* no. 3228(August 26):34–38.
Hilferding, Rudolf. 1981. *Finance Capital.* London: Routledge & Kegan Paul (orig. pub. 1910).
Homans, George C. 1984. *Coming to My Senses.* New Brunswick: Transaction Books.

Irons, Peter. 1983. *Justice at War*. New York: Oxford University Press.

Jencks, Christopher. 1987. "Genes & Crime." *New York Review* 34(February 12):33–41.

Kennedy, Mark C. 1988. "The New Global Network of Corporate Power and the Decline of National Self-Determination." *Contemporary Crises* 12:245–76.

Kerr, Clark. 1963. *The Uses of the University*. Cambridge: Harvard University Press.

———. 1989. "The Academic Ethic and University Teachers: A Disintegrating Profession." *Minerva* 27:139–56.

King, Frank H.H. 1991. *The Hong Kong Bank in the Period of Development and Nationalism, 1941–1984; From Regional Bank to Multinational Group*. Cambridge: Cambridge University Press.

Klausner, Samuel Z., and Victor M. Lidz, eds. 1986. *The Nationalization of the Social Sciences*. Philadelphia: University of Pennsylvania Press.

Knottnerus, J. David. 1987. "Status Attainment Research and Its Image of Society." *American Sociological Review* 52:113–21.

Knudsen, Dean D., and Ted R. Vaughan. 1969. "Quality in Graduate Education: A Re-evaluation of the Rankings of Sociology Departments in the Cartter Report." *The American Sociologist* 4:12–19.

Kreinin, Mordechai E. 1988. "How Closed Is the Japanese Market? Additional Evidence." *World Economy* 11:529–42.

Kurtz, Lester R. "War and Peace on the Sociological Agenda." pp. 61–98. In Terence C. Halliday and Morris Janowitz, eds. *Sociology and Its Publics*. Chicago: University of Chicago Press.

Kuttner, Robert. 1991. *The End of Laissez-Faire*. New York: Knopf.

Land, Kenneth. 1991. "On the Abolition of Sociology Departments: A Panel for Chairpersons." *Southern Sociologist* 23(Fall):9–10.

Levine, Felice. 1992. "The Executive Officer's Column." *Footnotes* 19 (January):2.

Littrell, W. Boyd. 1989. "New Technology, Bureaucracy, and the Social Construction of Medical Prices." *Journal of Applied Behavioral Science* 25:249–70.

Locke, Robert R. 1989. *Management and Higher Education Since 1940*. Cambridge: Cambridge University Press.

Lohr, Steve. 1991. "How B.C.C.I.'s Accounts Won Stamp of Approval." *New York Times* September 16, 1, C6.

McLanahan, Sara S. 1990. "The Two Faces of Divorce: Women's and Children's Interests." Pp. 193–207 in Joan Huber, ed. *Macro-Micro Linkages In Sociology*. Newbury Park: Sage.

Maier, Charles S. 1988. *The Unmasterable Past*. Cambridge: Harvard University Press.

Martindale, Don. 1976. *The Romance of a Profession: A Case History in the Sociology of Sociology*. St. Paul: Windflower Publishing.

Mayhew, Bruce. 1980. "Structuralism vs. Individualism." *Social Forces* 59: 335–75.

Mead, George H. 1934. *Mind, Self and Society*. Chicago: University of Chicago Press.

———. 1938. *The Philosophy of the Act*. Chicago: University of Chicago Press.

Merton, Robert K. 1973. *The Sociology of Science: Theoretical and Empirical Investigations*. Chicago: University of Chicago Press.

Mills, C. Wright. 1959. *The Sociological Imagination*. New York: Oxford University Press.

Minter, William. 1986. *King Solomon's Mines Revisited: Western Interests and the Burdened History of Southern Africa*. New York: Basic Books.

Morna, Colleen Lowe. 1991. "Scholarly Research Drying Up at African Universities as Financial and Political Problems Force Cutbacks." *Chronicle of Higher Education* 37 (August 7):A28–29.

Morgan, Gareth. 1986. *Images of Organization*. Newbury Park: Sage.

Murray, Alan. 1991. "Harvard, to the Dismay of U.S. Conservatives, May Replace Communism as Soviets' Planner." *Wall Street Journal* August 27, A14.

Okerson, Ann, and Kendon Stubbs. 1991. "The Library Doomsday Machine." *Publishers Weekly* 238:36–37.

Okimoto, Daniel O. 1989. *Between MIT and the Market*. Stanford: Stanford University Press.

Opp, Karl-Dieter. 1985. "Sociology and Economic Man." *Journal of Institutional and Theoretical Economics* 141:123–43.

Perrow, Charles. 1986. *Complex Organizations: A Critical Essay*. 3rd ed. New York: Random House.

Ratcliffe, R.G. 1991. "UT Uses Local Funds to Pay Perquisites." *Houston Chronicle* August 1, 1, 14A.

Raymond, Chris. 1991. "Psychologists Ponder Changes in Field as Discipline Enters Second Century." *Chronicle of Higher Education* 38(September 4): A10–11.

Read, Hill Paterson III., 1988. "A Research Empire for Roman." *Employee Assistance* 1:32.

Reich, Robert B. 1991. *The Work of Nations*. New York: Knopf.

Riecken, Henry W. 1986. "Underdogging: The Early Career of the Social Sciences in the NSF." Pp. 209–25 in Samuel Z. Klausner and Victor M. Lidz, eds. *The Nationalization of the Social Sciences*. Philadelphia: University of Pennsylvania Press.

Riley, Matilda White., ed. 1988. *Sociological Lives*. Newbury Park: Sage.

Ross, Dorothy. 1991. *The Origins of American Social Science*. Cambridge: Cambridge University Press.

Rubin, Allen, and Earl Babbie. 1989. *Research Methods for Social Work*. Belmont: Wadsworth.

Safire, William. 1991. "At P & G: It Sinks." *New York Times* September 5, A19.

"The Salomon Shocker: How Bad will it Get? 1991. *Business Week*, no. 3228(August 26):54–57.

Schmidt, William E. 1992. "Lenin to Stalin to Gorbachev: Read All about Them Here." *New York Times*, January 22, A4.

Schneider, Keith. 1991. "Military Has New Strategic Goal in Cleanup of Vast Toxic Waste." *New York Times* August 5, 1, C3.

Schwarcz, Vera. 1992. *Time for Telling the Truth Is Running Out*. New Haven: Yale University Press.

Schwertzer, Glenn E. 1989. *Techno-Diplomacy: U.S.-Soviet Confrontations in Science and Technology*. New York: Plenum.

Schwirian, Kent P., and Edward C. McDonagh. 1991. "Sociology PhDs in the 1990s." *Teaching Sociology* 19:424–29.

Sewell, William H. 1988. "The Changing Institutional Structure of Sociology and My Career." Pp. 119–44 in Matilda White Riley, ed. *Sociological Lives*. Newbury Park: Sage.

Shannon, Thomas R. 1989. *An Introduction to the World-System Perspective*. Boulder: Westview Press.

Sheehan, Neil. 1988. *A Bright Shining Lie: John Paul Vann and America in Vietnam*. New York: Random House.

Simon, Herbert A., and Victor A. Thompson. 1991. "Public Administration Revisited." *Society* 28(July-August):41–45.

Sjoberg, Gideon. 1976. "Social Research, Social Policy, and the Other Economy." Pp. 215–30 in W. Boyd Littrell and Gideon Sjoberg, eds. *Current Issues in Social Policy*. Beverly Hills: Sage.

———. ed. 1989. "Autobiography, Social Research, and the Organizational Context." Special Issue. *Journal of Applied Behavioral Science* 25:307–521.

Sjoberg, Gideon, and Leonard D Cain. 1971. "Negative Values, Counter System Models, and the Analysis of Social Systems." Pp. 212–29 in Herman Turk and Richard Simpson, eds. *Institutions and Social Exchange: The Sociologies of Talcott Parsons and George C. Homans*. Indianapolis: Bobbs-Merrill.

Sjoberg, Gideon, and Paula Jean Miller. 1973. "Social Research on Bureaucracy: Limitations and Opportunities." *Social Problems* 21:129–43.

Sjoberg, Gideon, Norma Williams, Ted R. Vaughan, and Andrée F. Sjoberg. 1991. "The Case Study Approach in Social Research: Basic Methodological Issues." Pp. 27–79 in Joe R. Feagin, Anthony M. Orum, and Gideon Sjoberg, eds. *A Case for the Case Study*. Chapel Hill: University of North Carolina Press.

Skocpol, Theda., ed. 1984. *Vision and Method in Historical Sociology*. New York: Cambridge University Press.

Smith, Bruce L.R. 1990. *American Science Policy Since World War II*. Washington, D.C.: Brookings Institution.

Smith, Robert W. 1989. *The Space Telescope: A Study of NASA, Science, Technology, and Politics*. Cambridge: Cambridge University Press.

Stern, Richard L., and Laura Jereski. 1991. "More Victims?" *Forbes* 148 (September 16):113.

Stinchcombe, Arthur L. 1990. *Information and Organizations*. Berkeley: University of California Press.

Sutton, Francis X., ed. 1990. *A World to Make: Development in Perspective*. New Brunswick: Transaction Books.

Teichova, Alice. 1986. "Multinationals in Perspective." Pp. 362–73 in Alice Teichova, Maurice Levy-Leboyer, and Helga Nussbaum, eds. *Multinational Enterprise in Historical Perspective*. Cambridge: Cambridge University Press.

Tilly, Charles. 1981. *As Sociology Meets History*. New York: Academic Press.

———. 1984. *Big Structures, Large Processes, Huge Comparisons*. New York: Russell Sage Foundation.

Turner, Jonathan H. 1989. "Sociology in the United States: Its Growth And Contemporary Profile." Pp. 220–42 in Nikolai Genov, ed. *National Traditions In Sociology*. Newbury Park: Sage.

Turner, Stephen P., and Jonathan H. Turner. 1990. *The Impossible Science: An Institutional Analysis of American Sociology*. Newbury Park: Sage.

"Universities under Siege." Special Issue. 1990. *Academe* 76(May-June):8–30.

Vaughan, Ted R., and Gideon Sjoberg. 1984. "The Individual and Bureaucracy: An Alternative Meadian Interpretation." *Journal of Applied Behavioral Science* 20:57–69.

Veblen, Thorstein. 1954. *The Higher Learning in America*. Stanford: Academic Reprints (orig. 1918).

Vessuri, Hebe M.C. 1986. "The Universities, Scientific Research and the National Interest in Latin America." *Minerva* 24:1–38.

Wachtel, Howard M. 1990. *The Money Mandarins: The Making of a Supranatural Economic Order*. Rev. ed. Armonk: M.E. Sharpe.

Waligorski, Conrad P. 1990. *Political Theory of Conservative Economists*. Lawrence: University Press of Kansas.

Wallerstein, Immanuel. 1983. *Historical Capitalism*. London: Verso.

———. 1987. "World Systems Analysis." Pp. 309–24 in Anthony Giddens and Jonathan Turner, eds. *Social Theory Today*. Stanford: Stanford University Press.

Williams, Norma, Gideon Sjoberg, and Andrée F. Sjoberg. 1983. "The Bureaucratic Personality: A Second Look." Pp. 173–89 in W. Boyd Littrell, Gideon Sjoberg, and Louis A. Zurcher, eds. *Bureaucracy as a Social Problem*. Greenwich: JAI Press.

Williams, Peter and David Wallace. 1989. *Unit 731; Japan's Secret Biological Warfare in World War II*. New York: Free Press.

Wilner, Patricia. 1985. "The Main Drift Of Sociology Between 1936 and 1982." *History of Sociology* 5:1–20.

Wilson, William Julius. 1987. *The Truly Disadvantaged*. Chicago: University of Chicago Press.

Wolfe, Alan. 1989. *Whose Keeper? Social Science and Moral Obligation*. Berkeley: University of California Press.

Wolin, Sheldon S. 1990. "Democracy in the Discourse of Postmodernism." *Social Research* 57:5–30.

Wright, Erik Olin. 1985. *Classes*. London: Verso.

| Chapter | **3** | **THE ETHICAL FOUNDATIONS OF SOCIOLOGY AND THE NECESSITY FOR A HUMAN RIGHTS ALTERNATIVE** |

Gideon Sjoberg and Ted R. Vaughan

This chapter has a complex, twofold objective. The first is to examine, in general terms, how sociologists have failed to explicate the ethical presuppositions of their discipline. Although members of the American Sociological Association claim to subscribe to a Code of Professional Ethics, and ethical issues are treated at least in passing in most textbooks on research methods, the fundamental assumptions regarding the ethics of sociological activities (and their link to the broader society and the global social order) typically have been ignored. Although a number of sociologists have come to employ the concepts of "morals" and of "ethics" rather freely in their scholarly accounts, the implications of these concepts for theory and research remain largely unexplored.[1]

The second objective is to sketch out an alternative approach to morals in sociology—one based on human rights rather than ethicist principles. Although human rights concerns have been addressed explicitly in declarations of the United Nations, and although this problem area has been widely debated on the world scene, American sociologists have conveniently sidestepped this major societal and global issue. *Human rights serve as a striking case study of how sociologists have disregarded a far-reaching cross-national or cross-cultural issue to which they are capable of making a substantial theoretical (and empirical) contribution.* The recent edited surveys of sociological theory by Ritzer (1990) and Giddens and Turner (1987) testify to the intellectual myopia of contemporary sociologists regarding human rights.

In formulating our argument we comment briefly on the differences between the ethicist and the human rights perspectives. Next we critically examine the prevailing orthodoxy within sociology—notably its claim to "value neutrality" and "objectivity." The data support the assertion that the stated ideal bears little or no resemblance to sociology-in-use, for ethical presuppositions permeate the discipline of sociology in the United States and elsewhere.

After briefly isolating the dominant ethical assumptions undergirding the theory and research of sociologists, we counterpose an alternative perspective—one based on human rights. Herein we can merely outline some of the essential

114

elements of a sociological theory of human rights. We then articulate the necessity for a human rights orientation by delineating a central moral issue of our age: bureaucratic domination. Such is supported by the existing ethicist framework and can be challenged only through an alternative moral theory. Our mode of reasoning, which we term "countersystem analysis" (Sjoberg and Cain 1971), exposes the weaknesses of the ethicist framework and points the way toward a meaningful alternative. Our analysis serves to expand on, and even restructure, Mills's (1959) "sociological imagination."

Conceptual Clarifications

Some conceptual clarifications are essential for understanding our argument. Our overall analysis is predicated on the observations of Alasdair MacIntyre (1981, 1982). This moral philosopher has reasoned, and in our judgment correctly so, that underlying every moral theory is an implicit social theory and undergirding every social theory is an implicit moral theory.

We use the concept "morals" to encompass both the ethicist and the human rights orientations. Sociologists have yet to grasp the essential difference between these two moral systems. While sociologists often speak of ethics without being aware of the particular ethical principles to which they subscribe, they are far less conversant with human rights. Most sociologists we have encountered are incredulous about our concern with a theory of human rights. A typical reaction has been, "Why investigate human rights?" American sociologists have thus far conceived of issues relating to human rights theory as standing outside the pale of proper social inquiry.

Although we find an interplay between the ethicist and the human rights traditions, the two can be distinguished in a rather well-defined way. In effect, the ethicist worldview rests on the principle of duties and assumes that as human agents carry out their duties to the community or to the nation-state they acquire rights. In contrast, the human rights tradition begins with the principle that human beings have rights simply because they are human beings. In this context duties serve to enhance one's rights, but they are not a precondition for them.[2]

In looking back on the history of social thought, we find that the ethicist position has been anchored in the philosophical heritage of the West (as well as other civilizations). It has served as the staple of moral theory from Aristotle to such diverse moral philosophers as Kant and the utilitarians. The ethicist worldview also is the foundation on which the writings of Durkheim, Weber, and Parsons rest. In fact, Durkheim had a well-defined interest in the sociology of ethics (Lukes 1972).

In contrast to the ethicist orientation, the principle of human rights has been articulated in the political wing of philosophical thought by Locke, among others, and it has been advanced by the practical and political activists associated with, for example, the French and American revolutions. This practical political dimension of the rights tradition finds expression in the modern era in the United Nations' Universal Declaration of Human Rights. This declaration was a response to the Nazis' destruction of the European Jews during World War II as well as to the revolt of colonial people against their European masters.

One question that often arises is: Just where does one locate civil rights in this debate? Although scholars, as we might expect, are not of one mind about this matter, we believe that the civil rights tradition has been more closely aligned, at least in the U.S. experience, with the ethicist rather than the human rights perspective. Civil rights, in both theory and practice, has for the most part conceived of rights as deriving from a citizen's adherence to duties relating to nation-states—not because one has these rights simply as a result of being human. These and other conceptual issues should become clearer as we elaborate our argument.

Value Neutrality as an Ideal in Sociology

Although moral inquiry has been an integral part of the sociological enterprise since the time of Auguste Comte and Herbert Spencer, we find after World War I the rise of two major, albeit divergent, theoretical traditions calling for value neutrality on the part of sociologists as scientists. The logical positivists, or logical empiricists, have championed this view; so too Weber and his followers have called with conviction for a value-neutral stance by sociologists. The principles undergirding these two intellectual orientations have been woven together in various, and at times contradictory, ways in social science in general and sociology in particular since World War II.

All too often, sociologists speak of positivism or logical empiricism as a homogeneous entity when, in fact, social theorists have not been of one mind in interpreting these concepts. There is the line of thought emanating from the British empiricists such as John Stuart Mill, William Jevons, and Karl Pearson, who have influenced sociological thought. We also can point to the strand of thinking associated with Percy William Bridgman and those who have championed the cause of "operationalism." While acknowledging the varieties of positivist thought, we focus our primary attention on the members of the Vienna Circle. Its supporters have deeply influenced the philosophy of science in the United States, which in turn has had a major impact on sociological theory and research. These theorists contend that the natural and the social sciences have a common methodological grounding and that metaphysics and moral judgments must be removed from consideration by scientists because these issues cannot be resolved through the scientific method. Admittedly some logical positivists have asserted that "the central problem of ethics concerns the causal explanation of behavior through scientific investigation" (Schlick 1959:263), but this viewpoint has had little or no impact on contemporary American sociology.

The positivist heritage regarding value neutrality has been congruent with the reasoning advanced by Max Weber and his followers. This congruence exists despite the marked differences between the positivists and the champions of the Weberian orientation. In part, Weber's argument regarding value neutrality reflects his efforts to provide the academics of his day with protection against intervention by external political forces within society; in part, his analysis is in keeping with his conception of bureaucracy wherein social scientists are expected to delineate for the managers the most efficient means by which to attain a given end. For Weber, scientific inquiry cannot determine the ends themselves but of necessity must focus on an evaluation of the effectiveness of the means.

Talcott Parsons, who is widely recognized as the sociologist who introduced Weber to American sociology, has defined the principle of value neutrality, or "scientific objectivity," as an ideal of sociological investigation, and his countless students have in general followed suit. Parsons (1967:139-65) at one point discussed Mannheim's concept of ideology and conceded that ideology may foster distortions in scientific reasoning, but ultimately for Parsons these are correctable.

Ironically, many Marxist sociologists who came to sociology in the 1970s and 1980s reinforced the belief in value neutrality in at least two respects. First, as Attewell (1984) has made explicit, many Marxists who have succeeded in academia often have done so by adopting the rigorous technical procedures of mainstream scholarship. Second, and less well understood, most Marxist sociologists have been faithful to that wing of Marxism which eschews ethics and human rights as basic topics of inquiry (cf. Lukes 1985). Marx himself gave short shrift to ethics. This resulted in part from Marx's conception of ethics (particularly the Kantian variety) as a rationalization for bourgeois intellectuals who refused to come to terms with the injustices that inhere in the capitalist order. So too, Marx (1972) was highly critical of the human rights principles that emerged from the French Revolution. Marxist sociologists, in keeping with this heritage, typically have focused on changes in class and power relationships. If these particular problems are resolved properly, ethical and human rights issues will take care of themselves.

Ethical Orientations in Contemporary Sociology

Earlier we mentioned that the American Sociological Association has adopted a Code of Professional Ethics as a guide for its activities. Yet many of its most well-known members insist on the value neutrality of their activities. Undoubtedly there are several ways to rationalize this seeming discrepancy between recognition of ethics as a guide for sociological activities and the claim that sociology as a science is value neutral. One tack in coping with this situation is to acknowledge, as does Parsons (1967:139-65), that ideological factors may distort scientific inquiry and, following this line of reasoning, the code can be viewed as a vehicle for reducing distortions. Another likely justification for the code is that it serves to legitimate sociological activities to members of the broader society. Thus, the code becomes a political tool to advance the goals of scientific sociology.

Whatever roundabout defense might be offered for the apparent discrepancy between adherence to an ethical code and an insistence that sociology must and can be value neutral, a careful analysis, on both theoretical and empirical grounds, supports the assertion that sociological inquiry is permeated by ethical assumptions. We are intent on outlining how ethical presuppositions lie at the core of reasoning in American sociology. The discipline is dominated by three major ethical orientations: a commitment to relativism, a commitment to a social system (or systems), and a belief in utilitarianism. We outline some essential features of each of these ethical orientations; yet in the process we take note of how they overlap or have been combined by various sociologists.

Ethical Relativism

A number of social scientists, including sociologists, prior to World War II openly espoused some form of ethical relativism. Anthropologists in particular were leaders in pushing forward this moral imperative. Certainly the principle of cultural relativism gave each culture (or subculture) its just deserts, and moral relativism thus served to open up social thought to a range of alternative ways of conceptualizing the nature of human nature and social reality. At its core, ethical relativism has called for tolerance of social and cultural patterns that differ sharply from those that sociologists generally support. It might also become the basis for challenging the moral superiority of one's own cultural system. The rise of Nazism and the resultant Holocaust undermined faith in ethical relativism (cf. Hatch 1983). A belief in this principle leads to a tacit acceptance or toleration of Hitler's destruction of the European Jews and other ethnic minorities, and therein lie fatal weaknesses of this moral system.

We witnessed considerable backtracking from the open espousal of ethical relativism in the post World War II era; yet ethical relativism never disappeared from sociology.[3] It has survived not only within the discipline but has experienced a revival among a group of sociologists who have been influenced by so-called postmodernist thought, which has fostered a variety of "debunking" efforts. The deconstructionists, for example, utilize certain rhetorical features of the text itself in order to refute its manifest content (Habermas 1987b:189). Yet this particular form of textual criticism becomes encased in a worldview dominated by nihilism (cf. Lehman 1991).

We can briefly document the place of ethical relativism in contemporary sociology by specifying particular theoretical and empirical traditions in which this perspective holds sway. Ethical relativism appears to have a stronghold in the sociological traditions associated with Goffman and Garfinkel as they seek to interpret micro relations. It also can be found in the social constructionist orientation toward social problems. So too, a number of macrosociologists, as becomes evident later, have adopted some form of ethical relativism.

Goffman serves as an informative starting point for recognizing one form of relativism that permeates a sizable subsector of the discipline. His moral assumptions have yet to be subjected to searching scrutiny. Although his writings are not of one cut of cloth, several facets of his analysis stand out. Goffman's agents adopt a form of "situational ethics"—a well-defined version of moral relativism—as they enhance their self-esteem or personal advantage through "image management." Social interaction in general, and the manipulation of others in particular, varies in accordance with changing social situations. Goffman has, in effect, combined situational ethics with a form of "utilitarianism" (discussed later) wherein agents maximize their social advantage or self-worth through manipulating others.

To anchor our argument more firmly in sociology, we single out Eliot Friedson's (1983) tribute to Goffman after the latter's death. For Friedson "Goffman's work is intensely moral in character" (1983:358) and he had a "deep moral sensibility" (1983:360). Although we recognize a case can be made for Goffman's moral concerns for the defense of self in his *Asylums* (1961), Friedson is illustrative of sociologists' failure to look closely at the underlying assumptions of Goffman's agents in his *The Presentation of Self in Everyday Life* (1959) and other works (e.g., Goffman 1967). He does not explain Goffman's tacit acceptance of the human agent who manipulates others for his or her gain and continually shifts tactics as situations vary. Friedson provides us with no hint of the moral difficulties associated with Goffman's commitment to situational ethics, which is combined with a particular form of utilitarianism.

Goffman's (1959) human agents who engage in "impression management" may well undercut the dignity of persons with whom they interact. Sociologists who reason that Goffman was simply describing "what exists" must answer why his analysis overlooked the effects of manipulation on the dignity of others. Goffman's use of the theater as an analogy for everyday life glosses over the moral issues embedded in his orientation. The audience in a theater expects to be "manipulated"—to be, for example, entertained. In everyday interaction this manipulation is of a different sort and may wreak social harm on the person or persons manipulated and thus exposed to possible exploitation.

Somewhat related to Goffman's perspective is the social constructionist orientation within the field of social problems. Spector and Kitsuse (1987) have been among the leading champions of this theoretical framework. They conceive of themselves as critics of the thesis that social problems arise as a result of "objective social conditions." For Spector and Kitsuse, social problems emerge as a result of a variety of "claims making" processes. Thus, child beating was at one time a nonproblem but came to be defined as a social problem. The claims making by particular groups in U.S. society led to this new definition of the situation.

In their advocacy of claims-making activities, Spector and Kitsuse approve of its relativist qualities. Sociologists, as these authors see it, can attain objectivity and avoid participating in the creation of social problems if they adopt this kind of orientation. Yet the moral implications of their mode of analysis, which is rather widespread in the study of social problems, may lead sociologists to trivialize moral issues of central import. The proponents of this orientation are unable to differentiate between the social and moral significance of claims-making activities concerning marijuana use and the U.S. bombing of Hiroshima and Nagasaki or the mass destruction of human beings in Cambodia in recent decades (cf. Chalk and Jonassohn 1990:398-407) or the disappearances in Argentina in the late 1970s and early 1980s (Simpson and Bennett 1985; Guest 1990).

The ethics of relativism is also alive and well among various macrosociologists. Jackall's (1988) research is a useful takeoff point, for he explicitly analyzes the morality or ethics of corporate managers. He insists he is simply describing "what is" with respect to "moral rules-in-use" among the managers of major corporations. But what if we look at sociologists like Jackall in their own mirror and apply their own logic to their own activities? When we do so, we discover that as sociologists their moral rules-in-use lead them to condone or accept racism in its virulent forms as well as the destruction of the environment by the managerial sector—whether corporate or governmental in nature.

A number of the issues regarding moral relativism become clearer as we consider sociologists' historical ethical commitment to various social systems, in particular the nation-state.

Ethical Commitment to a Social System

In the history of sociological theory and research, we perceive the pervasive role of the ethical commitment to social systems—be this a community, a large-scale organization (such as a bureaucracy), or, in particular, a nation-state. Most of the attention by sociologists, as well as moral philosophers, has been on the ethical underpinnings of community. Although the concept "community" has been widely debated, scholars often treat it as if its members share a common set of values as well as moral obligations.

Much of Durkheim's analysis is permeated with a version of the ethics of community (even societal community) life. Tönnies's distinction between *Gemeinschaft* and *Gesellschaft* contains a built-in concern with the changes in the moral order in face of modernity. When we turn to American sociology, the Chicago School was preoccupied (though largely in an unstated manner) with the breakdown of the ethical foundations of community, as urbanization came to dominate the social landscape in the early part of the twentieth century.

Recently we have experienced a revival of interest in "communitarian ethics" by a group of sociologists as well as moral philosophers. Many of these scholars have been responding to "individualistic liberalism" or the "new individualism" or "utilitarianism" (discussed later). In *After Virtue* (1981), MacIntyre, a moral philosopher, calls for a return to an idealized community of a bygone era in order to sustain the virtues espoused by Aristotle. As for sociologists, Bellah and his colleagues, in their *Habits of the Heart* (1985), have been labeled communitarians, although in their more recent work (Bellah et al. 1991) they have expressed reservations about this label for their analysis.

The proponents of communitarian ethics are rightly concerned with larger issues of the common good in contrast to what is good for individuals. Although Bellah et al., as well as other sociologists who have advocated some version of communitarianism (e.g., Wolfe 1989), are to be commended for advancing the cause of moral inquiry, we have significant reservations about their line of reasoning. One question we raise is, "Community for whom?" This must be addressed when communities are rent by racial and ethnic strife (to say nothing of class, gender, and the like). Who will set the standards for the common set of ethical obligations? Bellah et al. (1985) take the American middle class as their point of departure, and they do not consider the serious obstacles posed by the construction of common understandings across racial and ethnic lines. And we would remind ourselves that these issues go to the core of the ethical foundations of such social orders as the former Soviet Union, the former Yugoslavia, and the Middle East.

But more than racial and ethnic divisions pose a challenge to communitarian ethics. Bureaucratic organizations, with their hierarchy of authority and high degree of specialization and division of labor, have fractured community life, but sociologists have yet to investigate the resultant patterns either in theoretical or empirical terms. Moreover, the ethical commitment of the managerial sector is not to the community in some traditional sense but to the large-scale organization of which it is an integral part (cf. Jackall 1988). Many managers are deeply committed to what Talcott Parsons termed "system maintenance."[4]

As bureaucratic organizations come to have a life of their own on the international level, we witness the emergence of a transnational ethical commitment. Although this new order calls for qualifications in discussing the ethical commitment to the nation-state, the latter deserves special consideration because of its historical and contemporary impact on the ethical presuppositions of sociological theory and research.

Before we became aware of the import of human rights theory, we authored an essay on "The Sociology of Ethics and the Ethics of Sociologists" (Sjoberg and Vaughan 1971). We reasoned that a central ethical commitment of modern sociologists has been to the nation-state. Although sociologists have not been as explicit as have a number of political scientists in making the "national interest" the cornerstone for justifying many of their activities, sociologists have nonetheless adopted a form of nationalism and commitment to the power arrangements of their own nation-state as a guide for proper ethical conduct.

The ethics of the nation-state has been a guiding principle, implicitly or explicitly, for numerous sociologists. This includes the followers of Weber such as Parsons and Bendix, as well as positivists ranging from Lundberg to Coleman and Gibbs. Although in recent years we have experienced a weakening of nationalism and commitment to the ethical categories of the nation-state, we should not underestimate the depth of sociologists' commitment to this moral orientation.

A historical perspective provides us with a basis for charting this unexplored terrain. Parsons, and later Bendix, took the lead in bringing Weber to the attention of American sociologists, but both can be faulted for their unwillingness or, more likely, inability to confront Weber's adherence to the ethics of German nationalism and the state structure of his time. Wolfgang Mommsen's (1984) analysis of the intertwining of Weber's political theory with his deeply ingrained nationalism was sharply criticized when his book first appeared in the 1950s. But Mommsen's data are too compelling to be set aside. He documents Weber's avowed nationalism and even commitment to imperialism. According to Mommsen (1984:419):

> A pure separation of Max Weber the social scientist from Max Weber the politician may perhaps be expedient from the point of view of scholarly politics, but is an impossible task. If it were attempted consistently, it would lead to sterile interpretations of his sociological works as well as his political theories.

Parsons, like Weber, accepted the ethical categories (especially those of the legal apparatus) of the nation-state in his analysis, and his morality is made more understandable by the findings of Charles O'Connell, who brought to light how closely integrated Parsons was, at one point in his life, into the U.S. power structure, including the secret side of the military-intelligence complex. Some of his activities may have helped pave the way for ex-Nazi collaborators to enter the United States after World War II (Diamond 1992).

Parsons's ethical commitment to the nation-state (and to the system maintenance thereof) is clearly formulated in his discussion of sociology as a profession. Parsons (1959) emphasized the duties or responsibilities of sociologists to societal (i.e., nation-state) concerns. Moreover, as part of his analysis of the potential for full citizenship for the "Negro," Parsons (1967:463) writes:

> It has been stressed above that the American Revolutionary tradition has prepared this country for a position of leadership in the movement for equality for the new nations of the extra-European world.

He made this assertion without considering the negative consequences of America's military and economic power on the world scene.

As for the work of Bendix, another leading expositor of Weberian thought (Bendix 1964), we find in his autobiography (Bendix 1986, 1990) no reflection on his use of nation-state categories in his sociological analysis. He insisted that we must understand the development of nations by analyzing their social and cultural changes "in their own terms" (Bendix 1964), a form of analysis often termed "historicism." Moreover, Bendix seems to have had no second thoughts regarding the moral position of Weber, despite Mommsen's pioneering work. We thus find a victim of Nazism unable to examine the meaning of that tragic epoch in his sociological investigations. His inability to confront the link between sociologists and the ethical orientation of the nation-state for both Weber and himself speaks to the nature of American sociology during the era in which Bendix wrote.

We need not limit ourselves to sociologists closely linked to Weberian sociology. Another version of the commitment to the nation-state ethic is reflected in one wing of the Chicago School, particularly in the writings of Morris Janowitz. His *The Reconstruction of Patriotism* (1983) is a call for voluntary national service. More broadly, Janowitz is concerned with the issue of "civic education," which, again, has as its core an ethical grounding in the nation-state.

We also need to comment on the work of Theda Skocpol and her associates. The title of one of their edited books, *Bringing the State Back In* (Evans et al. 1985) speaks to their intellectual agenda. Except for Tilly and Stephan, the authors have little to say about the "dark side" of nation-state activities. Genocide, Nuremberg, and Watergate are absent from the Index. Thus, questions such as What are the limits to nation-state loyalty? What are the moral limits to state power and manipulation? are not even raised. Yet these issues are of central theoretical and empirical import in social research on the state in the contemporary world.

Nor have the avowed positivists escaped commitment to the ethical categories of the nation-state. In actuality, their particular commitment to "objectivity," which entails the use of highly technical and standardized procedures for achieving agreement on sociological principles or laws, well serves the administrative state. By and large, the avowed positivists are willing to work within the social categories of the corporate and state apparatus. This assertion finds support in their frequently unquestioned use of official statistics that typically reflect the social definition of the powerful organizational structures in U.S. society.

But positivists can be even more direct in their support of the ethics of the nation-state. Gibbs serves as a stark case in point, for he articulates his sociological position in a forceful manner. In Gibbs's (1975) work on deterrence, he assumes that the State (which he capitalizes) has the "ultimate duty" to control its citizens. In working out a preventive theory of crime, he advances the proposition: "The greater the celerity, certainty, and severity of punishment, the less the crime" (1975:222). On occasion, he hedges his views on deterrence, but nowhere does he systematically analyze the limits of the deterrence doctrine. He carefully sidesteps the issues relating to fairness and justice with respect to deterrence of criminal activities by the state apparatus. However Gibbs might protest, his writings provide a moral justification, both directly and indirectly, for the construction, in the past two decades, of an enormous prison complex in the United States, which the broader public perceives to be a deterrent to crime.

Looking back on the social and cultural situation within which social science came to be formed in the latter part of the nineteenth and early part of the twentieth century in the United States, we discover why the commitment to nation-state ideals has been so commonplace. During this era, social scientists, as critics, fared poorly within the university setting, and the early specialization of social science into disciplines served, as Furner (1975) has documented, to insulate social scientists from political attacks that undermined their place in the university.

These patterns became far more pronounced after World War II. First, the ideological fury of McCarthyism was unleashed against dissenters in university settings. Consequently, those who were prone to criticize existing internal power arrangements as well as the external power of the United States on the world scene were pushed out or reined in (Schrecher 1986). Second, in the decades after World War II, specialization within the social sciences, and sociology was no exception, was accentuated. This specialization, combined with the ideals of the natural science model—particularly with respect to objectivity and technically correct research procedures—helped integrate social scientists, including sociologists, into the organizational structures, both corporate and governmental, of the nation-state. For four decades, social scientists were committed to the Cold War and to the containment of the Soviet power bloc (cf. Lewis 1988). This pattern has wide-ranging implications that remain to be explored.

The postwar years also signaled the rise of managerial control within American universities. These bureaucratic managers, who have become closely intertwined with the dominant organizational structures of the nation-state, have had a built-in stake in "system maintenance"—in containing dissent and fostering technical social research perceived as "neutral" or supportive of existing power arrangements.

Utilitarianism

Utilitarianism is perhaps the dominant ethical commitment of contemporary American sociologists. Although Parsons, in his *The Structure of Social Action* (1937), challenged the foundations of utilitarian thought, and although both Durkheim and Weber reacted, from differing perspectives, against the utilitarian doctrine, the ethics of utilitarianism appear more widely accepted in the latter part of the twentieth century than the classical sociological theorists might ever have imagined.

The ethics of utilitarianism, on which we now elaborate, assume that the greatest good for the greatest number emerges from the individual's pursuit of his or her own self-interest. Although various contentious differences persist within this intellectual tradition, and although many present-day proponents of utilitarianism are likely to qualify their belief in this ethical doctrine, a number of domain assumptions are shared by advocates (including sociologists) of this ethical perspective.

One fundamental presupposition of utilitarians is that individuals are the ultimate unit of social reality and that they are committed to maximizing their self-interest, typically seeking to attain some form of "pleasure" and to avoid "pain." In the economic realm this means maximizing profit and minimizing financial losses. Among sociologists, what is maximized may be somewhat more complex in nature, but the pleasure-pain principle underlies the course of human action.

But why do individuals strive to maximize their self-interest? In the final analysis, the commitment to self-interest rests on the biopsychological nature of human agents. The biological and psychological makeup of humans is fixed and gives rise to the search for pleasure and the avoidance of pain. The utilitarians give short shrift to the shaping of human nature by social and cultural phenomena. Consequently, "motives" are a given, and values and beliefs become irrelevant to understanding human action.

A second fundamental tenet of utilitarianism is that as individuals pursue their self-interest through maximizing their "preferences," the broader social outcome, though unanticipated by any set of individuals, nonetheless results in the common good. In other words, the good society is an aggregate of isolated individuals each pursuing his or her own self-interest.

(One can readily perceive why utilitarianism has served the cause of the positivists. Individuals are separate units, and the whole is the sum of the parts. These domain assumptions lie at the core of probability sampling and statistical analysis. Coleman (1990:18) acknowledges the linkage between utility maximization and the "quantitative development of theory.")

The ethics of utilitarianism rest on the pursuit of self-interest, which leads to the greatest good for the greatest number—a "majoritarian perspective" to which we return later. In looking back on utilitarian thought, we find two major versions having influenced contemporary sociological theorizing.[5] One had its origins in the economic theory of Adam Smith, the other in the political theory of Jeremy Bentham. Both are concerned with the relation of individual actions to the public welfare. Although their conceptions of the relationships of individuals to the broader social order differ somewhat, each nonetheless was committed to the premise that pursuing self-interest leads to the greatest good for the greatest number.

Smith's utilitarianism emerged from his analysis of market relations characterized by a complex division of labor. In order to satisfy their material well-being, human beings naturally engage in exchange relations. To enhance their chances of satisfying their self-interest, they come to specialize in the production process. As specialization increases, the productivity of labor increases. Within this context, the societal welfare is enhanced as individuals pursue their own self-interest. In Halevy's (1955) terms, Adam Smith assumes a "natural identity of interests" as the activities of each person contribute without intention to the societal welfare.

Bentham's version of utilitarianism provided a different response to the relation between self-interest and the general welfare. He agrees with Smith's basic assumptions: Individuals inevitably "maximize" their pleasure (and avoid pain), and society is an aggregate of individuals. Still, Bentham did not anchor his analysis within the framework of the exchange relations that emerge as a result of the division of labor. For Bentham, self-interested actions of individuals do not naturally and automatically result in a common good. Instead, self-interest must be promoted through the legal and political system. Specifically, the legal apparatus must punish those individuals whose actions are socially injurious to the general welfare; the general welfare is identified with the interests of the majority. In Helevy's (1955) terms, Bentham's conceptualization rests on the "artificial identification of interests." The state becomes the source for sustaining this artificial identity of interests, a view that differs from Smith's natural identity of interests.

We have briefly discussed the Smith and Bentham intellectual traditions because one or both of these (or variants thereof) have shaped a large segment of theory and ethical reasoning within modern sociology. Although some scholars might quarrel with this assertion, it is striking how utilitarianism (under the guise, for example, of exchange theory or rational-choice theory) has permeated most subdisciplines within the field. One reason is that utilitarianism articulates well with the ideals associated with the natural science model (cf. Coleman 1990). By conceiving of individuals as "independent units," it is feasible for sociologists to rely on probability sampling and to employ sophisticated statistical procedures to test hypotheses in a "rigorous" manner.

Admittedly, the manner in which the Smith-Bentham heritage has been played out in contemporary sociology is, as implied, multifaceted in nature. Homans (1961), who did much to push forward one form of utilitarianism, relied heavily on Skinner's behavioristic psychology in formulating his theory of social exchange. More recently, Coleman (1990), while not committed to this version of psychology, is intent on advancing the utilitarian cause.

Opp (1985) has surveyed a range of research activities based on the "economic-man model." He argues that there is no basic incompatibility between the psychological perspective and those orientations that rely more directly on this model. Opp proceeds to specify some of the substantive fields in which the economic-man model has taken firm hold. One relates to the study of revolution and social movements. The research tradition associated with resource mobilization theory rests heavily on the economic-man heritage. Second, a group of sociologists have relied on this framework in the study of deviant behavior and crime. Opp gives primary attention to studies informed by anomie theory and contends that these can be derived, if one makes certain additional assumptions, from the economic model of man. Third, a considerable body of research related to social stratification is cast in this mold. Opp (1985:224) reasons that "there is a certain similarity between the Davis-Moore theory and price theory." He (1985:227) also observes that studies by Boudon have demonstrated that "'inequality of social opportunity' is an aggregate result of the actions of various individuals."

Additional data could be brought to bear to support Opp's contention that the economic-man model has permeated most subfields of sociology. In research on the family, exchange theory in a variety of forms holds sway, as sociologists seek to demonstrate the kinds of exchange relationships between men and women and the implications of these for marriage and the family (e.g., Collins 1988). Then, too, among demographers, one school of thought would have us believe that fertility patterns are based on some form of "economic calculus." When considering the number of offspring marital partners should produce, they calculate, prior to their bedroom activities, the costs and benefits of their action—so the "reasoning" runs.

Although Opp focuses on the economic-man model itself, we can readily trace various current sociological writings back to Bentham's conception of utilitarianism. Gibbs (1975) in his theorizing about deterrence of those who violate legal norms has explicitly associated himself with Jeremy Bentham.

Gibbs (1975:5) claims that Bentham came as close to a systematic theory as did Freud, Marx, Durkheim, Weber, or Parsons. It is evident that Gibbs has taken over the basic principles governing Bentham's conception of the control of crime, though he does not elaborate on Bentham's "hedonistic calculus."

On examining the larger picture, we find that the utilitarian doctrine is the theoretical and moral foundation for much of policy research and policy making by the U.S. government. Brandt (1983:37) writes:

> Nonphilosophers widely employ the general utilitarian framework in thinking about moral issues. It is obvious that "cost-benefit analysis" is used (doubtless often misused by construing it in a much over-simplified form) in evaluating government projects. The utilitarian conception appears to pervade the American Law Institute's recommendations for reform of the criminal law and it underlies the currently influential movement of "economic criticism" of the law. Indeed, in evaluating systems of "professional ethics" an assessment of the general costs and benefits of recognizing certain standards seems inescapable, although talk about "rights" is often introduced in this connection.

Brandt's comments signal two issues worthy of special mention. One, most evaluation research, which remains a salient aspect of applied sociology, rests primarily on utilitarianism. Programs on the national and local levels typically are judged to be effective by considering their "costs" and "benefits" for the majority of the populace. Second, and more important still, Brandt suggests that the ethical foundations of modern society are essentially utilitarian in nature. Thus, we find Reynolds (1979), a sociologist, writing about the ethics of sociology in utilitarian terms. This perspective has been accepted, almost without challenge or critical assessment, by mainstream sociology. Although for a time the logical positivists sought to separate ethics from utilitarianism, the two have always been intertwined, and recognition of this relationship seems more overt today than some decades ago. Still, the ethics of utilitarianism remain poorly understood by most sectors of the U.S. sociological community.

The Ethical Grounding of Sociology: A Recapitulation

The dominant ethical orientations in sociology have been linked together into differing constellations by sociologists. For example, Weber held, in varying degrees, to all three of the ethical orientations outlined here. His primary moral anchor was the German nation-state of the late nineteenth and early twentieth centuries. Consequently, he acknowledged one form of relativism, for he recognized the "sovereignty of nations" wherein each nation-state had its own autonomy and thus its own ethical moorings. (Yet Weber supported the imperialistic expansion of Germany as well.) In addition, for all of Weber's emphasis on bureaucracy, he countenanced, even supported, the role of the market, which for him existed within and was furthered by the bureaucratic apparatus. To the extent that the market is founded on utilitarian considerations, Weber introduced utilitarianism into his theorizing (though his perspective differed from that of the classical and neoclassical economists). Significantly, Parsons, Weber's ardent admirer, combined these ethical orientations as well. Parsons's belief in the American nation-state is clear enough. And although he championed the welfare state, which he perceived as moderating or constraining the negative effects of a "free market," he was nonetheless a supporter of capitalism, which to some degree is based on the utilitarianism he criticized. Although Parsons does not formulate his theory exactly as we have stated it, our interpretation is consistent with the general structure of his arguments.

Among the ardent positivists in sociology—Homans, Coleman, Gibbs, as well as many others—we find a commitment to some form of utilitarianism. Although they differ among themselves as to the kind of utilitarianism espoused, they stand in marked contrast to Parsons, for instance, in that they do not seriously qualify their belief in utilitarianism. At the same time these sociologists also adhere, each in his or her own way, to the ethics of the nation-state within which utilitarianism is seen to flourish.

Limitations of Current Ethical Orientations in Sociology

The existing ethical orientations in sociology contain serious flaws that have yet to be debated within the discipline. Although we have alluded to some of the strictures on the ethical premises of sociology, we now highlight them in more dramatic form. As for relativism, the Holocaust made it almost impossible for social scientists, including sociologists, to support the principle that ethical standards are relative— that the actions of the Nazis were not fundamentally immoral. So, too, the systematic destruction of the European Jews and other ethnic minorities by the Nazis has led to the questioning of nation-state morality. The Nazi experience demonstrates how scientists—for instance, the doctors depicted by Lifton (1986)—were firmly integrated into the political apparatus that engaged in mass destruction. Yet the commitment to the moral categories of the nation-state as the primary defense for participating in the mass killing of Jews and other ethnic groups was challenged by the Nuremberg trials after World War II. Although these trials were conducted by the victors as they judged the leadership that had been vanquished, the principle of "crimes against humanity" was set forth as a basis for punishing the architects of the Holocaust (cf. Luban 1987).

In a more specific sense, an ethical commitment to a social system (particularly a large-scale organization) often leads persons to justify their actions by contending, "I am obeying superior orders." However, such a defense by personnel in the corporate or governmental spheres can have grave consequences for individuals they influence or control. Unfortunately, sociologists have, with rare exceptions, failed to wrestle theoretically with these issues. We return to them when we critically evaluate the foundations of modern bureaucratic structures.

Another central dimension of modern sociology, utilitarianism, requires critical attention. Although utilitarianism, as noted, has experienced a resurgence in recent decades, it cannot shake a fundamental weakness—the inherent limitations of "majoritarianism." The principle of the "greatest good for the greatest number" ultimately provides no protection for minorities—be they ethnic groups, women, or intellectual dissidents. The will of the majority is all the more threatening to minorities, given the premise that each person is expected to pursue his or her self-interest. As the members of the majority (who possess social power) pursue their self-interest, they often do so at the expense of the politically and economically disadvantaged members of the social order. Inasmuch as utilitarianism has no built-in corrective to domination by majority rule, the position of minorities is further eroded.

That utilitarianism has in the past two decades been able to prosper within sociology speaks to the limited ethical sensibilities of many members of the discipline. It also reflects the emergence of a political environment that has provided renewed legitimacy to the free market and utilitarianism. Sociologists who are members of the American Sociological Association often issue public pronouncements regarding their concern with, for instance, ethnic minorities, but their theory and their methodology, in the main, belie their professed beliefs. In practice, the theoretical foundations of their research activities do not protect the disadvantaged from manipulation by the majoritarian control associated with utilitarianism. In fact, it lends credence, directly or indirectly, to this control. The debate about the tyranny of majoritarianism has yet to be joined in any meaningful way within large sectors of sociology. Nor can this be accomplished if sociologists insist on an unyielding belief in the natural science model (and its presuppositions that support, and are supported by, the utilitarian doctrine).

The present-day ethical orientations of contemporary sociologists should come into sharper focus as we detail some of the principles undergirding a morality founded on human rights.

The Human Rights Perspective: A Brief Overview

Here our intention is to point out how sociologists are in a position to contribute to the construction of a more meaningful moral orientation for today's world. A morality grounded in human rights has, as observed previously, its origins in both a theoretical and practical (or political) heritage. Although the theory of human rights has been traced back to natural law, modern human rights theorizing is associated most often with the likes of John Locke, who was intent on justifying the individual's "inalienable rights" as a basis for countering the political tyranny of state power. This theoretical tradition has found sustenance in the political doctrines of the French Declaration of the Rights of Man and the Citizen, which emerged from the French Revolution, and the Bill of Rights, which grew out of the American rebellion against British colonial domination.

From the time of the French and American revolutions to World War II, the principles relating to human rights languished. They never disappeared, but a morality predicated on human rights was not considered a viable alternative to the existing state of affairs. But, with the Holocaust carried out by the Nazis and the rebellion of colonial people against European rule, human rights emerged as a worldwide concern. The idea of human rights was legitimated in the Universal Declaration of Human Rights of the United Nations. This document, if studied carefully, can be perceived as a compromise between the "individual-based" rights of the West and the more "collectivist" orientation toward rights as held by the then communist bloc.

In the decades after World War II, theoretical analysis of human rights has taken place on a variety of fronts. In the United States a body of scholarship regarding human rights has been crafted primarily within political and legal theory.[6] At least two monographs are worthy of special mention. One is by Myres McDougal et al. (1980), *Human Rights and the World Public Order*. The basic thrust of the book is captured by the premise that "the observational standpoint to which we aspire is that of citizens of the larger community of humankind" (1980:xvii). Within this framework, the authors emphasize the importance of respect for others. This book, which surveys a rather wide range of practical issues, has had a significant influence in selected legal and political circles, especially in the area of international law.

A more widely debated work is Ronald Dworkin's (1977) *Taking Rights Seriously*. Dworkin has influenced our own thinking. Yet we take issue with his highly individualistic conception of the nature of human nature and social reality, and he is locked into Western social (even nation-state) categories. In essence, he has not provided an adequate theoretical grounding for his reasoning on rights. Still, Dworkin has striven to formulate a theory of rights based on the principle of "equal concern and respect." Unfortunately, the few sociologists who have attempted to utilize Dworkin's work often have misinterpreted his fundamental argument. We must not confuse his basic tenet with a stress on equality per se. Dworkin's reasoning is more subtle than this. The principle of equal concern and respect can be clarified in the context of age-status patterns. Very young children, for example, cannot be equal to adults, for they are incapable of caring for themselves and would die without the support of adults. Still, they should, in keeping with Dworkin's principle, be accorded equal concern and respect. So, too, the frail, dependent elderly should be treated in a similar manner (cf. Cain 1987).

We can further clarify the human rights perspective (and its implications) by contrasting it with the reasoning associated with civil rights. Civil rights typically have been justified within the framework of nation-state morality. In ideal-type terms, social scientists and legal scholars argue for civil rights on the grounds that minorities are citizens of the nation-state and thus they acquire the right to vote and participate on an "equal basis" in the social order. Underlying the efforts after World War II to establish civil rights, particularly for African Americans, was an appeal to the "higher values" associated with American society. Kluger (1977:710), after detailing the history of the Supreme Court's decision in *Brown v. Board of Education*, concludes that this opinion "represented nothing short of a reconsecration of American ideals." Sociologists such as Parsons (1967:422–65) have theorized about the rights of "Negroes" in the context of citizenship, which calls for inclusion of an ever-wider set of persons and groups into the activities of the nation-state. Although the concept of civil rights is a step forward in formulating an adequate moral theory, it nonetheless remains flawed by its linkage to nation-state categories per se. Unfortunately, many advocates of civil rights are unaware of the ethical underpinnings of their perspective.

To be sure, a belief in human rights that transcends national boundaries indirectly seeped into the Senate hearings regarding Robert Bork (nominated by President Reagan to be an associate justice of the U.S. Supreme Court). Bork, who contended that judicial decisions should be founded on the original intent of the framers of the Constitution, was above all else a believer in "majoritarianism." His critics, who ultimately blocked his nomination, were deeply dismayed by his stand on ethnic minorities and women. A few of them alluded to a more fundamental, transnational human rights moral standard when judging Bork's qualifications. Even so, justifications by the contesting parties generally were framed within the confines of the ethical presuppositions of U.S. society (U.S. Senate 1989).

The civil rights and human rights orientations as they have been articulated in practice differ in fundamental respects. Within the broader framework of human rights, persons are entitled to human dignity—to equal concern and respect—as human beings first and foremost, not just because they are citizens of the United States or any other nation. Within this framework, members of minority groups must first and foremost be accorded rights as human beings. Their rights are not simply accorded them by the majority.

Yet we are moving ahead of ourselves. We return to certain basics in order to establish a solid foundation on which we might construct a sociologically informed theory of human rights.

Toward a Sociological Theory of Rights

Sociologists stand in a favorable position to advance our understanding of the principles that must undergird an adequate theory of human rights. The efforts to establish human rights for the blacks in South Africa or the efforts to construct a sounder foundation for human rights for racial and ethnic minorities in the United States are not mere abstract concerns but relate directly to empirical problems that affect not only sociologists but also human beings in all societies.

Moreover, if we are to face up to the destruction of the environment by toxic wastes, the suffering produced by famines, as well as the potential for devastation by nuclear or chemical or biological warfare, then it becomes essential that we restructure the moral foundations not only of human action but also of the organizational structures in the modern world. Adherence to the ethics of the nation-state—with its underlying premise of "my nation right or wrong"—is grossly inadequate for constructing an alternative moral system and a supportive institutional structure to cope with these issues.

In considering what sociology can contribute to the advancement of human dignity, we must recognize that the concept of human rights, though widely discussed, is still in the process of emergence on the world scene. We readily acknowledge that the idea of human rights has been utilized as a political instrument, often to advance the power of the state. Thus, the Reagan administration, which theoretically was opposed to human rights, found itself employing the concept in a selective fashion in order to enhance U.S. power during the 1980s. Nevertheless, by relying on a human rights rhetoric, members of the Reagan administration provided an inadvertent legitimacy to this moral perspective.

The debate about rights in its various convoluted forms is in keeping with our view that a viable conception of human rights has yet to be constructed, much less implemented, on the world scene. Within this context, sociologists are in a position to contribute to refinement of the debate concerning an issue that affects the fate of humankind (Vaughan 1989).

But before proceeding with specifics, let us restate certain basic principles that already have been mentioned. Unlike the ethicists, who conceive of rights as derived from duties, we assert that human beings have the right to human status independently of their particular community or nation-state—a view in keeping with the Universal Declaration of Human Rights. A counterargument might be that such a premise is not empirical. But it is no less empirical than the premise that persons as citizens have duties from which they derive rights. It is simply that the latter articulates with the moral commitment of most persons (including sociologists) to the "community," notably the nation-state—not to humanity in a global context.

In formulating a more adequate conception of human rights, we must move forward on several fronts. First, we need to clarify what it means to be human.

We advance a conception of human agency that differs from the individualism that underlies not only utilitarianism but also, for instance, Dworkin's theory of human rights. We must come to terms with the fact that human agents not only respond to the social order but are proactive agents in shaping that order.

Second, human agents are embedded within a broader social context. Any adequate theory of human rights in today's world must confront the nature of bureaucratic organizations. We thus outline what we regard as the essential features of contemporary bureaucratic structures and, in turn, consider how human agents often respond to these structures but are also capable (if they act in concert) of remaking them. If we are to advance the rights of human agents, we must recognize that organizations must be held morally accountable. Ultimately to attain greater human rights—notably equal concern and respect— organizations must be remade. Such has occurred in the past, and thus there is no reason it cannot be achieved (though with great difficulty) in the future.

In dealing with the nature of human nature, we adopt a thoroughgoing sociological conception of what it means to be human. We build on a highly modified version of George Herbert Mead's theoretical framework. Our analysis is in keeping with the nature of empirical reality, but it opens up issues that lie at the core of human rights theorizing.

For Mead (1934) human beings are social in nature. Though they possess certain essential biological capabilities, individuals become human only through their interaction with other human agents. One comes to formulate a view of oneself only through interaction with others. One always depends on others, in greater or lesser degree. Mead's conceptualization is at odds with the individualistic bias in most Western thought. For example, as noted earlier, such sociologists as Goffman have discarded Mead's main principles as they became captive of a particular form of the "new individualism" with its own special version of "utilitarianism."

An adequate theory of human rights must be grounded in a conception of human nature that recognizes the interdependence of human beings. We do not deny individuality—but individuality itself emerges from human interaction with others. Nowadays, those who are committed to the "new individualism"— with its stress on narcissism and greed—fail to recognize that they indulge in their self-aggrandizement as a result of prior socialization as well as the social support of significant others and, most important, the less fortunate who carry out the "dirty work" that the privileged sectors take for granted.

Although we are deeply indebted to the writings of George Herbert Mead, we reformulate his theoretical reasoning. In keeping with a renewed interest in the mind by social scientists (Bruner 1990), we conceive of the "social mind"—not the "social self"—as central to the nature of human nature as well as to an adequate theory of human rights. The social mind—not language, not the social self—is the most distinctive characteristic of what it means to be human.

The social mind is characterized by a wide range of social capabilities (Vaughan and Sjoberg 1984). These include the ability to conceptualize, to create images, to draw inferences based on social observations, to rely on a social memory, and to employ such logics as typification, analogy, the relation of parts to wholes, deduction, as well as the dialectic. How one proceeds to think and reason, as well as the particular content of one's mode of reasoning, depends on the existence of a social mind. Mead (1934:88) rightly speaks of the mind as "arising and developing within the social process, within the matrix of social interaction." The formal educational system serves to illustrate this pattern. Persons are taught to employ different kinds of images to convey ideas and to employ different logics as they immerse themselves in the study of literature, on the one hand, and physics, on the other.

The social mind is the foundation for the development of the self. Through a complex reasoning process (which has yet to be explicated), we are able to take the roles of others, to think about how others might view oneself, and in turn to look back on oneself as object.

In the broadest sense, the central defining feature of the social mind is its reflectivity. Human agents stand apart from other species because they think about thinking. This means that human agents are not mirror images of their experiences. Instead, they can and do reflect on the social order in which they live and work—on their beliefs, values, and moral codes—and in the process they may seek to modify or change their activities. This reflectivity, we remind ourselves, does not occur in a vacuum. It depends on a social memory of past experiences, which then becomes the basis for critical reflection. Social memory is a capability of the social mind, and it emerges from, and is sustained by, social interaction.

Reflectivity also is intertwined with the process of justification, not only of one's own social identity but also of the broader social order, including persons who lie beyond one's "community." Human agents devote considerable effort to justifying their moral beliefs and their normative order, particularly when these are challenged by others.

Our perspective on human agency differs markedly from the biopsychological definition of human nature employed by the utilitarians, and it also gives far more attention to the proactive aspect of human agency than do those of Weber and Parsons and their many adherents.

We must come to comprehend the connection of the social mind to human rights. First, the ability to take the roles of others and to recognize another's humanity and commonality with oneself is an essential step in recognizing the rights of others, in treating others with equal concern and respect. In fact, the destruction of human rights occurs in situations in which human beings are defined as outside the human condition. In the extreme case of the Nazis, they first defined the Jews and other ethnic minorities as outside the category of human beings in order to proceed effectively with the "final solution"—the mass destruction of these people. But, even in lesser forms of human degradation that undermine human rights, the process of defining others as nonhuman is at work. In wartime the enemy typically is labeled as nonhuman in order that members of this group can be killed with impunity. So, too, with discrimination against racial and ethnic minorities, this process is justified by viewing others as having less than human status. Thus, for human rights to be attained, we must come to terms with, and then overcome, the social barriers to taking the roles of others who are socially and culturally different from ourselves (cf. Williams 1989).

Second, the attainment of human rights rests on human agents' being able to reflect critically about their own situation and communicate the results of their reflections to others. Although the communication of critical evaluations may threaten ongoing authority structures, it is through such a social process that human agents can transcend existing social arrangements and think about, and in turn construct, new organizational forms on the basis of new moral principles. Utilitarianism was created by human agents; contrary to its proponents, utilitarianism does not inhere in human nature. Therefore, it is in the realm of the possible to build a moral system based on human rights.

We are fully cognizant that for human agents to attain human dignity supportive structures must be created to provide "basic necessities" and to provide human agents with the opportunities to embark on the construction of alternative social arrangements. Without the proper kinds of social organization, reflectivity is greatly impaired or undermined (a problem to which we return).

Our attention is nonetheless riveted on the centrality of reflectivity with respect to the social mind. Because of reflectivity, human beings are capable of evaluating critically the social and cultural order and, over time, of constructing alternative social arrangements. The major effort to establish a viable human rights morality after World War II has been predicated on the fact that humans are capable of building a new moral system as well as creating the social conditions that support the principle of human rights. For instance, the Helsinki Agreement, although not a treaty per se, provided an external standard that at least some eastern European intellectuals employed in justifying their protests against the totalitarian order in which they lived. Yet we must not assume that the creation of alternatives itself is a viable moral act. Surely this was not the case with Nazism. The construction of alternative social arrangement must be evaluated in terms of advancing the principle of human rights.

When contemplating the nature of alternatives, we must not become captives of the iron cage and assume that formal rationality—or the search for the most efficient means to attain a given end—is the ultimate rationality. Weber recognized other modes of rational thought, but many social scientists have been trapped by the concept of formal rationality. But there is a need for—and the human capability of—other kinds of rational thought. One significant form of rationality was alluded to by George Herbert Mead but left undeveloped by him and his expositors. This form of rationality calls on persons to take into account an ever wider set of social perspectives, to be able to take the roles of multiple others, and to understand or comprehend both the *commonalities* and the *differences* among them. This rationality opens up the possibility that persons of divergent cultural and ethnic backgrounds are able to understand, even appreciate essential similarities among, social and cultural perspectives other than their own. Concomitantly, human agents need not insist that everyone be like everyone else. Yet through this inclusive form of rationality we can come to recognize (or construct) the core element of human rights that transcends specific societies and cultural settings—equal concern and respect for others (cf. Dworkin 1977).

Before articulating more fully the implications of our argument, we restate our themes for purposes of clarity. Human rights rest on the principle of human dignity—on the fact that rights accrue to human agents simply because of their human status (Donnelly 1989:12). Human dignity in turn rests on encouraging persons to reflect on their condition and construct alternative organizational forms that enhance their own dignity and self-respect—within the context of equal concern and respect for others. To the extent that persons take the roles of others, we can perceive that the destruction of the dignity of others undermines one's own dignity; humans are products of their interaction with, and dependency on, others. Writing off the dignity of others (defining them as nonhumans) destroys not only the dignity of others but also the dignity of oneself.

Our conception of human rights can be clarified in somewhat more concrete terms. We utilize the human rights perspective to evaluate the functioning of large-scale bureaucratic organizations with their emphasis on the rationalization process. Habermas (1984, 1987a) has written an extended critique of the rationalization process that he perceives as undermining people's "lifeworld" and communicative processes. (His concept of "lifeworld" is an ambiguous one, though it seems to refer to such social patterns as the family and civic culture.) Although our general goal is somewhat similar to that of Habermas, our approach differs markedly from his in the manner in which we articulate the problem. Habermas is still encased within a "systems" and an ethicist framework (Nielsen 1990). Moreover, his critique of bureaucracy and rationalization is cast in broad cultural terms. While we do not ignore the cultural element, we must pay special heed to the structural elements of bureaucracy if we are to come to grips with the role of this organizational form in the destruction of the politically and economically disadvantaged. The patterns we document have been overlooked by Habermas and other critics of the present-day bureaucratic or rationalization process.

The Growth of Modern Bureaucracy

We begin by taking note of the proliferation of bureaucratic organizations and their increased power within nation-states and within the transnational setting. We are sympathetic to aspects of Schumpeter's (1950) analysis, in which he anticipated how large-scale organizations eventually would blur the distinction between capitalism and socialism. We are of a mind that for all the talk of "liberation" from bureaucratic domination that has occurred in, say, eastern Europe in the late 1980s and early 1990s, the bureaucratic process (in a different form) will have a sobering, even negative, impact on the human condition in these societies if it is not dealt with in a creative manner.

Big government and big corporations currently dominate the social landscape in all highly advanced industrial nations. Moreover, we have during the past few decades witnessed the relentless growth of power and control by transnational organizations, many of which shape the lives of more people than do many nation-states. As these organizations have increased their power and control, we find nations—such as those associated with the European Community—seeking to integrate their economic (and even political) structures in a manner we have yet to grasp.

Within the global context, four powerful sets of transnational bureaucratic structures have come to the fore in recent decades. We briefly discuss each of these in more or less the descending order of their social power. First are those organizations associated with finance capital. Banking systems (including the World Bank and the International Monetary Fund) shape the economic and political and even cultural orientations of nation-states. Hilferding (1986) was far more prescient than his contemporaries when he recognized the power of finance capital as a social force in the modern world. For instance, many eastern European nations are nowadays being called on to remake their economic systems to qualify for much needed credit from the World Bank and other Western banking enterprises.

A second powerful constellation of large-scale bureaucratic structures has emerged in the form of the technological/scientific/education complex. Although this system is more loosely coupled than are banking enterprises, its power and influence stem from the fact that the modern economic (and military) systems depend on scientific innovation to shape the course of technology by which these systems expand and thrive.

A third set of transnational organizations has emerged around the mass media. This is especially important in shaping the nature of public opinion as well as generating the social forces associated with modern consumerism. The fourth bureaucratic complex is related to production of goods. This is the one that has received most of the attention by sociologists. But in terms of its power it is of lesser import than the three mentioned earlier.

A variety of interrelationships exist between nation-states and large-scale transnational bureaucratic structures. Whatever these may be, one pattern seems evident. Transnational structures, notably multinational corporations, often are able to escape the social and moral accountability demanded by the citizens of any nation-state. The leadership of these organizations may have no fundamental stake in improving certain social conditions in the nation in which they are based (Epstein 1990). This is all the more reason for constructing a transnational moral system that can rein in, and call into account, not only powerful nation-state organizations but also transnational ones, particularly as the latter exploit the less privileged Third World nations.

Human Rights and the Bureaucratic Process

At this point we circle back and fill in some gaps that have heretofore been taken for granted. Any adequate moral theory requires a thorough understanding of the relationships between human agents and the bureaucratic structure. Weber did not take up this issue. One has the distinct impression that, in Weber's eyes, human agents are incapable of resisting the iron cage of bureaucratic life. In turn, Mead, who contributed to our central understanding of the nature of human agents, had little to say about large-scale organizations. Thus, we now consider the intersection between human agents and bureaucracy, more specifically, how the social mind is shaped by and can aid in reshaping bureaucratic structures.

Human Agents and Organizational Structures

We begin with Weber's general characterization of bureaucracy. It is typified by a hierarchy of authority, a complex division of labor (notably a high degree of specialization within and among organizations), and a conception of rationality that calls for selecting the most efficient means of attaining a given end. Moreover, these patterns are associated with standardization (i.e., universalism) in the selection and promotion of personnel and the routinization of the activities of specialists, thereby fostering their coordination by those in positions of power and authority. (We use the term "rationalization" in two ways, as the context warrants: first, to refer narrowly to rationality based on efficiency, and, second, to refer broadly to the overall impact of bureaucracy.)

Human agents both shape and in turn are shaped by bureaucratic organizations and the enormous specialization of knowledge and activities that has been created by human agents over decades or even several centuries. Yet once these structures are in place, they mold the manner in which human agents interact with one another. One's location in the hierarchy of authority, as well as in the division of labor, affects the nature and quality of information at one's disposal. One's position in the bureaucratic structure also affects the nature of one's reflectivity, and thus the manner in which human agents can and will act on the information at their command.

We are intent on incorporating a modified Meadian conception of human agency, one that stresses the "social mind," into an analysis of bureaucratic organizations. When this is done, we find that organizations and human agents exist in a dialectical relationship with one another. Organizations are unable to carry out activities without human agents; however, bureaucratic structures have a reality somewhat apart from any human being or set of human beings. This can be perceived in the "reification" of organizational structures by human agents who speak of the police force, the corporation, the university, the department, and so on. But organizations are more than mere reifications. They have a reality apart from human agents in that they are phenomena that are both enabling and constraining (cf. Giddens 1984). Through bureaucratic organizations it is thus possible to mobilize a vast array of specialists (and resources) for the attainment of particular goals. In this sense, bureaucratic structures often have been judged to have "technical superiority" over other organizational forms. At the same time, they control and manipulate persons within their sphere of influence.

Although we emphasize the manner in which bureaucracy molds the nature of human interaction and the reflective capabilities of human agents, we recognize that bureaucratic structures can be restructured (often in a drastic manner) by human agents working in concert with one another. Thus, after World War II the victors dismantled Hitler's secret police and many segments of the Nazi system. So, too, it is of notable historical import that Nikita Khrushchev and his associates were able, for the most part, to rid the Soviet Union of slave labor camps, leading to fundamental changes in the system. Moreover, during the past few decades we have been observing the construction of a new economic and political entity—the European Community. Still, an asymmetrical relationship generally exists between bureaucratic structures and human agents, the latter being subject to considerable control by powerful organizations.

We are in effect discussing one facet of the micro-macro debate within sociology. We cannot, as Collins (1981) would have us do, reduce organizations to individuals. Yet we cannot study organizations without analyzing human agents. And we cannot, as Blau (1987) suggests, simply work either on the micro or the macro levels, for a number of major bureaucratic patterns relate to the interaction of agents with organizational structures. Blau (1974:9) has been concerned with the potentially dire impact of bureaucratic structures on the lives of human agents; however, in his later work (e.g., Blau 1975), his methodological commitment to a logico-deductive mode of reasoning made it impossible for him to examine, for instance, the role of powerful secrecy systems (discussed below) that have served to undermine the democratic process.[7]

Our orientation overlaps somewhat with that of Giddens's (1984) analysis of structuration. To his credit, Giddens (1985), unlike most contemporary social theorists, has given special attention to the use of violence by nation-states and to surveillance of the citizenry by the administrative apparatus. Nonetheless, he downplays the control and manipulation by contemporary bureaucratic structures. In addition, his conception of human nature is built on ego psychology, and by failing to come to terms with the social mind, Giddens is incapable of doing justice to the creative capacities of human agents.

Our general argument is that organizations and human agents exist in a dialectical relationship with one another. Neither can be reduced to the other. Thus, bureaucratic structures have a reality somewhat apart from any set of human beings. The hierarchical structure, the division of labor, and the efficiency principle shape the manner in which persons respond to a whole set of issues. But, human agents are capable of reshaping, albeit with great difficulty, bureaucratic structures.

A partial clarification of our perspective can be achieved by a brief analysis of "the market." The 1980s and early 1990s brought two patterns into sharp relief. One has been the failing of the command economy as practiced by the former Soviet bloc of nations. It has proved unfeasible for bureaucrats to set down effective rules that can govern the myriad decisions associated with a diverse and specialized economic system in an advanced industrial order. An overreaction to this situation has been the battle cry by numerous politicians and social scientists that the "free market" will cure the ills of the former Soviet Union and the nations of eastern Europe.

A second pattern emerged in the United States during the 1980s when a concerted effort was made to deregulate a number of economic activities. The enormous economic scandal relating to the Savings and Loan industry resulted, to a considerable degree, from a decline in governmental controls (Thomas 1991). This stands as an informative case study of finance capital corrupted by the greed of its leadership. We also have learned that many banking enterprises find it advantageous to seek protection by the nation-state in the event of failure, all the while also actively using offshore outlets, which escape regulation, when this serves their interests. While the privileged sector profited from the structural changes in the 1980s, we also witnessed a massive explosion of the truly economically disadvantaged, including the homeless.

The management of a market system (with its stress on the profit motive) within the context of large-scale bureaucratic structures has, except for a limited number of scholars such as Galbraith (1967) and Lindbloom (1977), escaped serious attention. The proponents of the free market are blind to the fact that economic activity is enabled as well as constrained by large-scale political and economic organizations even outside the former Soviet bloc (cf. Adams and Brock 1986). Powerful organizations, for instance, manage prices as well as demand. Littrell (1989) has demonstrated how the "demand" for medical technology in hospitals is constructed by managers, and they do so by manipulating "fictitious data." We also know that the procurement system of the military complex has never been based on the principle of supply and demand. This empirical phenomenon is conveniently overlooked by most economists as well as by sociologists such as Coleman (1990) and Collins (1990), who reason that exchange theory (or rational-choice theory) helps explain and understand the central issues associated with the modern-day political economy.

Our overriding contention is rather straightforward. Any effort to interpret economic activities must place the actions of human agents within a bureaucratic context. This requires a fuller understanding of the interaction of human agents within (and among) bureaucratic organizations. This holds true not only for the economic system but also for the educational system, the criminal justice system, and so on. We consider some of the issues that we believe must be given more careful attention if we are to come to terms with the interplay between human agents and bureaucracy.

Hierarchy, Discretion, and Blamability. Most commentators on bureaucracy, building on Weber, assume that members of the managerial sector, acting within the framework of the hierarchy of authority, delegate responsibility for carrying out required tasks to those below, primarily specialists. In the process, efficiency is enhanced. But they overlook several empirical realities associated with the hierarchy of authority. Relying on Thompson's (1961) insights, we find that managers in large-scale organizations are adept at the art of denying responsibility for any serious mistakes by members of the system. Instead, they blame their underlings for the failures of organizational activities. The process of delegating blame under the guise of responsibility sustains the hierarchy of authority.

We are not suggesting that street-level bureaucrats (cf. Lipsky 1980) cannot and do not attempt to act on behalf of their clients. But we do contend that their activities on behalf of clients—be these students or welfare recipients—are severely constrained. The teacher, for instance, in an underfunded school that serves the economically disadvantaged lacks the necessary resources (including time) to provide the truly disadvantaged with the special attention that might assist them in escaping their plight. In the final analysis, these students have less knowledge about how the system operates than do those who come from privileged environments wherein they are taught how to cope with the educational system, or, better yet, to manipulate it to their advantage. Nevertheless, the oppressed students are blamed for their failure to succeed within a structure that has constructed roadblocks against their possible success.

To grasp the full implications of the patterns we are describing we must look at the distribution of rules within bureaucratic structures. We readily discover that persons in powerful managerial positions not only are encased by fewer rules than those below but also have more discretion in the interpretation of these rules. The constraints imposed by rules and regulations increase as one moves down the hierarchy of authority. Even the ingenious street-level bureaucrat cannot overcome many of them. Thus, the personnel who often require the most discretion in dealing with the varied and difficult problems faced by the truly disadvantaged are limited by their position in the organizational apparatus. (We return to these issues in analyzing "social triage.")

Secrecy and the Bureaucratic Order. Weber took note of the role of secrecy in bureaucracy but did not elaborate on this social pattern. Most students of bureaucracy continue to avoid analyzing the widespread implications of secrecy, a fact readily discerned by examining such widely read books on large-scale organizations as those by Morgan (1986) and Perrow (1986). We must not confuse, as analysts of organizations are prone to do, secrecy systems with informal (as opposed to formal) activities. Secrecy systems, as illustrated by military structures or the secret police, may be highly formal, and those such as social cliques may be informal in nature.[8]

Secrecy systems underscore the proactive role of human agents (as well as the constraints on them) within organizational settings. One function of secrecy systems is to protect organizations from attack by groups in the interorganizational field who are intent on challenging their power and authority. Corporate secrets are therefore widespread, and they often are perceived as essential for protecting the bureaucratic system from unfair competition or for providing a corporation with a competitive edge. Thus, in the United States trade secrets have come to be shielded by the legal structure (Scheppele 1988). The function of secrecy in the military has been even more explicit.

A second reason for the emergence of secrecy stems from the inherent tensions that result from the contradictions between superordinates and subordinates. In somewhat oversimplified terms, the members of the managerial sector of bureaucracies create secrecy systems to protect their decision-making activities from scrutiny by specialists below. The latter are often in a position to challenge the manager's judgment, for they often possess technical knowledge that managers do not. To ward off potential criticisms, managers frequently insist that they and they alone are in a position to take the broad overview regarding organizational activities and place the activities of the subsystems in proper context. But how they arrive at their decisions generally is kept under wraps in order to fend off criticisms by hostile outsiders and by persons below who have specialized knowledge. Managers' ability to sustain their secrecy systems is enhanced by being able to delegate blamability to those below.

Persons in the lower reaches of the bureaucracy typically create secret arrangements as a defense against the arbitrary use of power by administrators. Specifically, underlings learn how to protect themselves from being blamed for certain actions. They conceal selected activities and knowledge from those in positions of managerial control.

As a consequence of the secrecy systems that emerge for coping with the organizational environment, as well as the secrecy arrangements of those above and below in the hierarchy of authority, we are confronted by the question of how order is sustained. One major social psychological glue for maintaining the bureaucratic stability is loyalty on the part of persons below, not just to the system but to their immediate superiors (Williams et al. 1983). The sanctions imposed on whistleblowers (or informers) attest to the significance attached to loyalty. So, too, if those lower in the hierarchy are loyal to their superiors, the latter need not be concerned with the secrecy arrangements created by the former. But if loyalty erodes, then questions arise about the legitimacy of the power of the managerial or administrative leadership.

Bureaucracy and Social Triage

We have cast into broad relief key elements of the bureaucratic structure. Now we are in a position to describe the manner in which the bureaucratic process generates major moral issues in the modern world—and clarify why in effect a standard of human rights must be developed in order to counter the built-in degradation of human dignity typical of modern bureaucratic structures.

There has been a long-standing controversy over the relationship of bureaucracy to democracy (Waldo 1977). Many "conservatives" are critical of the state or governmental bureaucracies but are tolerant of, or positive toward, corporate bureaucracies. "Liberals" generally are more positive about governmental bureaucratic controls but are more likely to be concerned about the rise of powerful corporate structures. Yet as we have suggested, the reality is that we must recognize an integration (of various sorts) of the state and the corporate apparatus in "capitalist societies." In the former Soviet bloc, the interlocking of public and private bureaucracies will continue even if the movement toward a so-called free-market orientation is realized to a considerable extent.

Our position, a rather unorthodox one, requires clarification. Our argument cuts across much of the traditional "liberal" versus "conservative" debate as it often has been defined. Although we are highly critical of bureaucracy, we acknowledge that the bureaucratization process (which both fosters and is fostered by technology and science) has increased the material well-being of many humans the world over. We disassociate ourselves from those scholars who adopt a romantic vision of the past. For example, Wallerstein (1983:40) states:

> Not only do I believe that the vast majority of the populations of the world are objectively and subjectively less well-off materially than in previous historical systems but, as we shall see, I think it can be argued that they have been politically less well off also.

This assertion is wrongheaded. Wallerstein ignores the enormity of the poverty in ancient civilizations and the minuscule number of privileged persons. Also, what about life in hunting and gathering societies? Does he wish to push humanity back into the realities of that kind of past? In a somewhat similar vein, MacIntyre's (1981) call for the resolution of contemporary ethical ills by a retreat into an idyllic past overlooks the plight of the "common man" of earlier eras. Wallerstein and MacIntyre adopt a kind of elitist worldview in their conception of past eras.

While having no desire to retreat into the past for a solution, we judge the gap between "human potential" and "social reality" to have increased, not lessened. Modernity has opened up possibilities not only for material comfort but also for people's potential control over their lives. However, it also has increased the potential—indeed the reality—of mass destruction of human beings on a global scale. A worldwide nuclear holocaust or biological warfare or the systematic destruction of the environment is not merely a vision of the science-fiction writer.[9] The potential for wiping out large segments of humanity could readily be transformed into reality by managers who control and manipulate powerful large-scale organizations.

Moreover, we find it morally unacceptable to praise (or even tacitly accept) the bureaucratic process as it is at present constituted. Data indicate that it is impossible for persons to be treated fairly, for universalistic criteria to be applied in a just manner, within bureaucratic structures. A form of "social triage" inheres in both the private and the public sectors (Sjoberg et al. 1984).

What is the meaning of "social triage"? We have appropriated this term from the medical setting (cf. Stoffle and Evans 1990:95). Personnel in emergency situations, as in wartime, are required to select among patients—some of whom are "hopelessly ill" or "maimed," and others who are more likely to respond to treatment. Using the standard of triage, medical care is rationed: The former are permitted to die, while the latter are provided treatment. Although the analogue to health care should not be drawn in a literal sense, the concept of social triage indicates the procedure by which bureaucratic decision makers respond to the truly disadvantaged—who often come to be defined as terminally ill or beyond rehabilitation.

The internal dynamics of the bureaucratic process contributes to social triage. Our assertion is buttressed by theoretical as well as empirical considerations. Several kinds of social triage command special attention. One concerns the manner in which the truly disadvantaged are sacrificed for the cause of efficiency as defined by the privileged managerial sector. A second relates to the treatment of various kinds of political and intellectual deviance, particularly those that challenge the structural relations that sustain triage.

William Julius Wilson (1987) has analyzed the plight of the truly disadvantaged in U.S. cities. But, like most sociologists, he fails to relate the plight of this group (in this instance, poor urban African Americans) to the larger rationalization process. Given the logic of modern bureaucratic structures, it is inefficient to assist the economically deprived. The economic costs of bringing about substantial advancement in the educational and economic well-being of blacks and other minorities would entail a restructuring of the U.S. bureaucratic system and financial "sacrifices" by the privileged sector who preside over the powerful bureaucratic structures. The economically advantaged would be called on, for instance, to reduce their conspicuous consumption.

Why, in the face of considerable economic growth during the 1980s, has the homeless sector of the population increased? It is not because societal resources are unavailable to enhance their economic situation. Instead, those who control the bureaucratic structures fall back on the claim of efficiency. Serving the disadvantaged detracts from the efficient management of the society as a whole. In the 1980s we observed the vulnerability of the welfare system in the United States to attack by the leadership of powerful organizational structures (cf. Katz 1989). The welfare bureaucrats and their clients do not wield the power held by members of the corporate sector.

Looking at the system from the bottom up, we find considerable data documenting, for example, the assertion that the poor pay more. They pay more interest when they purchase goods (Caplowitz 1963), and these goods typically are inferior in quality. In addition, a significant pattern in modern bureaucratic society, particularly in the economic sphere, is that many strategic services are most efficiently provided where economic enterprises cater to the privileged. A relatively few large depositors at banks thus are more profitable than hundreds of smaller ones. The paperwork associated with the latter reduces the banks' profits, and thus they find it more efficient to pay large depositors higher interest rates and provide them with less expensive checking services and so on. The ideology that "mass production" increases the economic quality of life can not be accepted at face value. Today, more sophisticated automobiles are being mass produced, but these require specialized and costly equipment for repairs. The day of the "shade tree mechanic" in the United States is coming to an end. In effect, transportation for the poor is being jeopardized by the mass production of luxury cars for the privileged, a process sustained in the name of increased rationalization (and profitability).

These aforementioned difficulties are not limited to the private sector. When government programs are targeted to assist the poor, the truly disadvantaged typically are cast aside. These programs in the United States often are justified in terms of cost benefit analysis within the political systems that create and fund them. This means that in efforts to upgrade the job skills of the poor, for example, a pattern of "creaming" is at work. Those who are most in need of training will not be served, for it is too costly to deal with the most disadvantaged sector of the society. It is possible to document a similar process at work in the educational sphere.

An even clearer pattern of triage emerges within the criminal justice system. Littrell (1979) has provided empirical evidence of how the politically and economically disadvantaged are judged guilty until they can prove themselves innocent. Because of their lack of legal (and other) resources, they are victims of the system. We have only to examine the growth of the prison population in the United States, wherein a disproportionate share of poor blacks and Hispanics are incarcerated, to recognize the gross injustices perpetuated by the criminal justice system. The U.S. prison system has, in the name of utilitarianism (and the protection of the majority), become, on a per capita basis, one of the largest, if not the largest, in the world (e.g., Wicker 1991).

These internal patterns in the United States have their counterparts on the global scene. The most poverty-stricken regions of the developing world are those receiving the least economic assistance.[10] If they are of no military or economic advantage to the powerful nations of the world, their citizens tend to be cast adrift. The plight of many people in Africa south of the Sahara attests to the social triage being practiced on a global basis. Thus, as the World Bank, the International Monetary Fund, and other banking enterprises cope with the burden of Third World debt, and insist on the implementation of certain political and economic policies as the basis for providing relief for this debt, the poor, in Africa and Latin America in particular, bear a disproportionate share of the economic and social burdens of such policies.

The area of agricultural production is illustrative of another aspect of how the poor are expected to suffer in behalf of the privileged. The pressures to produce crops for export are considerable, for these provide cash for farmers and for the nation as a whole. The demands for cash crops are increased within, for instance, Latin America by the growth of large-scale agribusinesses whose orientation is toward highly industrial societies. The resultant processes foster the shipping of cash crops abroad at the expense of the production of staples that are essential for the well-being of the local citizenry. The dynamics of decision making within transnational organizations are reinforced by the interaction patterns of the managerial sector. The primary contacts of these persons are with the small, privileged elite of the developing nations whose social linkages (and interests) are related more closely to powerful transnational organizations than to the broader citizenry of the nations they supposedly serve (cf. Colson 1982).

In view of the data for the United States and the global scene, we find that if the efficiency principle is relentlessly applied, the poor must fend for themselves. Once the rationalization process takes over, there is no sound social or moral basis for corporate and governmental organizations to support the truly disadvantaged. It is more efficient to let them die young.

The principle of majoritarianism—the greatest good for the greatest number—comes into play as an ethical justification for bureaucratic policies that support the practice of social triage. Who among the utilitarians in contemporary American sociology has addressed this problem? Not Homans, not Coleman, not Collins, nor others among this group. More generally, who among contemporary social theorists is coming to terms with this kind of problem? If, once again, we take the recent surveys edited by Ritzer (1990) and Giddens and Turner (1987) as evidence of the present state of social theory, the answer is no one. Even Habermas (1984; 1987a), as suggested earlier, has not examined the social processes embedded within the structure of bureaucratic organizations.

Still another aspect of social triage demands serious attention. This concerns the treatment of political and intellectual dissent. Here we uncover a different form of social triage from that already discussed, but one that relates back to the problems of the truly disadvantaged within American society and on the global scene.

Parsons dealt with a central empirical dimension of modern organizations (including the nation-state) when he discussed "system maintenance." But he did not consider the moral ramifications of his orientation, particularly its links to intellectual dissent. Admittedly, Parsons wrote about McCarthyism. Nevertheless, he had an aversion to examining bureaucratic power structures and how they manipulated and controlled political and cultural protesters. In general, American sociologists have been comfortable in discussing the repression of political dissent in totalitarian orders, but they have shied away from considering this process in their own society.

Considerable data reveal a long history of repression of political and intellectual dissent in an "open society" such as the United States. After World War I, a variety of radical groups were undercut by the formation of the FBI, which used the turmoil of that period to advance itself as a social-control agency. Symbolic of this repression was the treatment of Emma Goldman, the well-known anarchist/feminist. She was kept from reentering the United States after her disillusionment with the Soviet system.

Repression of various forms of dissent by government and corporate organizations occurred during the Great Depression, particularly with respect to persons who were seeking justice for the socially disadvantaged. The patterns of repression of intellectuals during the McCarthy era have received considerable attention by journalists and historians (Schrecher 1986). Much of the control during the Cold War was directed at those who might undermine system maintenance. In keeping with this phenomenon was the repression of civil rights activists who were striving to correct long-standing social and moral injustices. The wiretapping of Martin Luther King's personal life in order to discredit him is merely symptomatic of the social controls exerted on persons engaged in sustained efforts to achieve a more equitable society. This social control was carried out by federal and local agencies whose actions were cloaked in secrecy and thus not subject to moral accountability. The spinoffs of the "rupture" in the social fabric as a result of Watergate brought many of these activities to light.

Our intention is not to provide a systematic body of data relating to social triage but to illustrate that this phenomenon is built into bureaucracy. The sacrificing of the most disadvantaged members of the society for the benefit of the privileged—which serves to maintain both existing bureaucratic power arrangements and utilitarianism—is reinforced by repression of political and intellectual dissent, particularly from those who crusade in defense of the disadvantaged in U.S. society or on the world scene.

The Necessity for a Human Rights Perspective

Early on, we advanced certain elementary principles regarding the human rights perspective. Then we briefly surveyed the growing domination by the bureaucratic imperative in the modern world and have contended that moral problems are built into this apparatus. We also have suggested that the present ethicist orientation of modern sociology is grossly inadequate for coming to terms with, say, the issues surrounding social triage. In fact, the morality of utilitarianism and of system maintenance works against any solution to the problems confronting politically and economically disadvantaged peoples.

MacIntyre (1981) is one of the very few moral theorists to acknowledge some of the ethical dilemmas of modern bureaucracy (though his brief analysis differs markedly from our own). Unlike MacIntyre, we do not reject modernity and do not seek refuge in some small-scale idyllic past. Instead, we opt for a restructuring of existing organizational forms so that human rights can be more realistically attainable. We are convinced that sociologists can make a valuable contribution to the possible achievement of this objective.

The principle of human rights serves to counter not only the pattern of sacrificing the disadvantaged for the benefit of the majority but also the repression of those who engage in intellectual and political dissent in behalf of disadvantaged persons or groups. Senator Daniel Patrick Moynihan (1990) has contended that the national security state threatens the foundations of the democratic process. Thus, we are not alone in our concern about the repression of political and intellectual dissent. But to challenge this kind of organizational system requires a rethinking of the ethical foundations of the existing social order and the construction of a human rights alternative.

We must come to recognize that human beings have rights as human beings. This calls for equal concern and respect for all people. Although the principles surrounding human rights have been discussed by a variety of scholars, sociologists, as suggested, are in a favorable position not only to clarify the nature of the human nature that underlies this moral orientation but also to analyze the role of large-scale organizations in undermining human rights. It is in the latter arena that sociologists stand to make their most discerning contributions to formulating a more adequate theoretical foundation for the principle of human rights.

Our reasoning has led us to move beyond a highly individualistic conception of morality. In order to advance the cause of human rights we must recognize the social nature of human beings and their interdependency. We do not ignore the issue of duties, but we must examine duties through the prism of rights rather than look at rights through the prism of duties (as the ethicists do).

Any meaningful moral system based on human rights not only must take account of the rights of human agents but must come to terms with the moral accountability of large-scale organizations. Holding individuals accountable is grossly insufficient. Organizations must be restructured so as to advance the cause of human rights and human dignity. Such a view can be buttressed by considerable historical data. In order to eliminate slavery, organizations had to be reconstituted. Now in the late 1980s and early 1990s, the efforts of East Europeans to rid their societies of the worst features of the detested secret police, which was an integral aspect of these totalitarian regimes, have called for basic organizational changes.[11] So, too, if ethnic minorities and women are to attain human dignity within the United States and on the world scene, a fundamental organizational restructuring is in order. Remaking individual motives, while not irrelevant, will not suffice to come to grips with the issues we have discussed.

Conclusions and Implications

American sociologists have ignored a fundamental empirical and moral issue—human rights. To make our case we first outlined the ethical perspectives that inform sociological theory and research in the United States. Although most sociologists contend that they can and should sustain ethical neutrality in their research activities, the evidence overwhelmingly supports the assertion that in practice sociologists adhere to ethical relativism, an ethics of system maintenance, and utilitarianism (or various combinations thereof). The traditional scientist/citizen dichotomy cannot be supported on empirical or theoretical grounds. One reason is that underlying every social theory is a set of moral premises (and underlying every moral theory is a set of sociological premises).

Although the ideal of value neutrality has dominated the discipline since World War II, a few sociologists have challenged the prevailing orthodoxy. In recent years Robert Bellah and Alan Wolfe have been in the forefront of championing an alternative orientation for sociology. Bellah in particular has received critical acclaim within and outside the discipline for his challenge to utilitarianism. He and his associates are loosely associated with the ethics of "communitarianism." This ethical orientation, with its competing factions, has received considerable support from elements of the U.S. intellectual community (see, e.g., the signators to the "The Responsive Communitarian Platform," 1991/ 92).

Although we strongly commend Bellah and his associates (1985, 1991) for reopening the nature of moral debate in U.S. sociology, their ethical orientation does not (and from our perspective can not) come to terms with major changes on the world scene.[12] As we look at the global landscape, we find that bureaucratic organizations (and the rationalization process) are moving forward in a relentless manner. Concomitantly we are witnessing the rise of ethnic divisions (with resultant strife) throughout the world. Although the issue of ethnicity lies beyond the scope of our analysis herein, we assume that one reason for its widespread rise is that ethnic identity provides an important buffer against the rationalization process.

In order to come to terms with the moral consequences of the bureaucratization process (and its by-products), we are convinced that a major break with the ethicist heritage is essential. A moral perspective grounded in human rights serves as the most viable option. For us a morality based on human rights is a countersystem to existing ethicist perspectives. As a counterperspective, a human rights orientation becomes a standard by which we can critically evaluate the limitations of existing ethical traditions, and it provides us with a more viable moral foundation for humankind.

Current ethical traditions reinforce, rather than challenge, the bureaucratic process. Ethical relativism, the ethics of system commitment, and utilitarianism serve to justify social triage, which is part and parcel of the logic of the bureaucratization process. But what about the ethics of communitarianism? If we turn to Bellah et al. for guidance, we discover that they are on target when they criticize utilitarianism. When they speak of the "tyranny of the market" (Bellah et al. 1991), however, they fail to acknowledge that market forces function within, and often are defined by, large-scale bureaucratic structures. Although the communitarians are not of one mind, none of them appear to escape the pitfalls inherent in the ethics of system commitment. (And neither do theorists such as Habermas, who have leveled a frontal attack against various facets of the bureaucratization process.)

An adequate theory of morals must provide a sound basis for the rights of human agents (whose singularly most defining characteristic is the social mind). In the process we must come to terms with the accountability of, and the likely need to reconstitute, bureaucratic power relationships. An adequate theory of human rights should provide a transnational or transcultural standard by which we can critically evaluate the injustices wrought by the bureaucratic process (and it will also provide a basis for building bridges of understanding among divergent ethnic groups). *Current moral theory is grossly inadequate because of its failure to grapple directly with the moral accountability of bureaucratic organizations* (and other organizational forms). Again, by way of illustration, if American society is to adhere to the principle of human rights for its oppressed minorities, a large-scale restructuring of the criminal justice system is required; otherwise U.S. society will continue to warehouse ever increasing numbers of politically and economically disadvantaged persons in what seems likely to be the largest prison system (on a per capita basis) in the world. If we focus solely on the morality of human agents, we are unable to confront these larger organizational issues.

Although our alternative contains a utopian element, we should be aware of the fact that the growing concern with human rights within the "world community" for over four decades is an empirical, not just some fanciful theoretical, matter. Thus, we can observe efforts by diverse elements of humankind to create a moral system that will provide greater dignity for all human beings. Within this context, we remind ourselves, as Wolfe (1989) rightly observes, that moral systems are social constructions. Once we recognize this social fact, we can more readily appreciate why sociologists should be involved in the creation of a moral system based on human rights.

A commitment to human rights becomes a strategic means of coping, for instance, with genocide, with famine, with the potential for chemical or biological warfare or environmental disaster, as well as with racial and ethnic discrimination. All of these phenomena erode the very foundations of human dignity. Whether humankind will succeed in creating a more viable moral order is an open question, but a sustained effort should be made to do so—of that we have no doubt. The acceptance of the status quo by most sociologists who dominate the American sociological enterprise does not demonstrate that "what is" can, should, or will be. Although the intellectual challenge is a daunting one, sociologists should not shirk the task of examining, both theoretically and empirically, human rights on the national and international scene. Here is a striking instance wherein sociologists are in a position to advance fundamental democratic ideals.

Notes

1. Alexander, for one, uses the term "moral" in his work. For instance, he writes (1982:89): "Every social theory, of course, must evaluate action in terms of some standard of scientific accuracy and in terms of some substantive moral goal." However, he does not inform us about the meaning of morals or morality.

A small subgroup of contemporary American sociologists has examined moral and ethical issues in a direct manner. The most prominent of these are Bellah (1983) and Wolfe (1989). Moreover, the German social theorist Habermas has begun explicitly to discuss ethics (Nielsen 1990).

2. Some sociologists recently have begun to attach the concept of human rights to issues they once considered (and rightly so) to be ethical matters (cf. Galliher 1991). Unfortunately, this pattern limits our theoretical (and empirical) understanding of the central problems involved.

3. Gans (1990), an ex-president of the ASA, has spoken of his commitment to relativism and equality. Although he senses a dilemma in holding to both of these moral orientations, he apparently has not directly addressed the issues involved. His commitment to equality runs counter to a strong form of relativism.

4. A modest step in recognizing "obedience to the system" as a moral issue has been taken by, for example, Kelman and Hamilton (1989).

5. Our analysis builds on our paper "The Ethical Commitment of Sociologists to Utilitarianism: A Human Rights Critique." (Vaughan and Sjoberg 1988).

6. In addition to the literature cited herein, the following items are worthy of attention, for they point to the kinds of issues and debates that exist in the scholarly writings on human rights: Claude and Weston (1989); Henkin (1990); Fowler (1987); An-Na'im (1992); and Nickel (1987). Also see the *Human Rights Quarterly*.

7. Blau (1974:20) wrote: "The concentration of organizational power in the hands of a few men shielded from public surveillance and control poses a serious threat to democracy. Social action is needed to avert this threat, and so is knowledge about the internal structure of organizations and the structure of societies that is increasingly dominated by organizations." Blau's methodology did not permit him to consider the kinds of issues raised, for example, by Diamond (1992).

8. Although Coleman (1990) claims to discuss corporate actors, his methodological orientation precludes his analysis of the interaction between human agents and organizations. Thus, he is unable to confront such a problem as secrecy.

9. For an informative popular discussion of how toxic wastes are dumped on the less developed nations by the managers of corporations based in the highly developed nations see Moyers (1990). For analysis of one facet of the major environmental issue confronting humankind, see, for example, Maxwell (1991). See also the important article on the impact of radiation by the sociologist Erikson (1991).

10. We are unable to cite the vast literature on the global political economy. Our references are meant only to be suggestive of the kinds of materials we have consulted in formulating our generalizations. See, for example, Gill and Law (1988); Klitgaard (1991); Broad (1988); O'Cleireancain (1990); Petras and

Morley (1990); Sandbrook (1990); Ravenhill (1990); Felix (1990); and Epstein (1990-91).

None of these works analyze the relationship between bureaucracy and "social triage." However, the data presented lend considerable credence to our theoretical analysis. Even more striking documentation for our perspective has been provided by Lawrence Summers, chief economist of the World Bank. One of his memos was leaked to *The Economist*. According to a report on "The Environment" (1992:7), Summers reasoned as follows:

> First, the costs of pollution depend on earnings lost through death and injury. These earnings are lowest in the poorest countries. Therefore, 'I think the logic behind dumping a load of toxic waste in the lowest-wage country is impeccable and we should face up to that.' Second, the costs of pollution rise disproportionately as it grows, so polluting the cleanest parts of the world may be less harmful than making the dirty parts still filthier. Third, people value a clean environment more as their incomes rise. So if polluting industries move from rich countries to poor ones, the costs of pollution will decline.
>
> ... The idea that life is worth less in poor countries than rich is a curious one for a World Bank official to promote.

The logic of social triage is not a figment of our imagination.

11. After the crumbling of the totalitarian regimes in eastern Europe, the *New York Times* carried a number of accounts regarding the hatred of the citizenry of the secret police. The case of East Germany has received considerable attention. See, e.g., Kinzer (1991).

12. We agree with Bellah and his colleagues (1990) up to a point about the "tyranny of the market." We part company with these scholars because of their failure to recognize that the market is emmeshed in bureaucratic structures that then foster "social triage." Sociologists must rethink the relationships among the market, bureaucracy, and democracy (as well as human rights). Too many sociologists, in the name of objectivity, are apologists for the market. These include James Coleman, Randall Collins, and a host of others. In this setting, Bellah's work stands as a highly useful corrective.

The upheavals in the Soviet bloc afford sociologists with an opportunity to reformulate the theoretical foundations of how the market, bureaucracy, and democracy are interrelated. For example, Draper (1992) has observed how Sovietologists failed to anticipate the breakdown of the highly bureaucratized orders within the Soviet bloc. Now, ironically, many social scientists are clamoring for a market solution to the ills that beset these nations. However, sociologists (and other social scientists) have no effective theoretical framework for analyzing how to dismantle a highly centralized bureaucratic order. Thus, to suggest that the market per se will cure the ills of these nations strikes us as foolhardy. After all, the market is, to a considerable degree, being imposed on eastern Europe and the new nations of the former Soviet Union by large-scale financial organizations such as the IMF, as well as other transnational corporations. Just how democracy is expected to flourish under these circumstances should be of deep concern to sociologists. To assume that markets will lead to democracy when powerful bureaucratic organizations dominate the social landscape should be subjected to intense theoretical and empirical scrutiny.

But how do human rights enter into evaluating future policies in the Soviet bloc? We have serious misgivings about the ethics of utilitarianism. An ethics of "communitarianism" (or some version thereof) raises other serious problems. Within the latter framework, we have no external, transnational standard by which to create mutual understandings among the divergent ethnic groups in this region whose deep-seated hostility toward one another is long standing. Moreover, we have no moral standard by which to hold global bureaucratic organizations accountable for their activities. An ethics of communitarianism, a system-based ethics, is grossly inadequate under the aforementioned circumstances. Only by formulating a more adequate standard of human rights—one that is transnational in character—will we be able to come to terms with how to provide the people in eastern Europe and the new nations of the former Soviet Union with a measure of human dignity.

References

Adams, Walter, and James W. Brock. 1986. *The Bigness Complex*. New York: Pantheon.

Alexander, Jeffrey C. 1982. *Theoretical Logic in Sociology*. Vol. I. Berkeley: University of California Press.

An-Na'im, Abullahi Ahmed., ed. 1992. *Human Rights in Cross-Cultural Perspective*. Philadelphia: University of Pennsylvania Press.

Attewell, Paul A. 1984. *Radical Political Economy Since the Sixties*. New Brunswick: Rutgers University Press.

Bellah, Robert N. 1983. "Social Science as Moral Inquiry." Pp. 360–81 in Norma Haan, Robert N. Bellah, Paul Rabinow and William M. Sullivan eds. *Social Science as Moral Inquiry*. New York: Columbia University Press.

Bellah, Robert N., Richard Madsen, William M. Sullivan, Ann Swidler, and Steven M. Tipton. 1985. *Habits of the Heart*. Berkeley: University of California Press.

———. 1991. *The Good Society*. New York: Knopf.

Bendix, Reinhard. 1964. *Nation-Building and Citizenship*. New York: Wiley.

———. 1986. *From Berlin to Berkeley*. New Brunswick: Transaction Books.

———. 1990. "How I Became an American Sociologist." Pp. 452–75 in Bennett Berger, ed. *Authors of Their Own Lives*. Berkeley: University of California Press.

Blau, Peter M. 1974. *On the Nature of Organizations*. New York: Wiley.

———. 1975. *Inequality and Heterogeneity*. New York: Free Press.

———. 1987. "Microprocess and Macrostructure." Pp. 83–100 in Karen Cook, ed. *Social Exchange Theory*. Newbury Park: Sage.

Brandt, R.B. 1983. "The Real and Alleged Problems of Utilitarianism." *Hastings Center Report* 12:37–43.

Broad, Robin. 1988. *Unequal Alliance: The World Bank, The International Monetary Fund, and the Philippines*. Berkeley: University of California Press.

Bruner, Jerome S. 1990. *Arts of Meaning*. Cambridge: Harvard University Press.

Cain, Leonard D. 1987. "Alternative Perspectives on the Phenomena of Human Aging: Age Stratification and Age Status." *Journal of Applied Behavioral Science* 23:274–94.

Caplowitz, David. 1963. *The Poor Pay More*. New York: Free Press.

Chalk, Frank and Kurt Jonassohn. 1990. *The History and Sociology of Genocide*. New Haven: Yale University Press.

Claude, Richard Pierre, and Burns Weston, eds. 1989. *Human Rights in the World Community*. Philadelphia: University of Pennsylvania Press.

Coleman, James. 1990. *Foundations of Social Theory*. Cambridge: Harvard University Press.

Collins, Randall. 1981. "On the Micro-Foundations of Macro-Sociology." *American Journal of Sociology* 86:984–1014.

———. 1988. *Sociology of Marriage and the Family*. 2nd ed. Chicago: Nelson-Hall.

———. 1990. "Market Dynamics as the Engine of Historical Change." *Sociological Theory* 8:111–35.

Colson, Elizabeth. 1982. *Planned Change: The Creation of a New Community*. Berkeley: University of California, Institute of International Studies.

Diamond, Sigmund. 1992. *Compromised Campus: The Collaboration with the Intelligence Community, 1945–1955*. New York: Oxford University Press.

Donnelly, Jack. 1989. *Universal Human Rights in Theory and Practice*. Ithaca: Cornell University Press.

Draper, Theodore. 1992. "Who Killed Soviet Communism?" *New York Review* 39 (June 11):7–14.

Dworkin, Ronald. 1977. *Taking Rights Seriously*. Cambridge: Harvard University Press.

"The Environment." Special Survey. 1992. *The Economist* 323(May 30–June 14): 5–24.

Epstein, Gerald. 1990–91. "Debt, Lies, and Multinationals." *World Policy Journal* 8:27–59.

Erikson, Kai. 1991. "Radiation's Lingering Dread." *Bulletin of the Atomic Scientists* 47(March):34–39.

Evans, Peter B., Dietrich Rueschemeyer and Theda Skocpol, eds. 1985. *Bringing the State Back In*. Cambridge: Cambridge University Press.

Felix, David. 1990. "Latin America's Debt Crisis." *World Policy Journal* 7:733–72.

Fowler, Michael R. 1987. *Contending Approaches to Human Rights in U.S. Foreign Policy*. Lanham: University Press of America.

Friedson, Eliot. 1983. "Celebrating Erving Goffman." *Contemporary Sociology* 12:359–62.

Furner, Mary O. 1975. *Advocacy and Objectivity: A Crisis of Professionalization of American Social Science 1865–1905*. Lexington: University of Kentucky Press.

Galbraith, John Kenneth. 1967. *The New Industrial State*. Boston: Houghton Mifflin.

Galliher, John F., ed. 1991. *Deviant Behavior and Human Rights*. Englewood Cliffs: Prentice-Hall.

Gans, Herbert J. 1990. "Relativism, Equality, and Popular Culture." Pp. 432–51 in Bennett M. Berger, ed. *Authors of Their Own Lives*. Berkeley: University of California Press.

Gibbs, Jack P. 1975. *Crime, Punishment, and Deterrence*. New York: Elsevier.

Giddens, Anthony. 1984. *The Constitution of Society*. Berkeley: University of California Press.

———. 1985. *The Nation-State and Violence*. Berkeley: University of California Press.

Giddens, Anthony, and Jonathan Turner, eds. 1987. *Social Theory Today*. Stanford: Stanford University Press.

Gill, Stephan, and David Law. 1988. *The Global Political Economy*. Baltimore: Johns Hopkins University Press.

Goffman, Erving. 1959. *The Presentation of Self in Everyday Life*. New York: Doubleday Anchor.
———. 1961. *Asylums*. New York: Doubleday.
———. 1967. *Interaction Ritual*. Chicago: Aldine.
Guest, Iain. 1990. *Behind the Disappearances*. Philadelphia: University of Pennsylvania Press.
Habermas, Jürgen. 1984. *The Theory of Communicative Action: Reason and the Rationalization of Society*. Vol. I. Boston: Beacon Press.
———. 1987a. *The Theory of Communicative Action: Lifeworld and System: A Critique of Functionalist Reason*. Vol. II. Boston: Beacon Press.
———. 1987b. *The Philosophical Discourse of Modernity*. Cambridge: MIT Press.
Halevy, Elie. 1955. *The Growth of Philosophic Radicalism*. Boston: Beacon Press.
Hatch, Elvin. 1983. *Culture and Morality*. New York: Columbia University Press.
Henkin, Louis. 1990. *The Age of Rights*. New York: Columbia University Press.
Hilferding, Rudolf. 1986. *Finance Capital*. London: Routledge and Kegan Paul (orig. 1910).
Homans, George C. 1961. *Human Behavior: Its Elementary Forms*. New York: Harcourt, Brace and World.
Jackall, Robert. 1988. *Moral Mazes: The World of Corporate Managers*. New York: Oxford University Press.
Janowitz, Morris. 1983. *The Reconstruction of Patriotism: Education for Civic Consciousness*. Chicago: University of Chicago Press.
Katz, Michael B. 1989. *The Undeserving Poor*. New York: Pantheon.
Kelman, Herbert C., and V. Lee Hamilton. 1989. *Crimes of Obedience*. New Haven: Yale University Press.
Kinzer, Stephen. 1991. "Honecker's Flight Draws Bitterness." *New York Times* March 19, A6.
Klitgaard, Robert. 1991. "Adjusting to African Realities." *Wilson Quarterly* 15 (Winter):33–43.
Kluger, Richard. 1977. *Simple Justice*. New York: Vintage Books.
Lehman, David. 1991. *Signs of the Times: Deconstruction and the Fall of Paul de Man*. New York: Poseidon Press.
Lewis, Lionel S. 1988. *Cold War on Campus*. New Brunswick: Transaction Books.
Lifton, Robert Jay. 1986. *The Nazi Doctors*. New York: Basic Books.
Lindbloom, Charles E. 1977. *Politics and Markets*. New York: Basic Books.
Lipsky, Michael. 1980. *Street-Level Bureaucracy*. New York: Russell Sage Foundation.
Littrell, W. Boyd. 1979. *Bureaucratic Justice*. Beverly Hills: Sage.
———. 1989. "New Technology, Bureaucracy, and the Social Construction of Medical Prices." *Journal of Applied Behavioral Science* 25:249–70.
Luban, David. 1987. "The Legacies of Nuremberg." *Social Research* 54:779–829.
Lukes, Steven. 1972. *Emile Durkheim: His Life and His Work*. New York: Harper & Row.
———. 1985. *Marxism and Morality*. Oxford: Clarendon Press.
McDougal, Myres S., Harold D. Lasswell, and Lung-Chu Chen. 1980. *Human Rights and the World Public Order*. New Haven: Yale University Press.
MacIntyre, Alasdair. 1981. *After Virtue*. South Bend: University of Notre Dame Press.
———. 1982. "Risk, Harm, and Benefit Assessments as Instruments of Moral Evaluation." Pp. 175–89 in Tom Beauchamp, Ruth R. Faden, J. Ray Wallace, Jr., and LeRoy Walters, eds. *Ethical Issues in Social Science Research*. Baltimore: Johns Hopkins University Press.
Marx, Karl. 1972. "On the Jewish Question." Pp. 24–51 in Robert C. Tucker, ed. *The Marx-Engels Reader*. New York: Norton.
Maxwell, Kenneth. 1991. "The Tragedy of the Amazon." *New York Review* 38 (March 7):24–29.
Mead, George Herbert. 1934. *Mind, Self and Society*. Chicago: University of Chicago Press.
Mills, C. Wright. 1959. *The Sociological Imagination*. New York: Oxford University Press.
Mommsen, Wolfgang J. 1984. *Max Weber and German Politics 1890–1920*. Chicago: University of Chicago Press.

Morgan, Gareth. 1986. *Images of Organization*. Newbury Park: Sage.
Moyers, Bill. 1990. *Global Dumping Ground: The International Traffic in Hazardous Waste*. Cabin John, MD: Seven Locks Press.
Moynihan, Daniel Patrick. 1990. "The Peace Dividend." *New York Review* 37(June 28):3–4.
Nickel, James W. 1987. *Making Sense of Human Rights*. Berkeley: University of California Press.
Nielsen, Torben Hviid, Interviewer. 1990. "Jürgen Habermas: Morality, Society and Ethics." *Acta Sociologica* 33:93–114.
O'Cleireacain, Seamus. 1990. *Third World Debt and International Public Policy*. New York: Praeger.
Opp, Karl-Dieter. 1985. "Sociology and Economic Man." *Journal of Institutional and Theoretical Economics*, no. 141:213–43.
Parsons, Talcott. 1937. *The Structure of Social Action*. New York: McGraw-Hill.
———. 1959. "Some Problems Confronting Sociology as a Profession." *American Sociological Review* 24:547–59.
———. 1967. *Sociological Theory and Modern Society*. New York: Free Press.
Perrow, Charles. 1986. *Complex Organizations: A Critical Essay*. 3rd ed. New York: Random House.
Petras, James, and Morris Morley. 1990. *US Hegemony under Siege*. New York: Verso.
Ravenhill, John. 1990. "Reversing Africa's Economic Decline." *World Policy Journal* 7:703–32.
"The Responsive Communitarian Platform: Rights and Responsibilities." 1991/92. *Responsive Community* 2:4–20.
Reynolds, Paul D. 1979. *Ethical Dilemmas and Social Science Research*. San Francisco: Jossey-Bass.
Ritzer, George., ed. 1990. *Frontiers of Social Theory*. New York: Columbia University Press.
Sandbrook, Richard. 1990. "Taming the African Leviathan." *World Policy Journal* 7:673–702.
Scheppele, Kim Lane. 1988. *Legal Secrets*. Chicago: University of Chicago Press.
Schlick, Moritz. 1959. "What is the Aim of Ethics?" Pp. 247–63 in A.J. Ayer, ed. *Logical Positivism*. New York: Free Press.
Schrecher, Ellen W. 1986. *No Ivory Tower: McCarthyism and the Universities*. New York: Oxford University Press.
Schumpeter, Joseph. 1950. *Capitalism, Socialism, and Democracy*. 3rd ed. New York: Harper & Row.
Simpson, John, and Jana Bennett. 1985. *The Disappeared and Mothers of the Plaza*. New York: Penguin Books.
Sjoberg, Gideon, and Leonard D Cain. 1971. "Negative Values, Countersystem Models, and the Analysis of Social System." Pp. 212–29 in Herman Turk and Richard L. Simpson, eds. *Institutions and Social Exchange: The Sociologies of Talcott Parsons and George Homans*. Indianapolis: Bobbs-Merrill.
Sjoberg, Gideon, and Ted R. Vaughan. 1971. "The Sociology of Ethics and the Ethics of Sociologists." Pp. 259–76 in Edward Tiryakian, ed. *The Phenomenon of Sociology*. New York: Appleton-Century-Crofts.
Sjoberg, Gideon, Ted R. Vaughan, and Norma Williams. 1984. "Bureaucracy as a Moral Issue." *Journal of Applied Behavioral Science* 20:441–53.
Spector, Malcolm, and John I. Kitsuse. 1987. *Constructing Social Problems*. New York: Aldine de Gruyter.
Stoffle, Richard W., and Michael J. Evans. 1990. "Holistic Conservation and Cultural Triage: American Indian Perspectives on Cultural Resources." *Human Organization* 49:91–99.
Thomas, Michael M. 1991. "The Greatest American Shambles." *New York Review* 38(January 31):30–35.
Thompson, Victor A. 1961. *Modern Organization*. New York: Knopf.
U.S. Senate. 1989. *Hearings Before the Committee on the Judiciary: Nomination of Robert H. Bork to be Associate Justice of the Supreme Court of the United States*. 5 parts. September, 1987. Washington, D.C.: Government Printing Office.

Vaughan, Ted R. 1989. "Validity and Applied Social Research: A Theoretical Reassessment." *Journal of Applied Behavioral Science* 25:291–305.

Vaughan, Ted R., and Gideon Sjoberg. 1984. "The Individual and Bureaucracy: An Alternative Meadian Interpretation." *Journal of Applied Behavioral Science* 20:57–69.

———. 1988. "The Ethical Commitment of Sociologists to Utilitarianism: A Human Rights Critique." Paper presented at the annual meeting of the American Sociological Association, Atlanta.

Waldo, Dwight. 1977. *Democracy, Bureaucracy and Hypocrisy.* Berkeley: University of California, Institute of Governmental Studies.

Wallerstein, Immanuel. 1983. *Historical Capitalism.* London: Verso.

Wicker, Tom. 1991. "The Iron Medal." *New York Times*, January 9, A15.

Williams, Norma. 1989. "Role Taking and the Study of Majority/Minority Relationships." *Journal of Applied Behavioral Science* 25:175–86.

Williams, Norma, Gideon Sjoberg, and Andrée F. Sjoberg. 1983. "The Bureaucratic Personality: A Second Look." Pp. 173–189 in W. Boyd Littrell, Gideon Sjoberg, and Louis A. Zurcher, eds. *Bureaucracy as a Social Problem.* Greenwich: JAI Press.

Wilson, William Julius. 1987. *The Truly Disadvantaged.* Chicago: University of Chicago Press.

Wolfe, Alan. 1989. *Whose Keeper? Social Science and Moral Obligation.* Berkeley: University of California Press.

Chapter 4

ETHNICITY AND GENDER:
THE VIEW FROM ABOVE VERSUS
THE VIEW FROM BELOW*

Norma Williams and Andrée F. Sjoberg

During the past several decades a substantial number of social scientists have turned their attention to theoretical and methodological issues relating to the nexus between ethnicity and gender.[1] In the United States the civil rights movement of the 1950s and 1960s undermined a great deal of the conventional wisdom regarding research on racial and ethnic minorities. Next, the feminist movement that began in the 1960s brought forward still other issues. Somewhat later, and especially in the 1980s, a small group of scholars began to focus on women in particular ethnic groups and observed that these are persons who are "twice a minority"—who live their lives in a state of "double jeopardy." Yet despite the accumulation of an impressive body of scholarly work on the aforementioned issues, major theoretical, methodological, and substantive problems relating to ethnicity and gender remain to be addressed.

The issues regarding ethnicity and gender become all the more compelling when cast within a cross-national or cross-cultural perspective. Note the deep-seated ethnic and racial tensions in eastern Europe, the former Soviet Union, the Middle East, South Africa, India, and many other parts of the globe during the 1980s and 1990s. In these socio-cultural areas racial and ethnic conflict become intertwined with considerations of gender.

The Central Issue

This essay critically evaluates the research and theory on ethnicity and gender, especially the nexus between these two spheres. Ours is not a comprehesive survey. Instead, we focus on a much overlooked problem area. Specifically, we advance the thesis that the views of persons in positions of power and privilege typically differ from, and may even clash with, the perspectives of persons in socially disadvantaged situations (cf. Williams 1989b; Sjoberg et al. 1991). One kind of tension is associated with race and ethnicity; another relates specifically to gender. Moreover, both ethnicity and gender must be viewed within the context of broader social class and nationality considerations.

We analyze these matters not only within a societal context but also within a historical and comparative (or cross-cultural) perspective. To anchor our analysis in the ongoing debates within the social sciences, we begin by discussing Merton's widely cited article on "insiders and outsiders," as well as the more recent analysis by Patricia Hill Collins (1986) on "outsiders within." We then recast their conceptualizations in terms of our central thesis. Merton (1972) examined the position of the social researcher as "insider" and as "outsider" vis-à-vis the study of racial and ethnic groups. He was responding to the assertion that only black historians could study black history, that only black sociologists could study the social life of blacks, and so on. He concluded by calling for a dialogue between insiders and outsiders in any given realm of research. Yet for all his erudition, he did not examine the body of literature in anthropology that discusses a parallel problem. The debate about emics and etics had received considerable attention in anthropology during the 1960s (Headland et al. 1990). The concepts "emics" (relating to an insider vantage point) and "etics" (referring to an outsider vantage point) had first been advanced by Kenneth Pike as a result of his research in linguistics.

More recently, Patricia Hill Collins has redefined Merton's framework for African American women. She speaks of "Learning from the Outsider Within: The Sociological Significance of Black Feminist Thought" (1986) (cf. Collins 1990). Collins focuses on the marginality of African American female intellectuals or scholars. She also discusses black women's definition of oppression in relation to the black cultural heritage. These women's experience highlights the problems of relatively powerless outsiders within who challenge the dominant paradigm of a powerful insider community—namely, traditional academic social scientists.

Herein we reformulate the conceptual framework of Collins—and, more especially, Merton. Although both allude to power relations between researchers and the researched, this is not their primary focus. We explicitly analyze the contrasting perspectives of social scientists who view the social order from the vantage point of the privileged (a top-down perspective) and those who approach it from the perspective of the nonprivileged (a bottom-up orientation). Our reasoning parallels that of the Dutch anthropologist Willy Jansen (1989:290) who, employing somewhat different terminology when writing for *Current Issues in Women's History*, argues that

> the problem of ethnocentrism lies less in the difference between researcher and researched than in the power hierarchy this difference often creates, both on a personal and a social level. In order to redress this hierarchy, I would strongly advocate that more women study women (and men), more blacks study blacks (and whites). . . . If the foreign and the native researcher each have their specific advantages,

the ideal situation would be to combine these advantages in a complementary working relationship. Of course this is difficult to put into practice, given the hierarchical structures within which human beings work, but by making the effort we can learn much from each other.

In effect, if we conceive of insiders and outsiders in hierarchical rather than horizontal terms, we discover that Merton's insiders (black scholars) are really outsiders with respect to power and privilege, while his outsiders are insiders. In a sense, the black scholars were "outsider insiders," rather than, as Collins puts it, "outsiders within." In effect, Merton and his supporters were insiders with respect to power, outsiders with respect to the black cultural heritage.

Our reformulation of Merton allows us to consider a largely unexamined issue: the asymmetry between the orientations, knowledge, and actions of insiders (the privileged) and those of outsiders (the nonprivileged). We discuss the theoretical and methodological issues first with regard to race and ethnicity and then concerning gender. After that, we consider the complex intersection of these spheres, in the process taking account of class and power relationships within societies and on the wider international scene. In dealing with the views of the privileged as differing from, and at times conflicting with, the perspectives of the nonprivileged, we are attentive to the problems that ensue when scholars in positions of privilege seek to take the roles of persons who not only exercise less power than they do but also diverge from them culturally. In recent years anthropologists have self-consciously been concerned with the study of the "Other." Yet they have neglected to examine the fundamental difficulties of taking the roles of others, especially multiple others. And although a few historians have discussed the "bottom-up" view in their research, they have given insufficient attention to the theoretical and methodological barriers that arise in such an endeavor.

Taking the role of divergent Others becomes exceedingly difficult in situations where persons of power seek to understand those who are essentially powerless. Until social scientists acknowledge this reality they will be unable to increase our understanding of certain key issues relating to ethnic and race relations, particularly with respect to women who are in "double jeopardy."

On the matter of the orientations of the privileged (or the view from above) vis-à-vis the standpoint of the nonprivileged (the view from below), we must come to terms with the problems these contrasting perspectives pose for both collecting and analyzing social knowledge concerning ethnic minorities and women.

Our analysis involves a broad cross-cultural perspective. We cannot resolve the manifold problems regarding social knowledge on ethnicity and minority women; instead, our intention is to suggest a general framework for anyone willing to confront the highly charged social and moral issues associated with the interface between ethnicity and gender.

The Historical Setting: A Brief Overview

In order to contextualize our problem, we will briefly outline some of the social and cultural changes that have occurred since World War II. These global happenings have fundamentally altered the nature of racial and ethnic relations and the role of women in the modern world.

Certain events associated with World War II set racial and ethnic matters within a new social perspective. The ideology of European superiority (Adas 1989) came to be undermined in a serious way. Of starkest import was the rise of Nazism and the systematic destruction of European Jews. A major step in setting in motion the extermination of the Jews was defining them as nonhuman. The negative consequences of this action pushed racism to an extreme that could no longer be ignored by the world political and intellectual community. The German nation, which had contributed so substantially to the Western cultural heritage, contained within it devastating moral flaws. Moreover, collaboration with the Nazis by people from other European nations further compounded the problem.

Although hardly comparable to the Nazi destruction of the Jews, the racism associated with Japanese expansionism in the Far East prior to World War II has in recent years attracted serious attention in some sectors of the social science community (e.g., Dower 1986). Moreover, we cannot overlook the situation in the United States. The confinement of Japanese Americans in internment camps after the Japanese attack on Pearl Harbor proved a severe blow to the ideals that the nation had so frequently proclaimed.

After World War II, social relations in terms of ethnicity (and nationality) were heightened in various parts of the world. One major change involved the political revolt throughout Africa and much of Asia of colonial populations opposed to European domination. The erosion of colonial power that had been proceeding over several decades advanced rapidly in the immediate postwar period. The British Empire, as well as the French, the Dutch, and the Portuguese, underwent a steep political decline, although European cultural and economic influences persist to this day in the former colonies (Rich 1990).

Within the United States, the 1950s saw the emergence of the civil rights movement. Although this movement (with its varied and complex strands) has by no means achieved all of its main objectives, it has nonetheless had a profound effect on the political and cultural fabric of U.S. society. It has given a larger voice to the ethnic minorities who are of special concern in this essay.

Since World War II the study of racial and ethnic minorities has received considerable attention on the world scene (e.g., Tambiah 1989) and in the United

States. In this context we must now consider the problem of gender, which was brought to center stage by what a number of scholars refer to as "new wave feminism." The feminist question in Europe and the United States goes back mainly to struggles during the nineteenth century, but it is the new-wave feminism that is the focus of our attention. It has been, as we observe, a product of privileged women in the West, particularly in the United States. The new-wave feminism, for all the controversy it has engendered, has wrought considerable social and cultural change (including the backlash it has invited). And it has come to influence in diverse ways the manner in which gender issues are being reconstituted in certain parts of the world.

In addition, we can cite some significant comparative studies in the realm of gender (e.g., Tinker 1990). However, the efforts to integrate gender with race and ethnicity on a comparative basis are still in their infancy (e.g., Smith et al. 1988). It is the intersection of gender with race and ethnicity that, as we continue to emphasize, commands our attention.

With this general background in hand, let us examine the issues of race and ethnicity and then gender—and after that attempt to suggest ways to interweave them. Throughout, our central theme remains the asymmetry in orientations of persons above and persons below.

Race and Ethnicity

We return to Merton's influential essay on insiders and outsiders as a baseline for our analysis of selected theoretical and methodological issues in racial and ethnic relations. Merton, we remind ourselves, was responding to the challenges of a group of social scientists who, influenced by the civil rights movement in the United States, contended that only black scholars could study the black experience. Merton was disturbed by this line of reasoning. The argument that only insiders can study insiders with respect to racial and ethnic relations seriously undermines the social scientist's claim that they are capable of producing "objective scientific knowledge" on which all specialists can agree. Moreover, if carried to an extreme, the view that only insiders can study particular social and cultural systems would result in a "balkanization" of social knowledge with no shared body of human understanding.

Merton's position, which has been supported by William Julius Wilson (1974), is not without merit. While we agree with Merton about the need for a dialogue between researchers on the inside and those on the outside, Merton's analysis can be faulted on several grounds. It fails to examine explicitly how and why much of sociology in the United States has taken the vantage point of the privileged when analyzing ethnic minorities. The Chicago School, led by Robert Park, typically took a top-down orientation as it championed the primacy of the assimilation model. Its members assumed that racial and ethnic minorities would (and should) adopt the orientations of the more privileged white society. To this day, a host of sociologists and other social scientists cling to this model (e.g., Hirschman 1983).

Like the Chicago School, the functionalist school of Talcott Parsons (of which Merton was a member) advocated a modified version of the "assimilationist perspective." Parsons (1967), drawing on the concept of citizenship, perceived Negroes (his terminology) as ultimately becoming incorporated into the "American Dream," where persons enjoy equality of opportunity.

Merton, in effect, failed to consider why most American sociologists were unable, before the civil rights movement, to come to terms with many issues relating to disadvantaged racial and ethnic minorities. In part this reflects his particular interpretation of functional analysis. In an early, highly influential essay on deviance, Merton (1957:131-60) provides us with a clue as to his working assumptions about the social order. Although we must be careful not to overstate the case, in analyzing deviance, Merton tended to define as deviant persons who are unsuccessful with respect to social mobility. Thus, economically disadvantaged racial and ethnic minorities could be placed in this category. Actually, much social analysis has taken for granted the perspective of the societal power groups and tended to ignore the view from below.

One weakness of Merton's argument includes his failure to consider how outsiders (his insiders) must acquire some degree of political and intellectual power before their place in U.S. society can be redefined. As an instance, we can examine the role of Mexican Americans (or Chicanos), the second largest ethnic minority in the United States, during the past several decades. The shifting perspective of social scientists toward this group has been associated, to a degree at least, with the rise to social power of some Mexican American politicians and the emergence of certain Mexican American intellectuals. To be sure, a few Anglo social scientists, such as Joan Moore (1976), lent support to this group by correcting the social and historical record.

Rosaldo (1985) has documented some of these changes in anthropology and sociology that are intellectual by-products of the Chicano movement. A sociologist and an anthropologist, in a Chicano-based journal, *El Grito*, leveled the first sharp criticisms of the ethnographic literature. The authors were especially critical of such Anglo ethnographers as Rubel (1966) and Madsen (1964), whose works had defined Mexican American culture for numerous academics. Later, the highly respected Mexican American folklorist/anthropologist Paredes (1977) documented, in a reasoned manner, the failure of these scholars to understand many subtle, and not so subtle, facets of Mexican American language and culture. His critique should be read by anyone who doubts that "insiders" can contribute substantially to knowledge of their own cultural patterns.

More recently, a group of Chicano historians have been reinterpreting the history of Mexican Americans in the Southwest. De Leon (1983), in *They Called*

Them Greasers, attacks traditional historical accounts such as those by the preeminent western historian Walter Prescott Webb. Webb's research on the Texas Rangers has also been a focus of attack by the sociologist Samora and his associates (1979). Webb viewed the Texas Rangers from an Anglo, top-down perspective and failed to acknowledge the manner in which the actions of this law enforcement agency adversely affected many Mexican Americans.

The rewriting of the history of this ethnic group by Mexican American scholars and others is part of a larger effort at revisionist history regarding the American West more generally. Social scientists are increasingly taking account of Indians, women, and other groups who inhabited this geographic region prior to the Anglo conquest.

Given this situation, more research on the relations of Mexican Americans to Anglos is in order. For instance, certain features of culture that Anglos have assumed to be their own were borrowed from Mexicans and, later, Mexican Americans (cf. Williams 1990). As a striking example, many aspects of the "cowboy culture," popularly assumed to be Anglo, are almost certainly Mexican and Mexican American, though some of these can be traced farther back to Spain and perhaps beyond. Thus, certain facets of the Anglo culture into which Mexican Americans are supposedly being assimilated were originally part of the Mexican American heritage. That members of the majority culture have absorbed segments of the minority culture and then claimed them as their own (a pattern not unique to the U.S. West) raises still other questions about the relationship between insiders and outsiders—issues that still await attention.

The limitations of Merton's reasoning, which reflects the thinking of most social scientists, come into sharper focus when we place the insider-outsider debate within a cross-cultural perspective. We briefly consider the writings of anthropologists and those by one group of historians.

The question of the perspective of the privileged versus that of the nonprivileged is especially highlighted in the field of anthropology, which has been undergoing a struggle with self since the 1960s. A number of anthropologists have entered the fray. Asad (1973) and Berreman (1981) presented some of the early critiques of the discipline as they sought to take the vantage point of the Third World, rather than that of anthropologists in Europe and the United States. Although anthropologists' fieldwork represented an important step forward, in contrast, for example, to the observations of missionaries and travelers, their research on non-European peoples has been less than objective. As a specific instance, Geertz (1988) and Rosaldo (1986) have taken to task the renowned British anthropologist Evans-Pritchard. In his study of the Nuer of East Africa, Evans-Pritchard (1940) sought to enter the social world of the Nuer as a representative of a colonial power. Rosaldo's reading of Evans-Pritchard's widely cited ethnography on the Nuer reveals that as a result of his status this fieldworker was excluded from many spheres of activity of the persons he sought to study. The problem of the Eurocentric (or top-down) bias within anthropology still haunts one wing of that discipline (e.g., Ghosh 1991).[2]

Anthropology is not alone in this. A variety of historians have been subject to a barrage of criticisms for their flawed assessments of colonial peoples who are ethnically and racially different from themselves, and even for their interpretations of that seedbed of Western civilization: classical Greece. (Although these writings have not found their way into much sociological literature, they bear directly on sociological issues.)

Said's *Orientalism* (1979) is a landmark study. The author has tongue-lashed historians, especially those who specialize on the Middle East, contending that they have failed to portray fairly the subjects of their study, and that we learn more from them about privileged Europeans than about the groups they have supposedly been describing. Said perceived in this an unwarranted assumption of the superiority of European culture.

Not surprisingly, Said's work has elicited severe counterreactions. One criticism has been that Said ascribes no motive by scholars in the West other than that of domination; further, he fails to perceive the internal debate among Westerners over the proper approach to their subject matter. Also Said acknowledges no political or cultural divisions among the peoples whose cause he champions (Marcus and Fischer 1986).

Said's perspective has its flaws; nevertheless, he has changed the fundamental nature of the debate with respect to historical studies by Western scholars of societies in Africa and Asia (see e.g., Inden 1990). Consequently, the very concept of "Orientalism" has, because of the cultural legacy associated with it, come under heavy attack from a variety of scholars.

Somewhat in line with Said's critique has been the analysis of Adas (1989:9) concerning "attitudes toward non-Western peoples and cultures . . . held by literate members of the upper and middle classes of Western European societies." Adas (1989:15) contends:

> Scientific and technological superiority has often been put to questionable use by Europeans and North Americans interested in non-Western peoples and cultures. It has prompted disdain for African and Asian accomplishments, buttressed critiques of non-Western value systems and modes of organization, and *legitimized efforts to demonstrate the innate superiority of the white 'race' over the black, red, brown, and yellow.* (Italics added.)

In addition to the work of Said and Adas, we must not overlook Bernal's study of classical Greek civilization *Black Athena* (1987; 1991). Bernal devoted two decades of his life to research on China before turning his attention to late nineteenth- and twentieth-century historical writings on classical Greece. In his analysis he adopts an avowed sociology-of-knowledge perspective and defines himself as an "outsider" with respect to mainstream Greek scholarship (here the insider-outsider distinction is relevant not only for ethnicity and gender but also with respect to particular reference groups such as a given intellectual community).

Bernal is explicit about the influence of racism on European historians' top-down interpretation of Greek history. Briefly, he contends that classical Greek culture was not just Indo-European but was to a considerable extent shaped by African and Asian cultures. Even the idea of the polis, about which political and social theorists have written so much, is perhaps not Grecian but Phoenician in origin.

Bernal's reinterpretation of Greek culture is likely to remain essentially intact, despite certain modifications that will no doubt result from criticisms by specialists. We are thus witnessing a revision of certain basic assumptions about Western civilization—in this instance through recognition of the influx of non-European cultural traditions. Such a reinterpretation will have far-reaching consequences for traditional Western academic scholarship.

We can look forward to reinterpretations of the role of ethnic minorities in other civilizations as well. The second-named author has for some time been seeking to more accurately account for the historical development of Hinduism, a major world "religion," and of Indian civilization as a whole. She asserts that Hinduism, contrary to received wisdom, is not mainly Indo-Aryan (and thus ultimately European) in its origin and development but represents a synthesis of Aryan and non-Aryan elements, with the non-Aryan (mainly Dravidian) clearly predominating (Sjoberg 1990; 1992). One reason the Sanskrit-speaking Aryans have traditionally been perceived as the chief creators and developers of Hinduism is because European scholars came to define them as an extension of themselves. What is more important, speakers of Indo-Aryan languages have politically dominated the Indian subcontinent since their arrival almost 3500 years ago. The scriptures of Hinduism were until only a few centuries ago composed and transmitted in the ancient Indo-Aryan language Sanskrit. As a result, almost all the philosophical concepts of Hinduism today carry Sanskrit labels. This, unfortunately, has led scholars to assume that the concepts themselves are necessarily Indo-Aryan in origin. The majority are not. Social scientists who have not read Sapir (1949) tend to confuse linguistic symbols, or signs (the signifiers), with the cultural features to which they refer (the signified), a methodological issue of considerable consequence for social research on race and ethnic relations.

The writings of Said, Bernal, Adas, as well as anthropologists such as Wolf (1982), indicate that further reinterpretations of the social and cultural history of various racial and ethnic groups are likely to appear. These patterns will be heightened by the ongoing efforts of former colonial peoples—as, for example, in India—to write their own histories.

A striking case study of historical revisionism, resulting from the decline of one version of Eurocentric domination, has emerged in the past several decades among the Uzbeks of Central Asia, the largest non-Slavic minority in the former Soviet Union (e.g., Critchlow 1991: chap. 7). As a result of the breakup of the latter, the failure of the communist officialdom—based in Moscow and essentially Slavic or Eurocentric in orientation (but displaying its own special twist)— to understand the Uzbeks and other Turkic people of Central Asia has become apparent. Under Leonid Brezhnev, who directly preceded Gorbachev and whose policies (in an unanticipated way) led to the breakup of the Soviet Union, Uzbek intellectuals began rewriting their history in their own language, a fact that the Slavic ruling elite grasped only well after the process was under way. Even Gorbachev, who can be viewed as a visionary, seems to have had a serious blind spot when dealing with the Uzbeks and other Central Asian minorities. This rewriting of history, compressed within a brief time frame, highlights the role of shifts in power in the way social knowledge is constructed by "outsiders" as opposed to privileged "insiders." And this pattern, analogous to the one we discussed earlier for the United States, supports our central thesis: The perspective from above and that from below are generally asymmetrical. As we shall see, this asymmetry carries over to the analysis of gender.

Gender

The feminist movement that emerged in the 1960s in the United States and western Europe had a profound impact on the reinterpretation of gender roles within societies and on the world scene. Although the influence of gender studies seems to have been minimal in, for instance, the field of economics (Bergmann 1990), theory and research on gender have reshaped the nature of many substantive (as well as theoretical) issues in disciplines such as sociology, anthropology, and history (Zalk and Gordon-Kelter 1992).

In theoretical terms, gender studies have brought to the fore the importance of gender stratification (or patriarchy) in a variety of social settings in ways only dimly perceived a few decades ago. Concomitantly, theory and research on gender have also demonstrated that women are not the passive, "invisible" human agents male social scientists assumed a few decades ago. Moreover, most scholars have come to recognize that gender is a social construction and not some entity that inheres in the natural order of things.

Let us comment briefly on the impact of gender studies on selected fields. In sociology, Stacey and Thorne (1985) complained that gender research had not had the impact on the discipline they had anticipated. Nonetheless, research and theory have redefined many realms of social stratification, labor-force analysis, and even the analysis of organizations (e.g., Kanter 1977). As to the labor force, it is now evident that social policies have had different impacts on men and on women throughout their life cycles. In addition to conducting research on women's roles in the "public sphere," sociologists have come to view the family in a different light during recent decades. Thus, Talcott Parsons's theoretical formulations regarding family patterns (as well as age and status) have undergone extensive criticisms (e.g., Komarovsky 1991).

When we turn to U.S. history, we find that scholarship regarding women (with all its diverse strands) has reshaped the manner in which history is written today. Novick (1988:497), writing about the American historical profession, casts into sharp relief how women have been treated as nonpersons by traditional (male) historians.[3]

> Surely something was seriously amiss when twenty-four of the twenty-five leading American history texts published in the sixties and seventies devoted considerably less than 1 percent of their pages to women.

However, during the past several decades history regarding women (as well as ethnic minorities) has been redefined in a number of realms. For example, we have learned how scientists in the nineteenth century downgraded women (Russett 1989). Such research has implications not only for the study of history but also for an understanding of the nature of scientific activity. We must continually ask ourselves: How objective is the scientific research on gender (and race and ethnicity) today?

Currently, the history of women has moved forward on a variety of fronts. The diversity of the research is captured by the title of Stock-Morton's (1991) work, "Finding Our Own Ways: Different Paths to Women's History in the United States." Yet as Scott (1988) has underlined in a compelling manner, those who write about women's roles in history confront a fundamental dilemma. Many works seem rather narrow and descriptive. But to leave a mark on mainstream historical scholarship as traditionally defined by men calls for scholars concerned with women's place in history to address the theoretical structure and the basic concepts that undergird the historical enterprise.

When we turn from research on gender issues in the United States or western Europe to an investigation within a cross-cultural framework, we can readily discern in certain recent studies striking reinterpretations of gender-related issues. In a highly useful summary of research by anthropologists on women, di Leonardo (1991) documents how various subdisciplines of the field were restructured as a result of research during the 1970s. Di Leonardo (1991:8) speaks of how Jane Collier restructured political anthropology by redrawing "that discipline's map to include women's kinship struggles" and how Annette Weiner's research, following that of Malinowski on the Trobriand Islanders, gave us a new perspective on the Kula—a pattern of social exchange that challenges many fond premises of modern-day economists.

A dramatic illustration of how the map of anthropology regarding women has been redrawn concerns the study of peasant villages (Smith and Wiswell 1982). An American anthropologist, John Embree (1939), wrote a classic work on a village in Japan that he studied in the 1930s. His wife, though born in Siberia, had lived in Japan and spoke Japanese fluently. She pursued her own research in the same village setting. After the war, Embree died, and his widow (now Wiswell) took up her own academic career in comparative literature. After visiting Cornell University in the 1960s, she met the noted anthropologist Robert Smith and gave him her husband's, as well as her own, field notes. Smith discovered that John Embree (as a result of his theoretical framework but also because of the mind-set of male anthropologists at the time) neglected to use his wife's data on women. Smith and Wiswell (1982) then wrote *The Women of Suye Mura*, which presents a view of village life quite unlike that offered by anthropologists who carried out this kind of research in different parts of the world during the 1930s and 1940s.

If we step back a moment and survey gender research in the social sciences (cf. Zalk and Gordon-Kelter 1992), we conclude that the shift in power relationships by women in the broader society (in large part a result of the women's movement) has led to a substantial redefinition of the manner in which the social sciences have viewed women. Even in the face of the backlash against the women's movement in recent years (cf. Faludi 1991), it is difficult to imagine a return to the pre-1960 patterns. The shifting power relationships between men (the traditional insiders) and women (the outsiders) have played a considerable role in the changes that have occurred. Still, some central issues remain to be faced. We now turn our attention to these concerns.

Research on Women and Racial and Ethnic Minorities at a Critical Juncture

We have emphasized that the research on gender (or women's studies) during the past two decades or so has made substantial progress in restructuring many substantive and certain theoretical areas within sociology and other social sciences. Nevertheless, a frequent pattern in social inquiry has emerged: The very success of the dominant mode of inquiry has begun to expose some of its weaknesses, and these require special attention.

Research on gender and racial and ethnic minorities stands at a crossroads. A central question remains whether gender (or women's studies) will seriously incorporate issues relating to ethnicity into the existing theoretical and method-ological frameworks or whether the field will continue to work within the general paradigm that proved to be so successful during the 1970s and 1980s.

In order to examine the problem, we need to reflect on the state of current gender research. Broadly, we can delineate two main "schools" or wings of scholarly endeavor in this field. One wing of gender studies continues to work within the framework that emerged in the early 1970s. But a second became evident in the 1980s and especially in the early 1990s. This latter calls for a reformulation of the older paradigm and for restructuring gender studies so as to incorporate into one's analysis issues relating to women of differing racial and ethnic backgrounds (e.g., DuBois and Ruiz 1990). To do this effectively, however, requires that such issues as social class and nationality be addressed in a direct, not a tangential, manner.

In ideal-type terms, the original paradigm relied on the premise that "sisterhood is powerful" (e.g., Fox-Genovese 1990). Research and theory was predicated on the assumption that women share common interests and perspectives with one another that they do not with men. The existing system of patriarchy meant that women were in effect second-class citizens. And these patterns have persisted, albeit in different ways, across an array of social and cultural orders. In narrow terms this meant that male scholars had defined women for centuries essentially as nonpersons. Women scholars—be they adherents of Freudian feminism, Marxist feminism, postmodernist feminism, or whatever—thus shared a common focus of analysis.

This framework served in particular to advance the principle of "gender stratification." In the face of substantial resistance by supporters of entrenched intellectual traditions, the efforts of women scholars, as we have observed, has led to a rewriting of many aspects of the social sciences.

To understand the aforementioned scholarly activities, we place them within the social context in which they have emerged. Hazel S. Fisher (1971), one of the few social scientists to conduct research on the women's movement as it evolved in New York City during the late 1960s, documented the middle-class basis of that movement. She observed that women who were products, directly or indirectly, of this new-wave feminism made no systematic effort to incorporate into their agenda issues relevant to working-class women or women of racial and ethnic minorities. Although disagreements have existed among feminists (cf. Bannister 1991), the latter have been committed to demonstrating that men have discriminated against women.

Fisher's conclusions are congruent with those of Evans (1980), who reasoned that many of the leaders of the women's movement had participated in the civil rights movement. More recently, Fox-Genovese (1990:29) observed:

> The middle-class spokeswomen for the new women's movement, without fully recognizing what they were doing, established their own autobiographies as the benchmark for the experience of all women.

Although Fox-Genovese herself has been unable to avoid the trap into which she claims other scholars have fallen, certain facets of her arguments cannot be ignored.

That the women's movement has been a product of the U.S. middle class is reiterated by Buechler (1990:152):

> The truism about a white, middle-class movement was apt in the broadest sense because the aspirations of the earliest movement participants were a response to the specific situation of women who were relatively privileged by class and race but were unmistakably restricted on the basis of gender.

We thus contend that most of the leading scholars on gender issues have to a considerable degree had their research and theory shaped by their own life histories. And these are anchored in relatively privileged, middle-class circumstances. Scholars such as Carol Gilligan, Cynthia Fuchs Epstein, Dorothy Smith, Joan Scott, Jessie Bernard (and to a lesser degree Ester Boserup) have used their privileged backgrounds as benchmarks for their research and writing on gender.

The widely cited, and much discussed, work of Carol Gilligan (1982), *In a Different Voice*, is highly instructive. Gilligan perceives women as adhering to a moral vision—involving mainly the ethics of caring—which differs from that of men. Yet her research, based on U.S. college women, nowhere provides an understanding of the moral problems associated with politically and economically disadvantaged racial and ethnic minority women in the United States, to say nothing of women of color in developing societies. Consequently, Gilligan's moral vision is narrowly circumscribed; her ethics of caring rests on certain premises of privileged middle-class women in the United States.

To buttress our argument concerning the dominant wing in gender research, we next comment briefly on selected edited works in theory and methods. Although these tend to focus on sociology, they generally represent research in other social sciences as well.

Wallace's edited book, *Feminism and Sociological Theory* (1989) serves as a useful starting point. Here we pay special attention to the work of Dorothy E. Smith, a scholar often singled out as a leading feminist theorist in sociology.[4] Smith (1989:34) makes much of the concept of "standpoints" with respect to understanding women's perspectives. She writes:

> I have emphasized in my work a distinctive standpoint for women, not necessarily as a general attribute of women as a class of persons, but as a mode of experience that is distinctive to women and in important ways an experience that has marked us off from men and

continues to do so. . . This is an experience of work around particular individuals, particularly children; it is an experience grounded in a biological difference—our bodies give birth and men's do not—but through complex institutional mediations organized as caring and serving work directed toward *particular* others or groups of others . . .

Designing a sociology for a knower situated in the everyday/ everynight world of her actual lived experience means proceeding differently from the standard practice of sociology.

Smith (1989:36) proceeds to elaborate on her theoretical perspective by reasoning that "the particular version of the standpoint of women that I've worked with comes out of my own experience." We would be among the first to recognize the value of autobiographical accounts. Yet Smith has written a sociology from the standpoint of relatively privileged educated white women.

Chafetz (1989:136) reasons somewhat differently:

My theory of gender system maintenance and reproduction. . . asserts that superior male power, which exists by definition in gender-stratified societies, allows men to coerce women into assuming work roles that reinforce their disadvantaged status, at both the macro and the micro levels.

Given her perspective, Chafetz (1989:157) calls for a major restructuring of the gender division of labor, "especially the demand for substantially greater access of women to elite positions." Although some facets of Chafetz's argument have merit, we find her top-down ideology disturbing. At the very time we have been witnessing the "feminization of poverty" on a massive scale, Chafetz glosses over this empirical reality (cf. Chafetz 1990). Her writings demonstrate no fundamental social understanding or moral compassion for women of color who suffer from economic and political deprivation, who must first and foremost be concerned with feeding themselves and their children.

Although exceptions to the dominant paradigm have emerged (e.g., Gorelick 1991), the collections by Nielsen (1990) and Fonow and Cook (1991) document our overall thesis regarding the lack of attention to the asymmetry between the orientations of privileged and nonprivileged women, particularly women of color. In Nielsen's work, one chapter includes an analysis of class in Germany, but the book does not confront the issues that we deem to be of central methodological concern. In the useful collection by Fonow and Cook, *Beyond Methodology* (1991), the editors (1991:1-15) stake out, in their introductory essay, a claim for feminist methodology. They speak of the consciousness of oppression leading to new insights. Yet they do not take into account how oppression may vary within and among social orders. This collection includes an essay by Patricia Hill Collins and one by Cannon et al., but none appears on Third World women. Even with respect to these essays, Fonow and Cook do not deal directly with the issues regarding research on nonprivileged women of color.[5] Ironically, neither Nielson nor Fonow and Cook consider the arguments that have been made for a sociology based not on gender but on race and ethnicity (e.g., Blea 1988; cf. Merton 1972).

Up to this point we have argued (admittedly in adumbrated fashion) that the dominant paradigm in gender studies has reflected a privileged, largely middle-class perspective. This orientation is best seen in the light of various emerging criticisms of gender research. We begin with scholars who have addressed issues in the United States and then consider those concerned with Third World women.

Although some women of color offered dissenting views in the 1970s, their voices became more pronounced in the 1980s. One of the leading lights in challenging the dominant paradigm has been the African American scholar bell hooks (e.g., 1984). Today, more scholars question the earlier paradigm regarding gender studies. As an instance, Albrecht and Brewer (1990:11), have advanced serious criticisms of it, observing that "women's activism and the development of feminist theory came hand in hand." Within this context the authors (1990:11) reason, in the light of writings by women of color in the 1980s, that

> the racism of the U.S. white women's movement could no longer be swept under the rug. No longer could gender alone be the defining element of the women's movement. White feminists had come to define gender as narrowly as the white women's experience. What emerged from the critique of women of color was the simultaneity of multiple oppressions of women's lives.

With respect to women of color, the work of Collins, *Black Feminist Thought* (1990), will have considerable impact on gender studies. Collins proceeds on the premise that knowledge assumes vital importance in social domination as well as in social resistance. In keeping with this view, she is highly critical of the Eurocentric male domination of current knowledge systems, observing that those who challenge these systems, such as black women, are often ostracized.

In the face of this Eurocentric domination, she adopted a conceptual framework based on "standpoints"—here, the black women's experience. Collins (1990:234) writes: "Despite African-American women's potential power to reveal new insights about the matrix of domination, a Black women's standpoint is only one angle of vision. Thus Black feminist thought represents a partial perspective." While we readily acknowledge the creative nature of Collins's work, we fear that her conceptualization ultimately will undermine her objective. Her particular view of standpoints leads to a relativization of social knowledge. The black women's standpoint comes to be one among a host of others. Thus, Smith (1989), and to a much lesser degree Harding (1991), can attach the black women's standpoint onto their own standpoints without probing into the serious conflicts that may exist between the views of privileged women (and men) and those of women of economically and politically disadvantaged racial and ethnic groups.

To bring out these issues more clearly, we again rely on a cross-cultural perspective wherein we attempt to see ourselves in the mirror of others. Here Ramazanoglu's (1989:125) observations are relevant:

> Black and third-world criticisms of new-wave feminism identify the assumption of common sisterhood in white feminism as rooted in a narrow version of western experience. These critics challenge new-wave feminist conceptions of women's oppression by arguing that women's domination by men, although very general, is not the only form of oppression that exists. Privileged white, western women are unusual in that sexism is the main form of oppression that they experience.

Mohanty (1991:53), who has attracted considerable attention in various scholarly circles, reasons along somewhat similar lines.

> I argue that assumptions of privilege and ethnocentric universality, on the one hand, and inadequate self-consciousness about the effect of Western scholarship on the "third world" in the context of a world system dominated by the West, on the other, characterize a sizable extent of Western feminist work on women in the third world.

Mohanty makes a special effort to observe that the perspectives of Western feminism are far from monolithic. Yet their overall effects are quite similar. Moreover, Mohanty criticizes the middle-class urban African or Asian scholars who write about their rural or working-class sisters, for they use their own experiences as a standard when evaluating the plight of disadvantaged women. She fails to acknowledge, however, that in part this stems from the dependency of Third World scholars on their Western counterparts for the production of certain forms of knowledge.

A few other scholars have called on Western specialists on gender to demonstrate greater critical awareness of the fact that their scholarship has developed in the context of special economic and social privilege and that this scholarship "owes its support to the existence of other populations who continue to experience daily exclusions of various kinds" (Chow 1991:98).

Where Do We Go from Here?

We are committed to the view that theory and research on gender must be integrated into race and ethnicity (as well as class and nationality) on both the international and the national planes (cf. Maynard 1990).[6] In the process we must be cognizant of our central thesis regarding the asymmetry between the viewpoints and interests of privileged women (and men) and the perspectives of the nonprivileged.

When we seek to integrate gender with race and ethnicity, however, we encounter manifold complexities. For example, political and religious systems vary considerably across cultures (and subcultures) in the manner in which gender and racial and ethnic issues are defined and redefined over time.[7]

In an attempt to integrate the research on gender and on race and ethnicity, we delineate selected patterns that seem to transcend the apparently endless social and cultural complexity that characterizes gender relationships. We tentatively outline patterns on the cultural level and then indicate how these are interrelated with systems of social stratification and social power.

Concerning cultural change in colonial India, Mani (1990:90) observed:

> Women become emblematic of tradition, and the reworking of tradition is largely conducted through debating the rights and status of women in society.

Mani's general perspective, though contentious, clarifies a number of empirical issues regarding the role of women in divergent sociocultural settings. Disagreement over the roles and activities of women is particularly intense because women symbolize certain core values relating to family and children (an aspect of the "sacred"). Within this framework, Desai's (1992) observations concerning cultural responses to women which transcend diverse cultural systems support Mani's theoretical premise. As Desai (1992:45) puts it, "modernization required criticism of tradition, while nationalism demanded its glorification." We can modify and extend this thesis by taking into account not only nationalism but also social and ethnic identity. In a number of instances, nationalism and ethnic identity have gone hand in hand; in other instances, maintenance of racial and ethnic identity may run counter to the dominant power orientations within the nation-state.

The problems facing women in a society's struggle between modernity and tradition (a slight variation on the Desai thesis) have been highlighted in twentieth-century Iran. The sociologist Najmabadi (1991) asserts that Iranian men who were exposed to modernization wanted a modern female counterpart, and government policy early in the century supported this goal. Yet Najmabadi (1991:70) observes: "The boundaries of the new were shaped in tension with another set of symbols: women simultaneously became the symbolic location of social morality and cultural conservatism," and, further, women were confronted with "becoming modern yet remaining modest and authentic."

With the rise of the Islamic Republic of Iran in the late 1970s, God and State became one. In the process, the traditional values associated with women were reconstituted (e.g., even educated women were required to wear the traditional modest garb in public), and many of their activities were sharply curtailed, especially in the public sphere. Within the patriarchal system that has dominated the Islamic Republic, women have been called on to sacrifice for a greater cause—the rejection of Western beliefs and values, which have been defined as evil.

In most societies the tensions over the roles and status of women are not as stark as in Iran, but the contest between modernity and tradition persists. To be sure, the situation is complicated by the ongoing reconstruction of what is meant by "tradition" (cf. Hobsbawm and Ranger 1983). Yet to understand the conflict between tradition and modernity in concrete terms, we must first analyze stratification systems on both the national and the international levels. That is, to grasp the interrelationships between gender issues and racial and ethnic relations we must conceptualize these realms within the context of social power and social class. How women as carriers of tradition (and morality) are defined varies in terms of complex stratification patterns and power relationships.

In recent years one group of scholars of gender have focused on colonialism (e.g., Strobel 1991). The role of women in European colonialism tells us much about the ruling group and provides us with indirect information about the ruled. Although subservient to men, particularly in the public sphere, European women were nonetheless a part of the power structure that controlled colonized men and women. These women helped to shape, directly and indirectly, the nature of colonial domination. According to Stoler (1991:87), "White prestige became redefined by the conventions that would safeguard the moral respectability, cultural identity, and physical well-being of its agents, with which European women were charged." In this instance, women were the carriers of salient features of the cultural tradition that legitimized European power and privilege and fostered racism.

Other issues relating to colonialism and gender merit attention. For example, Burton (1990) has provided data on how the nineteenth-century feminist movement in England used Indian women not to advance the latter's cause but as a means for promoting the cause of women at the core of the empire. She (1990:306) concludes that

> nineteenth-century feminists sought empowerment by a variety of means—education, the vote, welfare legislation—not the least of which was by allying their cause with British imperial rule. The

international feminist vision which reformers . . . cherished held the promise of global sisterhood based on equality and 'womanly values.' That promise went largely unfulfilled because their feminism, like Victorian cultural ideology, depended on the existence of classes and races whose powerlessness defined and guaranteed all kinds of hegemonies. These included the construction and domination of Indian women as the female Other by white western feminists.

Present-day students of gender should be mindful of the potential trap into which their research might lead them and use certain lessons from the past to avoid these dangers.

Stratification on the international level (or what some scholars refer to as "informal colonialism"), remains with us today. Enloe (1990), in a pioneering work, *Bananas, Beaches & Bases*, provides us with insights into how the gender division of labor is being played out on the world scene. These patterns tend to be overlooked by students of gender. Obvious examples of the gendered division of labor include those associated with tourism and with U.S. military bases abroad (a sensitive and little-discussed topic).

Enloe (1990:199) stresses that the world economic system affects women of different classes and ethnic backgrounds in divergent ways:

Middle-class women in countries such as Mexico and Sri Lanka have different kinds of stakes in the present system than do working-class and peasant women. This is compounded by societies' ethnic and racial barriers—between Hispanicized and Indian Mexican women, and Tamil and Singhalese Sri Lankan women, for instance. International debt may affect all women in Mexico, but not to the same degree or in the same ways.

Enloe's broad generalizations are given specificity in Stephen's *Zapotec Women* (1991). We learn a great deal about the efforts by the Zapotec Indians to sustain their ethnic identity within Mexican society. In the process we observe how the Zapotecs have relied on their ethnic heritage in order to produce, for instance, handmade shawls, blankets, and rugs for an international market. Within the community studied, a gendered division of labor clearly exists, but it differs by class groups, and the makeup of these classes has shifted over time. In turn, Zapotec women are far more marginalized than urban middle-class women in Mexico as a whole.

The need to integrate gender with race and ethnicity, as well as with class, seems evident in many other social orders. Bardhan (1991:169) observing the multilayered systems of hierarchy in South Asia, India in particular, asserts:

It is thus incorrect, misleading, and a little obfuscating to speak of women as a class, either in terms of economic exploitation or as a community of shared interests and problems. Women in general may be more oppressed than men, but the nature and extent of the oppression differs according to their class location; the oppression is perpetuated by men as well as by women.

In her implicit challenge to the premises underlying a considerable body of gender research in the United States, Bardhan (1991: 170) observes:

> Last, but not the least important in South Asia, the effect of caste/ethnic/religious violence on women's lives as mothers, wives, sisters, and daughters is not class-neutral; it is far more severe for the poor within each community.

The plight of economic and politically disadvantaged minority women in India differs from that of more privileged women, although both are restricted by the patriarchal order.

This leads us to an issue alluded to by Bardhan but undeveloped by her or by most specialists on women's issues. Class and power are employed not just by men but also by women in order to preserve positions of privilege (even though privileged women also must function within a patriarchal system).

The situation in Chile in the late 1970s and 1980s, while not directly related to race and ethnicity, is highly instructive with respect to class, gender, and women's issues. In the 1970s, the military, led by General Pinochet, overthrew the government of Salvador Allende—a regime viewed as fostering communism. The power structure under Pinochet's regime instituted various forms of oppression. According to Constable and Valenzuela (1991:160-61).

> One of the most ambitious efforts to change the Chilean mentality was aimed at women. Traditionally preoccupied with order and stability, wives and mothers had been a key element of support for the coup. . .
>
> It was first Lady Lucia Hiriart, however, who took up the banner of feminine support for military rule, reigning over a network of forty-nine charities. . . . These agencies, managed by wives of military officials, mirrored the official chain of command, and their parallel army of volunteer housewives, dressed in neat, smock-like 'uniforms,' grew to a force of over twenty thousand.

The authors (1991:161) go on to observe that one goal of this group was charity: "ladies in lilac or pink helping the elderly or teaching poor women a craft." But there was a second, parallel goal: to promote and reward loyalty to the regime; to inculcate anticommunist and 'family' values; and to replace an egalitarian model of civic participation with a vertical one.

If we return to our earlier reasoning, we see how women, as symbols of tradition, have played a role in a variety of power struggles. In this instance, women of privilege, espousing one view of morality, imposed their perspective on less privileged women (cf. Strobel 1991). Although the elite women were themselves subservient to their husbands, they nonetheless actively participated in constructing and maintaining Pinochet's military rule.

The essential patterns illustrated by Pinochet's Chile are far from unique, though they often remain unexamined. Planter women in the American South had a special stake in maintaining slavery. In the words of Fox-Genovese (1988:334).

> Slaveholding women did not share their slaves' opposition to slavery. . . . Slavery, with all its abuses, constituted the fabric of their beloved country—the warp and woof of their social position, their personal relations, their very identities.

Blee's research in *Women of the Klan* (1991), specifically the Ku Klux Klan in Indiana in the 1920s, points to another variant of the nexus between gender and ethnicity. She speaks of the Klan as advancing Protestant white women's rights. The women in this group "could safeguard women's suffrage and expand women's other legal rights while working to preserve white Protestant supremacy" (1991:1). Blee (1991:72) also refers to "the ferocity of its [the Klan's] insistence that women show their support for women's rights by lashing out against immigrants, blacks, Catholics, and Jews." Here the role of women as symbols of morality was articulated within class, race, and power relationships. The women of the Klan were pitted against not only other women but also, and especially, against minority males.

In contrast, women have often played an unheralded role in movements of liberation. The role of African American women in the civil rights movement of the 1950s and 1960s is yet to be analyzed and appreciated (Lawson 1991:467). A somewhat similar pattern holds for South Africa in more recent times (Walker 1991). While recognizing women's contributions to freedom,[8] however, we must not ignore the reality that some privileged women have played (and continue to play) an active role in the oppression of other women (and men), especially those who belong to racial and ethnic minority groups.

Our analysis began with the premise that women have been carriers of morality (most notably that relating to children and the family). Yet the definition of morality is played out within the framework of a multifaceted (and at times convoluted) system of gender stratification. Nevertheless, within this complexity a rather persistent tension obtains between the top-down and the bottom-up views of gender relationships.

Methodological Issues in Research on Racial and Ethnic Minority Women

Moving forward, we need to clarify the difficulties associated with our central thesis that the orientations of privileged persons and groups often diverge from, and may stand in opposition to, the views of the economically and politically disadvantaged. Formidable barriers arise in carrying out fieldwork and in the interpretation of historical and even contemporary records. One group of anthropologists, given the cultural chasms with which they have had to deal, have essentially thrown up their hands in frustration. "Some feminist anthropologists ... have argued that cross-cultural comparisons of women's status are impossible in any event, [and constitute] the arrogant imposition of philistine Western grids on deeply divergent cultural understandings" (di Leonardo 1991:14). While we acknowledge the enormity of the sociocultural barriers social scientists are likely to encounter in their research—the cultural categories of economically disadvantaged respondents diverge markedly from the researcher's taken-for-granted premises—we reject the extreme relativism of this assertion. However difficult it may be, human beings, especially if they are reflective about the inherent difficulties of the task, can establish some common ground across wide social and cultural hiatuses, for they share some fundamental similarities in that they speak languages that are mutually translatable, and they engage in the construction or the reconstitution of social and cultural orders. To deny these similarities would be to empirically and morally give up on the possibility of people coexisting relatively peaceably in a complex multicultural global order.

Herein we can merely sketch out selected methodological issues relating to a bottom-up vs. a top-down perspective. Still, research problems arise because of the asymmetry in these orientations. Let us consider first the problems inherent in taking the roles of Others and then deal briefly with a related question of interpreting historical and contemporary records.

Taking the Roles of Others

Apart from a few anthropologists, mainstream scholars on race and ethnicity and gender have sought to avoid the methodological dilemma that commands our attention. Taking the roles of Others, though basic to the fieldwork process, has received surprisingly limited attention in publications on the research process (Williams 1989b). Charles Cooley and George Herbert Mead, who examined this problem area theoretically, did so with regard to a homogeneous social setting, notably the Anglo society of their day. Moreover, Goffman (1959), whose views regarding the presentation of self, or image management, have been widely influential among social scientists, deflected attention from an understanding of social and culturally divergent Others. He openly adopted the perspective of the privileged Anglo middle class (cf. Williams 1989a) and seemed intent on explicating how privileged persons can, within the context of a highly individualized society, manage their impressions so as to enhance their own personal well-being. His actors concern themselves not with understanding others but with manipulating them to their own advantage. Regrettably, the unquestioned adoption of Goffman's framework by social researchers reflects the latter's own privileged position in U.S. society.

When taking the roles of Others whose status and culture diverge markedly from one's own, researchers must make a special effort to explicate their premises to themselves and their respondents. They must recognize that stereotypes of disadvantaged Others by persons in positions of power can be used as a means for sustaining positions of privilege (Herzfeld 1987). Consequently, they must be wary of false stereotypes when studying class, gender, and racial and ethnic minorities.

In developing our perspective we deal first with selected micro dimensions and then move to the macro level, all the while recognizing that the two intersect.

We draw on Rollins's (1985) informative research on domestics and their employers to clarify one facet of our argument. Although Rollins did not detail the broader methodological implications of her findings, she observed that domestics had much greater sensitivity concerning their employers than their employers had about them. They were keenly intent on taking the roles of their employers, as a means of adapting to the demands placed on them—and, more broadly, as a means of survival. Still, it is unlikely that the domestics understood the roles of their employers beyond the household setting.

In contrast, the employers made no real effort to understand their domestics. Had they done so, they would have had to confront the latter's everyday life circumstances, which would have been discomfiting and even threatening on a personal level. It was easier for them to make demands of their servants without seeking to understand the latter's ongoing struggles.

The difficulties of taking the roles of Others are exacerbated when investigating previously unexamined roles (cf. Fischer 1986). Preconceived assumptions often stand in the way of the acquisition of sound social knowledge. For example, Williams (1990) faced this problem directly when studying working-class Mexican American women. At first she assumed, because of expectations gleaned from the sociological literature and because the women's role-making patterns did not conform to those of the Mexican American professional class, that these women did not actively engage in remaking their roles. But after critical reflection, she realized that these women indeed engaged in role making but that they did so in ways different from those of more advantaged women—a pattern that tends to be overlooked in social science literature.

In more general terms, we must recognize that when researchers study persons of much lower status and divergent cultural backgrounds, the latter are likely to be suspicious, even resistant, to providing certain information about themselves and their culture.[9] Rosaldo (1986) observed how Evans-Pritchard (1940), in his widely cited research on the Nuer (a tribal group in East Africa), failed to understand the reasons for the evasiveness of some of his respondents. Rosaldo rightly interprets the reactions of the Nuer as realistic efforts to protect themselves and their culture from unwarranted intrusion, for Evans-Pritchard was an "agent" of a colonial power that had engaged in conflict with them. Why should the respondents reveal themselves fully to persons whom they may rightfully distrust?[10]

When conducting research on racial or ethnic minorities, we are interacting with persons who sustain some form of Du Bois's (1973:3) "double-con-sciousness." Minorities seek to preserve their social identity and at the same time adapt to the controls exerted on them by persons in positions of social power. As for minority women, the researcher must be prepared to take the roles of multiple Others—not just a single unitary Other. Women of color respond in both reactive and proactive ways not only to the patriarchy within their own ethnic group but also to the power group of the society in which the minority group is embedded. The social researcher, then, must be prepared to take the multiple roles of Others whose expectations are at times contradictory. Minority women experience multiple forms of social oppression: from the patriarchy within their own setting, as a result of ethnic discrimination in the broader society, and because of social-class considerations within their subgroup as well as in the broader society. And however well intentioned the researcher, respondents will likely identify him or her with the societal power arrangements that are the source of oppression for them. It would be informative to learn just how researchers and the researched have responded to these situations.

Turning from micro to broader macro issues, we should, as suggested earlier, be mindful of the researcher's position within the social order to which he or she belongs. Researchers on gender take into consideration the responses of women as they have sought to carry out research on male domination in historical or contemporary settings. The problem becomes greatly compounded when one studies women who are members of racial and ethnic minorities. The values and power relations of the broader social order and of one's own academic setting can lead the researcher astray when studying minority women.

Two different kinds of case studies should help clarify our perspective. The first concerns India. The two leading cultural traditions in the Indian subcontinent are the Indo-Aryan and the Dravidian. The latter, the older tradition, is perpetuated by about a third of India's population. Dravidians today are concentrated mainly in the South, though their ancestors must originally have populated much of the North as well. A number of scholars have observed striking differences in gender patterns between North and South India. Goody (1990), an eminent anthropologist, has summarized some of the main features. But he stumbles in his attempt to account for these contrasts. Significantly, the kinship systems and marriage patterns of North and South strongly contrast. Yet he fails to acknowledge that the differences between North and South are the product not just of "material conditions" but also of something broader: two fundamentally different cultural traditions—the Aryan and the Dravidian. Goody has, in fact, been ill served by Indologists, who have typically refused to recognize the importance of the Dravidian culture and the impact it has had on Indian civilization in general and on Hinduism in particular. Indeed, they have tended to treat the Dravidians as persons of little importance whose culture, they assume, has been mainly shaped by the dominant Indo-Aryans. The Aryan bias in the study of India seems even greater than the "Aryan" bias that Bernal (1987; 1991) argues has led to false interpretations of Greek civilization that have functioned as received wisdom since the latter part of the eighteenth century.

European scholars' interpretation of Indian history was strongly colored by the discovery that the Old Indo-Aryan language, Sanskrit, shared a common ancestor with most of the languages of Europe. This has led scholars to impose an Indo-Aryan interpretation on Indian history and culture that tends to minimize the impact of the Dravidian people, the ancestors of whom had settled in the Indian subcontinent before the arrival of the Aryans. One result is that the patterns concerning women in Dravidian culture differ markedly from those in the Indo-Aryan cultural setting and are still not properly appreciated. This illustrates how gender researchers can unwittingly become captives of some broader ideological orientation.

A more dramatic instance of the way a power structure can distort one's understanding of minority women can be found in the aftermath of Japanese colonial rule of Korea. Recently, on an anniversary of the bombing of Hiroshima and Nagasaki, some Korean women brought suit against the Japanese government for its earlier official policy of forcing prostitution on young Korean girls (some of whom are still alive). That such a policy was approved by the military leaders has been documented by a Japanese historian (Sanger 1992a, 1992b). Given the power structure of Japan in the post World War II years, this information has only recently come to light. Such occurred as a result of a "social rupture" in the body politic and the courage of the aforementioned historian. The prime minister, on an official visit to Korea, subsequently apologized for the past policies of the Japanese government. But why this suppression of information for so many decades? The formal acknowledgment of the mistreatment of disadvantaged Others opens up wounds with respect to Japanese colonialism in Korea. The colonialist policy concerning women among the conquered reflects adversely on the legitimacy of the current power arrangements within and outside Japan.

But we must not single out the Japanese. For example, the exploitation in Kuwait of ethnic women immigrants from other parts of Asia came to the attention of an international audience only with the rupture in power relations that resulted from the Persian Gulf War. As to the United States, the role of its military bases abroad and the effect of these on the women of the host countries has been barely discussed. Enloe (1990) is one of the few students of gender to have attempted this; however, her discussion focuses more on Europe than on Asia, and she downplays the racial and ethnic dimensions of the problem. As the United States reduces its military presence in Korea, the Philippines, and elsewhere in Asia, we assume that scholars will begin to analyze the treatment of Others by the military. Such works will engender controversy, for they raise questions about past U.S. policies with respect to oppressed minority women. But it is not just sexual exploitation that is at issue. What is the responsibility of the U.S. government or society toward the children fathered by U.S. military personnel in Vietnam and elsewhere—and toward the mothers of these children? Certain other aspects of the roles of ethnic minority women are unlikely to be examined until the current values and power arrangements enable social scientists and others to take the roles of women of color in the United States and on the global scene.

Problems in the Use of Historical and Contemporary Records

In our discussion of taking the roles of divergent Others, we have touched on the matter of the historical data. We now briefly consider this topic. Social scientists, after all, need to rely not just on fieldwork but also on historical materials in their study of ethnic minority women. Yet when dealing with these records serious obstacles arise that merit attention. Here all we can do is suggest a direction for future analysis.

When utilizing historical and even current records on racial and ethnic groups, and especially on women, we confront the question: How and for what reasons are particular documents constructed, and why is it that some have been preserved and others lost?[11] This question has not been adequately addressed by historiographers or other social scientists. Yet it is vital for the investigation of women who are members of racial and ethnic minorities.

It is usually taken for granted that history is compiled by persons who wield power. Most historical accounts, therefore, have been written from a top-down perspective. To adequately address this problem area one must consider the nature of historical records over a long time period—and in cross-cultural perspective. We can, for heuristic purposes, distinguish between the records from preindustrial civilized societies and the data obtained on modern social orders that rest on a scientific and industrial base. In preindustrial civilized societies—such as China, India, or those in the Middle East—written records were created and preserved by a tiny segment of the population: the literati. And they were intended for rather narrow purposes: for administrative ends—for example, to facilitate taxation and commerce—or for religious/philosophical purposes, including legitimization of the power and privilege of the ruling elite.

For preindustrial civilized societies very early records must be distinguished from later ones. Although all the materials from preindustrial civilizations tend to be fragmentary, generally the farther one goes back in time, the more elusive the data. The earliest written records are so skimpy and uneven in coverage that historians have debated the reliability of using these materials in attempts to reconstruct patterns of life in the earliest cities and societies (e.g., Hallo 1990). Nevertheless, we can derive a modicum of understanding of early civilizations by piecing together archeological and written records.

Still another issue concerns the wide variations in the availability of records on preindustrial civilized orders. This has resulted in part from the kinds of materials on which writing was inscribed. The baked clay tablets of the Middle East have survived far longer and in greater numbers than have the bark and, especially, palm leaf records that have long been traditional in India.

Variability in the quality and quantity of historical records has also been a product of fortuitous historical events. For example, almost all the Mayan books were savaged by the Spanish conquerors, who were intent on stamping out the local religion. So, too, the great library at Alexandria was destroyed in the early centuries of Christianity as a result of religious political struggles. On the other hand, conflagrations in Crete and Mycenaean Greece during the mid-second millennium B.C.E. led to the preservation of numerous clay tablets that, ironically, were apparently intended to be discarded; the baking process dramatically extended their lifetime. More generally, however, the ravages of war have led to widespread destruction of historical records in many parts of the world. All of this has had the effect of structuring our knowledge of peoples of the preindustrial past.

What do our observations on the fragmentary nature, as well as variability, of data from the past mean for research on racial and ethnic minorities and gender? Nowadays numerous efforts are being made to reconstruct the role of women in preindustrial civilized societies. However, the texts were written by the literati, who were part of the small ruling class and almost exclusively male. Ordinary people, especially ethnic minorities (and the women even more so), were essentially nonpersons. Admittedly, the religious and philosophical literature contains some depictions of women of the privileged sector. Nevertheless, only fleeting glimpses of the everyday life of even these women have been preserved. One must, in the words of Tharu and Lalita (1991), "read against the grain" in order to acquire even a limited understanding of what women's lives were like. Most religious and philosophical discussions of women were reflections of male authors' idealized views of primarily elite women and their place in the order of things. However, Bernal (1987, 1991), in his work on classical Greek civilization, demonstrated the feasibility of piecing together a variety of data in order to discern patterns regarding the interaction of divergent cultural (and racial and ethnic) traditions. But even here, little can be learned about women.

In all, it is important to understand how and why the records of preindustrial civilizations were constructed, as well as the controversies over the reliability of the data, when we attempt to generalize concerning the history of racial and ethnic minorities and of gender issues.[12] Indeed, we must exercise caution when using even relatively recent records, especially those pertaining to women—a problem that is especially acute for understanding politically and economically disadvantaged minority women.

With the rise of the scientific/industrial complex in the West—a complex process stimulated earlier by, for instance, the borrowing of many patterns from the Arabs—a vast expansion of literacy took place. The development of the printing process involving movable type and the spread of formal education led to a burgeoning of written records that continues to escalate to this day. As the Europeans extended their influence (most often through conquest), these patterns became worldwide.

The records of Europeans concerning their cultures and the people they encountered require careful attention from specialists on gender and racial and ethnic issues. True, during the European colonial expansion the conquerors imposed their own social categories on the conquered; but now for almost the first time, we have substantial information not merely about the upper classes but also to some extent about the everyday life of ordinary people, persons whom the elite within the conquered areas had virtually ignored. This pattern resulted in a body of data that, among other things, provide us with information about minority peoples, and to some extent women, that might not otherwise exist.

Taking India as a case study, we can usefully distinguish among the writings of Westerners such as travelers, missionaries, administrators, historians and anthropologists.[13] Each of these groups composed accounts based on different premises as they recorded their observations about an Other they barely understood. The validity of these data in part must be evaluated in terms of how and why particular authors composed their works. One of the most distinctive facets of British colonial rule in India is the manner in which scholars such as Sir William Jones, in the late eighteenth century, and Max Müller, in the nineteenth century, directly and indirectly encouraged the elite segment of Indian society to delve into its past. Müller set out to translate and publicize the ancient Vedic texts, which were composed in Sanskrit (a language that, as we observed, is related to most of those in Europe). His Eurocentric bias is apparent enough, but his complex role in stimulating a particular historical consciousness among educated Indians has only recently begun to be examined. Ultimately, elements of the Indian elite rewrote their history from what was in a broad sense a bottom-up perspective. This served as a vital stimulus to their search for independence from the colonial master. In India we have an example of the complex interaction between outsiders and insiders in the formation of social knowledge; the power struggle between the two assumed a variety of forms to which Merton seemed oblivious.

But to return momentarily to Europe and the United States. The dissemination of literacy to many of the nonprivileged (of whom there are several layers) has not led to the acquisition of sufficient information on these members of society. Historians such as E.P. Thompson (1964) and Eric Hobsbawm (1985) have championed the writing of history as seen from below. But they have neglected to deal adequately with the problem of serious gaps in the written records, even with respect to the past few centuries. As Scott (1988) has observed, Thompson did not do justice to gender issues in his major endeavor on the English working class. Viewing the past from the vantage point of the present, we find that it is extremely difficult to acquire valid knowledge about lower-status persons (including members of the working class)—and especially ethnic minorities—in the United States and Western Europe. This makes us somewhat skeptical concerning the materials on the aforementioned groups of a century or two ago.[14] Consider the blacks, or African Americans, during slavery in the United States. From one perspective, a substantial body of data concerning them is available. However, most of this material was constructed by the white elite. Despite the vital data contained in slave narratives, an adequate understanding of the experiences of the nonliterate slaves, including most of the women, may never be attainable.

Even given the formidable obstacles encountered in writing history from below, efforts can be made to close the gaps in our understanding.

When we come to the matter of ethnic minority women we must be prepared to face special difficulties. Thus, although Scott (1988) has criticized Thompson for his inattention to gender, she herself seems to be insufficiently sensitive to women of color when she discusses historical research. As minority women come to be heard, a still different kind of history will likely be written.

Numerous other facets of research on ethnic minorities require explication. Statistical data recorded for the oppressed sectors of society must be interpreted with care. One of Scott's (1988) contributions to the analysis of gender has been her examination of how and why administrative organizations such as those in mid-nineteenth-century France constructed statistical reports relating to gender.

190   A CRITIQUE OF CONTEMPORARY AMERICAN SOCIOLOGY

In her critical examination of the Paris Chamber of Commerce's *La statistique de l'industrie à Paris*, she observes that statistics served to legitimate the claims of bourgeois administrators. For Scott (1988:115) the statistical reports "are neither totally neutral collections of fact nor simply ideological impositions. Rather they are ways of establishing the authority of certain visions of social order." Yet "when the Statistique's administrative polemic uses had long been outdated, historians searching for unimpeachable data took the report at face value, incorporating its documentation without questioning its categories and interpretations" (1988:137).

The issues Scott has raised for "official statistics" in mid-nineteenth-century Paris can be generalized to other societies and to present-day advanced industrial orders. In an earlier publication (Sjoberg et al. 1991) we observed that, to judge by the existing data, members of the very top and the very bottom of U.S. society are the least likely to respond to social surveys (Goyder 1987). Yet these surveys often form the basis for the "official statistics" on which rests a significant amount of social research regarding racial and ethnic relations and gender.

In the light of Scott's analysis, the data from the U.S. census, for instance, should not be immune to careful scrutiny. Moore (1976) has observed how the concept Mexican American (and now Hispanic) has been manipulated over time by the Bureau of the Census. Perhaps the concern over the undercount in the 1990 census will finally rivet attention on the problems associated with the failure to collect data on both men and women in politically and economically disadvantaged minority groups. In this context we wonder aloud about Wilson's (1987) highly regarded study *The Truly Disadvantaged*. His heavy reliance on official statistics leads us to suspect that he failed to examine the most disadvantaged sector of the truly disadvantaged. As for developing societies, the gross inadequacy of official data on disadvantaged minority groups is clearly apparent and in need of critical analysis. But it is not just statistical data that require scrutiny in any study of the nexus between gender and racial and ethnic minorities. Similar critical examinations are required in the case of newspaper reports and the like. Some of the most "vulnerable" sectors of the U.S. population have not received the careful attention they deserve; at the same time, we may have insufficient data on the power groups who make the critical decisions regarding the fate of the disadvantaged members of society.

Broader Implications

Such questions as "How are data collected?" "How are they constructed?" "Which groups suffer most from neglect?" should be in the forefront of research on the intersection of gender and racial and ethnic relations. Our working thesis is that the data collected on women of color often do little or nothing to advance their cause; instead, they seem to enhance the positions of the researchers who collect and analyze these materials. There is also a tendency for educated persons to study "exotic" marginal members of society rather than groups whom the privileged have a greater stake in controlling. Social scientists are reluctant to take the roles of Others where knowledge of such persons could undermine the legitimacy of the upper sectors of society.

Conclusions and Implications

Our main objective has been to critically evaluate certain fundamental theoretical and methodological issues regarding research on gender and on racial and ethnic minorities. Social scientists in general, and sociologists in particular, have yet to address many salient problems relating to this worldwide problem area.

Merton's well-known essay on insiders and outsiders has served as our primary point of departure. We have recast his analysis, for it fails to treat the centrality of power relations between insiders (the privileged) and outsiders (the nonprivileged). Merton, reflecting the views of most social scientists, seems unaware of the role of privileged researchers in justifying, directly or indirectly, the existing power arrangements. In effect, oppressed ethnic minorities fail to receive a fair hearing within the social science community and the broader society. Given Merton's framework, he cannot come to terms with the fact that the interests, knowledge, and activities of the privileged often diverge markedly from, or are at odds with, those of the nonprivileged.

After sketching out certain fundamental changes in the patterns of race and ethnicity, as well as gender, on the global scene since World War II, we considered recent scholarly efforts to reevaluate the nature of racial and ethnic relations, particularly the Eurocentric bias within the social sciences, and some of the counterreactions to this top-down orientation.

Turning to gender, we outlined two schools of thought. The first, which held sway within new-wave feminism, has been anchored in a middle- or upper-middle-class perspective. The second challenges the first in both the United States and on the world scene. As this latter orientation has gained legitimacy in recent years, the divergencies between the view from above and the view from below, particularly in the data they yield on women who are members of nonprivileged racial and ethnic minorities, are now more clearly discernible.

Not just theoretical but also methodological issues relating to women of color demand special attention. We have emphasized the difficulties of integrating the analysis of gender with that for ethnicity, class, and even nationality. If we are to achieve such an integration, we must recognize the multifaceted nature of gender stratification—all the while perceiving the asymmetry between the views from above and those from below.

Many current research procedures do not permit social scientists to address the issues we have considered. Methods such as social surveys or experimentation emphasize standardization. Adherents of these approaches lose sight of the existence of multilayered definitions of gender relations and thus impose a false order on existing social relations. The situation is compounded by the fact that the use of standardized research procedures is associated with a commitment to specialization—for example, a focus on gender (or some facet thereof) to the exclusion of ethnicity.

One useful alternative to current practices is the employment of in-depth case studies, with respect to both historical and contemporary patterns. A number of these have been carried out, especially by historians and anthropologists. Yet many such works suffer from a failure to place the problems being analyzed within a general cross-cultural framework. Social scientists too often intentionally or unintentionally emphasize the unique while ignoring the general. But can one define what is unique except in terms of some underlying generalities? Certainly most American sociologists can be criticized for their failure to take a cross-cultural perspective with respect to gender, ethnicity, and class.

In seeking to analyze the interrelationships of gender, ethnicity, and class, we must be ever aware of the difficulties of taking the roles of Others, particularly of Others who remain relatively powerless and whose cultural patterns diverge from one's own.[15] The barriers to mutual understanding should not be underestimated.

One role that social scientists (including sociologists) can and should play is in providing a voice for disadvantaged minorities, especially women. But this can be achieved only through taking the roles of these persons and setting their worldview within a framework that takes account of how they are treated by persons in positions of societal power and authority.[16]

In addition, if research on gender and ethnicity is to advance, social scientists must also come to terms with how and why various kinds of historical data have been collected and constructed. Also, we need to consider seriously the data that do not get recorded. The historical record largely reflects the view from above, and when ordinary people are considered, they are usually seen through the lenses of the privileged stratum. The implications of this situation await careful analysis.

Some readers may judge our analysis to be too critical of gender studies during the past two decades. We readily acknowledge the fact that these highly significant research efforts have served as the basis for our critical dialogue. Yet if gender studies are to advance, a special effort must be made to break with the dominant worldview, which takes privileged women as its main point of departure. We also need to grasp the perspectives of dispossessed women, especially members of racial and ethnic minorities. They must be given a voice within the framework of national and international large-scale bureaucratic structures—concerning the pervasive nature of which these women (as well as many social scientists) seem only dimly aware.

Embedded in the foregoing reasoning is an agenda for future research. Social scientists, including sociologists, must seek to comprehend the problems of racial and ethnic women within the context of large-scale organizations. Such structures effectively constrain the actions of these women, while the latter are striving to gain control over their lives. Today we are witnessing the emergence of large-scale international organizations that intersect with national organizations in complex ways. The research by, for instance, Stephen (1991) on Zapotec Indian women in Mexico provides glimpses into these patterns. A further imperative concerns the need for specialists on gender as it relates to racial and ethnic minorities to come to terms with the issue of human rights. Students of gender have rarely been concerned with the rights of women (or of men) as human beings. A human rights perspective will more readily than any other moral orientation incorporate the concerns of racial and ethnic minority women.

Moreover, if research on minorities and gender is to make a compelling contribution to scholarly and practical endeavors and avoid marginalization, social scientists must examine core theoretical and methodological issues, many of which can properly be addressed only from an interdisciplinary perspective. For example, Scott (1988) recognizes that if historians of gender are to have their work taken seriously by their colleagues, they must do more than carry out research on specialized topics; they must also confront conceptual issues that undergird the historical enterprise.

In analyzing the intersection of gender and race and ethnicity, we cannot paper over the tensions and conflicts that pervade the world scene. If we are to come to terms with the emerging world community, we must be willing to search for common ground to achieving mutual understanding. First and foremost is respect for the human rights of others. The study of differences and commonalities must go hand in hand. We do not underestimate the formidable barriers to achieving our overall objective. But, given the present trends in the United States and on the global scene, this task takes on even greater urgency. In the process, current conceptions of gender (as well as of race and ethnicity) will of necessity undergo profound revision.

Acknowledgements

We are especially grateful to Vicki L. Ruiz for her highly constructive criticisms, and we thank Gideon Sjoberg for his sustained effort in helping to integrate our respective orientations and data into a coherent argument.

*For over a decade the first-named author, a sociologist, has carried out intensive fieldwork in various communities in Texas on undocumented workers from Mexico, on the Mexican American family and on the Mexican American elderly. One of her areas of specialization is race and ethnic relations. The second-named author's training is in linguistics and anthropology. She has written on such major ethnic minorities as the Uzbeks of Central Asia and the Dravidians of India and has had a longstanding interest in cross-cultural analysis (especially of societies in Asia). This essay is an outgrowth of our ongoing research endeavors as well as of our prior collaboration (e.g., Sjoberg, Williams, Vaughan, and Sjoberg 1991).

Notes

1. Such terms as *feminism, gender* and *women's studies* have been a matter of extensive debate in the literature. We rely primarily on the concept of "gender" but refer to the other terms where it seems appropriate. Admittedly, still other distinctions have been drawn in the rapidly growing body of writings in this area. For example, Alvarez (1990), in her research on Brazil, distinguished between feminist issues (those pertaining to more privileged women) and feminine issues (those referring to working-class women).

2. We need more information on the negative impact of researchers on those researched in other societies. Yet we must also be wary of assuming that all social research has had a negative impact on the people studied. The latter may use that research in highly creative ways as a means of furthering their own goals. See, e.g., Wiswell (1988) and Smith (1988).

3.The following observations by Stannard (1991:381) underline Novick's generalizations not only with respect to gender but also with reference to ethnic minorities:

American history has come a long way in the past quarter century. It was, after all, 1965 when Samuel Eliot Morison published his enormously successful and widely praised *Oxford History of the American People*—an 1,100-page work that relegated the women's suffrage amendment of the Constitution to half a sentence in a chapter entitled 'Bootlegging and Other Sports,' and intimated that most blacks were pleased and contented as slaves. And this was an avant-garde position for Morison, commonly regarded as the pre-eminent American historian of his time: in earlier versions of the same text he had referred to blacks collectively as 'Sambo,' as 'childlike, improvident, humorous, prevaricating, and superstitious' creatures; when confined to slavery, he had stated flatly, blacks were 'adequately fed, well cared for, and apparently happy.'

If space permitted we could provide far more documentation in support of our contention that U.S. history, as seen from the perspective of gender and of racial and ethnic minorities, has been rewritten during the past three decades—though the intersection of these realms has not received due attention.

4. For a discussion of Smith's theory, see the "Symposium on Dorothy E. Smith" (1992).

5. The recent work by Reinharz (1992) refers to problems associated with studying women who are members of racial and ethnic minorities within the United States and in a cross-cultural context. But, the author has failed to incorporate critical methodological issues (including those we raise herein) into the themes of her book; consequently, Reinharz's formulation requires fundamental revision.

6. Maynard (1990:280), reviewing trends in gender studies, contends that "probably the most serious and important on-going debate taking place amongst those studying gender concerns the inherent racism of many approaches to the subject." She rightly acknowledges the lead taken by black women in challenging the dominant paradigm in women's studies that held sway during the 1970s and 1980s. But she includes the works of all women of color under the framework of "black critique." Maynard's subsequent analysis thus glosses over divergent historical and cultural heritages that must be given due attention if we are to advance our understanding of the nexus between gender and ethnicity.

7. In this survey essay we can hardly do justice to the variations in women's issues that can be attributed to "nationality" differences. The particular way women's roles in Japan have been changing is one such significant topic. Japan is a highly industrialized nation; yet a patriarchal system is still very much in evidence (e.g., Kelly 1991). The changes in Japan over time (Bernstein 1991), as well as the role of Japanese women today (Tamanoi 1990), are quite unlike the patterns in the United States and western Europe and raise many unresolved questions concerning the link between industrialization and the "freedom" of women in the public sphere.

The role of women in the former Soviet Union also deserves special consideration (e.g., Attwood 1990). The question needs to be asked, "What was the impact of Soviet communism on gender roles?" One of the most intriguing problems concerns recent and ongoing changes in women's roles in the Muslim Turkic societies of Central Asia.

8. A set of brief case studies illustrating women's role in revolutionary movements in a number of societies appears in a special journal issue on women activists edited by Diamond (1990).

9. Although the study by Alvarez (1990) on women's movements in Brazil provides much valuable data, it is significant that the author gave very limited attention to the black women's movement in that country. We infer from her comments that it was easier to gain access to data on movements carried out by the society's more privileged women.

10. Most researchers who discuss research methods as these relate to the study of gender and racial and ethnic minorities seem unaware of the various forms of resistance that subordinates employ in their interaction with dominant groups. Scott's (1990) discussion of the "arts of resistance"—though not focused on gender and ethnicity—needs to be incorporated (with modifications) into our understanding of the research process, particularly with respect to what it means to take the roles of divergent Others. We must recognize, for example, that the deference accorded by subordinates to privileged researchers may serve to hide their actual "backstage" orientations. Penetrating the social worlds of the nonprivileged, ethnic minorities in particular, may be more difficult to achieve than most specialists on research methods would acknowledge.

11. Many issues regarding the study of preindustrial civilized orders demand clarification if social scientists are to discuss these societies in a meaningful way. One concerns the complex interrelationship between oral and written traditions. See, e.g., Finley (1985) on these and related problem areas.

12. Historians often must draw on contemporary data when writing about the past, but this fact tends to go unnoted in works on research methods. In the edited book *Marriage and Inequality in Chinese Society*, which focuses primarily on historical research, Ebrey (1991:6-7) observes that:

> Our current knowledge of Chinese marriage is based largely on observations made during the last century by social scientists. Given the many continuities in Chinese marriage practices, these studies provide considerable insight into earlier periods. Yet they are no substitute for historical research. . . . The historians writing here have had to decide how well the terms and concepts commonly used by anthropologists convey what they know of past societies.

The methodological issues raised must be incorporated into historical research on women.

13. A number of historians are seeking to evaluate the validity of various travel accounts by Europeans concerning areas such as the Middle East. See, e.g., Murphey (1990).

14. Tilly (1986:11-52) emphasizes that we do have data on "ordinary" people. Still, he recognizes that members of the elite had narratives written about them (or else they wrote about themselves), whereas ordinary people left no such

records. This poses major difficulties when contrasting the views from above with those from below in sixteenth-century Europe and later.

We also question Tilly's proclivity to downplay the significant gaps in the data on certain groups of ordinary people. For the United States, as an example, we must recognize the inadequacy of historical information on nonprivileged persons—particularly ethnic minorities—even for the nineteenth century. The dearth of knowledge about Mexican Americans in the U.S. Southwest dramatizes how oppressed groups are unable to accumulate more than a fragmentary history of themselves. Their "social memory" has in large part been obliterated by the power elite.

15. While recognizing the efforts by racial and ethnic women to attain a measure of dignity in their lives, we must be wary of romanticizing the role of the oppressed (Pettman 1991). The pain and suffering of women in traditional orders has been noted by researchers such as Potter and Potter (1990).

16. If social researchers are to give a voice to subordinate ethnic minorities, they must rethink the relationships between the self and others. For a perceptive analysis of this issue, see Tedlock (1991).

England (1992:33), in a highly informative discussion of research on Mayan linguistics, points to other issues that must be considered: "The role of linguistics can be seen as a scholarly role *within* a given political and social context. In many cases, this implies working with a subordinate language, which further implies intellectual, scholarly, and political responsibilities to that language and the people who speak it. These responsibilities are not the same as those we have when we work with dominant languages. We are asked, at the very least, to recognize the social and political roles we play and not to pretend that our role is 'purely scientific' and neutral."

References

Adas, Michael. 1989. *Machines as the Measure of Men: Science, Technology, and Ideologies of Western Dominance.* Ithaca: Cornell University Press.

Albrecht, Lisa, and Rose M. Brewer. 1990. "Bridges of Power: Women's Multicultural Alliances for Social Change." Pp. 2–22 in Lisa Albrecht and Rose M. Brewer, eds. *Bridges of Power.* Santa Cruz: New Society Publishers.

Alvarez, Sonia E. 1990. *Engendering Democracy in Brazil: Women's Movements in Transition Politics.* Princeton: Princeton University Press.

Asad, Talal., ed. 1973. *Anthropology and the Colonial Encounter.* London: Ithaca Press.

Attwood, Lynne. 1990. *The New Soviet Man and Woman.* Bloomington: Indiana University Press.

Bannister, Robert C. 1991. *Jessie Bernard.* New Brunswick: Rutgers University Press.

Bardhan, Kalpana. 1991. "Women and Feminism in a Stratified Society: Recent Developments in India." Pp. 163–97 in Sally J.M. Sutherland, ed. *Bridging Worlds: Studies on Women in South Asia.* Berkeley: Center for South and Southeast Asia Studies, Universityof California.

Bergmann, Barbara R. 1990. "Editorial." *Women's Studies Quarterly* 38:3–4.

Bernal, Martin. 1987. *Black Athena: The Afroasiatic Roots of Classical Civilization.* Vol. I. New Brunswick: Rutgers University Press.

———. 1991. *Black Athena: The Afroasiatic Roots of Classical Civilization.* Vol. II. New Brunswick: Rutgers University Press.

Bernstein, Gail Lee., ed. 1991. *Recreating Japanese Women, 1600–1945.* Berkeley: University of California Press.

Berreman, Gerald. 1981. *The Politics of Truth.* New Delhi: South Asian Publishers.

Blea, Irene. 1988. *Toward a Chicano Social Science.* Westport: Greenwood Press.

Blee, Kathleen M. 1991. *Women of the Klan: Racism and Gender in the 1920s.* Berkeley: University of California Press.

Buechler, Steven M. 1990. *Women's Movements in the United States.* New Brunswick: Rutgers University Press.

Burton, Antoinette M. 1990. "The White Woman's Burden: British Feminists and the Indian Woman, 1865–1915." *Women's Studies International Forum* 13:295–308.

Chafetz, Janet Saltzman. 1989. "Gender Equality: Toward a Theory of Change." Pp. 135–60 in Ruth Wallace, ed. *Feminism and Sociological Theory.* Newbury Park: Sage.

———. 1990. *Gender Equity: An Integrated Theory of Stability and Change.* Newbury Park: Sage.

Chow, Rey. 1991. "Violence in the Other Country: China as Crisis, Spectacle, and Women." Pp. 81–101 in Chandra Talpade Mohanty,Ann Russo, and Lourdes Torres, eds. *Third World Women and the Politics of Feminism.* Bloomington: Indiana University Press.

Collins, Patricia Hill. 1986. "Learning from the Outsider Within: The Sociological Significance of Black Feminist Thought." *Social Problems* 33:14–32.

———. 1990. *Black Feminist Thought.* Cambridge: Unwin Hyman.

Constable, Pamela, and Arturo Valenzuela. 1991. *Chile Under Pinochet: A Nation of Enemies.* New York. Norton.

Critchlow, James. 1991. *Nationalism in Uzbekistan.* Boulder: Westview Press.

De Leon, Arnoldo. 1983. *They Called Them Greasers.* Austin: University of Texas Press.

Desai, Anita. 1992. "Women Well Set Free!" *New York Review* 39 (January 16):42–45.

Diamond, M.J., ed. 1990. "Women and Revolution." Special Issue. *Dialectical Anthropology* 15:89–267.

Di Leonardo, Micaela. 1991. "Introduction: Gender, Culture, and Political Economy." Pp. 1–48 in Micaela di Leonardo, ed. *Gender at the Crossroads of Knowledge.* Berkeley: University of California Press.

Dower, John W. 1986. *War without Mercy: Race and Power in the Pacific War.* New York: Pantheon.

Du Bois, Ellen Carol, and Vicki L. Ruiz, eds. 1990. *Unequal Sisters: A Multicultural Reader in U.S. Women's History.* New York: Routledge.

Du Bois, W.E.B. 1973. *The Souls of Black Folk.* Millwood, N.Y.: Kraus-Thomson (orig. 1903).

Ebrey, Patricia Buckley. 1991. "Introduction." Pp. 1–24 in Rubie S. Watson and Patricia Buckley Ebrey, eds. *Marriage and Inequality in Chinese Society.* Berkeley: University of California Press.

Embree, John. 1939. *Suye Mura: A Japanese Village.* Chicago: University of Chicago Press.

England, Nora C. 1992. "Doing Mayan Linguistics in Guatemala." *Language* 68:29–35.

Enloe, Cynthia. 1990. *Bananas, Beaches & Bases.* Berkeley: University of California Press.

Evans, Sarah. 1980. *Personal Politics.* New York: Vintage.

Evans-Pritchard, E.E. 1940. *The Nuer.* Oxford: Clarendon Press.

Faludi, Susan. 1991. *Backlash.* New York: Crown.

Finley, M.I. 1986. *Ancient History: Evidence and Models*. New York: Viking Press.

Fischer, Michael M.J. 1986. "Ethnicity and the Post-Modern Arts of Memory." Pp. 194–233 in James Clifford and George E. Marcus, eds. *Writing Culture*. Berkeley: University of California Press.

Fisher, Hazel S. 1971. "The Women's Liberation Movement in the Process of Emergence: An Analysis of the Spokeswomen's Negative Valuations, Definition of Issues, and Images of the Future." Ph.D. dissertation, City University of New York.

Folbre, Nancy, and Marjorie Abel. 1989. "Women's Work and Women's Households: Gender Bias in the U.S. Census." *Social Research* 56:545–69.

Fonow, Mary Margaret and Judith A. Cook, eds. 1991. *Beyond Methodology*. Bloomington: Indiana University Press.

Fox-Genovese, Elizabeth. 1988. *Within the Plantation Household: Black and White Women of the Old South*. Chapel Hill: University of North Carolina Press.

———. 1990. *Feminism Without Illusions: A Critique of Individualism*. Chapel Hill: University of North Carolina Press.

Geertz, Clifford. 1988. *Works and Lives: The Anthropologist as Author*. Stanford: Stanford University Press.

Ghosh, Anjan. 1991. "The Stricture of Structure, or the Appropriation of Anthropological Theory." *Review* 14:55–77.

Gilligan, Carol. 1982. *In a Different Voice*. Cambridge: Harvard University Press.

Goffman, Erving. 1959. *The Presentation of Self in Everyday Life*. Garden City: Doubleday Anchor.

Goody, Jack. 1990. *The Oriental, the Ancient and the Primitive: Systems of Marriage and Family in the Pre-industrial Societies of Eurasia*. Cambridge: Cambridge University Press.

Gorelick, Sherry. 1991. "Contradictions of Feminist Methodology." *Gender & Society* 5:459–77.

Goyder, John. 1987. *The Silent Majority: Nonresponders on Sample Surveys*. Boulder: Westview Press.

Hallo, William W. 1990. "The Limits of Scepticism." *Journal of the American Oriental Society* 110:187–99.

Harding. Sandra. 1991. *Whose Science? Whose Knowledge?* Ithaca: Cornell University Press.

Headland, Thomas N., Kenneth L. Pike, and Marvin Harris, eds. 1990. *Emics and Etics: The Insider/ Outsider Debate*. Newbury Park: Sage.

Hedges, Chris. 1992. "Foreign Women Lured into Bondage in Kuwait." *New York Times* January 5, A4.

Herzfeld, Michael. 1987. *Anthropology through the Looking Glass: Critical Ethnography in the Margins of Europe*. Cambridge: Cambridge University Press.

Hirschman, Charles. 1983. "America's Melting Pot Reconsidered." *Annual Review of Sociology* 9:397–423.

Hobsbawn, Eric J. 1985. "History from Below—Some Reflections." Pp.63–73 in Frederick Krantz, ed. *History from Below: Studies in Popular Protest and Popular Ideology in Honour of George Rudé*. Montreal: Concordia University.

Hobsbawn, Eric, and Terrence Ranger, eds. 1983. *The Invention of Tradition*. Cambridge: Cambridge University Press.

hooks, bell. 1984. *Feminist Theory: From Margin to Center*. Boston: South End Press.

Inden, Ronald. 1990. *Imagining India*. Cambridge: Blackwell.

Jansen, Willy. 1989. "Ethnocentrism in the Study of Algerian Women." Pp. 289–310 in Arina Angerman, Geerte Binnema, Annemieke Keunen, Vefie Poels, and Jacqueline Zirkzee, eds. *Current Issues in Women's History*. London: Routledge.

Kanter, Rosabeth. 1977. *Men and Women of the Corporation*. New York: Basic Books.

Kelly, William W. 1991. "Directions in the Anthropology of Contemporary Japan." *Annual Review of Anthropology* 20:395–431.

Komarovsky, Mirra. 1991. "Some Reflections on the Feminist Scholarship in Sociology." *Annual Review of Sociology* 17:1–25.

Lawson, Steven F. 1991. "Freedom Then, Freedom Now: The Historiography of the Civil Rights Movement." *American Historical Review* 96:456–71.

Madsen, William. 1964. *The Mexican-Americans of South Texas*. New York: Holt, Rinehart, and Winston.

Mani, Lata. 1990. "Contentious Traditions: the Debate on *Sati* in Colonial India." Pp. 88–126 in Kumkum Sangari and Sudesh Vaid, eds. *Recasting Women*. New Brunswick: Rutgers University Press.

Marcus, George E., and Michael M.J. Fischer. 1986. *Anthropology as Cultural Critique*. Chicago: University of Chicago Press.

Maynard, Mary. 1990. "The Re-shaping of Sociology? Trends in the Study of Gender." *Sociology* 24:269–90.

Merton, Robert K. 1957. *Social Theory and Social Structure*. Rev. and enl. ed. New York: Free Press.

————. 1972. "Insiders and Outsiders: A Chapter in the Sociology of Knowledge." *American Journal of Sociology* 78:9–47.

Mohanty, Chandra Talpade. 1991. "Under Western Eyes: Feminist Scholarship and Colonial Discourses." Pp. 51–80 in Chandra Talpade Mohanty, Ann Russo, and Lourdes Torres, eds. *Third World Women and the Politics of Feminism*. Bloomington: Indiana University Press.

Moore, Joan. 1976. *Mexican Americans*. Englewood Cliffs, N.J.: Prentice-Hall.

Murphey, Rhoads. 1990. "Bigots or Informed Observers? A Periodization of Pre-Colonial English and European Writing on the Middle East. *Journal of the American Oriental Society* 110:291–303.

Najmabadi, Afsaneh. 1991. "Hazards of Modernity and Morality: Women, State and Ideology in Contemporary Iran." Pp. 48–76 in Deniz Kandiyoti, ed. *Women, Islam and the State*. Philadelphia:Temple University Press.

Nielsen, Joyce McCarl., ed. 1990. *Feminist Research Methods*. Boulder: Westview Press.

Novick, Peter. 1988. *That Noble Dream: The "Objectivity Question" and the American Historical Profession*. Cambridge: Cambridge University Press.

Paredes, Americo. 1977. "On Ethnographic Work among Minority Groups."*New Scholar* 6:1–32.

Parsons, Talcott. 1967. "Full Citizenship for the Negro American?" Pp. 422–65 in Talcott Parsons. *Sociological Theory and Modern Society*. New York: Free Press.

Pettman, Jan. 1991. "Racism, Sexism and Sociology." Pp. 187–97 in Gill Bottomley, Marie de Lepervanche, and Jeannie Martin, eds. *Intersexions*. North Sydney: Allen and Unwin.

Potter, Sulamith Heins, and Jack M. Potter. 1990. *China's Peasants*. Cambridge: Cambridge University Press.

Ramazanoglu, Caroline. 1989. *Feminism and the Contradictions of Oppression*. London: Routledge.

Reinharz, Shulamit. 1992. *Feminist Methods in Social Research*. New York: Oxford University Press.

Rich, Paul B. 1990. *Race and Empire in British Politics*. 2nd ed. Cambridge: Cambridge University Press.

Rollins, Judith. 1985. *Between Women*. Philadelphia: Temple University Press.

Rosaldo, Renato. 1985. "Chicano Studies, 1970–1984."*Annual Review of Anthropology* 14:405–27.

————. 1986. "From the Door of His Tent: The Fieldworker and the Inquisition." Pp. 77–97 in James Clifford and George Marcus, eds. *Writing Culture*. Berkeley: University of California Press.

Rubel, Arthur. 1966. *Across the Tracks: Mexican Americans in a Texas City*. Austin: University of Texas Press.

Russett, Cynthia. 1989. *Sexual Science: The Victorian Construction of Womanhood*. Cambridge: Harvard University Press.

Sacks, Karen Brodkin. 1989. "Toward a Unified Theory of Class, Race, and Gender." *American Ethnologist* 16:534–50.

Said, Edward W. 1979. *Orientalism*. New York: Vintage.

Samora, Julian, Joe Bernal, and Albert Pena. 1979. *Gunpowder Justice: A Reassessment of the Texas Rangers*. Notre Dame: University of Notre Dame Press.

Sanger, David E. 1992a. "Japan Admits Koreans Were Forced into Brothels." *New York Times*. January 14, A6.

————. 1992b. "Historian Expresses a Brutal Chapter." *New York Times* January 27, A4.

Sapir, Edward. 1949. *Selected Writings in Language, Culture, and Personality*. Berkeley: University of California Press.

Scott, James C. 1990. *Domination and the Arts of Resistance*. New Haven: Yale University Press.

Scott, Joan Wallach. 1988. *Gender and the Politics of History*. New York: Columbia University Press.

Sjoberg, Andrée F. 1990. "The Dravidian Contribution to the Development of Indian Civilization: A Call for a Reassessment." *Comparative Civilizations Review*, no. 23:40–74.

————. 1992. "The Impact of Dravidian on Indo-Aryan: An Overview." Pp. 507–29 in Edgar C. Polomé and Werner Winter, eds. *Reconstructing Languages and Cultures*. Berlin: Mouton de Gruyter.

Sjoberg, Gideon, Norma Williams, Ted R. Vaughan, and Andrée F. Sjoberg. 1991. "The Case Study Approach in Social Research: Some Basic Methodological Issues." Pp. 27–79 in Joe R. Feagin, Anthony M. Orum, and Gideon Sjoberg, eds. *A Case for the Case Study*. Chapel Hill: University of North Carolina Press.

Smith, Dorothy E. 1989. "Sociological Theory: Methods of Writing Patriarchy." Pp. 34–64 in Ruth A. Wallace, ed. *Feminism and Sociological Theory*. Newbury Park: Sage.

Smith, Joan, Jane Collins, Terence K. Hopkins, and Akbar Muhammad, eds. 1988. *Racism, Sexism, and the World-System*. New York: Greenwood Press.

Smith, Robert J. 1988. "Postscript." *American Ethnologist* 15:380–84.

Smith, Robert J., and Ella Lury Wiswell. 1982. *The Women of Suye Mura*. Chicago: University of Chicago Press.

Stacey, Judith, and Barrie Thorne. 1985. "The Missing Feminist Revolution in Sociology." *Social Problems* 32:310–16.

Stannard, David E. 1991. "Recounting the Fables of Savagery: Native Infanticide and the Functions of Political Myth." *Journal of American Studies* 25:381–418.

Stephen, Lynn. 1991. *Zapotec Women*. Austin: University of Texas Press.

Stock–Morton, Phyllis. 1991. "Finding Our Own Ways: Different Paths to Women's History in the United States." Pp. 59–77 in Karen Offen, Ruth Roach Pierson, and Jane Rendall, eds. *Writing Women's History: International Perspectives*. Bloomington: Indiana University Press.

Stoler, Ann Laura. 1991. "Carnal Knowledge and Imperial Power: Gender, Race, and Morality in Colonial Asia." Pp. 51–101 in Micaela di Leonardo, ed. *Gender at the Crossroads of Knowledge*. Berkeley: University of California Press.

Strobel, Margaret. 1991. *European Women and the Second British Empire*. Bloomington: Indiana University Press.

"Symposium on Dorothy E. Smith" 1992. *Sociological Theory* 10:60–98.

Tamanoi, Mariko Asano. 1990. "Women's Voices: Their Critique of Anthropology in Japan." *Annual Review of Anthropology* 19:17–37.

Tambiah, Stanley J. 1989. "Ethnic Conflict in the World Today." *American Ethnologist* 16:335–49.

Tedlock, Barbara. 1991. "From Participant Observation to the Observation of Participation: The Emergence of Narrative Ethnography." *Journal of Anthropological Research* 47:69–94.

Tharu, Susie, and K. Lalita. 1991. "Literature of the Ancient and Medieval Periods: Reading Against the Orientalist Grain." Pp. 41–64 in Susie Tharu and K. Lalita, eds. *Women Writing in India. 600 B.C. to the Present*. Vol. I. New York: Feminist Press.

Thompson, E.P. 1964. *The Making of the English Working Class*. New York: Pantheon.

Tilly, Charles. 1985. "Retrieving European Lives." Pp. 11–52 in Olivier Zunz, ed. *Reliving the Past.* Chapel Hill: University of North Carolina Press.

Tinker, Irene, ed. 1990. *Persistent Inequalities.* New York: Oxford University Press.

Walker, Cherryl. 1991. *Women and Resistance in South Africa.* New York: Monthly Review Press.

Wallace, Ruth A., ed. 1989. *Feminism and Sociological Theory.* Newbury Park: Sage.

Williams, Norma. 1989a. "Theoretical and Methodological Issues in the Study of Role Making." Pp. 167–84 in Norman Denzin, ed. *Studies in Symbolic Interaction: A Research Annual.* Vol. 10. Greenwich: JAI Press.

———. 1989b. "Role Taking and the Study of Majority/Minority Relationships." *Journal of Applied Behavioral Science* 25:175–86.

———. 1990. *The Mexican American Family: Tradition and Change.* Dix Hills, N.Y.: General Hall.

Wilson, William Julius. 1974. "The New Black Sociology: Reflections on the 'Insiders and Outsiders' Controversy." Pp. 322–38 in James E. Blackwell and Morris Janowitz, eds. *Black Sociologists: Historical and Contemporary Perspectives.* Chicago: University of Chicago Press.

———. 1987. *The Truly Disadvantaged.* Chicago: University of Chicago Press.

Wiswell, Ella L. 1988. "Suye Mura Fifty Years Later." *American Ethnologist* 15:369–80.

Wolf, Eric R. 1982. *Europe and the People without History.* Berkeley: University of California Press.

Zalk, Sue Rosenberg, and Janice Gordon-Kelter, eds. 1992. *Revolutions in Knowledge: Feminism in the Social Sciences.* Boulder: Westview Press.

PART II

INTRODUCTION

The second set of chapters in this book elaborates on the themes in the first section and on other topics as well. Although we do not recapitulate our discussion of the critical tradition outlined in the Introduction to the first part, it serves as a theoretical backdrop for this section. We can thus move directly to the contributions themselves. Although each chapter should be read in its own terms, we believe certain interrelated themes deserve to be underscored.

The chapters by Littrell and Saxton are a follow-up to the critique of the natural science model detailed in the earlier chapters. Littrell has provided striking evidence, based on his own research experience, that demonstrates that the natural science model, as it has been interpreted by sociologists, rests on a "consensus model" of social research. Most researchers—and sociologists are no exception—assume that the researched will cooperate with them. Many sociologists proceed as if this cooperation is part of the natural order of things, even after they encounter the problem of nonrespondents in social surveys.

Littrell's investigations reveal that the premise of cooperation between researcher and the researched is empirically incorrect for strategic kinds of sociological research. For instance, persons in powerful large-scale organizations typically conceal data from outsiders: social researchers, policy makers, and the broader citizenry. Current textbooks on research methods do not inform students of the social reality they are likely to encounter if they are concerned with gathering meaningful data about the nature of powerful organizations in modern societies. Under these circumstances, sociologists can do little to advance the cause of democracy—if, indeed, one assumes that democracy rests on a high degree of openness with respect to debate about issues, including relevant information about them. Thus, we find Littrell committed to a normative sociology.

Littrell points to selected ways current social barriers to the study of powerful organizations might be circumvented, but he also discusses some of the perils in doing so. He is concerned, too, with the role of sociological researchers in colleges and universities outside the orbit of research universities. He makes a case that the former may have opportunities to carry out research that sociologists in the latter setting may be more constrained from conducting.

Saxton picks up on selected aspects of Littrell's argument but takes them in a different direction. Saxton is deeply troubled by the future of sociology at comprehensive universities and liberal arts colleges. For him, sociologists, in order to sustain and justify the existence of the discipline, must be able to make a difference within their own setting. Therefore, he calls on sociologists to become "citizen-scholars." In this capacity, sociologists are able to integrate their teaching, research, and community activities and thereby make their presence felt within the social setting in which they live and work. He perceives this goal as most effectively achieved by adopting a symbolic interactionist perspective.

Saxton has isolated a set of social issues that deserves careful consideration by all sociologists. The majority of sociologists who occupy academic positions teach at nonresearch universities. Yet they often attempt to emulate the activities of members of the "elite" departments from which they have received their degrees. But sociologists at comprehensive universities and colleges do not command the resources of their research-based colleagues. All too frequently, sociologists in these former settings have not reflected on the possibility of creating new roles for themselves—roles that advance the calling of sociology (and of civic discourse) within comprehensive universities and colleges. Their socialization into positive science (Saxton's terminology) means that they are ill prepared to rethink their role and contribute substantially not only to their local or regional setting but also to the larger sociological enterprise. Most of the leaders of the American Sociological Association advocate the role model of sociologists at elite universities. But such a definition of the situation can be self-defeating. If sociologists become citizen-scholars they have a countertradition to draw upon. They can anchor themselves in the intellectual heritage of the American pragmatists, and they will in effect do what Robert Bellah and his colleagues believe sociologists should be doing in order to create the "good society."

We have juxtaposed Knottnerus's chapter and those by Littrell and Saxton. Knottnerus provides us with an understanding of how the Department of Sociology at the University of Wisconsin at Madison—the No. 1 ranked department in the United States in terms of prestige—was able to legitimate itself. Sewell, who was its builder and guiding spirit, justified his research activities, as well as those of many of his colleagues and students, by making the claim that the "status-attainment model" was based on rigorous quantitative research methods.

What Knottnerus indicates is that the status-attainment model was supported by, and in turn supported, the dominant images of the American society in Sewell's era. This model resonated with the ideal of upward mobility for many Americans. Concomitantly, the scientific methods Sewell advocated were justified in the eyes of his fellow sociologists and the funding agencies. Thus, Sewell's findings, and the research procedures on which they rested, were "validated" by the images of American society of his day. As the American society of the 1950s and 1960s has undergone profound change, many sectors of the U.S. population are far less optimistic about their upward mobility than when Sewell wrote. In the light of new social and cultural circumstances, the validity of the status-attainment model is being challenged by various social scientists. More than ever, we must ask ourselves questions Sewell seldom, if ever, addressed. For example, is the status-attainment model generalizable to other social orders? We hypothesize that this model is largely irrelevant for studying the former Soviet Union, rent as it is by deep ethnic divisions and facing fundamental revisions in the organizational structure that supported the traditional stratification system. Race and ethnic conflict, as well as the role of large-scale organizations in stratification arrangements, were not part of Sewell's image of American society or of the model on which his reputation rested. One by-product of Knottnerus's analysis is a subtle questioning of the natural science model as practiced by Sewell.

We turn from a discussion of sociological research at a prestige research university and consider the plight of sociologists who live and work on the margins of academia or who function as applied sociologists outside academia. The problems of these sociologists, which are often brushed aside by sociologists at research universities, are considered by Hartung and by Lyson and Squires.

Beth Hartung focuses on the temporaries—the least visible and most vulnerable members of the teaching faculty. Her research suggests that these persons are difficult to locate through probability sampling. Because of Hartung's chapter, we are able to consider sociologists not only from the vantage point of the privileged sector of academia but from the perspective of its most marginal members.

In our judgment the failure of the American Sociological Association to give due attention to this group indicates, indirectly at least, as much about the leadership of the ASA as it does about the temporaries. By playing down the plight of the invisible professoriate, the privileged sector of the ASA may in the long run undermine some of its own privileges. They must recognize that their students need to be placed, and most newly minted doctorates will not find positions in the research universities from which they receive their degrees. Graduate students, in particular, need more information about the whys and wherefores of the existence of temporaries.

From our perspective, Hartung's chapter relates back to the bottom-up vs. top-down orientation in social research articulated in chapter 4. This chapter also is linked to the chapter on the bureaucratization of sociology (chapter 2). We would surmise, on the basis of existing theory and data, that temporaries serve the "interests" of the managers of contemporary colleges and universities. The managers save money by employing temporaries, and, more important, they achieve greater social control over a set of vulnerable employees.

The chapter by Lyson and Squires deals with sociologists who are engaged in applied pursuits outside academia. As they observe, the emphasis on training sociologists for applied positions is a worthy calling. We also subscribe to their view that these sociologists must be more than mere technicians. In order to apply sociological knowledge in an effective manner, they must be trained to use their sociological imagination, and this involves a grounding in fundamental theoretical traditions within the discipline. These sociologists should ideally be reflectively aware of the constraints and opportunities of the organizational settings in which they work. Again, the problems raised by Lyson and Squires seem to be given scant attention by the American Sociological Association or in the curricula of many departments of sociology.

Dioff follows up one aspect of a theme developed in chapter 4: the bottom-up versus the top-down perspective. His primary focus is on examining American sociology from the vantage point of the Third World. This problem area will increasingly plague American sociology as the gap between highly industrialized and developing nations grows rather than lessens. We must be able to perceive ourselves through the eyes of our politically and economically disadvantaged colleagues in other nations and not simply impose our views on them.

We conclude with Galliher and Nelson's chapter on the convoluted history of *The American Sociologist*. This journal, of which Talcott Parsons was the first editor, was deemed inappropriate to the mission of the American Sociological Association. It was thus terminated for reasons, as Galliher and Nelson suggest, that are somewhat ambiguous. To be sure, Transaction Publications now publishes it, but its circulation has dropped and it does not have the power base of the ASA.

The history of *The American Sociologist* (TAS) provides us with knowledge about the ASA and its leadership. At the very time that the executive office of the ASA acknowledges that sociology as a discipline faces serious problems, sociologists have no official outlet in the ASA for articles that analyze the current state of the discipline—and its future direction—in a scholar manner. *Footnotes* does not provide an adequate form for reasoned and sustained debate about alternative directions of the discipline with respect to theory, research, and practice. In effect the leadership of the ASA saw fit to marginalize debate about the foundations of the discipline itself. The effort to inhibit intellectual dissent makes this kind of edited book all the more necessary. We sincerely hope the contributions to this volume will be read within this social context.

5

BUREAUCRATIC SECRETS AND ADVERSARIAL METHODS OF SOCIAL RESEARCH

Boyd Littrell

In this chapter I consider a methodological issue having to do with the relation between bureaucratic power and social science. The issue concerns what methods sociologists (and other social scientists) may use to collect data when powerful organizations resist being studied. Sociologists' responses to powerful resistance and, therefore, the politics of social research and its consequences for sociological knowledge form the inquiry of the chapter.

Admittedly power and the politics of social research have been widely discussed (see, e.g., Denzin 1989; Emerson 1983; Starr and Collier 1989; Sjoberg 1967). I add to this work a discussion of "adversary methods" and then turn to their far reaching methodological implications. The basic presupposition underlying the chapter is that no independent social science can exist without adversary methods. Any social science without such methods will be subordinated to existing structures of power. And to the degree any social science is subordinated to power, it cannot develop independent or "disinterested" theories of social relations.

I believe adversary methods will be more important in the future because bureaucratic structures of power increasingly will control more detailed information about more detailed aspects of personal and collective life. New technologies make this information more malleable, and they have made it more valuable. The growing volume of information, its malleability, and its utility for legitimating power make the control of information and adversary methods especially important in a bureaucratic era.

My discussion of adversary methods develops variations on a familiar criticism of modern science.[1] This criticism warns that social context makes scientists and science less "objective" than many want to believe. The more specific variation developed here is that bureaucratic organizations now form the most important social context of science. Bureaucratic organizations have distinctive requirements for survival, and I believe science increasingly is pressed into the service of those requirements. In doing so, bureaucracy subordinates science to its own ends. In this respect, at least, what is true of science generally also is true of sociology.

207

Adversary methods are intended to address the bureaucratic subordination of science. The theme is developed in five sections. It begins with a working definition of adversary methods; then it offers a case study of a research project where adversary methods were used. The case study provides concrete circumstances and establishes a shared context for three more theoretical sections that follow. In "Adversary Methods, the Role of the Researcher and the Social Construction of Data," I examine distinctive ways researchers must think abut their role and its relation to data. In "The Bureaucratic Secret and the Methodological Significance of Bureaucracy," I examine why agents of bureaucratic organizations may be especially resistant to researchers. Finally, in "Sociology, Adversary Methods, and Democratic Society," I propose a normative conception of sociology that both justifies and limits the use of adversary methods.

Adversary and Cooperative Methods of Social Research

A working definition of adversary methods draws on Denzin's discussion of the research act. Denzin emphasizes the importance of the social relationship between researcher and researched. He assumes that data are the products of negotiations between researchers and researched, and that the "research act" (or the acts that comprise it) affects the social milieu under investigation. Adversary methods require the same assumptions but require three additional ones. They must be considered (1) when social groups or their agents define researchers as antagonists; (2) when agents act to block, misdirect, or mislead researchers; and (3) when researchers decide to proceed with projects, despite opposition.

One may characterize the relations of a research act along many dimensions. But adversary methods suggest a dimension of "cooperation/antagonism" between researcher and researched. The typology outlined in figure 5.1 usefully characterizes this dimension.[2]

Cell 4 describes an adversary research act as one of mutual antagonism between researcher and researched. Researchers must, in this situation, consider adversary methods in order to sustain a research project.

Adversary methods are rarely discussed by social scientists. Researchers are more likely to withdraw from mutually antagonistic settings than to sustain projects in them. In fact, most widely accepted methods of research presuppose the cooperative relations suggested by cell 1. In such cases researchers have agreed with the researched about access, about the spaces in which they may circulate, about the kinds of information they may collect, and often about arrangements for publication of findings.

The cooperative assumption is accepted so widely that sociologists virtually define research methods as techniques for assuring themselves and others that their presence does not distort a research milieu or else that they can measure those distortions and adjust their analyses so as to remove the distorting effects of their presence. Such a conception of methods simply ignores purposive efforts to mislead researchers and direct attempts to hide important information from them.

Figure 5.1. The Research Act:
Cooperation/Antagonism

Researcher's Relationship to Researched

	Cooperative	Antagonistic
Cooperative	1	2
Researched Relationship to Researcher		
Antagonistic	3	4 Adversary Methods.

If illusory thinking consists in believing something to be true because one wants or needs it to be so, the cooperative assumption may lead to illusion. The cooperative assumption teases researchers into the belief that widely accepted methods automatically produce objective information or its best approximation. We might call the belief that methods appropriate to cooperative settings are to be preferred for all settings the "illusion of good methods".

The illusion of good methods has strong psychological and organizational supports. The illusion of good methods supports researchers' psychological need to believe that widely accepted methods employed in self-disciplined and self-restrained ways will bring under their control the objectivity science requires. Organizations also support the illusion of good methods. Cooperative research settings often provide the quickest and most desirable rewards. Cooperative research has helped U.S. sociology find its place in the web of bureaucratic relations that have been emerging especially since World War II. In his farewell to the nation, President Eisenhower, who was neither a radical nor a methodologist, warned against the organizational supports for cooperation and about their effect on science. He stated (quoted in Cousins 1987:74):

... the free university, historically the fountainhead of free ideas and scientific discovery, has experienced a revolution in the conduct of research.

Partly because of the huge costs involved, a government contract becomes virtually a substitute for intellectual curiosity . . .

The prospect of domination of the nation's scholars by Federal employment, project allocations, and the power of money is ever present—and is gravely to be regarded.

In summary, in this section I have drawn a distinction between adversary and cooperative methods of research. The distinction is rooted in different relations between researchers and researched. While I have not rejected the value of widely accepted methods of research designed for cooperative settings, I have warned against the illusion that methods designed for cooperative settings are always better or even appropriate.

The distinction between adversary and cooperative settings is the first step needed to support the argument that no independent sociology can exist unless it is capable of conducting (and in fact does conduct) research against the resistance of powerful "others." The next section presents a brief case study of an adversary setting where adversary methods were employed.

White Paper II: A Brief History of a Research Project

In 1980, the planning committee of the Health Planning Council of the Midlands (HPCM) in Omaha decided to examine why hospital prices in Omaha were, comparatively speaking, extremely high. HPCM was a federally chartered Health Service Agency established under provisions of the National Health Planning and Resources Development Act of 1974, (U.S. Congress 1976). Analysis of hospital costs were part of the agency's health planning and cost-reduction mandate. (In order to avoid the ambiguity of the word "costs" here, I refer to money consumers pay to purchase hospital services, rather than to money hospitals spend in order to provide those services.)

Dr. David Ambrose, then chair of HPCM's planning committee, was asked to direct the study. The committee finished its work by submitting to the HPCM board a White Paper. The main conclusion of the study was that Omaha had 700 or more excess hospital beds. This, the report claimed, led to wasteful duplication and underutilization of space, equipment, and in turn led to very high prices for hospital services.

The planning committee sought data from local hospitals and from relevant provider associations. These associations often declined to provide any information. Sometimes they provided alternative or partial information. These refusals were seen by researchers as the initial acts of resistance by providers.

The planning committee developed the *White Paper* from HPCM's own sources of information, which included information from state government and other public sources. The principal recommendation of the *White Paper* was that about 700 hospital beds (the equivalent of two medium-size hospitals) should be delicensed. The recommendation was controversial and angered many providers and other prominent citizens. The HPCM board, like the boards of most HSAs, was powerfully influenced by providers (see, e.g., Enthoven 1980:101-5; Aaron and Schwartz 1984:5) and refused to adopt the *White Paper* as an official planning document.

Critics on the HPCM board, who were often providers, argued that the *White Paper* had ignored other possible explanations of high costs. The planning committee acknowledged that other factors did affect costs but claimed these factors were roughly randomly distributed through the crucial variable, which was the number of hospital beds. The committee also argued that other explanations of high costs were irrelevant to the central conclusion that many hospital beds should be eliminated in order to reduce duplication. Providers indirectly acknowledged the problem by privately offering to "close" but not delicense about 300 beds. HPCM rejected that offer because the beds providers offered up already were empty because of citywide underutilization. HPCM's longer-range agenda was to eliminate *licensed* beds in order to establish a more reasonable estimate of future needs and, thereby, eventually to reduce the future building of hospital capacity in the metropolitan area.

Researchers interpreted the board's refusal to adopt the *White Paper* as a second act of resistance coordinated by providers on the board. Soon after the HPCM board shelved the *White Paper*, I was invited to participate on a task force whose purpose was to prepare a far more comprehensive analysis of the relationship between Omaha's excessive supply of resources and its very high hospital costs. The final report of this group was formally titled *White Paper II* (Health Planning Council of the Midlands 1987).

Members of the task force discussed provider resistance at their first meeting. They agreed to accept hospital cooperation if offered, but agreed that they should expect antagonism and should proceed with or without provider cooperation. That decision made, the project moved rapidly toward an adversarial setting.

Hospital representatives on the HPCM board suggested that we develop a cooperative relationship. They offered a "more appropriate methodology," and suggested that we schedule meetings to work through the extensive documentation needed to implement that methodology. Members of the task force agreed, but set out criteria by which to judge the nature of the cooperation. Crucial among these criteria was that hospitals provide data from their records to the task force.

The new "model for planning" proved not to be a model for analyzing communitywide hospital costs at all. When providers' representatives were asked to provide data, they waffled, promised to get back to us, and later declined. Members of the task force concluded that "analysis paralysis" had developed, broke off the meetings, and designed the new project. With this decision, the research project became fully adversarial.

Months later, HPCM obtained correspondence that confirmed researchers' suspicions about the offer of a "new methodology." The Omaha Medical Providers Association (OMPA, a fictional name) had conducted meetings about the task force's efforts and distributed written summaries to its members. The letters (nicknamed "the deep throat letters" because of the way they came into our possession) provide a rare glimpse of powerful organizations at work to thwart researchers. The subcommittee acknowledged a basic dilemma with respect to the earlier *White Paper*: "If the `White Paper' is given to the news media in its current form the (OMPA) would be able to expose it for the inaccurate and fallacious information it contains; although if the (OMPA) helps HPCM staff eliminate these inaccuracies and the paper is then published, it could then prove embarrassing to the (OMPA) and the various hospitals within the community."

During the next several days OMPA's subcommittee developed a three-pronged plan to attack HPCM's task force. First, they decided to introduce "a copy of the `Implications of Cost Effectiveness Analysis of Medical Technology ...' The assessment includes a main report and five supporting papers." This was the "more appropriate methodology" that led HPCM researchers to conclude providers were trying to create analysis paralysis.

Second, the subcommittee proposed to move Dr. Ambrose away from the *White Paper* project ". . . without embarrassment and *not to eliminate the inaccuracies in the 'White Paper,' but to have all these inaccuracies delineated and prepared in such a manner to expose the true incompetency that exists within the HPCM staff.*" (Italics added.) These remarks ignore the fact that HPCM researchers had requested information from hospitals in the first place in order to prevent inaccuracies.

Third, the subcommittee recommended that a public relations campaign be designed "to gain public support for the [local] hospitals by delineating what the hospitals have done for the community as opposed to what HPCM has done for the community."

Clearly, the research setting had become adversarial, and this shaped the research design of the *White Paper II* project. Researchers could not obtain measures of case mix, charges, and diagnoses that a cooperative situation might have produced. Instead, we developed a design that compared hospital costs and several other variables in several midwestern cities. The nature of the design restricted many of our conclusions to those that were appropriate for ordinal measures. We could determine Omaha's rank order among an array of cities, and we knew such information would allow us to draw broad conclusions about factors related to medical costs.

When *White Paper II* was finished it was nearly 180 pages long. It consisted of 50 pages of text and about 130 pages of detailed comparative information on eighteen midwestern cities. The project showed that Omaha had far more medical resources and that users of Omaha hospitals paid far higher prices than patients in comparable cities. *White Paper II* originally announced that area hospitals charged about $67 million (later revised to about $55 million) in excess of what consumers in comparable cities were charged. To put that figure in some perspective, a few years later a legislative task force estimated the cost of providing medical service to all Nebraskans at poverty or Medicaid levels to be about $58 million (not adjusted for inflation).

In keeping with HPCM's charter, several copies of *White Paper II* were issued to the press, to providers, and to others who had shown continuing interest in hospital costs. Also in keeping with the charter, HPCM called a press conference to announce the release of *White Paper II*, and to announce the date for a public hearing. Comments and testimony were invited from providers and the public. The findings announced at the press conference prompted yet more antagonism.

In response to HPCM's announcement, OMPA called a press conference to announce it had hired a big eight accounting firm to discredit *White Paper II*. Hospital representatives tried to discredit the findings in public statements. Both sides held additional press conferences. The conflict was very sharp and lasted for several months during 1981. The accounting firm's report was announced at an OMPA press conference, where HPCM researchers challenged both the firm's findings and its methods.

We return to the case study later. But it already has served four important purposes for my argument that sociology must institutionalize ways of conducting adversary research as a condition of its independence. First, as an empirical case of an adversary setting, it bars the criticism that adversary settings are merely plausible abstractions. Second, the discussion describes how real agents of powerful organizations attempted to stop, divert, and resist a legitimate research project. Third, the case study points to the necessity of devising alternative research designs to cope with adversary settings. Fourth, the use of press conferences foretells something about methods researchers can employ in adversary settings.

In order to explore these matters further, the case study must be set in a broader methodological perspective. The role of the researcher, the nature of data, and the kinds of conclusions one may draw involve methodological issues as well as technical concerns. The following section examines adversary methods in the context of these methodological concerns.

Adversary Methods, the Role of the Researcher, and Social Construction of Data

Adversary research involves more than selecting one rather than another method from the shed of sociological tools. Researchers in adversary settings must consider different issues. Differentials of power change the role of the researcher and the social construction of data.

The Researcher's Power Base

When research settings become mutually antagonistic, the relative power of the antagonists may determine entirely (and will always affect) the outcome of the research. The relative power of researcher and researched, in turn, depends primarily on the institutional supports of the antagonists. Researchers must compare their power bases (Sjoberg and Miller 1973) with those of the researched in order to determine what data, if any, they can obtain. If researchers can develop useful data, they must consider how the differentials of power affect the selection of methods and the collection of data. And these considerations shape the range of possible conclusions researchers may draw.

Structural considerations largely determine sociologists' power bases and explain why sociologists are poorly prepared for adversary research. Most sociologists who conduct research (other than for personal or instructional purposes) work in one of five settings that have weak power bases: government service; private corporations or practices; elite universities or foundations; nonelite doctoral degree departments; or four year "comprehensive" colleges and universities.

Most sociologists who work in government service occupy powerful enough institutional bases for cooperative research, but weak ones for adversary research. Government agencies must operate within a complex system of rules; their research budgets are allocated with an eye to current administration policies; and they are sensitive to political pressures. They must strive to be, or appear to be, neutral in the face of competing constituencies. They tend (imperfectly) to protect themselves and their agencies by funding "sure things." Government employees face clear restrictions on what they may investigate and even more limiting restrictions on what they may say about their research.

Clear exceptions to these generalizations about government agencies can be found, notably in law-enforcement agencies. The Internal Revenue Service (IRS) and the Securities and Exchange Commission (SEC), for example, conduct research against the wishes of very powerful organizations. But law-enforcement agencies have technical limitations as research tools. Investigations often are guided by narrowly defined rules of procedure and evidence; they often must be conducted secretly over long periods of time; and they may exclude sociologically relevant information if it has little or no legal importance. Thus, while information from government investigations may provide useful sociological data, they do not provide a very solid basis for designing sociological research.

Sociologists in private corporations and private practice face fewer and less complex rules, but they are more sensitive to corporate control and public goodwill. Sociologists in corporations usually work within a system that legitimates controversy only at very high levels. The incomes of sociologists in private practice are particularly responsive to community "goodwill," which tough controversy inevitably jeopardizes.

Sociologists in elite universities and foundations face pressures similar to their colleagues in government agencies and corporations. Such organizations routinely look to elite universities and foundations for research and development advice. Sociologists working in those settings serve in a similar capacity to that of private consultants and often perform important public service. While the prestige of elite institutions provides sociologists with a small measure of freedom, the boundaries of that freedom in practice are determined by the governmental and corporate interests that fund their projects.[3]

Foundations, like governments, can fund research against the opposition of powerful groups. More often, however, foundations in search of "the biggest bang for their bucks" fund research that will have an immediate impact. While working on *White Paper II*, for example, the American Hospital Association (AHA) and the Robert Wood Johnson foundations both sponsored programs designed to explore the control of high hospital costs. Both programs required cooperation among researchers, state and local governments, and providers as a criterion of selection. While both research programs served important purposes, the requirement of cooperation eliminated the possibility of adversary research.

Unlike elite universities, doctoral-granting nonelite universities are not consulted automatically by government and corporations. They compete fiercely with one another for funds from these sources.[4] That competition drives researchers away from controversy because controversial research *may* be viewed as risky by governments and foundations. In addition, the centerist pressures exerted by institutional review boards, by peer-review practices, and by administrators pose formidable barriers.

Sociologists at four-year colleges and universities usually have heavier teaching loads, smaller research budgets, fewer computing facilities, and no specialized research centers. At some of these institutions, faculty members must set good examples for students, and adversary projects rarely are considered to be good examples. Although sociologists in such universities may find ways to conduct adversary projects, limitations of time and resources dictate that these projects nearly always will be small ones.

Sociologists' professional associations offer no assistance. They have no legal departments, no legal defense funds, and provide little or no assistance in brokering these services with public-interest organizations. Only as I wrote the final draft of this chapter, some eight years after *White Paper II* was completed, did I think of calling the American Sociological Association for assistance with potential legal difficulties. At the time, however, I did contact a public-interest law firm in Washington, D.C.

To summarize, most of the places where sociologists work offer sufficient power bases for cooperative research, but very little power for adversary research. Sociologists have little or no help from their professional associations. At present, then, sociologists who face antagonism must either withdraw from their research or find other power bases.

Given the costs of building organizations from the ground up, the most practical choice will be to join forces with existing organizations. But leaving academic settings takes sociologists yet another step away from conventional research. Stepping outside the academic setting to join HPCM's task force made it possible to evade the intense cooperative pressures imposed by the relation between big money and big education. But it also forced changes in the researcher's role and in the collection of data.

Public Participation and the Role of the Researcher

Although HPCM had little power to enforce its health planning recommendations, it had several resources for research. It had a small staff and a small research budget to carry through its planning responsibilities. HPCM had experts in the field of hospital administration. It received copies of hospital utilization and cost reports from state government. It received copies of pending legislation, announcements of numerous policy changes from state and federal governments, and information from state agencies that monitored or regulated medical practice. Finally, HPCM brought together consumers and providers in regular meetings that academic sociologists could not call independently. Such meetings provided opportunities to observe and participate in extensive discussions by a variety of knowledgeable persons about the delivery of medical service. That participation, in turn, provided a great deal of knowledge about the social organization of medical services. In brief, HPCM provided a small, specialized research center.

Participation at HPCM provided a good operating base for research, but it also reshaped the role of the researcher. HPCM partially altered the institutional identity of the academic researchers. The new identity brought both assets and liabilities. The partially changed identity helped legitimate my own involvement in health planning, in ways academic settings could not. It also meant that I had to do the work on my own time.

Participation at HPCM diluted the researcher's role as "expert" by mixing it with the role of citizen. That change, ironically, helped rather than inhibited the research. People outside academic settings hold different views of expertise than do academic insiders. Academic outsiders recognize, for example, that "expertise" is bought and sold so regularly and with such ease that it has primarily tactical value. While real skills are respected, "experts" very often are not. That is more apt to be true of sociologists than of lawyers, financial experts, accountants, actuaries, and the like. Social scientists, for example, are apt to be considered experts in such "peripheral" areas as human resources. An interested citizen, however, who comfortably trades technical punches with people who claim to be experts, can benefit from a broader social ambivalence toward "experts."

HPCM's institutional identity also enabled the three primarily academic researchers to distance ourselves from our universities. *White Paper II* triggered bitter controversy in Omaha, but it did not attract the formal concern of university officials that it probably would have, had the project been university-sponsored research.[5]

The HPCM identity reshaped the researchers' roles in other ways. Sometimes it required that the researchers become public and controversial, rather than private and detached. Although much work was done in seclusion, some of it had to be done in public. The researchers were accountable both to an interested public and to technical standards. The project had to be defended both on television and in private discussions among experts. These different criteria of accountability pose problems for which no easy answers exist.[6]

Finally, the role of researcher was stretched in ways that initially appeared to be beyond the scope of the *White Paper II* project. In exchange for the resources HPCM provided, the academic researchers donated time to other HPCM projects. In addition to service on the HPCM board, HPCM's director of planning and one or more of us met with leaders from four labor unions to discuss the effect of rising hospital costs on their pension and welfare funds. This led to four separate analyses of Omaha unions' hospital cost experience. We met with the management of Nebraska Blue Cross/Blue Shield to discuss and compare estimates of excessive hospital charges; and we met with other organizations as well.

"Community participation," it seems, requires participation in the community in senses quite different from many discussions of participant observation. Community participation stretched and expanded the researchers' role. The analysis of union data and the discussions with Blue Cross/Blue Shield and other organizations produced systematic data that later served as checks on *White Paper II*. Discussions with news reporters and state officials also added information to the *White Paper II* project. This stretching of the researchers' roles affected the social construction of data, the next issue to be discussed.

Public Participation and the Social Construction
of Data by Adversary Methods

All social science data are constructed within the context of the research act. In cooperative settings, this can be done with relative ease and data can be constructed differently than in adversarial settings. Researchers in cooperative settings often can define problems in ways that permit them to use any of a variety of research methods. They may select methods for their statistical power or their contextual richness. They may build redundant measures into their projects. In adversary settings, however, one must learn what information can be obtained and then convert this information into data by working it into a partly fixed and partly evolving research design. HPCM researchers developed guidelines for the *White Paper II* project. Much later, however, we learned that some data from labor unions applied directly to the issue the task force was examining. In adversary settings data emerge in ways that cannot be predetermined.

The give and take of public participation led to three specific adversary methods. Press conferences, public hearings and litigation were added to investigative reporters' techniques (Patner 1988; Sjoberg and Miller 1973) as methods of adversary research. The HPCM project illustrates how such tools, rooted in public participation, became methods for the construction of sociological data.

White Paper II initially estimated excessive hospital charges to have been about $67 million. That much money was newsworthy. Reporters began independent investigations to check HPCM's findings. Although they did not produce a great deal of independent data, they did produce crucial bits and pieces of information. Their findings and their questions often helped us check our own work.

Much information was exchanged with reporters in "coded" conversations. Within the shared context of the setting, for example, a reporter's question "What do you make of Dr. X's new equipment?" had clearly understood meanings. It meant first, "Have you heard that Dr. X has new equipment?" And second, it meant "What does that imply about her association with hospital Y?" Such conversations guided both reporters and researchers into new areas of inquiry. On one occasion a reporter asked us to help him interpret hospital financial statements they had obtained through the Freedom of Information Act. In doing so, he gave us financial information about hospitals from a different source with which to compare our own.

The duel of press conferences moved into high gear when OMPA's accounting firm finished its evaluation of *White Paper II*. OMPA called a press conference at which two of the accounting firm's local executives spoke for several minutes. The accounting firm proposed that HPCM should change our estimate of the total amount of excess charges. They rightly noted that HPCM's work was based on a calendar year. They observed, again correctly, that Omaha's hospitals operated on fiscal years ending in different months, and that our use of the calendar year failed to reflect that fact. On this basis they recommended a downward adjustment of approximately $500,000, to which HPCM agreed. The press conference developed new financial data, and it improved HPCM's analysis.

The accounting firm also reported that it had used HPCM's data, even though it had direct access to information from the hospitals. Had HPCM's estimate been significantly overstated, the firm could have produced new information to demonstrate that fact. It did not do so.

To summarize, press conferences served as a research method. They produced new data that helped HPCM to improve its analysis. The use of press conferences as a method for data collection differs from their use for public relations or political purposes. It is a powerful, though limited, tool for sociologists who face adversary settings.

A public hearing became a second adversarial method for building data. HPCM's charter required it to hold public hearings in order to offer supporters and critics an opportunity to present supporting or contradictory evidence. HPCM's hearing produced crucially important data that supported *White Paper IIs* analysis. The labor unions and other organizations we had worked with— work that expanded the role of the researchers—presented their own analyses of excessive costs.

A senior executive with Blue Cross/Blue Shield of Nebraska testified at the public hearing. He opened his testimony with a carefully worded statement in support of HPCM's findings (Health Planning Council of the Midlands 1981:J1): "*White Paper II* is, in our opinion, a sincere attempt to address the question of community need, and it should not be dismissed on the basis that some may view it as inflammatory in certain respects or inaccurate in others. It squares generally with our publicized position, and we support it as a basis for honest appraisal by all parties concerned with this community's hospital needs."

This statement, though guarded, was very important. The executive represented an insurance company with powerful provider ties. Although his appearance at the hearing involved personal risks, its broadly stated support provided important confirmation of the general analysis presented in *White Paper II*. Blue Cross/Blue Shield continuously analyzes its own very large base of patient data. Had *White Paper II* been seriously wrong, the company's data would have alerted him, and he would have avoided the hearing.

The public hearing produced other data as well. The Western Electric Corporation presented independently developed data based on its own insurance experience. They compared average dollar amounts spent per employee in Omaha with that spent in their plants in other U.S. cities. Claims paid at the Omaha works were "28.2 percent higher than the . . . average" in 1979 and 43 percent higher in 1980 (Health Planning Council of the Midlands 1981:J-7).

Some of the labor unions we met with developed comparative data with locals in other cities. One union reported the cost charged per hour for health benefits to be about 49 percent higher in Omaha than the average hourly charge for locals in comparable cities in a five-state region. Three other unions reported similar differences (Health Planning Council of the Midlands 1981:J14-22).

To summarize, the public hearing provided an opportunity to produce new data from sources other than HPCM's. In that way, the public hearing allowed HPCM researchers to address questions of validity. HPCM's data and data from these other organizations consistently pointed to excess charges in Omaha of about one-third. The public hearing provided an occasion for others to introduce these new data.

Litigation, the third and last method of adversarial research, was suggested during the Omaha project. Although it never materialized, litigation is so obvious a source of data and raises such important issues for researchers in adversary settings that it must be mentioned. The subject arose at a HPCM board meeting. A middle manager from a hospital, who also served on the board, sat down beside me and asked if I had ever thought about being sued by the hospitals. He added that he would have sued us "just to keep you busy" and to discredit the effort. A few weeks later, another provider asked a similar question. Whether these questions were "messages" or simply part of the needling produced by the antagonistic setting, I did not know then and do not know now. I responded in both cases by saying we were prepared to be and willing to be sued. (I had made initial preparations with two nationally known law firms outside Omaha.) I added that counterlitigation and subpoena power would force the hospitals to produce data we had been seeking from the outset.

Litigation is costly and wasteful of time and energy. But researchers in adversary settings must be prepared to face it. It is a powerful tool of intimidation with which to resist researchers. Researchers also may have to determine when they should employ litigation to force data from organizations.

To discuss litigation as a method of adversary research raises crucial questions for individual sociologists and for the discipline. The integrity of the research process, the interests being served, and protection of the public from researchers whose motives are base, foolish, or mistaken must be analyzed. Crucial moral and methodological matters hang in the balance. But litigation presents issues sociologists in adversarial settings cannot ignore.

To summarize, the researcher's power base poses a special issue in adversarial settings. It raises questions about the traditional institutional bases for sociological research. It affects research design. It involves community participation, including cooperation with reporters, corporations, agencies of state and local governments, and labor unions as a means of forcing data from resistant organizations. These activities all helped HPCM researchers to identify independent data to triangulate those data with HPCM's own findings. Press conferences and public hearings were vital methods for gathering those data.

The last two sections of this chapter address fundamental methodological concerns: the meaning of adversary methods within the context of particular social institutions and in the yet larger context of a theory of knowledge. Adversary methods grow as responses to power. Because power in modern societies is institutionalized primarily in bureaucratic organizations, one should expect adversary research to emerge in research about bureaucratic organizations. The methodological importance of bureaucracy, then, occupies a special place in a discussion of adversary methods.

The Bureaucratic Secret and the Methodological Importance of Bureaucracy

Modern bureaucracy rests on authority, and, as Weber emphasized, authority is a form of power that requires legitimacy. Legitimacy, in turn, depends upon either the consent or the acquiescence of those who are dominated. Control of information has become a crucial means for engineering consent and acquiesence. Managers are so anxious to control information that they have introduced such terms as "disinformation," "spin," and "spin doctors" into the language. The practices of advertising agencies, public relations departments, and public relations firms further attest to the importance of twisting information to serve power. Although managers have other reasons to protect information, such concerns will seldom lead to antagonistic relations. Most sociologists, for example, would agree with managers about protecting the confidentiality of personal information and would work with them to avoid antagonism over that issue.

Bureaucratic domination requires managers to engineer consent by using formal criteria. This, in turn, leads managers to trace their decisions and their justifications of their operations to studies, data, and expertise—in brief, to applied science. Such formal standards encourage voluntary compliance over the long term by those to whom power is applied. Formal criteria provide managers with a vocabulary of motives that is "disinterested" and "necessary," given a set of "brute facts."

Yet the necessity of justifying decisions by means of formal, rational criteria may place managers in a motivational bind. Managers often must act on imperatives that have clearly "interested" motivations, or for which no formal justification can be found. Such situations create "the manager's bind." Managers who face this bind must legitimate their actions by a means they cannot employ. Managers often respond to this bind by creating bureaucratic secrets. *Bureaucratic secrets* differ from the many mundane secrets found in bureaucracies and everywhere else.[7] They are created to hide gaps in the requirement of formal justification for decisions. Bureaucratic secrets protect managers and officials from public scrutiny. Bureaucratic secrets are always tactical. What Weber (1978:225) wrote about official secrets applies to bureaucratic secrets as well: "It stands in relation to technical knowledge in somewhat the same position as commercial secrets do to technological training. It is a product of the striving for power."

Because all managers depend upon some bureaucratic secrets, seemingly innocent information holds greater importance for them than researchers might suspect. Social researchers may expose bureaucratic secrets or they may represent a symbolic threat[8] to them. Researchers may expose bureaucratic secrets on purpose or by accident, but from the manager's point of view, that distinction makes no difference.

Adversary research settings may emerge because the researchers and the researched hold different commitments and face different consequences for the failure of bureaucratic secrets. Managers are responsible for holding organizations together; sociologists are not. Managers must live with problems created by the exposure of bureaucratic secrets; sociologists do not. The likelihood of adversary settings will increase as one studies the higher reaches of bureaucratic power because managers' binds are more urgent and more complex there.

Bureaucratic secrets pose different, but no less "interested," problems for sociologists. If sociologists fail to distinguish the facade of information surrounding bureaucratic secrets from descriptions of fact, sociologists will create erroneous data and false theories of human behavior. They will fail to create an intellectually independent discipline. Finally, sociologists, like managers, dislike being made to look silly. In order to avoid these fates, sociologists may become determined about revealing bureaucratic secrets. Thus, sociologists have a social stake in bureaucratic secrets.

Managers create bureaucratic secrets in at least four ways. They lie (Becker 1967; Bok 1978; Frankfurt 1987), they "bullshit" (Frankfurt 1987), they play hypothetical games (Littrell 1989), and they stonewall. We turn to each of these techniques in order.

Becker's (1967:241) "hierarchy of credibility" helps explain how lies serve as bureaucratic secrets. Becker wrote (1967:242): "Because they are responsible

. . . officials usually have to lie". "Officials must lie because things are seldom as they ought to be."

Higher-level officials are especially apt to lie because of the "hierarchy of credibility." Becker (1967:241) defined this idea as an assumption, explicit or tacit, that "in any system of ranked groups, participants take it as given that members of the highest group have the right to define the way things really are." In bureaucratic organizations managers may officially hold that right.

The "deep throat correspondence" revealed lying in Omaha. OMPA claimed to have information that would correct alleged errors in the original *White Paper*. But the author of the letters claimed they hid the true information for tactical purposes. Hiding the truth for tactical reasons is the defining feature of a lie.

Philosopher Harry Frankfurt (1987) distinguished lies from bullshit, a second method for sustaining bureaucratic secrets. While liars respect the truth enough to lead others away from it for tactical reasons, bullshitters have no interest in the truth at all. Bullshitters, Frankfurt explains, say what they say primarily to look or sound good. The pose is tactically more important for bullshitters than the truth or lack of it.

OMPA's public relations plan to discredit HPCM illustrates the use of bullshit to hide a bureaucratic secret. When OMPA agreed to mount a public relations campaign to present hospitals favorably and HPCM unfavorably, they were concerned with a pose, or an image, not with the truth about Omaha's hospital costs. Although one can imagine hospital officials who might have been concerned to know the truth, the OMPA public relations plan rejected a search for truth in favor of maintaining appearances.

Hypothetical games are a third method for hiding bureaucratic secrets. Hypothetical games consist of applying analyses of hypothetical data to real situations or of applying real data to hypothetical situations in order to advance one's own agenda. Elsewhere (Littrell 1989), I analyzed the use of a hypothetical game by a consortium of hospitals to justify the purchase of costly new technology. In that case, real "inpatient" data were used to "estimate demand" for a costly machine. But hospital managers knew the equipment was intended for use primarily by "outpatients." The data were real, but they were applied to a hypothetical situation. In the Omaha project, OMPA's attempt to divert researchers with an irrelevant methodology was an attempt to develop a hypothetical game.[9]

Stonewalling, the fourth method for hiding bureaucratic secrets, consists in simply refusing to provide any information at all. Several hospitals rejected requests by HPCM researchers for data relevant to the research project. Nor would they work with HPCM to develop comparable data. In the "deep throat" correspondence, OMPA representatives wrote about their decision not to try to improve HPCM's analysis. And when HPCM requested information for its analysis, the hospitals often "stonewalled" the requests.

To summarize, information, data, research, and expertise are fundamental features of modern societies both because they have technical value and because they legitimatize bureaucratic power. Technical information is malleable and may be twisted to serve either its technical task or its legitimatizing one. Managers often press technical information and expertise to serve the task of legitimatizing power by supporting bureaucratic secrets. Both the functional importance and the fragility of bureaucratic secrets increase the likelihood that adversary relations between researchers and officials, especially higher-level officials, will occur. This often will predispose agents of bureaucratic organizations to define researchers as real or symbolic adversaries.

Unless sociologists have a methodology that guides them in forcing information in the face of resistance, they risk their capacity to collect information, they compromise the knowledge they construct, and they jeopardize the independence of knowledge that science requires. Yet virtually no guidance exists. Sociologists usually work from weak power bases. Their professional associations offer little or no help. There is no discussion of the impact of power on methods in research methods textbooks. There is no preparation or guidance about when to submit to power or about when and how to resist it. In brief, sociologists have no methodology for research in antagonistic settings.

The absence of discussions of adversary methods may make sociologists less thoughtful and more dangerous. Sociologists, for example, are no more immune to ignorance and ulterior motives than anyone else. Sociologists are as obligated to limit the use of adversary methods as they are to develop and use them. But this too presupposes a methodology of adversary methods.

The final section of the chapter suggests how wider moral and intellectual standards might shape both the uses and limitations of adversary methods. These considerations close the methodological circle: Methods for research assume meaning only when they are set in the contexts of the society and the theory of knowledge for which they are created.

Sociology, Adversary Methods, and Democratic Society

Sociologists who face resistance to their research either must accept the information organization's pump out or they must be able to force other information from organizations for independent analyses. No thinking person at this time in history can accept at face value the information organizations pump out. Lies, bullshit, hypothetical games, and stonewalling are so widespread and well recognized that they may constitute necessary conditions of bureaucratic administration. Evidence of deception has poured out of eastern Europe. It has been pouring out of the U.S. government, from NASA's Hubble trouble and the HUD scandal to the continuous stream of impropriety in defense contracting. The

AMA's attempts to smear the Canadian health insurance system and the fraud in the Savings and Loan industry make it clear that the private sector, including the not-for-profit part of it, as well as governments, survive in part by hiding bureaucratic secrets. Add to this the grotesque behavior of the military bureaucracy and the secret police in South America, the stream of lies from South Africa, Israel, and China, and the suggestion that lies, bullshit, hypothetical games, and stonewalling are necessary in bureaucratic systems is at least plausible.

Sociologists must be able to force information from powerful organizations or else they cannot develop independent theories of social life. Yet no society can give sociologists an unrestricted license to force information from individuals or organizations. In such a society sociologists would become the secret police.

Adversary methods force sociologists to consider what kind of society makes an independent sociology possible. Clearly such a sociology requires a democratic society. The simultaneous emergence of modern sociology and democratic revolutions of the eighteenth century may be more than coincidental. To the degree that a democratic society forms a necessary condition of an independent sociology, sociologists must consider their obligations to democratic societies. Sociologists must be free to force information from organizations, and they must do so within the limits of a democratic society. Four considerations must shape the limits of our use of adversary methods.

1. Democracy, accountability, and public interest   From the outset, theories of democracy have been preoccupied with theories of "downward accountability." Downward accountability requires justification for the use of power to those upon whom power is used. The principle of downward accountability counters the bureaucratic theory of upward accountability based on the subordination of specialized work. Sociologists who seek to justify adversary methods must appeal to this principle of the downward accountability of power.

The idea of "public interest" rooted in law and political theory links democratic authority, downward accountability, and the use of adversary methods. A justification for the use of adversary methods must begin with a clear statement of the part one's research plays in advancing a public interest. The use of HPCM as a research base linked the *White Paper II* project to a statutory foundation for claiming a public interest. The research was an expected part of the work to be done by an HSA with a federal charter. Although the current practices of a government or corporation cannot serve as the only standard of public interest, they provide useful starting points. Sociologists who link adversary research to a public interest may begin to justify the uses and limits of adversary methods.

2. Democracy, authority, and individual persons   A second principle democratic societies advance is that the integrity of individual persons must be protected from the arbitrary use of power. All major statements of human rights express this principle. It is the cornerstone of a democratic society. Sociologists who employ adversary methods of research must limit the use of such methods at the point of safeguarding the integrity of individual persons. A methodology of adversary methods might begin by distinguishing agents of organizations from private persons, and by distinguishing statements made in the name of agency from private statements. At the same time, private persons must accept that a democratic society requires agents of corporations and governments to submit to public accountability. These two concerns about the place of individuals in democratic societies pose a useful and permanent dilemma.

The currently accepted practice of reporting collective summaries of information, rather than individual responses from research projects, may contribute part of the solution to the dilemma. The use of public as distinct from private information contributes another part of the solution. Statements issued in press conferences and public hearings are examples of information that agents of organizations themselves introduce for public purposes.

3. Sociology, public interest, and public participation   I have discussed benefits and problems associated with public participation. Public participation may help limit abuses of adversary methods. Participation in local, statewide, and national organizations can help define common practices for advancing public interest. Such organizations might review the use of adversary methods of research and agree to sponsor or cosponsor parts of the research. Their legal departments can provide counsel about the use of such methods.

Public participation poses issues for individual sociologists and for sociologists collectively. The Omaha project illustrates how public participation helped legitimize an individual sociologist's work. It helps to emancipate sociologists from the growing isolation and increasingly restrictive environments of universities and provides links to a larger public.

Sociologists' professional associations also need to consider the collective importance of participation. The Code of Ethics will need revision. Legal guidelines for the use of adversary methods will have to be developed. Standards for limiting and authorizing adversary methods need to be developed. These concerns are increasingly important as restrictions on independent research grow in a bureaucratic era.

4. Sociology as a science of democratic society   This chapter is based on the assumption that sociology now, and for the foreseeable future, should define itself as the science of democratic societies. This does not mean that sociology applies only to those Western industrialized societies that call themselves democratic. "Democratic society" refers to a normative standard that requires sociologists to analyze the contributions and the limitations of social practices for building channels of downward accountability of power and for assuring the social integrity of individual persons.

This concern with democratic values is not new to discussions of values implied in science. Nor is it new to sociology. Durkheim, Weber, Schumpeter, and Marx considered these matters. Durkheim's preoccupation with the normative standards of modern societies was a fundamental theme in nearly all his work. All the early social science disciplines explored the relations among industrial development, democratic theory, and their own existence.

Bureaucratic assumptions about authority are fundamentally antidemocratic. The decline of democratic principles in both socialist and capitalist societies throughout the twentieth century can be explained in part by the expansion of bureaucratic power. The socialist societies, just before their collapse, were forced to assess more soberly their internal demands to democratize the state along lines their own critics had proposed for years (see, e.g., Sik 1981). Ironically, the capitalist societies, which pridefully define democracy in terms of themselves, have yet to confront the totalitarian potential in concentrations of private power and to recognize the need to democratize this power.

The suggestion that sociology operate, provisionally at least, as a science of democratic societies presents an alternative to the natural science model. That model has neither fared well in identifying laws, nor has it developed a unified approach to explanation, though it has achieved much as a descriptive science. Anthropologist Clifford Geertz (1983:4) summarized the plight of the natural science model in the social sciences:

> The penetration of the social sciences by the views of such philosophers as Heidegger, Wittgenstein, Gadamer, or Ricoeur, or such critics as Burke, Frye, Jameson, or Fish, and such all purpose subversives as Foucault, Habermas, Barthes, or Kuhn makes a simple return to a technological conception of those sciences highly improbable. Caught up in some of the more shaking originalities of the twentieth century, the study of society seems on the way to becoming seriously irregular.

Faced, as the world now is, with globalized bureaucratic domination, faced with ever more "shaking originalities" and faced with the growing "irregularity" of the social sciences, a redefinition of sociology as a science of democratic society offers sociologists a meaningful alternative to the natural science mode. Adversary methods are necessary in order to fulfill such a vision of society and to advance an independent sociology in an era of bureaucratic domination.

Acknowledgements

I would like to thank Ted Vaughan, Larry Reynolds, and especially Gideon Sjoberg for generous substantive comments and editorial suggestions.

Notes

1. Both empirical and philosophical versions of this criticism of science are often made. The infamous Tuskegee Institute's study of the effects of untreated syphilis on black men long after an effective treatment had been discovered points to the effect of racism on science. More recently, concerns have been voiced about the underrepresentation of women as subjects of federally funded research, including medical research. Many other examples can be cited. Widely known philosophical statements of the criticism have been stated by Kuhn and Feyerabend.

The influence of bureaucracy on science has been most clearly developed in discussions of "Big Science." Smith's (1989) *The Space Telescope*, a discussion of NASA's space telescope, Price's (1967) *Little Science, Big Science*, and Weinberg's (1967) *Reflections on Big Science* are major scholarly treatments of issues that grow from the influence of bureaucratic organizations on science. The issue has appeared in more popular publications as well. Broad (1990) and Browne (1990) have written lengthy articles for the *New York Times* occasional series "Big Science: Is it Worth the Price?" Kelves's (1990) "Begetting Big Science"is a long review essay of Hielbron and Sidel's *Lawrence and His Laboratory, vol. 1*. Although none of the authors develops the theory of bureaucratic influences, the issues they discuss concerning the division of labor, authority, management and money are clearly the concerns of bureaucratic administration.

2. The typology presented in figure 5.1 is only partly analyzed in this chapter. A complete analysis of that typology lies beyond the purpose of the chapter, though it would be informative. A complete analysis would require development of the logical implications of each cell, the classification of specific research projects into each cell, and an analysis of differences in the processes and outcomes of research conducted in each setting.

Although a complete analysis of the typology was not attempted here, the chapter is organized around basic principles for analyzing typologies. The meaning of the conditions described by cell 4 is explicated; an empirical case that fulfills those conditions is presented; a theoretical explanation of the settings that produce the conditions described in cell four is offered; the effect of those conditions on the behavior of researchers is discussed. The use of the typology, then, is more than heuristic, although the typology is not completely analyzed.

3. Charles Lindblom's discussion of "polyarchies" (1977:131-57) as systems where several hierarchies of power interact while limiting the range of choices at the bottom of those hierarchial structures is an analysis of matters that are assumed here. His analysis of "The Privileged Position of Business" (1977:170-200) is particularly relevant. Lindblom's own treatment at Yale after he published *Politics and Markets* is evidence that social scientists at elite

universities face sharp sanctions over merely controversial matters, to say nothing of openly adversarial research projects. For quite different discussions of this theme by I.F. Stone, see Patner (1988); *see also* Veblen (1965).

4. The intensity of this competition was sketched in the GAO report *University Funding*, (U.S. General Accounting Office, 1987:13) prepared at Senator Mark Hatfield's request. In the years 1967 and 1984, 86 and 88 percent of federal R&D budgets went to 100 universities and colleges. Of that, 42 and 45 percent, in respective years, went to the top twenty institutions. That means that 80 percent of the top 100 universities competed for less than 60 percent of the federal dollars. If one thinks of universities that are not in the top twenty as "nonelite" universities, the competition such universities face for federal funds is fierce.

5. Two weeks before *White Paper II* was released, I told the chancellor of the University of Nebraska at Omaha about the report. He served on the board of a local hospital, and I did not want him to be caught unaware. I did not provide a copy of the report, but I outlined its main findings. I emphasized that this was done in my capacity as citizen, rather than as professor, and I emphasized that the project was not university-sponsored research. It was my hope that the information would provide the chancellor maneuvering room in his multiple roles. Some pressure was exerted after *White Paper II*, though none of that pressure was passed on to me or to Dr. Ambrose, the other UNO professor who worked on the project.

6. The problem of public discussion of scientific issues has no simple answer, and it is becoming more difficult. Controversy over AIDS research suggests that funding for research and publication of results was very slow to emerge. Earlier exposure of those issues certainly would have been in the public interest. The uses of publicity around the Jarvik artificial heart was sensationalist and well beyond what was necessary to inform the public about scientific findings. Questions have been raised about the degree to which the Jarvik publicity served corporate, rather than scientific, purposes. Similar questions have been raised about publicity surrounding the research on cold fusion and high-critical-temperature superconductivity. The foundations of science are very much at issue in all such cases.

7. For a different yet related analysis of secrets and the social sciences, see Bok (1983, esp. 102-15, 230-48). Bok relates secrets to power and to social science, though she makes only a weak distinction between collective and individualistic issues. She develops no discussion of bureaucracy. Schepple (1988:1-2, 301-8) presents a discussion of secrecy and the social sciences more closely related to my own, though she does not directly address bureaucracy as a system of power nor how its irrationalities may call forth bureaucratic secrets. Schepple's [1988:308] conclusion about the functional importance of secrets is similar to this one, though general: "On one hand, they [secrets] make social

control and social structure possible. But on the other hand, they provide opportunities for undermining the existing order and creating alternative forms."

Becker (1967), Sjoberg and Miller (1973), Lowery (1973), and Frankfurt (1987) develop discussions of secrecy that are directly related to the concerns of this chapter. These sources, more than those cited earlier, have influenced my own idea of bureaucratic secrets and their importance for social research.

8. The idea of "symbolic threat" is borrowed directly from Skolnick (1975:45-8, 105-9), who explained the generalized suspicion that characterizes police officers' responses to those with whom they must deal. Police officers know they face real assailants from time to time, but they have no way of knowing who might become such an assailant. Therefore, all people with whom they must deal become "symbolic" assailants, at least until police officers clearly understand that those people will cooperate with the officers' occupational requirement to take control of messy situations.

Bureaucratic managers, similarly, may consider researchers to be either real or symbolic threats to bureaucratic secrets. In either case, bureaucratic managers may have reasons to be suspicious of all researchers and to resist them.

9. Hypothetical games appear to be a widespread method for hiding bureaucratic secrets. Reisner (1986) analyzed similar practices by the Bureau of Reclamation and the Army Corps of Engineers in order to justify building dams. NASA used them to justify a manned space-flight program [Littrell 1987; Trento 1987; U.S. Congress, 1986]. Gibson's (1986) analysis of body counts, and especially the air war in Vietnam, describes the use of hypothetical games in the military.

REFERENCES

Aaron, Henry J., and William B. Schwartz. 1984. *The Painful Prescription: Rationing Hospital Care.* Washington D.C.: Brookings Institution.

Becker, Howard S. 1967. "Whose Side Are We On?" *Social Problems* 14:239–47.

Bok, Sissela. 1978. *Lying: Moral Choice in Public and Private Life.* New York: Pantheon.

———. 1983. *Secrets: On the Ethics of Concealment and Revelation.* New York: Random House.

Broad, William J. 1990. "Greater Sums for New Research Pose a Threat to Basic Science. *New York Times* May 27, A1, 12.

Browne, Malcolm. 1990. "Super Collider's Rising Cost Provokes Opposition." *New York Times* May 29, B5, B8.

Denzin, Norman K. 1989. *The Research Act: A Theoretical Introduction to Sociological Methods.* 3rd ed. Englewood Cliffs, N.J.: Prentice-Hall.

Eisenhower, Dwight D. 1961. "Farewell Address." Quoted in Norman Cousins (1987). *The Pathology of Power.* New York: Norton.

Emerson, Robert M. 1983. *Contemporary Field Research.* Boston: Little, Brown.

Enthoven, Alain. 1980. *Health Plan: The Only Practical Solution to the Cost Of Medical Care.* Reading, Mass: Addison-Wesley.

Feyerabend, Paul. 1978. *Against Method.* London: Verso.

Frankfurt, Harry. 1987. "On Bullshit." Pp. 117–33 in *The Importance of What We Care About.* New York: Cambridge University Press.

Geertz, Clifford. 1983. *Local Knowledge: Further Essays in Interpretative Anthropology.* New York: Basic Books.

Gibson, James William. 1986. *The Perfect War: Technowar in Viet Nam.* Boston: Atlantic Monthly Press.

Health Planning Council of the Midlands. 1981. *White Paper II.* Photocopy available from University of Nebraska at Omaha Library or from the author.

Hielbron, J.L., and Robert Sidel. 1990. *Lawrence and His Laboratory.* Berkeley: University of California Press.

Kelves, Daniel J. 1990. "Begetting Big Science." *New York Review of Books* October 25, 6–10.

Kuhn, Thomas D. 1970. *The Structure of Scientific Revolutions.* 2nd ed. Chicago: University of Chicago Press.

Lindblom, Charles. 1977. *Politics and Markets: The World's Political-Economic Systems.* New York: Basic Books.

Littrell, W. Boyd. 1989. "New Technology, Bureaucracy, and the Social Construction of Medical Prices." *Journal of Applied Behavioral Science* 25:249–69.

————. 1987. "Shuttle Trouble: Notes on the Bureaucratization of Deviance." Paper presented at the annual meetings of the Midwest Sociological Society, Chicago.

Lowery, Ritchie P. 1972. "Toward a Sociology of Secrecy and Security Systems." *Social Problems* 19:437–50.

Patner, Andrew. 1988. *I.F. Stone: A Portrait.* New York: Doubleday.

Price, Derek de Solla. 1967. *Little Science, Big Science.* Cambridge: MIT Press.

Reisner, Marc. 1986. *Cadillac Desert.* New York: Viking/Penguin.

Schepple, Kim Lane. 1988. *Legal Secrets: Equality and Efficiency in the Common Law.* Chicago: University of Chicago Press.

Sik, Ota. 1981. *The Communist Power System.* New York: Praeger (orig. pub 1976).

Sjoberg, Gideon., ed. 1967. *Ethics, Politics, and Social Research.* Cambridge: Schenkman.

Sjoberg, Gideon, and Paula Jean Miller. 1973. "Social Research on Bureaucracy: Limitations and Opportunities." *Social Problems* 21:129–43.

Skolnick, Jerome S. 1975. *Justice without Trial: Law Enforcement in a Democratic Society.* 2nd ed. New York: John Williwaw.

Smith, Robert. 1989. *The Space Telescope: A Study of NASA, Science Technology, and Politics.* New York: Cambridge University Press.

Starr, June, and Jane F. Collier, eds. 1989. *History and Power in the Study of Law: New Directions in Legal Anthropology.* Ithaca: Cornell University Press.

Trento, Joseph. 1987. *Prescription for Disaster.* New York: Crown.

U.S. Congress. 1976. "The National Health Planning and Resources Act." *Statutes at Large* 88, sec. 641. Washington, D.C.: Government Printing Office.

————. 1986. *Investigation of the Challenger Accident.* (House Report 99–1016). Report of the Committee on Science and Technology, House of Representatives, October 29. Washington, D.C.: Government Printing Office. (House Report 99–1016).

U.S. General Accounting Office. 1987. *University Funding: Patterns of Distribution of Federal Research Funds to Universities.* (GAO/RCED-87-67BR).

Veblen, Thorstein B. 1965. *The Higher Learning in America.* New York: Augustus M. Kelly (orig. pub. 1918).

Weber, Max. 1978. *Economy and Society.* Berkeley: University of California Press.

Weinberg, Alvin W. 1967. *Reflections on Big Science.* Cambridge: MIT Press.

Chapter **6**   SOCIOLOGIST AS CITIZEN-
SCHOLAR: A SYMBOLIC
INTERACTIONIST ALTERNATIVE
TO NORMAL SOCIOLOGY

Stanley L. Saxton

The sociological community must mount a challenge to "normal sociology."[1] A split labor force is developing in the discipline. Typically, sociologists doing normal sociology are positioned in major research universities. They use a positivist approach to serve the information needs of their clients, usually government agencies. Another and much larger group of sociologists pursue their craft in comprehensive universities and liberal arts and community colleges. Primarily, these sociologists are teaching scholars who serve the interests and needs of students and the academic and local communities.[2]

The conditions of work, interests, and needs of these two groups of sociologists are increasingly disparate. The faculty at comprehensive universities and liberal arts and community colleges do not have the time, funds, facilities, or assistants necessary to conduct normal sociology research. These sociologists are excluded from knowledge production as defined by the major sociological journals. Further, knowledge produced by sociologists in research universities is increasingly irrelevant to the teaching and research needs of the majority of their colleagues (cf. Feagin et al. 1991). The discipline requires an active and aggressive alternative to normal sociology.

One vital alternative to normal sociology is sociology from a Symbolic Interactionist (hereafter SI) perspective. Marxist or neo-Marxist perspectives are informative, but historical events have made them less influential. Functionalism, under the able efforts of Jeffrey Alexander (1985), is attempting a resurgence but it still suffers from the dilemmas that led to the sharp decline in its influence a few decades ago. For sociology to serve all its members and the broader social order, the SI perspective should be employed. The SI perspective can best integrate the commitments to teaching, research, and community service. These commitments are essential to the advancement of sociology and the community.

Normal Sociology

In his introduction to *The Handbook of Sociology*, Neil Smelser (1988) describes the influences producing normal sociology. He first reviews the history of competing theoretical perspectives and methodological positions within the discipline. Then, Smelser (1988:13) observes that the strongest and most influential voice in sociology throughout this century, despite critiques and laments, has been "sociology as an empirical, if not positive, science. . . . [Sociology] chose the route to intellectual legitimacy by modeling itself on the established sciences and insisting that it too was a positive science."

Smelser argues that this strong voice in sociology is a consequence of three persistent conditions facing the discipline. First, by becoming a positive science, sociology is more readily accepted as a legitimate academic discipline within a university system dominated by the natural sciences. Second, the state requires facts in order to make objective decisions justifying the allocation of funds and rationalizing a variety of social programs to serve public policy objectives. The state's need for "facts about society" provides an opportunity for sociology to produce "objective facts." As a discipline committed to being a positive science, sociology can be relied upon to provide factual information serving the needs of the state. Third, the social and behavioral sciences are a part of the National Science Foundation. NSF grants and all other federal granting agencies' allocations are typically reviewed by congressional and executive branch oversight committees: "The view of the social and behavioral sciences in the halls of government is fraught with ambivalence" (Smelser 1988:14). The social and behavioral sciences occupy a very minor place in federal government grants and contracts. But perhaps because they are considered "soft" and not really "scientific," they are a lightning rod for critical review and even, on occasion, ridicule by oversight committees.

Smelser (1988:16) describes the response of the discipline to the above set of influences:

> The main temptations generated by these pressures on the behavioral social sciences are two: first, to maintain as low a profile as possible, to avoid political notice and . . . survive; and second, to present themselves as respectably and undangerously as possible and thereby to curry political and budgetary support. The main response to these temptations according to my observations is for the spokespersons of the behavioral and social sciences to represent themselves as adhering to the model of positive science.

The persistence of positivism is not the consequence of scholarly debates concerning the theoretical adequacy or validity and reliability of current research efforts. Instead, quantitative positivism is a consequence of external influences and the protection of funding interests. In effect, Smelser describes the discipline of sociology as being shaped by the needs of the state and the interests of the research university.

Sociology as a positive science, or normal sociology, primarily serves political interests and dominates the discipline. Smelser (1988:15) continues:

> In the end, of course, this response emerges as a victory of the positive-science emphasis, and as a kind of marriage of convenience between the behavioral and social science investigators in the academy on the one hand and the Washington social-science establishment on the other—a marriage that encourages those in the academy to support so-called hard behavioral and social scientific investigations because such a policy encourages funding agencies to give research grants to such investigators because it provides evidence that their own standards are strictly "scientific."

Smelser's analysis is candid and insightful. He has been in a position to observe these trends in the discipline, and I suspect his interpretation of the linkages and their influences upon the discipline are accurate. There is an opportunistic collusion between academic administrators, quantitative researchers in the discipline, and the Washington social-scientific establishment. Each serves the interests of the other. It is in their collective interest to continue this triangle of accommodation. The recent hiring of a former officer of the National Science Foundation to be the executive director of the American Sociological Association (ASA) is symptomatic of the trinity of mutual interests that Smelser describes.

The following questions arise: Does the set of influences described here serve the discipline and its members? Who among us finds it necessary to curry governmental favor? Who most cares about government officials' definition of their research? Smelser's analysis focuses on how the needs and interests of sociologists at research universities have powerfully influenced the direction of the discipline as a whole. But, their needs and interests do not correspond with the needs and interests of the vast majority of sociologists who are teaching scholars. Moreover, the needs and interests of sociologists at major universities do not necessarily advance the cause of sociology as a scholarly discipline nor the quality of life of members of the society.

The discipline of sociology should not adopt the position of positive science only because it is the route to serving the interests of the state and the financial needs of the research university. The discipline cannot be led by powerful members captured by the politics of science. We need to support research that (1) diagnoses the problems and recommends potential solutions for the general community (Bellah et al. 1985, 1991), (2) investigates alternative research methodologies (Feagin et al. 1991), (3) supports a variety of theory building research programs (Couch et al. 1986), and (4) recognizes the legitimacy of questions appropriate for qualitative and interpretive research methodologies

(Van Maanen 1988). We need discussion about differences and relative strengths of competing positions.[3] Such debate will clarify the positions and the consequences of assuming one position over the other for all members of the profession. There are alternatives to normal sociology, and we must promote these alternatives with great vigor. I advance SI as the alternative perspective that will best serve the vast majority of sociologists and the academic and social communities in which they work.

Symbolic Interactionism (SI)

Symbolic interactionism is a theoretical and methodological approach used by sociologists to practice their scholarly craft. Members of the SI tradition are interested in developing a better understanding and explanation of social order and change. They are particularly concerned with the relationship between the individual and society.

Proponents of the SI perspective advocate advancing sociology through research using theoretical assumptions and methodological techniques that are distinct from those used in doing normal sociology. The philosophical assumptions, theoretical formulations and major concepts, and methodology of the SI approach are clearly described by a number of authorities (Blumer 1969a; Couch et al. 1986; Denzin 1978; Fine 1990b; Kuhn 1964; Manis and Meltzer 1972; Reynolds 1993; Rose 1962; Stryker 1981). A reproduction of these discussions is outside the scope and purpose of this paper. However, a description of the central features of SI is provided as a foundation for the remainder of this essay. As Sheldon Stryker (1981:3) notes, "There is considerable internal variation in the content of symbolic interactionism. While there is a core set of theoretical assumptions and concepts which most, if not all, working within the framework accept and use, there are other theoretical ideas relatively peculiar to one or another version."

Building from the pragmatist tradition (Cooley 1902; Dewey 1922; James 1987; Mead 1934), SI scholars develop theory and research to advance understanding of the complex processual nature of human activity.

Theoretical Approach

SI focuses study on human agency and activity. It takes up the challenge of understanding and accounting for the direction of individual activity, within the context of social interaction, the forms of interpersonal relationships, the organization of coordinated activity and the structure of interrelated activities, called organizations. More specifically, SI scholars argue that (1) human activity is purposeful and self-directed (Blumer 1969b); (2) the relational forms that shape the interaction between two persons and coordinate the activity within small groups can be uncovered (Couch et al. 1986); and (3) it is possible to identify and describe the processes of negotiation that organize the joint activity of large numbers of people (Hall 1987).

SI Assumptions

Activity is constructed by self-reflective, directing, and purposeful actors. Ongoing action is constructed from the definitions of the situation (Blumer 1969a; Thomas and Znaniecki 1918), the experience of prior activity (Couch and Katovich 1991), and the joint activity of others (Miller et al. 1975). Unlike Einstein, interactionists assume that "nature throws dice." SI is not bedeviled by the experience of uncertainty. In fact, SI embraces uncertainty as a fundamental condition of human existence (Dewey 1922; Shalin 1986). Because uncertainty, like activity, is ubiquitous, humans are always interacting with themselves and others as they cope with physical and social environmental factors in constant flux.

Further, human beings create meaning as they individually and collectively weave their way through the routines and the problematics of social life. The relevance and definitions of objects vary as individuals and groups negotiate the implications of new purposes and encounter unanticipated obstacles or novel conditions that influence their activity. One only has to experience a troubling relationship, a new war, altered conditions of work, or difficulty with children to become aware of these processes firsthand. SI assumes that these processes and comparable experiences are the routine nature of everyday life for almost everyone. How individuals, small groups, communities, and collectivities detect change, redefine objects, create new meanings, alter their plans of action, and change the direction and pace of activity are the features of social life that are to be investigated.

SI Methods

The research methodology of SI is consistent with the theoretical assumptions outlined in the previous section. Data generating methodologies and the modes of analyzing social data have been developed to study self-directed activity. Interactionists often observe how activity unfolds in natural settings through field studies. They collect first-person descriptions of activity through in-depth interview studies. They create activity settings in the laboratory permitting the collection of video- or audiotaped activity. On occasion they use answers to questions gathered from survey questionnaires. Interest in accounting for self-directed, purposeful activity occurring within natural environments requires that the research be as consistent with these conditions as is possible. In most SI research, qualitative analysis techniques are used to reduce, organize, and analyze data (Denzin 1989; Scheff 1990). New concepts are being introduced to better understand topics of study involving these processes (Hall 1987). New lines of inquiry are being developed to expand our understanding of social experience (Ellis 1991; Franks and McCarthy 1989). New methods of investigation are being employed (Katovich et al. 1986; Saxton and Couch 1975) and new ways of presenting research findings are being explored (Becker et al. 1989). Today, the work flowing from the SI position is rich with variety, but for the most part it can trace its origins to the theoretical and methodological principles advanced by Herbert Blumer.

Herbert Blumer: The Exemplar of SI

Herbert Blumer's life work is examined for two main reasons. First, Blumer was the leading interpreter of George Herbert Mead's writings for sociological discourse. His theoretical analysis and methodological contributions are worthy of careful attention in their own right. Second, Blumer's life highlights how the SI perspective can be integrated with broader teaching and citizenship activities. Blumer's activities as scholar, administrator, and citizen are of a whole cut of cloth. He was a "citizen- scholar" and serves as an exemplar for an alternative kind of sociology that needs to be resurrected.

Herbert Blumer (1900-1987) was an enigma of intellectual and physical power combined. People knew he was a former professional football player and were even more aware of his critical mind and articulate discourse. He studied with many of the famed Chicago School sociologists and received his Ph.D. from the University of Chicago in 1928. Blumer worked directly with George Herbert Mead and is said to have been at his side just before Mead's death.

Blumer spent most of his academic career in sociology at the University of Chicago. In 1952 he moved to the University of California, Berkeley, where he became chair of the department. He took the lead in building one of the most distinguished sociology departments in the United States. What is striking about his role as chair was his willingness to recruit a diverse group of prominent sociologists, many of whom were at odds with his perspective.

Blumer's role as chair was only one of his many contributions to sociology. He served as editor of the *American Journal of Sociology*, president of the Society for the Study of Social Problems in 1954, and president of the American Sociological Association in 1955. Blumer also attained considerable acclaim as a labor mediator. During the 1940s, he was appointed to a three-member panel to arbitrate the labor union strike against U.S. Steel. Little has been written by sociologists about Blumer's role as a labor mediator. Yet, by helping to resolve labor conflicts, Blumer came to understand firsthand the social process that informed his theoretical and methodological orientation.

As an educator, Blumer left a lasting impact on sociology. In particular, he influenced (in greater or lesser degree) a group of students at Chicago in the late 1940s and early 1950s including Ralph Turner, Lewis Killian, Tamotsu Shibutani, Joseph Gusfield, Charles Bolton, Anselm Strauss, Howard Becker, and Bernard Meltzer. They wielded considerable influence in sociology, especially during the 1950s and 1960s.

In keeping with Blumer's role as teacher, he also was supportive of a number of sociologists who did not identify with SI. His willingness to sponsor activities of various members of the discipline is reflected by the fact that he wrote the lead article for the first issue of the *Pacific Sociological Review* as well as the *Sociological Quarterly*. He lent his considerable prestige to assist these new publications in establishing legitimacy.

I have already mentioned that Blumer made central contributions to sociological theory. His interpretation or reformulation of Mead's writings laid the foundation for SI theory within sociology. The emphasis on the self in sociology, for instance, owes much to Blumer's careful theoretical investigations.

Blumer's intellectual position within the discipline is salient in other respects as well. His methodological writings (Blumer 1931, 1969b) are deserving of far more attention than they have received from either Symbolic Interactionists or their critics. Blumer crafted a methodology that was in keeping with his assumptions of society as process. He seriously questioned the foundations of the emerging dominance of quantitative sociology. For example, in his critique of operationalism, Blumer advanced the counterperspective that sociologists must rely on "sensitizing concepts."

More generally, Blumer was a critic of positive science, although *not* of empirical investigation. He was also a critic of functionalism. He sought to carve out an alternative to the two major paradigms of the post World War II era. His criticisms were pointed, but he never stooped to ad hominem arguments. He was true to the calling of a citizen-scholar. The pragmatist position that ongoing debate is a means of advancing not only the role of social knowledge but also the quality of social democracy was a central part of Blumer's life.

There are sociologists who argue that Blumer never put his theory (or methods) into practice. Yet a broader view of his life's work shows that Blumer the sociologist was consistent with Blumer the chairperson and labor mediator. He was able to practice sociology in a manner that was not petty or demeaning to his cause or to persons with whom he disagreed. He had the ability to step back and reflect on himself in the context of those with whom he interacted.

Blumer's concern for substantive problems of his day is documented in his essays on labor relations, public opinion, social problems, and race and ethnic relations (e.g., Blumer 1990, 1971, 1948, 1939). These essays are being rediscovered (Maines 1988), and they point to the fact that Blumer's SI perspective (though not as integrated as one might wish) was capable of addressing theoretical, methodological, and substantive issues.

Blumer's work is at present being reevaluated and recast. This is consistent with his theoretical heritage. It is difficult to imagine that Blumer expected the course of scholarly endeavor to be otherwise. Although Blumer has been the central figure in bringing Mead's work into sociology, Mead as well as other pragmatists, such as his good friend and colleague John Dewey, are being rehabilitated by a wide variety of scholars. The prominent German theorist Jurgen Habermas, for one, placed Mead alongside Emile Durkheim and Talcott Parsons as master theorists on whom Habermas draws in critically evaluating the growing bureaucratic domination of what he terms "the life world." And although Bellah et al. (1991) are not especially sympathetic to Mead, they rely rather heavily on Dewey in calling on social scientists to become involved in the creation of the "good society."

But let us return to Blumer's place in the history of sociology. He formulated a sociological version of the Meadian heritage and was a representative of the citizen-scholar. While many SI scholars have achieved national reputations for excellence in their work, no one has come forward to take Blumer's place as a mediator between SI and sociology. As the influence of Blumer waned and as the direction of sociological theory and research in America changed in the 1970s, the relationship between SI and the rest of sociology underwent a fundamental transformation.

The Society for the Study of Symbolic Interaction

The Society for the Study of Symbolic Interaction (SSSI) is a scholarly society devoted to serving the interests of SI; it has a membership of about four hundred. SSSI sponsors the journal *Symbolic Interaction* and organizes an annual meeting. It administers funds used to support the annual Gregory Stone Symposium and represents the interests of SI at regional sociological meetings and in related societies.

If the members of the American Sociological Association had been supportive of the interests of Symbolic Interactionists as a critical minority in the discipline, SSSI would never have been organized. But, in the early 1970s being a minority within sociology became particularly onerous for some prominent SI advocates. The talk in 1973 was that the discipline of sociology was bent on the destruction of SI. Nicholas Mullins (1973:98) argued that SI, as the loyal opposition, was about to die out:

> It is clear that the original ideas within symbolic interactionism, like those of standard American sociology, have run their course intellectually and socially. Some symbolic interactionists are still actively publishing and, as a theory of social psychology, symbolic interactionism still has respectability. .... As a change maker and general orientation for sociology and as the loyal opposition to structural functionalism, however, it has come to an end.

Also in 1973, the *American Sociological Review* published a paper by Joan Huber that attempted to delegitimate the research by adherents to the SI perspective. Huber reaffirmed the role of positive science in sociology and more or less dismissed those who worked within the qualitative tradition. For example, Huber (1973:282) wrote:

> But the practitioners of SI remain nervous lest their reports be confused with mere journalism. Their fear is justified. What is needed is a frank confrontation with a major legacy of pragmatism. In the absence of theory, the social givens of researcher and the participants serve as a theoretical framework giving the research a bias which reflects the climate of opinion in the discipline and the distribution of power in the interactive setting.

The impact of this article arose primarily from its publication in the *ASR*, not from its persuasive argument.

In addition to the writings of Mullins and Huber, adherents of the SI perspective were increasingly dissatisfied with the perceived editorial policy of *Sociometry* (later to be named the *Social Psychology Quarterly*). The assumption of many Symbolic Interactionists was that the editors were biased against their work and favored quantitative research reports based on experimental or survey methodologies.

These attacks were too much for Carl Couch, University of Iowa, and Gregory Stone, University of Minnesota. In 1973, both Couch and Stone were well-published, respected scholars. They had successfully produced and were then advising a large number of Ph.D. candidates. Both were completely committed to the SI perspective and felt that the powerful members of the American Sociological Association were purposefully acting in a manner that was doing serious damage to the SI tradition.

Whenever SI people got together, there was critically playful talk of the other sociology. Nevertheless, before, during, and after the 1973 Midwest meetings, talk about the Mullins chapter and the Huber article was not playful. SI people were angry and determined to preserve an intellectual tradition in sociology (Couch 1991; Denzin 1992). These conditions fostered a shared concern. That concern was the beginning of an episode of collective action to sustain SI as a vital perspective.

After much discussion during the Midwest meetings in 1973, a course of action was tentatively decided on. Carl Couch and Gregory Stone would write a proposal for ASA funds to hold a seminar on the status of SI in sociology. Gregory Stone was to look into what was needed to build a scholarly society of SI members, that is, matters of incorporating, funding, and the like. Many others were involved in the discussions, but these two individuals were the most important actors at the Midwest meetings in 1973. At that time, with widespread agreement that the ASA was politically hostile toward SI, the sentiment to do something to support SI was very strong. A number of people were willing to act together in an organized effort to strengthen SI. Of particular importance to the continuity of these initial activities was the work of Richard Travisano, University of Rhode Island, who shouldered the responsibility for creating a newsletter that would carry the intentions of the Midwest working group to a wider audience.

The Couch and Stone application to the ASA was funded. The first SI symposium was held at the University of Minnesota. In addition to Couch and Stone, Herbert Blumer and about twenty other Symbolic Interactionists convened to give papers and discuss the future of the perspective. Carl Couch organized the second SI symposium, held at the University of Iowa in May 1975. Both symposiums were intellectually exciting. The intense personal interaction provided a strong sense of solidarity for sociologists committed to the SI perspective. They had worked together to organize what all agreed were very successful paper sessions. SI was not dead; it was alive and thriving.

Throughout 1973, Gregory Stone had been investigating the corporate status of a formal organization, a Society of Symbolic Interactionists. At the 1974 Midwest meetings, Stone recommended that an SI organization be incorporated in the state of Minnesota, that recruitment of members should begin, and that a journal be sponsored by the new society. The decision was made to pursue building a society independent of the ASA in lieu of a section within the structure of the ASA. A working group was asked to draft a formal constitution, begin the incorporation process, and actively recruit members. All along, Travisano recorded these discussions and decisions and published them in the newsletter, which by summer 1974 had a mailing list of persons located all across the nation and involved in the full variety of SI expressions.

The SSSI has been a successful organizational base for SI scholars. The journal *Symbolic Interaction* has provided an outlet for articles that are in keeping with the SI orientation. Symbolic Interaction recently moved from a semiannual to a quarterly publication. SSSI annual meetings provide the opportunity for SSSI members to present and discuss their work and to reaffirm their identity and solidarity. The annual Stone Symposium has provided an additional outlet for presenting papers, discussing work in progress, and networking among SI scholars. In 1990, the SSSI agreed to sponsor mini symposiums to support small gatherings for focused discussion of specific issues or problems.

The collective action that began in 1973 has resulted in a robust organization that supports SI. Ironically, the success of the SSSI has had an unintended consequence that is detrimental to the future of SI and to the discipline of sociology. The activities of SSSI have marginalized the SI perspective from the larger discipline.

In an essay titled "The Greying of SI" (Saxton 1989b; see also Saxton 1989a), I argued that the membership of SSSI seemed to be getting older and that the number of graduate students interested in the SI approach seemed fewer than in prior years. Further, graduate departments where students can be trained in the SI tradition have virtually disappeared. Fifteen years ago, the Universities of Iowa, Illinois, Minnesota, California at San Diego, Texas, and others had a critical mass of faculty who offered sophisticated training in the SI perspective. Today, none of these departments can provide the same opportunities. To my knowledge, no new departments are replacing the above departments as centers for graduate work in the SI tradition. The question is, "Will the SI tradition be reproduced with new members engaged in the work required to further develop the perspective?"

SSSI has not acted to create graduate training centers, nor has it offered training seminars. Further, SSSI has not expanded its efforts to recruit sociologists dissatisfied with the direction of normal sociology. While it is not accurate to characterize the SSSI as an exclusive scholarly society, members of the SSSI have not defined the organization as representing the interests of sociologists using interpretive, qualitative research techniques. The SSSI can and should, in my judgment, broaden its appeal to sociologists dissatisfied with normal sociology.

I suspect that the SSSI has not broadened its base of appeal because leading SI scholars have become increasingly isolated from the issues and debates in the discipline of sociology. The current leaders of the SI effort have been drawn into the supportive circle of membership in SSSI and have become increasingly less willing to be a vocal opposition resisting the dominance of normal sociology. In this sense they have not sought to carry on the role played by Herbert Blumer.

For example, very few SI scholars are involved in current discussions of the relationship between microsociology and macrosociology (Alexander et al. 1987; Collins 1981; Fine 1990a; Maines 1982). This is a central theoretical issue in sociology and a natural arena of inquiry for members of the SI perspective (Fine 1990a). Moreover, the proponents of SI have not mounted the kind of critique, based on theoretically informed research, that is necessary to demonstrate the serious weakness of the articles being published in the *Social Psychology Quarterly* (sponsored by the ASA). In the studies in this journal, individuals have been removed from their social context, and the result has been disastrous for our understanding of contemporary society. Proponents of SI have a great deal to say about the "individualism" vs. "communitarian" debate that is now the concern of a number of prominent scholars.

SI: The Essential Alternative

SI must not allow sociology to be shaped by the triangle of political interests defined by (1) the needs of the state for objective information, (2) the appetites of research universities for overhead funds, or (3) the search for scientific legitimacy by research university faculty. The SI perspective can and must become a significant participant in the reproduction of the discipline. The SSSI, which serves as home base for the SI perspective, must now be mobilized to lead the return of SI as a strong critical voice in the discipline of sociology.

The SSSI can reach out to sociologists teaching in comprehensive universities and liberal arts colleges who have the resources to conduct qualitative, interpretive sociological research. The SSSI can act to broaden its membership of women and minority-group members who find it difficult to crack the "old boy" circle of prestigious influentials in the larger discipline. The SSSI can sponsor workshops and special summer training sessions in the techniques of depth interviewing, field research, and videotape research. These sessions and workshops can be offered just before or during our annual national meeting or at the annual Stone Symposium meetings. The SSSI newsletter can become more active in identifying and advertising available faculty positions, and the SSSI could become a more powerful voice promoting SI through special mailings of the SI newsletter or issues of *Symbolic Interaction* to appropriate groups of sociologists across the nation. SI scholars must renew interest in the affairs of the ASA. Sponsoring a section within the structure of the ASA must be reconsidered. There are enough members of the SSSI and enough latent interest in the SI perspective to continue support of the SSSI and sponsor a SI section within the ASA. With an ASA section, more SI sessions would be scheduled at the national meetings. Members of SI who continue their membership in the ASA would be natural links between the two organizations. The visibility of SI would be heightened and SI members might take more interest in the politics of the ASA and perhaps become more influential in shaping the future of sociology. At the least, members of the SSSI should join the Social Psychology section of the ASA. With a large number of SI scholars involved, they could become influential in selecting the editor of the *Social Psychology Quarterly*. The current editorial practices support normal sociology in the extreme. All these measures should be taken to reestablish SI as a presence in the reproduction of sociology.

The most effective strategy, in my judgment, is to create another collective action in the 1990s around an alternative vision for conducting the craft of sociology. Members of the SSSI have the intellectual and organizational resources to define and support forms of sociological excellence different from the work of normal sociology. I offer a brief description of one such alternative approach.

Sociologists as Citizen–Scholars

I am convinced that sociologists must become what I call "citizen-scholars," using Blumer as the major role model. The citizen-scholar approach to the craft of sociology is based upon four principles. First, society generally and local communities specifically are always in the process of being reconstructed. The task of the citizen-scholar is to study processes with sufficient depth to understand the central mechanisms of change and stability. The objective of this analysis is to identify the robust structures of stability and the processes and points of change in the evolution of community life. This premise suggests that it is possible and reasonable to intervene in these processes and structures for purposes of enhancing the quality of community or broader regional life.

Second, the most effective approach to the development of long-term understanding of community stability and change is empirical research employing the appropriate techniques of the scientific method including qualitative and interpretive data-gathering and analysis techniques. The objective of such research is continually to increase the sophistication of understanding about processes in the community, rather than be satisfied with a cross-sectional analysis of a single theoretical question or problem. The approach I advocate perceives research in the community as an ongoing activity that involves the accumulation of information leading to a better understanding of basic community processes that reproduce existing social arrangements. The community becomes a research site for theoretically informed, empirical research projects organized with the objective of creating a higher quality community life. (I emphasize research on processes in the community and region and not just community studies, though these studies would not be ruled out.)

Third, communities and regions are not simple reflections of national patterns. Social scientists, as well as policy makers, cannot generalize from national data in order to understand local communities or the regions in which these are embedded. Instead, it is through the thick description of ongoing processes on the local level that we come to understand the interrelationships of demographic characteristics, power relations, local economic activities, and historical circumstances.

Knowledge of general societal principles, in and of themselves, is insufficient for effective understanding for how lives are shaped in the community context. At the same time, attention to localities (cf. Bellah et al. 1991) does not mean that we ignore the broader societal and global processes. To understand the meaning of these extracommunity processes, we must investigate how they are constructed and reconstructed on the local levels by purposive human beings. The sociologists who, as citizen-scholars, study the community context do not thereby become "locals," but they come to understand the impact of "cosmopolitan" processes in a meaningful sociological way. Thus, the citizen-scholar is in a position to criticize the conventional wisdom constructed on "national data sets."

Finally, community research also means that sociologists should think about their craft from a holistic perspective that includes using their activities as teachers, members of voluntary associations, and so on to aid in the construction of knowledge about the social worlds. Research is not an activity to be set apart from teaching and community activities.

What makes the activities of the citizen-scholar possible is that the research being carried out, while labor intensive, requires relatively little funding. Qualitative research on community processes can be readily employed by a wide range of sociologists who can thereby be both consumers and producers of social knowledge.

SI and the Citizen-Scholar

At its best, SI scholarship produces information that adds to our understanding of how people in everyday life construct activities in their natural social settings (Adler and Adler 1991; Denzin 1987; Farberman 1975; Katovich and Reese 1987; Scheff 1990). In principle, any sociologist trained in the craft of qualitative research can make a significant contribution to this body of knowledge. Appropriate research sites are available to any sociologist equipped with theoretical insight and the curiosity to understand the construction of social life better. The results of this work have the virtue of being informed by generic theoretical understanding combined with local knowledge, that is, detailed thick descriptions of the setting within which social activity is created. This combination produces results that are relevant to local parties and the general audience of scholars interested in the same issues. This means that sociologists have the opportunity to serve the information needs of locals as well as the scholarly interests of SI and of the discipline of sociology. The fact that this research serves the simultaneous purpose of informing the local actors and developing generic principles is the key to its being a strong competitor of normal sociology.

Empirical research reports in the major sociological journals are esoteric. They serve the information needs of a small, highly specialized audience. Further, normal sociology findings address theoretical questions and employ research methodologies that are politically noncontroversial and thereby devoid of major theoretical and substantive implications, particularly for issues regarding local conditions. The demographic, political, and cultural conditions of a local community are sufficiently particularized so that findings based on general theoretical models and national data samples are of little, if any, use for local or regional parties. Sociologists should take on the task of interpreting how national and international trends translate into useful information for local parties through community research.

Ideally, an effective strategy would be for departments of sociology to abandon their loose collection of individual scholars pursuing their own individual intellectual interests in favor of a more collective enterprise that provides more systematic knowledge of local settings. Given the atomized nature of most academic departments, a coordinated, cooperative approach is not likely to exist. Members of departments of sociology could make significant contributions to the information required to understand local social issues and problems better. Departments of sociology could provide informational services that combine the general knowledge of the discipline with specialized knowledge of the local community for purposes of improving the community's quality of life.

Because they do not now provide this service, sociology departments risk becoming increasingly irrelevant to the production of useful knowledge in contemporary society. I do not think this trend augurs well for the future of the discipline in the next century. I am deeply concerned that if departments of sociology at comprehensive and liberal arts institutions were disbanded, six months later few members of the academic or local community would know they were gone, and still fewer would care. In contrast, the academic community and the federal bureaucracy would miss departments of sociology at research universities, which do provide needed information and bring in needed overhead funds. Providing useful knowledge about local and regional communities can be the mission of sociology faculties of liberal arts and comprehensive institutions.

Conclusions and Implications

My central thesis has been that normal sociology must be challenged on theoretical and empirical grounds. Sociologists whose work does not conform to normal sociology must take an active role in reshaping the nature of social knowledge and, ultimately, the existing power arrangements within the discipline.

If normal sociology is not effectively reconstituted, an increasingly larger majority of sociologists will find it difficult to participate in the production of sociological knowledge. As long as normal sociology continues to dominate the discipline, some of sociology's most important purposes (e.g., cultural criticism) will continue to be neglected. Finally, many important theoretical questions and issues cannot be investigated by employing quantitative methods based on social surveys or laboratory experiments. In any event, qualitative research will not receive the hearing it deserves unless major journals are willing to change their policies and publish this kind of research.

I have argued that normal sociology serves the interests of sociologists at research universities and their clients—most notably state and federal agencies. The faculty members employed by liberal arts colleges and comprehensive universities commonly do not have the resources to conduct research based on the premises of normal sociology. Young faculty members, those who are members of minority groups, and sociologists who emphasize teaching are reduced to becoming consumers and disseminators—not producers—of sociological knowledge. In addition, the knowledge produced by sociologists at major research universities often may be irrelevant to the academic activities of the majority of sociologists. The majority of faculty are being marginalized just when they are being held increasingly accountable for producing knowledge for purposes of acquiring tenure and being promoted.

Qualitative field studies and interpretive essays of contemporary issues are scholarly activities that best fit the conditions of work of the educator-researcher. Many significant theoretical questions can be addressed through qualitative and interpretive scholarly endeavors. These endeavors also are the basis for reasoned social criticism. Yet this kind of work does not conform to the expectations of normal sociology.

The conditions of work for a small but powerful minority of sociologists at research universities need not and should not imprint the whole discipline. Sociologists should not abandon their long-standing tradition of being committed to an inclusive academic discipline. To counter the dominance of normal sociology, we need to recognize the politics of science (e.g., Gergen 1982) and to organize support for alternatives to normal sociology.

Herein I have argued that the most reasonable alternative to normal sociology is the Symbolic Interactionist perspective. SI is the only operating perspective in the discipline broad enough to support the use of qualitative methods and interpretive frameworks as well as more traditional quantitative work. The general objective should be to strengthen the recognition of and support for alternatives to normal sociology that better serve the full range of conditions of work, intellectual interests, and forms of scientific inquiry in the discipline.

In developing an alternative sociology, I am calling for sociologists to become citizen-scholars and for the Society for the Study of Symbolic Interaction to take the lead in advancing this model of sociological activity. I have briefly described the origins and foundations of Symbolic Interactionism. Until the late 1960s, it was generally viewed as a legitimate form of sociological inquiry. Thereafter, it was largely disregarded, which promoted the formation of the SSSI, the organization that has kept the SI tradition alive. Now is the time for members of this organization to move beyond playing a defensive role in sociology and reengage the discipline. SSSI can demonstrate how the sociologist as citizen-scholar can integrate research, teaching, and civic activities as Blumer did.

The activities of sociologists as citizen-scholars should be:

1. Sociologists must carry out qualitative research in their local and regional settings. Local communities do not reproduce national or global trends in any neat and simple manner. Therefore, it is incumbent on sociologists to carry out research in community and regional settings in order to challenge or modify the generalizations constructed on the basis of social surveys of the society as a whole. We need to understand the social processes by which human arrangements are constructed and reconstructed in the context of a variety of communities and regions. By carrying out qualitative research studies on a variety of issues in local communities, sociologists not only can mount a challenge to the current generalizations that dominate the discipline but also can redefine what passes for sociological knowledge.

2. The type of in-depth qualitative research advocated also makes it possible for sociologists to relate teaching to research in a more meaningful way. Introductory textbooks or readers in a variety of subdisciplines illustrate that sociologists as teachers rely on qualitative research. At present, the majority of articles published in the major sociological journals are highly quantitative; thus, most are irrelevant to the teaching enterprise. For sociologists acting as citizen-scholars, research activities become an integral part of one's teaching endeavors.

3. By participating in the construction of a higher quality of life in the local academic and community setting, sociologists can legitimate the discipline of sociology on the local and regional levels. The ASA, as far as I can determine, has given almost no attention to this issue because the primary focus of the ASA is on the interests of sociologists at major research universities. If only those interests are served, the discipline eventually will become very small in numbers and in contributions to our society. Graduate students need to be trained to become technically competent so that they can carry out the activities of citizen-scholars.

The time is ripe to mount a major challenge to normal sociology. The SI perspective is the basis for launching a critique of normal sociology. We must work together as citizen-scholars in order to construct a sociological discipline that is meaningful to the majority of sociologists—not merely sociologists at major research institutions. If this is done, sociology will prosper, and sociologists as citizen-scholars once again will make sociology an exciting discipline in which to carry out their various endeavors.

Acknowledgements

*In large part, what is of value in this essay is due to the patience, persistence, and insightful editorial skill of Gideon Sjoberg. Without his help and encouragement I do not think this essay would have been completed. My colleague Fred Pestello also made helpful comments along the way. To the degree that this essay reads smoothly, it is due to the marvelous editorial skills of my daughter Kathleen E. (Saxton) Ferrante. I am responsible for what is wrongheaded and clumsy about this work.

Notes

1. Judging from publications in the major journals, sociology is a well-established positive science. Numerous articles developed from research grants indicate that sociologists find clients willing to fund their research. Faculty at research universities secure research funds, produce research, and publish their findings. The following picture emerges: Sociologists, using well-established data-gathering and analytical techniques, are investigating topics for clients who have questions about social life. Sociology has been "normalized."

2. Teacher scholars, working in comprehensive universities and liberal arts colleges, are coming under increasing pressure to publish in refereed journals. The conditions of work at these institutions militate against producing "normal sociology" research acceptable to the editors of major journals. It seems that college and comprehensive university administrators are using the major research university as their model of excellence. The conditions of work for the teacher-scholar are dramatically different than for the researcher-scholar, i.e., teaching load, committee work, graduate students acting as teaching and research assistants, and commitment to having face-to-face interaction with undergraduate students. The teacher-scholar will continue to experience the contradiction between what is expected and the conditions of work allowing for the reasonable fulfillment of those expectations.

3. Since the mid-1960s, theoretical development in the discipline has been diverse. Competition between perspectives has been reasonably vigorous. Ritzer (1990) suggests that recent theoretical developments have tended to move in the direction of syntheses. This is not to suggest that a grand theoretical perspective, i.e., a winner, has emerged. Instead, the recent tendency is to break the boundaries of theoretical positions for purposes of taking advantage of the ideas and insights of competing positions. In addition, a number of theorists are working simultaneously on common themes, e.g., the micro-macro issue. These developments in theory should be extended to varieties of research.

REFERENCES

Adler, Peter, and Patricia A. Adler. 1991. *Backboards and Blackboards: College Athletes and Role Engulfment*. New York: Columbia University Press.

Alexander, Jeffrey A. 1985. *Neofunctionalism*. Newbury Park, Calif.: Sage.

Alexander, Jeffrey A., Bernhard Giesen, Richard Munch, and Neil J. Smelser eds. 1987. *The Micro-Macro Link*. Berkeley: University of California Press.

Becker, Howard S., M.M. McCall, and L.V. Morris. 1989. "Theatres and Communities: Three Scenes." *Social Problems* 36:93–116.

Bellah, Robert N. 1985. *Habits of the Heart*. Berkeley: University of California Press.

Bellah, Robert N., Richard Madsen, William M. Sullivan, Ann Swidler and Steven M. Tipton. 1991. *The Good Society*. New York: Knopf.

Blumer, Herbert. 1931. "Science without Concepts." *American Journal of Sociology* 36:515–33.

———. 1939. "The Nature of Racial Prejudice." *Social Processes in Hawaii* 5:11–21.

———. 1948. "Public Opinion and Public Opinion Polling." *American Sociological Review* 13:542–54.

———. 1969a. *Symbolic Interactionism*. Englewood Cliffs, N.J.: Prentice-Hall.

———. 1969b. "Sociological Analysis and the Variable." Pp. 127–139 in Herbert Blumer, *Symbolic Interactionism*. Englewood Cliffs, N.J.: Prentice-Hall.

———. 1971. "Social Problems as Collective Behavior." *Social Problems* 18:298–306.

———. 1990. *Industrialization as an Agent of Social Change: A Critical Analysis*. Hawthorne, N.Y.: Aldine.

Collins, Randall. 1981. "On the Microfoundations of Macro Sociology." *American Journal of Sociology* 86:984–1014.

Cooley, Charles H. 1902. *Human Nature and Social Order*. New York: Scribner.

Couch, Carl J. 1991. Conversation with Dr. Couch about his activities in the formation of the Society for the Study of Symbolic Interaction.

Couch, Carl J., and Michael Katovich. 1991. "Common and Shared Pasts: The Basis for Routine Situated Encounters." Manuscript.

Couch, Carl, Stanley L. Saxton, and Michael A. Katovich, eds. 1986. *Studies in Symbolic Interaction—the Iowa School*. Parts A and B. Greenwich, Conn.: JAI Press.

Denzin, Norman K. 1978. *The Research Act*. 2nd ed. New York: McGraw-Hill.

———. 1987. *The Recovering Alcoholic*. Newbury Park, Calif.: Sage.

———. 1989. *Interpretive Interactionism*. Newbury Park, Calif.: Sage.

———. 1992. Discussion with Dr. Denzin concerning his recollections about the beginning and early years of the Society for the Study of Symbolic Interaction.

Dewey, John. 1922. *Human Nature and Conduct*. New York: Holt.

Ellis, Carolyn. 1991. "Sociological Introspection and Emotional Experience." *Symbolic Interaction* 14:23–50.

Farberman, Harvey. 1975. "A Criminogenic Market Structure: The Automobile Industry." *Sociological Quarterly* 16:438–57.

Feagin, Joe E., Anthony M. Orum and Gideon Sjoberg eds. 1991. *A Case for the Case Study*. Chapel Hill: University of North Carolina Press.

Fine, Gary A. 1990a. "Agency, Structure, and Comparative Contexts: Toward a Synthetic Interactionism." Paper.

———. 1990b. "Symbolic Interactionism in the Post-Blumerian age." Pp. 117–57 in George Ritzer, ed. *Frontiers of Social Theory: The New Syntheses*. New York: Columbia University Press.

Franks, David D. and E. Doyle McCarthy, eds. 1989. *The Sociology of Emotions: Original Essays and Research Papers*. Greenwich, Conn.: JAI Press.

Gergen, Kenneth J. 1982. *Towards Transformation in Social Knowledge*. New York: Springer-Verlag.

Hall, Peter. 1987. "Interactionism and the Study of Social Organization." *Sociological Quarterly* 28:1–22.

Huber, Joan. 1973. "Symbolic Interaction as a Pragmatic Perspective: The Basis of Emergent Theory." *American Sociological Review* 38:278–84.

James, William. 1987. "Pragmatism." Pp. 479–557 in *William James: Writings 1902–1910*. New York: Library of America.

Katovich, Michael A., and William A. Reese. 1987. "The Regular: Full-time Identities and Membership in an Urban Bar." *Journal of Contemporary Ethnography* 16:308–43.

Katovich, Michael A., Stanley L. Saxton, and Joel O. Powell. 1986. "Naturalism in the Laboratory." Pp. 79–88 in Carl J. Couch, Stanley L. Saxton, and Michael A. Katovich, eds. *Studies in Symbolic Interaction: The Iowa School*. Greenwich, Conn.: JAI Press.

Kuhn, Manford. 1964. "Major Trends in Symbolic Interaction Theory in the Past Twenty-five Years." *Sociological Quarterly* 5:61–84.

Maines, David. 1982. "In Search of Mesostructure: Studies in the Negotiated Order." *Urban Life* 11:267–79.

———. 1988. "Myth, Text, and Interactionist Complicity in the Neglect of Blumer's Macrosociology." *Symbolic Interaction* 11:43–58.

Manis, Jerome G. and Bernard N. Meltzer, eds. 1972. *Symbolic Interaction: A Reader in Social Psychology*. 2nd ed. Boston: Allyn and Bacon.

Mead, George H. 1934. *Mind, Self, and Society*. Chicago: University of Chicago Press.

Miller, Dan E., Robert A. Hintz, and Carl J. Couch. 1975. "The Elements and Structure of Openings." Pp. 1–24 in Carl J. Couch and Robert A. Hintz, eds. *Constructing Social Life*. Champaign: Stipes.

Mullins N.C. 1973. *Theories and Theory Groups in Contemporary American Sociology*. New York: Harper & Row.

Reynolds, Larry T. 1993. *Interactionism: Exposition and Critique*. 3rd ed. Dix Hills, N.Y.: General Hall.

Ritzer, George, ed. 1990. *Frontiers of Social Theory: The New Syntheses*. New York: Columbia University Press.

Rose, Arnold, ed. 1962. *Human Behavior and Social Processes*. Boston: Houghton Mifflin.

Saxton, Stanley L. 1989. "Knowledge and Power: Reading the Symbolic Interaction Journal Texts." Pp. 9–24 in Norman K. Denzin, ed. *Studies in Symbolic Interaction*. Vol. 10. Greenwich, Conn.: JAI Press.

———. 1987. "Stan Saxton's Turn: The Greying of SI." *SSSI Notes*. Vol. 13, no. 3:3–5.

Saxton, Stanley L., and Carl J. Couch. 1975. "Recording Social Interaction." Pp. 255–62 in Carl J. Couch and Robert A. Hintz, eds. *Constructing Social Life*. Champaign: Stipes.

Scheff, Thomas J. 1990. *Microsociology: Discourse, Emotion and Social Structure*. Chicago: University of Chicago Press.

Shalin, D.N. 1986. "Pragmatism and Social Interactionism." *American Sociological Review* 51:9–29.

Smelser, Neil J., ed. 1988. *The Handbook of Sociology*. Newbury Park, Calif.: Sage.

Stryker, Sheldon. 1981. "Symbolic Interactionism: Theories and Variations." Pp. 3–29 in Morris Rosenberg and Ralph H. Turner, eds. *Social Psychology: Sociological Perspectives*. New York: Basic Books.

Thomas, W.I., and F. Znaniecki. 1918. *The Polish Peasant in Europe and America*. 5 vols. Boston: Little, Brown.

Van Maanen, John. 1988. *Tales of the Field: On Writing Ethnography*. Chicago: University of Chicago Press.

Chapter 7

THE RISE OF THE WISCONSIN SCHOOL OF STATUS ATTAINMENT RESEARCH

J. David Knottnerus

In recent years, the Department of Sociology at the University of Wisconsin has ranked No. 1 in prestige ratings of sociology departments in the United States. For this reason, this chapter examines a major facet of this department—the status-attainment research tradition—and addresses the question of how the department acquired such a high degree of prestige over the past several decades.

The status-attainment research tradition at the University of Wisconsin was spearheaded by William Sewell and his associates. From the 1960s to the present, the Wisconsin School has concentrated on mobility processes and produced much research, while stimulating related investigations into status-attainment processes at other institutions (e.g., Sewell et al. 1969; Sewell et al. 1970; Sewell and Hauser 1972, 1975; Duncan et al. 1972; Featherman and Hauser 1978). Sewell and the other scholars who have followed in his footsteps at Wisconsin have produced one of the most extensive research programs in contemporary sociology (see the review by Kerckhoff 1984).

The question that naturally arises is how did this research program in the sociology department at the University of Wisconsin acquire the prominent position it holds today within the field of social stratification and sociology as a whole. In addressing this question there are a number of legitimate ways by which a sociology of sociology analysis can be conducted.

One method would be to place the Wisconsin School and the Sewell model of status-attainment processes in their *historical context*. Attention would be especially directed to three points: the informal social organization of this emerging research program, the appeal of the program's methodology, and the funding of its research and the perceived relevance of the research tradition for various social problems and issues.

Another way to conduct a sociology of sociology analysis is to examine how a research and/or theoretical program exhibits an affinity with certain themes, arguments, and conceptual images within the *intellectual currents of its time*. I give greatest attention to this issue by focusing upon how the Sewell model of attainment processes articulated with certain popular images of society of its era. I argue that the affinity of the model with certain themes in the intellectual milieu of postwar (World War II) sociology was a major reason why the Sewell model and Wisconsin research program came to dominate the field of sociology in the 1970s and early 1980s. Today, however, the Sewell model is being increasingly criticized. I suggest that one reason for this is because the model is not consistent with certain images of American society and social structure that are coming to the fore. Brief mention is given to some of the changes in theoretical developments and research that seem needed if the Wisconsin School is to retain its place in the sociological enterprise.

Historical Context

In examining the historical context in which the status-attainment tradition emerged, it is perhaps appropriate first to describe the social organization of this research program and to identify the major figures contributing to its growth. This research program grew out of the efforts of a number of scholars who collaborated on many projects through the years and for the most part have worked at the University of Wisconsin.

Fortunately, David Featherman (1981) has succinctly described the key developments in this regard. O.D. Duncan (who was to play a major role in initiating the modern era of status-attainment research) was an undergraduate student of William Sewell's at Oklahoma A & M (now Oklahoma State University). Through the years, they remained in correspondence as Duncan did his graduate work and occupied several faculty positions, eventually settling at the University of Michigan. In 1946 Sewell moved to Wisconsin. After studying under Duncan at Michigan, Robert Hauser and David Featherman obtained positions at Wisconsin. Sewell and Hauser collaborated on a number of long-term mobility research projects, as did Featherman and Hauser. Furthermore, a former student of Sewell's, Archibald O. Haller, was to take a position at Wisconsin and conduct a variety of mobility studies. These scholars and their students formed a strong social network that fostered communication, intellectual stimulation, and a host of research projects.

A second factor that contributed to the rise of the status-attainment program was the methodological procedure used in the research. Status-attainment's methodology made it possible for research to be conducted in a cumulative manner and thus contributed to the "scientific" appeal of the program to many in the social science community. This, in turn, enhanced the ability of the program to obtain funding for its studies. More precisely, in *The American Occupational Structure* Blau and Duncan (1967) utilized path analysis (a regression methodology) to represent status attainment as a multivariate, casual process. Variables, such as father's occupation and education, were incorporated incrementally into models describing the factors that influence son's educational and occupational attainments. In a similar manner, Sewell and his associates used data collected from sources such as his longitudinal study of Wisconsin high school seniors to develop path models of status attainment. From these efforts emerged a number of complicated models of the social and psychological influences involved in attainment processes (Sewell and Hauser 1980), which contributed to a growing, cumulative research program.

Related to this point is the fact that more recent critics of the status-attainment tradition often have used the statistical methods developed in status-attainment research. For example, Wright (1980) has used structural variables in structural equation models of the status-attainment process. Scholars such as Featherman (1981) have argued that this shows that the status-attainment tradition has contributed to the development of a cumulative social science. What this research program did was to create a methodology and general approach to the study of attainment processes that has allowed different perspectives to be researched and discussed systematically.

Finally, it should be recognized that status-attainment research at the University of Wisconsin and elsewhere was developed during a unique period in American history. In the 1960s attention to social problems and issues was at a peak. These concerns ranged from civil rights problems to the policies of John F. Kennedy and Lyndon Johnson that were aimed at mitigating social and economic inequalities such as poverty. Status-attainment models of the life cycle and the factors influencing attainment directly contributed to debates focused on social inequality and the lack of mobility experienced by various members of society such as racial groups (Featherman 1981).

In this same time period, as pointed out by Mullins and Mullins (1973), the large surveys carried out by status-attainment researchers such as Sewell, Hauser, and Blau and Duncan were made possible by certain technological developments and increased funding for social research. In the early 1960s computers became available to university researchers. The introduction of such technology allowed status-attainment researchers to process their large collections of data much more quickly and efficiently. Large amounts of money initially were obtained from the National Institutes of Health (NIH). At the same time, the Kennedy administration's support of government programs aimed at social change enhanced opportunities for research. Gradually, monies also became more available from the National Science Foundation (NSF) and other funding organizations. These funding sources helped provide direct and indirect support for many status-attainment research projects.

Examination of the historical context in which the Wisconsin school of status attainment research arose thus reveals several significant influences. They range from the works of particular scholars, their social networks and ties, to the scientific nature of the research program and the available financial resources that made it possible for this research tradition to proliferate. In addition to these concrete developments, however, it is also argued that the rapid and extensive development of this research tradition occurred because it rests on a set of conceptual assumptions that are highly consistent with certain themes popular in the intellectual currents of contemporary sociology. The remainder of this chapter considers the nature of this influence and its implications for status attainment research.

Status-Attainment's Image of Society and Modern Social Thought

As discussed elsewhere (Knottnerus 1987, 1991), status-attainment research, particularly in its early formulations by the Wisconsin School and other key scholars such as Blau and Duncan (1967; Duncan 1968), rests upon certain assumptions other than structural-functional theory (Horan 1978). More precisely, the depiction of society underlying the status-attainment tradition is an optimistic image of modern, mass, industrial society.

At the heart of this image is the concept of universalism that emphasizes that modern society is characterized by features such as increasing differentiation, rationality, and efficiency. The social structure is pictured as having a complex division of labor, an increasing middle mass of workers, and as being technologically sophisticated. Furthermore, social structure is described as possessing high rates of mobility and providing opportunities for all persons. In essence, social structure is pictured as a fluid system where people are free to seek their goals, especially their occupational goals, in the growing middle tier. It is a system presumedly unique to the modern industrial world, characterized by an increasingly homogeneous social body in terms of occupational levels and lifestyle.

The social actors in this structure are depicted as motivated by the desire to attain occupational status, material goods, and so on. Such an orientation is a direct outgrowth of rational or universalist standards of evaluation that guide actors. A prime example of this dynamic would be the gratification people derive from obtaining material consumer items that are valued status symbols.

This image of society underlying the early formulations of the status-attainment tradition provided the conceptual foundation for the research of William Sewell and others who formed the Wisconsin School. In other words, what the Wisconsin School did was to clarify how the attainment process operates. That is because the research conducted by Blau and Duncan showed that educational attainment mediates to a large degree between parental position and son's occupational attainment. Sewell and others examined this process in much greater detail showing the many ways that father's occupation influences educational and occupational attainments.

Their research showed that social-psychological mechanisms play a major role in the status-attainment process (for a discussion of this research, see Haller 1982). These mechanisms include significant others, aspirations, performance, and ability. Aspirations and significant others such as peers and parents, are the most important factors. Drawing on symbolic interactionism, it was argued that aspirations are formed in social interaction, basically due to the evaluations received by significant others. Academic performance also contributes to the formation of self-evaluations. Ultimately, the aspirations formed in the early part of life through social interaction with others will influence educational and occupational attainments in later life.

What this research did was to describe in detail the dynamics by which the image of society underlying the status-attainment tradition operates. Based upon the Wisconsin School's research efforts, an explanation was put forth for how universalistic values are or are not transmitted to individuals. Actors are socialized into the value of achievement through the influence of the family, school, and significant others. Aspirations and abilities then shape attainments. It is a formulation that complements and builds on the image of society in the status-attainment program. Actors socialized into and propelled by universalist values such as achievement are able to freely seek their goals in the fluid structure of mass, industrial society.

Since these early studies, a variety of research efforts have been conducted. While it is impossible to discuss all these studies, several lines of work that will very likely guide future research endeavors deserve attention. For example, Alexander and Pallas (1983) have specified in greater detail the interactionist dynamic focused on by the Wisconsin research program. At the same time, other studies of some of the factors shaping individual attainments have taken a different approach. As noted by Campbell (1983), various studies show that status-attainment research is moving toward earlier stages of the life cycle. The goal of this research is to achieve a more complete understanding of the social-psychological processes involved in attainment by expanding the time frame of observation. For instance, the research of Mercy and Steelman (1982) suggests that early childhood experience may influence ability at an early age.

Clearly, this research and status-attainment's underlying image of society emphasize that the attributes of individuals are important. Moreover, certain social settings undoubtedly exhibit an open quality that makes the drive to achieve the crucial and distinguishing characteristic in such an environment. Nevertheless, questions remain. In addition to the need to extend and refine formulations that focus on the influences on achievement motivation, another key concern is whether in certain circumstances the social context in which individual actors are embedded shapes status-attainment. Does the social structure impinge on actors' educational and occupational attainments in certain settings, and if so, how?

Reflecting the fact that the status-attainment tradition is large and extensive, some research in recent years has included structural factors in its analyses of attainment. Indeed, such efforts have been undertaken by some of the original members of the Wisconsin School. For example, Haller (e.g., Pastore and Haller 1982; Bills et al. 1985) has examined the impact of class origin and class position on attainment processes in societies other than the United States. Recent research has investigated how these processes vary by different regional levels of socioeconomic development and/or industrialization in countries such as Brazil.

Despite these and other studies, the effects of social structural factors still have not been investigated sufficiently by status-attainment researchers, especially in their early work and formulations. That this is so is in large part caused by the image of society underlying the early works of the status-attainment tradition with its depiction of modern industrial society as fluid, increasingly middle mass, and populated by actors possessing to varying degrees values such as desire to achieve. Why such an assumption underlies this research tradition takes us to the next issue concerning the era in which this research program arose and its affinity to certain ideas that enjoyed widespread popularity in the social sciences during this time period.

Several intellectual themes in sociology after World War II are consistent with this image of society, the most important being mass-society theory. Generally, the many scholars who contributed to the perspective known as mass-society theory argued that class distinctions in America were decreasing as people were increasingly merging into an expanding middle class. More precisely, two distinct versions of this theory can be discerned in the literature (Knottnerus 1987).

A negative version of mass-society theory has focused on the idea that in modern industrial society the increasing mass of people are marked by a leveling of their cultural tastes and norms. While differences exist among theorists in their various formulations, people often are pictured as fragmented, isolated, adrift, anxious, politically alienated and/or ineffectual, and easily manipulated by political leaders (Lederer 1940; Mannheim 1940; Fromm 1941; Arendt 1951; Rosenberg and White 1957; Kornhauser 1959; Ortega Y Gasset 1960; Stein et al. 1960; Olson 1963; Marcuse 1964).[1]

The second version of mass-society theory presents a more positive interpretation of modern society. The optimistic version of mass-society theory (Wilensky 1964; Nisbet 1959; Bell 1949, 1960; Parsons 1954; Barber 1968; Drucker 1953; Gaibraith 1958), contributing to the image of society underlying status-attainment research, suggested that postwar America was witnessing the growth of a more *homogeneous middle mass* (for a discussion of this thesis, see Pease, Form, and Rytina 1970; Huber and Form 1973). While differences exist among individual scholars, the basic argument was that in the affluent years following World War II, America was becoming classless as economic and political inequalities decreased and the homogeneous middle class grew in size. Developments such as an increasing division of labor, the rise of industry, bureaucratization, education, urbanization, professionalization, and the spread of impersonal norms and nonascriptive standards of achievement were bringing about this transformation in the social and economic structure of modern America. Usually, the United States was viewed as the world leader in regard to such developments.

Parsons (1954:430-36) expressed some of the major ideas of this perspective when he suggested that the American stratification system was fluid and loose, lacked a rigid hierarchy of prestige except in a very broad sense, and possessed opportunities for upward mobility due to increases in economic productivity and the increased importance of education for mobility. In describing the occupational structure, he argued that the occupational pyramid was declining. Social trends such as automation were causing the bottom of the occupational pyramid to disappear. This, along with the fact that the top of the pyramid is quite diffuse, Parsons argued, meant that America was becoming more and more middle class.

Another scholar who articulated many of the themes of optimistic, mass-society theory was Wilensky (1964; Wilensky and Lebeaux 1965), who argued that as the United States became more industrialized it was becoming increasingly middle class. Industrialization, the growth of complex formal organizations, increasing specialization in occupations, and other developments such as continued technological innovations were contributing to the upgrading of the economic system, resulting in greater equality in income distribution. More specifically, the growth of the middle class reflected changes in the occupational structure, including a transition in the United States to tertiary industries, the greater need for white-collar jobs in professional and clerical areas, and the increasing numbers of skilled manual workers.

Wilensky, like others, also suggested that the increasing distribution of occupational positions in the middle class was caused by increasing specialization. As part of this development, the skilled working class was steadily becoming part of the middle mass. As the income of the working class improved, differences between nonmanual and manual work disappeared (Mayer 1959; Lenski 1966). It was further argued that manual workers were becoming middle class in their economic status and overall lifestyle because modernization was doing away with low-skill jobs and increasing employment in the white-collar arena of clerical and administrative work.

To summarize, various authors under different labels, such as postindustrial-society theory, affluent-society theory, service-class-society theory, postcapitalist-society theory, and end-of-ideology theory, have contributed to this general perspective, which also has been referred to as the class convergence model (Blumberg 1980). What this perspective emphasized was that class differences were being reduced and huge portions of the population were becoming affluent (see, e.g., Mayer 1963; Blumberg 1974; Aron 1968; Kristol 1978). Other key issues were discussed by Bell in *The Coming of Post-Industrial Society* (1973), where he argued that as America has become a mass society, it has become extremely mobile, both socially and spatially (showing that the class structure has not become rigid as some had argued in the 1940s and 1950s), and this development has involved the movement from a primary to a secondary to a tertiary economy. Complementing these points was the idea that knowledge and information have become quite important, as reflected in the rapid growth of the white-collar middle class (Drucker 1958). The result of these various developments was the growing massification of modern industrial society, an idea shaping the status-attainment research program.

Finally, it should be noted that the image of society underlying early attainment research is compatible with certain general intellectual themes in American sociology extending back to the beginning of the twentieth century. One scholar who voiced such ideas and influenced early status-attainment researchers was Charles Cooley (Knottnerus 1987). Cooley (1909, 1918) voiced certain sentiments typical of his peers of the time, such as Ross, Ward, Small, and Sumner. Among all these authors one finds to varying degrees (see Pease et al. 1970; Huber and Form 1973; Page 1969) an optimism about the stratification system and the "classless" quality of the middle class in America. In their view the opportunity existed for large proportions of the population to be upwardly mobile in our society. One of the benefits of our social-political-economic system, they believed, was a limitation on the extent that inequalities could form. Such ideas, which in many ways overlap with the dominant American ethic of equality of opportunity for all (in which success is presumedly the result of individual attributes such as hard work and skill, while failure connotes lack of ambition and ability), also have contributed to the distinct image of society found in early attainment research.[2]

The conceptualization of society underlying the status-attainment tradition, therefore, is consistent with and reflects several themes dominant in the intellectual environment of postwar sociology. The affinity of this image of society with mass society theory and certain themes in American sociology (and our culture at large) throughout the twentieth century is a major reason why the research program of Sewell and the Wisconsin School had come to dominate the field of sociology by the 1970s and early 1980s.

Limitations of the Status-attainment Research Program and Its Image of Society

Despite the dominance of the Wisconsin School in sociology, criticism of this research program has been growing. A major reason for these criticisms is that the image of society underlying the status-attainment tradition is not consistent with certain images of the class and/or occupational structure of American society that have been coming to the fore in recent years. For that reason, a brief examination of some of these alternative conceptions of the social structure and/ or changes occurring in American society would contribute to a sociology of sociology interpretation of what has been taking place and what may need to occur in the future to status-attainment research.

As previously discussed, early status-attainment formulations do have a conception of social structure (contrary to the common assumption that this tradition either has no conception of social structure or, if it does, its conception is simply a product of structural functionalism). This conception of social structure articulated within the image of modern, mass, industrial society is characterized by growing universalism, differentiation, fluidity, and homogeneity. Similar to certain assumptions made in classical economics, social structure is pictured as a series of occupations that vary in pay and prestige and are located in the expanding middle range. When examined in its totality, the social structure of modern industrial society is essentially depicted as a finely graded continuum of occupational positions diffused throughout the middle tier. Of course, the open quality of the system means that a large and growing proportion of actors are free to seek their occupational niche within this series of positions in the bulging middle of the class structure.

In contrast to this conception, a number of alternative perspectives have emerged in recent years that stress that different factors in society affect the availability of positions in the social structure. In other words, some have argued that attainment processes depend on the structure of positions available to actors and the factors that facilitate or limit their attempts to attain these positions. This "structuralist" perspective has taken different forms and has led to different kinds of structural research. While there is no need (or space) to conduct a review of all this research, several well-known perspectives present conceptualizations of the social structure that clearly are different from status-attainment's depiction of structure. Three major perspectives can be identified in the labor market: industrially segmented labor markets, organizational structures, and social class.

Industrial segmentation asserts that the labor market is not open and homogeneous, but is partitioned into different sectors that influence individual opportunities for mobility and the overall quality of people's lives. The most-well-known version is the dual economy model (Averitt 1968; Doeringer and Piore 1971). It suggests that the market is composed of two segments. In the primary labor market workers receive salaries, benefits, and promotions based on their abilities and experience. In contrast to this stable work structure, workers in the secondary labor market are paid less, receive fewer benefits and promotions, and experience greater uncertainty in their work lives because ability has little bearing on advancement. Support for this argument has been found by different researchers (Osterman 1975; Beck et al. 1978; Bibb and Form 1977). Nevertheless, questions remain because others have failed to find support for this perspective (Kaufman et al. 1981).

An alternative to the segmentation thesis is found in the works of Baron and Bielby (1980, 1984), who argue that the organizational structure of the work setting affects attainment processes. What is important are the ways rewards and work are affected by the way the work setting is structured, how technology is used, and what strategies of power and dominance are found there. The usual object of analysis is the firm. The subject of organizational processes and structure is a large one and involves many dimensions, including the basic one of organization size. A growing literature attests to the appeal of this perspective while indicating that much more research into such issues is needed (Stolzenberg 1978).

The third structuralist perspective focuses on the class structure of the labor market. Wright's work (Wright and Perrone 1977; Wright 1978) exemplifies this orientation. He builds on Marx's model of class while giving explicit attention to the role of authority in modern organizations. Three new class positions are identified, which fall between the original three positions discussed by Marx. Between the proletariat and the bourgeoisie are the managers. Small employers are between the petty bourgeoisie and the bourgeoisie. Lastly, between the proletariat and the petty bourgeoisie are the semiautonomous wage earners. These three class positions described by Wright are subjected to conflicting pressures because they are both dominating and dominated by other classes. One's position in the class structure, it is suggested, will influence attainment processes and outcomes such as earned income.

In their unique way, then, each perspective argues that actors' opportunities for mobility are influenced by structural constraints in society. Of course, many questions surround these approaches (Baron and Bielby 1980), and some research has not supported these perspectives. Nevertheless, each perspective has generated a significant amount of attention and support from scholars investigating attainment processes. Undoubtedly, this is partly because each approach directs attention to various dimensions of the social structure not examined by early status-attainment research.

In addition to the Wisconsin School not placing sufficient attention on these structural factors, another issue has significant implications for the status-attainment tradition. This issue concerns the possibility that historical changes in the American social and economic order are affecting attainment processes in ways not envisioned by the status-attainment tradition. As previously discussed, early status-attainment formulations characterize the class/occupational structure of America as expanding in the middle levels with opportunities for mobility increasing and the quality of life for the masses steadily improving. Such a conceptualization may have been a valid portrayal of conditions in the United

States for several decades after World War II, which was a period of accelerated economic growth. It is conceivable, however, that the class structure of the United States is changing and no longer fits a scenario emphasizing a growing middle class.

Indeed, evidence from a variety of sources has in recent years suggested that the middle class is shrinking and the lower- and upper-class levels are becoming more polarized in the United States (Kuttner 1983). This issue has spawned debate in both academic and public arenas (for a sophisticated analysis of these trends, see Levy 1987). Some (Rosenthal 1985) contend that this is a false interpretation of recent trends. Others have marshaled a persuasive array of evidence and arguments that suggests otherwise.

While a review of this literature would be inappropriate at this time, a few examples may be mentioned (for reviews of this research, see Knapp 1987; Knottnerus 1991). A number of studies examining family incomes have described a decrease in the middle class over the last one to two decades (Thurow 1984). Although the exact proportions vary, a large number of studies argue that family income inequality has been increasing since at least the middle of the 1970s. Others, using different criteria, have made the same observation. Looking at lifestyle and the purchase of consumer items, Steinberg (1983) argues that the middle mass market is shrinking and that, therefore the market increasingly is becoming centered on lower- or upper-income tiers. Finally, in a related but different kind of analysis, Bluestone and Harrison (1986) have focused on the jobs being created in the American economy and have argued that many new jobs are low paying, which exacerbates the trend to a polarized labor market.

Assuming that changes are taking place in the socioeconomic order, the question arises as to why this is the case. The reasons offered are varied, ranging from slow economic growth, the increase of baby-boomers in the workforce, the globalization of the economy and its impact on modern industrial nations, to the shift from a manufacturing economy to a service economy. Some would argue that factors such as these, particularly those structural developments concerning alterations in the industrial economy (e.g., Bluestone and Harrison 1982), are affecting the class structure of the United States. Of course, the relatively recent character of these trends means that their future course of development is uncertain. The evidence to date suggests, however, that there is a significant likelihood of their continuing in the near future. Such a transformation of the class structure of America contrasts sharply with the image of a growing middle mass that underlies status-attainment research.

These changes in the images of the class and/or occupational structures of American society could have significant implications for the Sewell/Wisconsin model of status-attainment because such developments may contribute to a decline in the importance of this model in the years ahead. If the early status-attainment program was based on an image of society that enjoyed strong support in the years in which the program rose to ascendance, then it would seem likely that, as other images of society and social structure gain greater credence, the formulations of the Sewell/Wisconsin approach might have less appeal and might exercise less influence in the intellectual environment of contemporary sociology.

Given the validity of these observations, certain fundamental changes in the ways that society and social structure are conceptualized would seem desirable if this program is to sustain its place in the sociological world of ideas and research. What these changes would entail requires detailed elaboration of those areas in which theory development and research should focus (Knottnerus 1991). Briefly, such a reformulation would require attention being placed not only on the role of the individual actor but also on the various relevant structural dimensions of the socioeconomic order. At the same time, a more comprehensive framework for depicting societal and attainment processes should recognize that national labor markets are influenced by the international economic system and historical developments that can alter how societies and their class arrangements are structured.

Summary and Conclusions

In conclusion, many factors can play a role in the emergence of a research or theoretical school. This is certainly the case with the Wisconsin School's rise to prominence and the No. 1 ranking accorded the Department of Sociology at the University of Wisconsin. Part of the reason for its dominant position in contemporary sociology is the result of several historical factors. These include the informal social organization of the early research program, as centered around William Sewell, the appeal of its methodology, the available funding for its research projects, and the perceived relevance of the program for various social problems.

The utilization of rigorous quantitative procedures by Sewell and his associates was in keeping with the general trend in sociology in the post World War II period. The scientific approach legitimatized Sewell's findings among many of his colleagues and with funding agencies. Sewell, and the Wisconsin School of which he was chief architect, demonstrated the utility of sophisticated quantitative procedures in addressing what was then regarded as a salient feature of social mobility and stratification in the United States.[3]

Sewell's findings and his rigorous quantitative approach can be investigated from another vantage point. From a sociology of sociology perspective, research and/or theoretical schools may or may not exhibit an affinity with dominant themes, assumptions, and arguments in the social milieu of its time. When a research program articulates with a popular image of society, the appeal of that program is heightened. Status-attainment research is an excellent example of this dynamic because its affinity with a very popular conception of modern industrial society in the post world War II era enabled it to come to the fore in sociology during the past several decades.

Our analysis assumes that research findings, however quantitative in nature, rest in part for their "validity" on certain images of society and conceptual assumptions, even when these are not explicitly stated. This is the case with the status-attainment model, for it was founded on a distinct conception of society— the optimistic image of modern, mass, industrial society. That this image has exhibited a powerful and widespread appeal in sociology and many other social sciences over the past four decades had a rather direct bearing on the acceptance of the findings of the status-attainment model and the consequent rise in influence of the Wisconsin School.

If we pursue this reasoning further, we discern an interaction among Sewell's findings, his use of quantitative techniques, and the images of society. The "validity" of the findings were not merely a result of his use of rigorous quantitative procedures. For one thing, the early "sample" on which Sewell based his findings did not reflect the ethnic diversity common to many other regions in the United States. Instead, the research procedures were validated because the findings of the status-attainment model articulated with the ideal images within American society during (and just after) the time when Sewell and his associates were carrying out their research.

The thesis that I have advanced gains credence if we consider the changing images of American society during the 1980s and early 1990s. During the 1980s it was not the middle class that experienced upward mobility but the very privileged sector of American society. Tentative evidence suggests that ever larger sectors of American society no longer take their own or their children's upward mobility for granted. If these trends continue, we are likely to witness a serious questioning by sociologists and other social scientists of the findings regarding social mobility and stratification in America. In the process we are likely to find researchers questioning Sewell's research procedures as well.

If we consider the Department of Sociology at Wisconsin-Madison within a sociology of knowledge framework, we are able to gain a fuller understanding of how the enormous prestige of the Department was attained. This was in part a product of the confluence of Sewell's research program with the images of American society in the era in which he carried out his main sociological research.

More generally, a careful investigation of the status-attainment model, from a sociology-of-sociology perspective, provides us with a clearer understanding of how particular research programs come to be accepted or validated by the sociological community.

NOTES

1. For an in-depth analysis of this critical mass society thesis as found in social literature, see Giner (1976).

2. With its emphasis on individual factors and the open, fluid quality of society, the formulations of the status-attainment tradition coincide in many ways with the Horatio Alger conception of individual success and failure that has been a widely held belief in American culture for many years.

3. Sewell's autobiographical account (Sewell 1988) lends credence to the arguments of this paper. For instance, in his autobiography Sewell describes how the Wisconsin School built on the work of Blau and Duncan (1967) by introducing social-psychological factors as mediators between origins and attainment outcomes. Furthermore, in this essay Sewell describes his efforts to change the institutional structure of social scientific research at both Wisconsin and the national level. In the attempt to win recognition for sociology as a legitimate science, Sewell actively sought (especially while chair of the Department of Sociology at Wisconsin) to increase funding for sociological research by promoting scientific, quantitative research in areas such as social psychology, social stratification, and demography and ecology. As institutional scientific research gradually expanded to include social science research, the Wisconsin School was well positioned to compete successfully for these funding opportunities. Indeed, one might suggest that the Department of Sociology at Wisconsin stood at the forefront of what Sewell has referred to as the "quantitative scientific revolution in [American] sociology" (Sewell 1988:140).

REFERENCES

Alexander, Karl L. and Aaron M. Pallas. 1983. "Bringing the Arrows Back In: On the Recursivity Assumptions in School Process Models." *Social Forces* 62:32–53.

Arendt, Hannah. 1951. *The Origins of Totalitarianism*. New York: Harcourt,Brace.

Aron, Raymond. 1968. *Progress and Disillusion: The Dialectics of Modern Society*. New York: Praeger.

Averitt, Robert T. 1968. *The Dual Economy*. New York: McGraw-Hill.

Barber, Bernard. 1968. "Social Stratification Structure and Trends of Social Mobility in Western Society." Pp. 184–95 in Talcott Parsons, ed. *American Sociology: Perspectives, Problems, Methods*. New York: Basic Books.

Baron, James N., and William T. Bielby. 1980. "Bringing the Firms Back In: Stratification, Segmentation, and Organization of Work." *American Sociological Review* 45:737–65.

———. 1984. "The Organization of Work in a Segmented Economy." *American Sociological Review* 49:454–73.

Beck, E.M., Patrick M. Horan, and Charles Tolbert II. 1978. "Stratification in a Dual Economy." *American Sociological Review* 43:704–20.

Bell, Daniel. 1949. "America's Un-Marxist Revolution." *Commentary* 12:207–15.

————. 1960. *The End of Ideology: On the Exhaustion of Political Ideas in the Fifties.* Glencoe, Ill.: Free Press.

————. 1973. *The Coming of Post-Industrial Society.* New York: Basic Books.

Bibb, Robert and William H. Form. 1977. "The Effects of Industrial, Occupational, and Sex Stratification on Wages in Blue-Collar Markets." *Social Forces* 55:974–96.

Bills, David B., Archibald O. Haller, Jonathan Kelley, Mary B. Olson, and Jose Pastore. 1985. "Class, Class Origins, Regional Socioeconomic Development and the Status Attainment of Brazilian Men." *Research in Social Stratification and Mobility.* Vol. 4. Greenwich, Conn.: JAI Press.

Blau, Peter M. and Otis Dudley Duncan. 1967. *The American Occupational Structure.* New York: Wiley.

Bluestone, Barry, and Bennett Harrison. 1982. *The Deindustrialization of America.* New York: Basic Books.

————. 1986. "The Great American Job Machine." Washington, D.C.: Joint Economic Committee of Congress.

Blumberg, Paul. 1974. "The Decline and Fall of the Status Symbol: Some Thoughts on Status in a Postindustrial Society." *Social Problems* 21:480–94.

————. 1980. *Inequality in an Age of Decline.* New York: Oxford University Press.

Campbell, Richard T. 1983. "Status Attainment Research: End of the Beginning or Beginning of the End?" *Sociology of Education* 56:47–62.

Cooley, Charles H.. 1909. *Social Organization: A Study of the Larger Mind.* New York: Scribner.

————. 1918. *Social Process.* New York: Scribner.

Doeringer, Peter B., and Michael J. Piore. 1971. *Internal Labor Markets and Manpower Analysis.* Lexington, Mass.: Heath.

Drucker, Peter F. 1953. "The Employee Society." *American Journal of Sociology* 58:358–63.

————. 1971. "The New [Middle-Class] Majority." *The Listener* (a BBC publication), October 23 and 30, 1958, reprinted in Edgar Schuler et. al., *Readings in Sociology.* 4th ed. New York: Crowell.

Duncan, Otis Dudley. 1968. "Social Stratification and Mobility: Problems in the Measurement of Trends." Pp 675–719 in E.B. Sheldon and W.E. Moore, eds. *Indicators of Social Change.* New York: Russell Sage Foundation.

Duncan, Otis Dudley, David L. Featherman, and Beverly Duncan. 1972. *Socio-economic Background and Achievement.* New York: Seminar Press.

Featherman, David L. 1981. "Stratification and Social Mobility: Two Decades of Cumulative Social Science." Pp. 79–100 in James F. Short, Jr., ed. *The State of Sociology: Problems and Prospects.* Beverly Hills: Sage.

Featherman, David L., and Robert M. Hauser. 1978. *Opportunity and Change.* New York: Academic Press.

Fromm, Erich. 1941. *Escape from Freedom.* New York: Rinehart.

Gailbrath, John K. 1958. *The Affluent Society.* Boston: Houghton Mifflin.

Giner, Salvador. 1976. *Mass Society.* New York: Academic Press.

Haller, Archibald O.. 1982. "Reflections on the Social Psychology of Status Attainment." Pp. 3–28 in Robert M. Hauser, David Mechanic, Archibald O. Haller, and Taissa S. Hauser, eds. *Social Structure and Behavior: Essays in Honor of William Hamilton Sewell.* New York: Academic Press.

Horan, Patrick M. 1978. "Is Status Attainment Research Atheoretical?" *American Sociological Review* 43:534–41.

Huber, Joan and William H. Form. 1973. *Income and Ideology: An Analysis of the American Political Formula.* New York: Free Press.

Kaufman, Robert L., Randy Hodson, and Neil Fligstein. 1981. "Defrocking Dualism: A New Approach to Defining Industrial Sectors." *Social Science Research* 10:1–13.

Kerckhoff, Alan C. 1984. "The Current State of Social Mobility Research." *Sociological Quarterly* 25:139–53.

Knapp, Tim. 1987. "Deindustrialization and the Declining Middle Class." Paper presented at the 51st meeting of the Midwest Sociological Society, April 15–18, Chicago.

Knottnerus, J. David. 1987. "Status Attainment Research and Its Image of Society." *American Sociological Review* 52:113–21.

———. 1991. "Status Attainment's Image of Society: Individual Factors, Structural Effects, and the Transformation of the Class Structure." *Sociological Spectrum* 11:147–76.

Kornhauser, William. 1959. *The Politics of Mass Society.* New York: Free Press.

Kristol, Irving. 1978. *Two Cheers for Capitalism.* New York: Basic Books.

Kuttner, Robert. 1983. "The Declining Middle." *Atlantic Monthly* 252:60–72.

Lederer, Emil. 1940. *State of the Masses: The Threat of the Classless Society.* New York: Norton.

Lenski, Gerhard E. 1966. *Power and Privilege: A Theory of Social Stratification.* New York: McGraw-Hill.

Levy, Frank. 1987. *Dollars and Dreams: The Changing American Income Distribution.* New York: Russell Sage Foundation.

Mannheim, Karl. 1940. *Man and Society in an Age of Reconstruction.* New York: Harcourt, Brace.

Mayer, Kurt. 1959. "Diminishing Class Differentials in the United States." *Kyklos* 12:606–26.

———. 1963. "The Changing Shape of the American Class Structure." *Social Research* 30:460–68.

Marcuse, Herbert. 1964. *One Dimensional Man: Studies in the Ideology of Advanced Industrial Society.* Boston: Beacon Press.

Mercy, James A. and LaLa Carr Steelman. 1982. "Familial Influence on the Intellectual Attainment of Children." *American Sociological Review* 47:532–42.

Mullins, Nicholas C., and Carolyn J. Mullins. 1973. *Theories and Theory Groups in Contemporary Sociology.* New York: Harper & Row.

Nisbet, Robert A. 1959. "The Decline and Fall of Social Class." *Pacific Sociological Review* 2:11–17.

Olson, Philip., ed. 1963. *America as a Mass Society.* New York: Free Press.

Ortega Y Gasset, J. 1960. *La Rebelion de las Masas.* Madrid: Revista de Occidente. 34th ed. (orig. pub. 1929).

Osterman, Paul. 1975. "An Empirical Study of Labor Market Segmentation." *Industrial and Labor Relations Review* 28:506–23.

Page, Charles H. 1969. *Class and American Sociology: From Ward to Ross.* New York: Schocken.

Parsons, Talcott. 1954. "A Revised Analytical Approach to the Theory of Social Stratification." Pp. 386–439 in Talcott Parsons, *Essays in Sociological Theory.* New York: Free Press.

Pastore, Jose, and Archibald O. Haller. 1982. "Social Mobility under Labor Market Segmentation in Brazil." Pp. 113–40 in Robert M. Hauser, David Mechanic, Archibald O. Haller, and Taissa S. Hauser, eds. *Social Structure and Behavior: Essays in Honor of William Hamilton Sewell.* New York: Academic Press.

Pease, John, William H. Form, and Joan Huber Rytina. 1970. "Ideological Currents in American Stratification Literature." *American Sociologist* 5:127–37.

Rosenberg, Bernard, and David M. White, eds. 1957. *Mass Culture.* Glencoe, Ill.: Free Press.

Rosenthal, Neal H. 1985. "The Shrinking Middle Class: Myth or Reality? *Monthly Labor Review* 108:3–10.

Sewell, William H., Archibald O. Haller, and George W. Ohlendorf. 1970. "The Educational and Early Occupational Status Attainment Process: Replication and Revision." *American Sociological Review* 35:1014–27.

———, Archibald O. Haller, and Alejandro Portes. 1969. "The Educational and Early Occupational Attainment Process." *American Sociological Review* 34:82–92.

————, and Robert Hauser. 1972. "Causes and Consequences of Higher Education: Models of the Status Attainment Process." *American Journal of Agricultural Economics* 54:851–61.

————. 1975. *Education, Occupation, and Earnings: Achievement in the Early Career.* New York: Academic Press.

————. 1980. "The Wisconsin Longitudinal Study of Social and Psychological Factors in Aspirations and Achievements." *Research in Sociology of Education and Socialization* 1:59–99.

————. 1988. "The Changing Institutional Structure of Sociology and My Career." Pp. 119–44 in Matilda White Riley, ed. *Sociological Lives.* Newbury Park, Calif.: Sage.

Stein, Maurice, Arthur Vidich, and David M. White, eds. 1960. *Identity and Anxiety.* Glencoe, Ill.: Free Press.

Steinberg, Bruce. 1983. "The Mass Market Is Splitting Apart." *Fortune* 108:76–82.

Stolzenberg, Ross M.. 1978. "Bringing the Boss Back In: Employer Size, Employee Schooling, and Sociological Achievement." *American Sociological Review* 43:813–28.

Thurow, Lester C. 1984. "The Disappearance of the Middle Class." *New York Times* February 6, F3.

Wilensky, Harold L. 1964. "Mass Society and Mass Culture: Interdependence or Independence?" *American Sociological Review* 29:173–97.

Wilensky, Harold L., and Charles N. Lebeaux. 1965. *Industrial Society and Social Welfare.* New York: Free Press.

Wright, Erik Olin. 1978. "Race, Class and Income Inequality." *American Journal of Sociology* 83:1368–97.

————. 1980. *Class Structure and Income Determination.* New York: Academic Press.

Wright, Erik Olin and Luca Perrone. 1977. "Marxist Class Categories and Income Inequality." *American Sociological Review* 42:32–55.

| Chapter | **8** | ACADEMIC LABOR MARKETS AND THE SOCIOLOGY TEMPORARY |

Beth Hartung[*]

In 1965, *Time* magazine reported the ascent of an assistant professor of sociology who was offered fourteen jobs in a single year. His top offer was $18,000.[1] Some twenty-five years later, the young (or not so young) sociologist seeking entry-level appointment faces a different labor market. Even exceptional students from highly regarded programs are unlikely to receive as many lucrative job offers as they begin their careers. The "average" student may be fortunate to find any kind of academic employment. According to the National Center for Education Statistics, 20 percent of new Ph.D.s in the social sciences in 1988 were still seeking employment when the degree was awarded (NCES 1990:273).

Despite concern about an aging professoriate and younger faculty to replace them (Gee 1988; Skelley 1990), in this fiscally troubled decade, many sociologists who are unable to find secure employment start careers in part- or full-time temporary appointments. Some build careers off the tenure track. One scholar estimates that temporary faculty constitute 35 percent of all faculty teaching at colleges and universities (Arden 1988). Other estimates are more modest (see NCES 1990:221). Nevertheless, some systems have become heavily dependent on temporary faculty to meet classes. In the California State University, for example, part- and full-time lecturers made up almost half the faculty in 1987-88 (California Commission on Higher Education 1987).

Of course, temporary faculty are themselves a diverse group. Some are students finishing degrees, others do not have terminal degrees, or are retired from full-time teaching, or have other full-time employment (see Tuchman and Tuchman 1980). The most dissatisfied temporary faculty members are those with terminal degrees who cannot find full employment (Rosenblum and Rosenblum 1990:151-64).

This essay examines the human and career consequences of being a temporary in sociology.[2] Thus, it also is an essay about structuring an academic career. In 1988 and 1989, I surveyed and spoke with sociologists marginalized by a bad job market, declining university resources, uneducated mentors, the "wrong" specializations, lifestyle limitations (both voluntary and involuntary), and other factors. Their comments are reported here, organized by the length of time and the circumstances that place them outside the "normal" academic marketplace.

The longer they teach in nontenureable appointments, the more marginal they become. Timing, then, helps construct normalcy or deviance in a sociological career (see Reese and Katovich 1989).

What do sociologists in temporary positions tell us about the structure of the academy and the nature of doing sociology? Certainly they lead us to question how doing sociology has been confined to the colleges and universities where 75 percent of all sociologists earn their keep (Gans 1989). Moreover, they read the academy, and the future of sociology, from the bottom up. An examination of the role of temporary faculty members and their impact on the discipline starts with looking at (1) the expansion of sociology since World War II and the impact of more sociologists on the intellectual life of the discipline; and (2) how the academy works as an employer of intellectual talent.

The Expansion of Sociology/The Retrenchment of the Academy

The 1965 Ph.D. whose career opportunities were profiled in *Time* was a beneficiary of the post War expansion of the academy and of sociology. Table 8.1 shows that the peak year for undergraduate sociology degrees was 1973-74. Only two years later, the year in which Ph.D. production was at its highest, undergraduate degrees in sociology declined precipitously. In the fifteen years between 1974 and 1988, undergraduate degrees awarded in sociology dropped by 63 percent, M.A. degrees by 55 percent, but Ph.D.s dropped by only 28 percent (though Ph.D. production has slowed since 1985). The relatively high numbers of Ph.D.s balanced against declining demand for undergraduate instruction was a formula for under- and unemployment, a problem the discipline addressed only belatedly.[3] But the employment problems of young sociologists were only part of the malaise afflicting sociology throughout the 1980s. Resources became tighter even as the community of sociologists competing for resources grew. Research funds for social science were cut 30 percent between 1980 and 1989. Major centers of graduate education were threatened with closing, and some departments were disbanded. Pragmatic undergraduates chose fields that they perceived led more directly into employment than the social sciences (Berger 1989). There was grumbling about the caliber of students in graduate programs. Scores on the Graduate Record Exam declined, leading Hubert Blalock to state bluntly, "Sociology is not a high quality discipline" (Blalock 1989:457).[4]

Of more pressing concern to many sociologists, though certainly related to the intellectual abilities of its practitioners, is whether the discipline still has good ideas. In his presidential address to the American Sociological Association, Herbert Gans noted that sociologists play a smaller role in the intellectual life of this country than they might (Gans 1989:1). At the same time, sociologists have multiplied. The community of sociologists has grown from 2000-3000 to more than 10,000 since 1965, and the need to stand out in the crowd has promoted a differentiation of specialties (Collins 1986:1339-41). There is marked disagreement about whether this is a good thing (Collins 1986) or a bad thing (see Denzin 1987 and Collins 1987).

Worries about the quality of sociology, as measured by its students, its impact on policy and social commentary, and ground-breaking intellectual work, must be seen against the larger backdrop of U.S. higher education since the

Table 8.1
Earned Degrees in Sociology Conferred by Institutions
of Higher Education, 1949–50 to 1987–88

Year of Degree	B.A./B.S.	M.A.	Ph.D.
1949–50	7,870	552	98
1959–60	7,147	440	161
1969–70	30,436	1,813	534
1970–71	33,263	1,808	574
1971–72	35,216	1,944	636
1972–73	35,436	1,923	583
1973–74	35,491	2,196	632
1974–75	31,488	2,112	693
1975–76	27,634	2,009	729
1976–77	24,713	1,830	714
1977–78	22,750	1,611	599
1978–79	20,285	1,415	612
1979–80	18,881	1,314	583
1980–81	17,272	1,240	610
1981–82	16,042	1,145	558
1982–83	14,105	1,112	552
1983–84	13,145	1,008	520
1984–85	11,968	1,022	480
1985–86	12,271	965	504
1986–87	12,231	950	451
1987–88	13,000	982	452

Source: *Digest of Education Statistics*. (Washington, D.C.: National Center for Education Statistics, U.S. Department of Education, 1990), 272, table 261.

early 1970s. University administrators shaped the job market in sociology and other academic disciplines by their hiring practices. Reacting to predictions of declining undergraduate enrollment in the traditional-aged cohort of 18-24 year olds, universities hired large numbers of part-time and full-time lecturers (Franklin et al. 1988:15) instead of committing positions to faculty members they feared they could not tenure. Creating these appointments was seen as a necessary evil so that academic institutions could survive the hard times anticipated in the 1980s. When enrollments did not decline, universities continued to rely on temporary labor.

In their discussion of the university as an organizational labor market with internal and external sectors, Rosenblum and Rosenblum (1990) suggest that the proportion of "contractually limited" faculty has not changed greatly since the late 1960s. What *has* changed is the composition of persons available to do part-time and full-time temporary work. The Rosenblums' discussion of Canadian academics suggests that this faculty is relatively inexperienced (less than three years of teaching experience), over thirty-five, female, and married. While faculty members in temporary appointments are much less likely to have the Ph.D. than those tenured or on tenure track, increasing numbers do have terminal degrees. Table 8.2 shows that part-time faculty in U.S. institutions are well-educated and middle-aged, and that women are disproportionately represented. About one-third of part-timers have professional or doctoral degrees (28 percent) and 42 percent hold the master's degree.

Internal and External Labor Markets

A temporary faculty that looks more and more like a permanent faculty occupies a separate labor market with its own rules, but with very few rights. Temporary faculty members have been described as occupying a secondary labor market, as opposed to a primary market (Hartung 1985; Roemer and Schnitz 1982), or an external labor market (Rosenblum and Rosenblum 1990; Doeringer and Piore 1971) because of the parameters of temporary academic employment. These parameters include: a nonpermeable barrier between the secure internal marketplace and the external marketplace; poorer working conditions, pay, and other resources; and a low ceiling for career prospects and mobility.

Temporary or adjunct faculty members frequently are hired at the last minute or even after classes have begun. Hiring practices in this labor market are capricious, particularly for part-timers (full-timers have more advantages) (Abel 1984). Temporary faculty members have few choices about what classes they teach, their schedule of courses, or even *if* they will teach, since their hiring is contingent on enrollment (Franklin et al. 1988). They rarely get to teach in their areas of specialization and, in sociology, often teach multiple sections of large introductory courses. In addition, at many institutions full-time temporaries teach more courses than their tenured counterparts because their classes are weighted differently.

For teaching more classes and larger classes, full-time temporaries earn less than beginning assistant professors (Rosenblum and Rosenblum 1990). Part-timers are the most poorly paid of all academics. Their labor is contracted on a per class basis. Most part-timers, regardless of skill and experience, earn $1000 to $2000 per class (Franklin, et al. 1988).

Table 8.2
Part-Time Regular Instructional Faculty in Higher Education by Selected Characteristics, Fall 1987

	Number	Percent
Sex		
Male	99,000	56.7
Female	75,000	43.3
Total	174,000	100.0
Age		
Under 35	26,000	15.9
35–39	39,000	22.4
40–44	34,000	19.4
45–49	25,000	14.2
50–54	19,000	11.0
55–59	12,000	6.8
60+	19,000	10.9
Degree		
Doctoral	26,000	15.2
Professional	22,000	12.9
Master's	70,000	41.9
Graduate work	13,000	7.6
Bachelor's	28,000	16.9
Some college	9,000	5.2

Source: *Digest of Education Statistics* (Washington, D.C.: National Center for Education Statistics, U.S. Department of Education, 1990), 222, table 210.

Although temporary faculty may be responsible for more students than their tenured colleagues, they usually share an office with several other part-timers— if office space can be found. Some departments do not provide basic clerical services like typing and duplicating exams and syllabi. Some part-timers complain that they do not even have an office phone to receive calls from students (see VanArsdale 1978; Roemer and Schnitz 1982; Abel 1984; Wallace 1984).

Access to other institutional resources are limited as well. Part-timers rarely receive any benefits—such as retirement or medical insurance—and most faculty members off the tenure track cannot apply for university monies. Nontenure-track faculty members, regardless of the length of time they serve an institution, often are not eligible for university grants or teaching awards. Pursuing one's own research becomes extremely difficult.

Being a temporary for several years can have devastating effects. Self-esteem, a realistic assessment of ability and competence, and other prerequisites to scholarship can suffer. Such feelings and self-assessments can become a self-fulfilling prophecy, particularly for sociologists who serve a department for several years, but are not considered seriously for permanent employment. Feelings of exclusion, of being an outsider, persist. Even full-time temporaries note that colleagues may not think to encourage joint research efforts, as might be the case with faculty perceived to be part of the ongoing life of the department (cf. Katovich and Hardesty 1986).

No one can document how many sociologists teaching off the tenure track want a tenured position. Similarly, no one knows how many have been marginalized by a poor job market, meager talents, personality problems, or less desirable specializations and research. The ASA has no statistics on how many graduate students failed to finish dissertations through the 1970s and 1980s, discouraged by the limited employment prospects waiting for them. Even locating temporary faculty can be a challenge. Many do not appear in an institution's faculty directory. They may no longer belong to expensive professional associations. Once located, they may be sensitive about divulging their career histories. According to the sociologists I talked to, some have simply disappeared and are no longer in touch with more fortunate friends and colleagues.

Research Methods

The difficulties forced me to rely on a convenience sample of temporary faculty. The Chancellor's Office for the California State University, which is the largest state university system in the world and my employer, provided me with the names of all persons teaching off the tenure track in departments of sociology. In the then-nineteen campus[5] California State University, there were seventeen sociology departments. During the fall of 1988, 90 temporary positions in sociology were filled by seven full-time and seventy-four part-time teachers (some individuals were teaching at two or more branch campuses). Excluding the adjunct faculty members on my own campus, I contacted these persons with an open-ended questionnaire. Seven were returned outright with no forwarding address; twenty-five returned completed questionnaires. Additionally, I asked each respondent for the names of other persons who might be willing to tell their stories in a letter or by responding to a questionnaire. Several names were duplicated so that my final N from a universe of about ninety part-time and full-time sociologists was thirty-three. I also talked with several persons at length by phone, resulting in very informative case material.

Virtually all the respondents are from California, where, as several people noted, competition for academic jobs may be stiffer than elsewhere in the country. Over half graduated from nationally ranked public and private graduate institutions such as Berkeley, Arizona, Texas, Washington, and Brandeis. Two-thirds of the sociologists who responded were women. The median age was forty-one, the median degree year was 1985, and the average respondent had been teaching for about three and a half years. The courses these respondents reported teaching most frequently were introductory sociology, gender/sex roles, sociology of the family, social problems, and research methods. The top areas of research specializations they named were gender, medical sociology, criminology and deviance, theory, and social psychology. Six respondents were ABD (and still officially students) or teaching with a master's degree and no further graduate work. Only one sociologist said she chose part-time, nontenure track employment. For the other respondents, the disadvantages of nontenure track appointments outweighed any advantages. Even so, not everyone dissatisfied with their employment was actively seeking more permanent work.

Findings

The remainder of this essay examines academic careers off the tenure track. As mentioned earlier, case materials are organized by the length of time the respondent has spent in the temporary market and thus the distance from a normal academic career, but the reader should bear in mind that these categories are not rigid. Time off the tenure track helps to tell the stories drawn from extensive written comments on the surveys as well as personal correspondence and follow-up phone interviews with willing persons.

Transitional Temporaries: New Ph.D.s and ABDs

Six respondents had earned Ph.D.s since 1987 and two expected degrees in 1989. Two recent graduates had secured tenure track positions (including one

ABD candidate[6]), two were not actively searching for work, and the other four hoped to find secure employment. Nor surprisingly, how these recent entrants saw the job market in sociology ranged from poor, to OK, to much improved in recent years—depending on their own experiences and those of other students in their graduate program. A graduate of one of the top programs in the country reported that 60 percent of his cohort took post-doctoral positions or part-time teaching after earning their doctorates, but he believes graduates from his program are getting more interviews than was true for earlier cohorts. Another graduate from the same program stated that the market for sociologists is improving as a result of retirements and expanding enrollments.

Their perceptions were not shared by graduates from less prestigious programs. Students from middle-ranked graduate programs report fewer opportunities. One young ABD said, "No new positions are opening up in sociology [in the CSU] . . . When someone retires or leaves (or dies) even that position is closed." The other ABD in this group added, "Our discipline is in big trouble. Shrinking enrollments and lost turf battles with other disciplines steadily erode our ground."

While no one in this group was pleased about a temporary position, a couple of respondents conceded that it could be used to launch a career. A 1988 graduate suggested temporary positions could be made into "launching positions," rather than liabilities. This could be accomplished, he said, by close mentoring by senior faculty. "The temporary position should be more like a post-doc; departments can `produce' candidates for regular positions using temporary positions as training slots."

Beginning a career in a temporary position, even the relatively advantaged full-time temporary position, involves several drawbacks. Respondents commented on the diminishing likelihood of getting on tenure track with each passing year. This is an outcome of heavy workloads in temporary positions and of prejudices about Ph.D.s who hold such appointments. A 1988 graduate said that her three new course preparations left little time for professional activities in her first year out of graduate school. Another part-timer wrote that "the workload is such that earning a living can prohibit research or even serious study."

Successful launching from a temporary position in a crowded market involves some record of original scholarship (more likely for Ph.D.s with recent dissertations), some teaching experience, and the ability to go where the jobs are. It also involves realistic, sometimes painful, assessments of the future. One part-timer who taught for four years at her institution found a tenure track position elsewhere. She wrote, "Although [my department] really liked me, I knew in my heart of hearts that they would never hire me when the retirements start."

A temporary appointment offers ample opportunity for getting teaching experience and may be useful to persons whose teaching opportunities in graduate school were limited. This was true for one young Ph.D., who wrote: "I sought part-time, temporary work after failing to get [a] tenure track position due to lack of teaching experience. It worked (I used them; they didn't use me) and I ended up with two full-time offers." Others commented that temporary appointments are a place to develop teaching skills, try different techniques, and experiment. But candidates eager to make the transition can bog down in the immediate rewards of teaching to the detriment of research. Temporary faculty members know this, and expressed these assessments: "At some point . . . teaching takes up too much of your time and energy and thus takes away from research, writing . . . and time with friends." And, "The `publish or perish' virus has infested the teaching-oriented Cal. State system. Those people who have the least teaching experience and the most publications get the job. It's a shame really."

Persons who finished doctorates in the late 1980s expected a limited job market. Unlike their predecessors of the 1970s, they may not blame themselves for being unable to find employment. However, limited employment options can result in lethargy and can slow progress in scholarship or a nearly completed degree. One respondent's case is instructive of these dangers. She entered graduate school in a cohort of eighteen students in 1982. Seven years later, two had completed Ph.D.s. The rest had left the program or technically still were students. The respondent hoped to finish her Ph.D. in 1989, although she had just started her dissertation research that year. In the meantime, she had one on-site interview for a full-time renewable temporary position in a women's studies program and a local job offer that involved teaching two courses in the fall and three in the spring for a salary of $13,000. Of the latter job, she was told that "this is really a position for someone who has another income."

She left the city where she attended graduate school to take a part-time teaching job and that slowed down her degree progress. Like many graduate students nearing the end of a doctoral program, she felt she received minimal support from the faculty there. Anticipating the end of her doctoral work, she said she has already started to look into other jobs besides teaching. Piecing together part-time jobs while working on her dissertation was hard. Looking ahead to the future, she said, "I don't want to kill myself. I don't want to work as hard as I did in graduate school."

When her part-time teaching job ended, she worked as a waitress and as a secretary, and applied for eighty teaching jobs all over the country. Her mentors have told her and other students not to take nontenure-track jobs because they say they will never be taken seriously in the field.

Most new Ph.D.s fear starting a career off the tenure track. Their fears are not unfounded. A 1989 graduate, still looking for work at the time of this survey, wrote that if one continues in temporary positions past receipt of the Ph.D., "[it] will probably be seen as a sign of incompetence." This was echoed by a 1988 graduate, who said, "I sense that a long career of temporary teaching can result in a person being stigmatized as less qualified than regular instructors."

The recent Ph.D. who is able to move, who actively publishes, and who is a competent teacher is the most likely of the two groups discussed here to make the transition to tenure track in a year or two. The catch for that Ph.D. is that not everyone in his or her cohort will find tenure track appointments. When one is temporary, one never knows exactly how long job insecurity will extend.

Permanent Temporaries

Twenty-two respondents qualify as permanent temporaries. The likelihood that they will move into permanent positions declines with each year, although many have served their departments longer than permanent junior faculty. A question that many might raise, looking at this group, is why they continue to teach under such poor conditions. Why not simply leave college teaching and do something else? Each of these respondents would answer the question differently. And although most of these sociologists are all too aware that the odds of entering sociology's mainstream decline with time spent at the periphery, they tell some remarkable success stories. One respondent took his first tenure track position six years after he earned a Ph.D. Another sociologist who lived on part-time teaching and soft money for twelve years after earning his doctorate was finally hired in a permanent capacity.

More realistically, after being a temporary for several years it becomes nearly impossible to move to more secure employment. Those with older Ph.D.s (awarded in the 1970s) have different perceptions of *why* they have not found employment than those with more recent degrees. This section presents two categories of individuals who, for all intents and purposes, have entered the permanent temporary market.

First is the special case of academic women married to academic men. In a dual career marriage, women's careers often take a back seat to a husband's career (and if this were not so, there would be more dual career women married to other academics in the transitional group). Second, there are those who have been in the temporary market for so long (more than ten years) that their escape to something more permanent is highly unlikely. They represent the "lost generation" that commentators wrote about in the 1980s.

The Women

Women are overrepresented in temporary positions for a variety of reasons. Women graduate students kept graduate program enrollments strong in the

1980s as men who might have entered graduate programs sought work elsewhere. Since the late 1970s, the proportion of all Ph.D.s awarded women increased by 36 percent, while the proportion awarded men declined by 14 percent (Coyle 1986). Indeed, women earned 35 percent of all Ph.D.s in 1987-88, and 45 percent of social science Ph.D.s. Women sociologists, like other women scholars, are at greater risk of underemployment and marginal employment because of the real numbers of women earning terminal degrees, institutional sexism (Hartung 1987), and the different form women's careers can take because of children and mate.

Thirty-five percent of the temporaries in this sample were married to other academics, usually men whose careers were established. They are the group most likely to build careers as local adjunct faculty. Although not all of the immobile were women and not all were married, women more often than men reported sacrificing a "normal" career for their spouse or family. Only two men in this study mentioned that a wife's employment or school-aged children limited their freedom to move. Instead of commuting long distances for a tenure track job or uprooting a spouse established in his career, the women in this group took local, temporary employment.

Dual career couples are becoming more common, but wives are often the academics who sacrifice their careers. Only exceptional couples, where both parties are committed to furthering the careers of both and have the economic security to take risks, resolve career issues equitably (see Adler et al. 1989). For most academic couples, disadvantages are not shared (Smart and Smart 1990:36). Kauffman and Perry (1989) suggest that mobility as an employment issue is minimized because the "moving ethic" is accepted in academia. The wife who postpones her own graduate work while her husband finishes his Ph.D. may finish graduate school where he *starts* his career. Some institutions will avoid hiring spouses or scholars whose degrees were earned locally (Kauffman and Perry 1989).

Aisenburg and Harrington (1988) suggest academic women are caught between two contradictory cultural plots. In the first, the feminine "love plot," the end goal is marriage and domesticity; the "quest plot" is the one associated with men and has a knowledge goal at the end of a personal journey. Many women sociologists make an uneasy choice between maintaining a personal life and having a career. Several respondents spoke about these difficult choices.

One respondent who earned her Ph.D. in 1985 and who was a star student in her doctoral program has never had a permanent appointment. She and her spouse decided moving was unrealistic for them: "Since he's a full professor (white male, only somewhat published) with some agony we decided not to put me on the job market. [We] couldn't afford living on a beginning assistant professor's salary with two kids." Another sociologist who had not looked for permanent positions since earning her degree said that while her husband has always been supportive, "he has his own career to consider. Let's face it, two-career families create problems."

For many couples, physical separation is the only way both partners can have full-time careers. This is less of an option for couples with young children, but even couples without children may not want to live apart. A sociologist with eight years of part-time teaching would like a full-time appointment, but she is unwilling to leave her academic husband. Another who taught part-time in the program where she earned her degree did not want to leave her family and commute. She was still bitter about how others responded to her choice: "The worst part was the lack of support from many so-called feminists. I was informed that I wasn't really serious about my work and that I was ruining my chances for getting tenure anywhere. In addition I was told that I was making it difficult for other female Ph.D. students to be taken seriously."

Unfortunately, this last statement probably is accurate. Individual women's choices are still generalized to all women, even in a field increasingly peopled by women. In valuing her family over her career, this women made a choice about her priorities—a choice not always respected by men or women, and certainly not a choice in keeping with the usual academic career.

Immobility can lead to mistreatment and unprofessionalism. The case of the sociologist who agonized and decided not to enter the job market because of her full professor husband suggests just how hard immobility can be. She had been teaching part-time in sociology and in women's studies for nine years when a full-time position opened in her institution. She applied for the job, but later heard the personnel committee had not considered her application. She said, "I had heard temporary lecturers are disadvantaged as too close to the department, and I understand the importance of infusing new ideas." But she felt her department had made an *a priori* assumption about her candidacy that was not based on her service to the department at that time. Moreover, they were legally bound to read her application. She filed a grievance and got the position (which was for one year only), but at the cost of her physical and mental health. She still teaches in the department part-time.

Tenured colleagues may treat local scholars with condescension, as if getting a doctorate is a sign of dilettantism. The new tenure track colleague of the respondent who filed the grievance was told that "there were no [other] women" in the department despite the evident presence of two women part-timers with Ph.D.s. Thus, part-timers are "invisible. The language used excludes us. As part-time workers we are perceived as part-time people . . . half-time people are more committed than full-time temporaries. They have a long-term relationship [with their institution]."

Another sociologist who taught as a temporary and whose husband also was on staff in her department said, "I was *never* treated as a colleague or valued person; [I was] labeled early on as a 'troublemaker' because I was a feminist [although I] was probably treated less shabbily than I'd have been if they weren't concerned about my husband leaving."

Even those sociologists who did not feel alienated from colleagues noted they were still not a "real" part of the department. Katovich and Hardesty suggest that friendships developing between the temporary and his or her colleagues are bounded by the length of contract. They call this absence of a proscribed future "the long goodbye" (1986:338). For local scholars who cannot move, the long goodbye may extend for years. They also tend not to be seen or encouraged as scholars. This is especially true if they are married to another faculty member, or are teaching in the department where they have been a student. The respondent quoted earlier who taught in the department where she had earned her degree said of her two years off the tenure track, "Not one of my fellow faculty suggested we work together on research or a paper." Her "fellow faculty members" probably were not defining her as a "real" colleague, but as a student.

This group is not optimistic about finding permanent academic work. Unlike their peers from the 1970s (see below), some of whom left tenure track appointments or at least had job offers, this group has not ever been on tenure track, and may never be. Most of them are not seeking permanent work outside their local area. As one respondent put it, "I know I am stuck." Many had families before they returned to graduate school or had spouses with more advanced careers. Economic imperatives and the desire to remain with a spouse means career "choices" are simplified but no less painful.

The Lost Generation

Persons earning Ph.D.s in the 1970s who are still teaching in the temporary market are probably a relatively small group. (There were five in this sample, and two were teaching part-time after voluntarily leaving tenured positions.) Most of their peers either left academia or took less desirable teaching jobs where they now are tenured. This earliest cohort of permanent temporaries has been designated the "lost generation" (Bowen 1981). They faced a terrible job market in the early 1970s, and they did not know how far-reaching their decisions at the beginning of their careers would be. For the first time since the early 1960s, not all sociologists were getting good jobs with an earned doctorate. Some in the lost generation decided to hold out, to wait until the academic market got better. Instead, it got worse. A sociologist who earned her degree in 1974 explained, "There was never any discussion on the part of faculty about the job market. We didn't know until we started looking for jobs how bad it was. We discovered all at once that it was just horrible." She continued, "Just about everywhere I've been, nobody has been hired full-time since the late 1960s. Institutions were only hiring temporaries and part-timers. I've known lots and lots of people who've dropped out."

One of her peers, a friend from graduate school, took a replacement position in 1973 because he "wanted to stay in California, and we all thought ˋsomething will come up.'" Instead, by 1975 the market for sociologists was extremely poor. One Bay Area school where he applied had 450 applicants for a single opening in the late 1970s. In the intervening years, he continued to apply widely for academic positions (though primarily in the west). He says, "I've been in the top categories where I've applied. That keeps me going."

A number of forces act against the lost generation: their age (the youngest are in their middle forties) and the age of their degrees, whether or not they have been able to continue with their research, the kind of research they do, and their willingness (at midlife) to move to another part of the country and start over in an entry level position. Said one, "I keep thinking I'm not going to do this anymore." The psychological strains and the constant financial pressures are burdensome, she said, and yet "I love sociology and teaching. As long as there's any possibility, I keep going. At some point I may become less enchanted." While their experiences as individuals have been quite different, this group's careers have been marked by similar events: permanent temporary status for several years at the same state colleges; being passed over for tenure track openings in favor of younger, less expensive (and less experienced) colleagues; and being passed over for full-time temporary openings.

The respondent quoted earlier left a tenure track job at a good public university ten years ago. She left because she was unhappy there and because she did not believe she would be tenured. When she returned to California in the late 1970s, she found a brisk competition for jobs. She was hired as a lecturer in the state university system and was fairly content at two of the three campuses that employed her. At her last part-time job, she understood she would be hired on a permanent basis if there was ever an opening. For years there were no openings. Recently, though, her department had advertised two positions, one of which suited her. She applied as did the other temporaries in the department. Her interview went well, but the job was offered to an outside candidate—a young women with a new Ph.D. When that candidate refused the job, the department lost the appointment altogether.

Another sociologist in this group graduated in 1973 and was never on a tenure track. He described himself as "about three standard deviations from the mean" because of his experiences in the academic market. One feature distinguishing him from his peers in the temporary marketplace is the scholarship he produced without economic or institutional support. He has published two books and ten articles in as many years, and several short essays which appeared in major metropolitan newspapers and journals of opinion. He is driven, in part, by his opposition to the affirmative action policies he believes have disadvantaged him and others he knows. This is his story.

When he graduated, he restricted his serious job hunting to California. By 1977, he was unemployed when his replacement position at a private college ended. The following year he began to teach part-time at one of two state universities, where he remained for ten years. He had no appointment for the coming academic year when we spoke and was considering leaving sociology and earning another doctorate.

He faults the ASA for its failure to restrict the flow of terminal degree holders when so many have been unable to get jobs. The ASA, he says, is "heavily into denial" since it does not acknowledge limited opportunities in academic sociology. The professional association is "locked into political orthodoxy" and systematically has covered up the damage to entire cohorts of sociologists. He alleges that academic sociologists have knuckled under to pressure from administrators to hire sociologists only in affirmative action preference categories, especially in public systems of higher education serving large numbers of minority students. This is his moral crusade, and he believes he has paid a price in jobs lost.

On job interviews, he has been asked not to discuss his critique of affirmative action for fear that he will be labeled racist and discredited. He feels his choice of unpopular and impolitic research questions, combined with entering the market at the wrong time, have kept him from the tenure track.[7]

Not all graduates of the 1970s are unhappy about a career in temporary appointments. A 1972 graduate, now sixty, has chosen part-time teaching. "I feel a bit uncomfortable about this as I know a number of part-time teachers who are far from happy with their lot," she said. "I chose to give up a position at a good school because I wanted to write and do some other things. I love teaching, though, and didn't want to abandon that. . . . For me [this] has worked well. I am well-treated and appear to be respected here."

She has continued to publish and present papers as well as write nonacademic pieces, so she feels part of an academic community that many of her peers find excludes them. "I have not particularly wanted a full-time, tenure track position—which is just as well, considering the dearth of jobs!"

She is unique among her peers, most of whom continue to search for full-time and part-time, tenure track and nontenure track jobs. For the lost generation of sociologists, hope is the companion of financial insecurity. Additionally, tension between them and their colleagues is exacerbated because, says one, "[Tenured faculty] tend to view temporaries as second rate . . . They have no idea how rotten the job market is. If you are a temporary too long, the assumption is that something is wrong with you." Another 1974 graduate who taught part-time for ten years says bluntly of his department, "As far as departmental life is concerned, I am *not* included . . . They don't care about me, so I don't care about them."

Of course, not all temporary jobs are created equal, nor are all temporaries. Some departments, and colleagues, are more appreciative than others. One respondent has found that even in the best of situations, permanent faculty "don't realize or seem concerned about how little part-timers earn. We tend not to complain, because we don't want to lose our jobs." Finances are a constant, nagging struggle. One respondent, who labeled himself a "permanent temporary," said the most pressing problem for him was the disparity between his earnings and those of his tenured colleagues.

Conclusions and Speculations

In this essay, I describe different paths to employment in sociology off the tenure track, and I analyze the role of temporaries specific to sociology. Information about this group is limited and it is impossible to draw a probability sample from their numbers. Nevertheless, two points emerge from this discussion that need not depend on the validity of the sample: first, the heterogenous nature of temporaries in sociology; and second, the homogamous nature of their grievances as exploited workers.

I identify two kinds of temporaries in sociology: those who may be in transition to permanent (tenure-track) employment, and those who will be permanently temporary. Of the permanent temporaries, women are the most significant group. A second subtype are members of the lost generation of the 1970s. Recent Ph.D.s appear most able to move out of the temporary market, though no one has examined the longer-term implications of such extended apprenticeship on academic careers. Married women and mothers in dual-career couples are sociologists who have been discarded or demeaned as local scholars even as sociology becomes more feminized. And finally, the lost generation are the most embittered because they saw what an academic life could have been, expected it would be theirs, and watched it pass them by. Thus, there can be no single composite of the "temporary" in sociology.

Despite diversity, temporaries share similar grievances. Three kinds of grievances are implicit in this analysis: (1) not having one's contributions to a department or program acknowledged; (2) inadequate salary and benefits; and (3) being denigrated as local scholars.

Many faculty members complained that they were not treated as colleagues whose work is important. Ironically, since temporary faculty members are more likely to teach introductory courses that recruit new generations of sociologists, they may have contact with more students than regular faculty. Closely related to lack of acknowledgment is poor pay and benefits, a constant source of worry for sociologists in temporary appointments. If there is no faculty union, part-timers are unlikely to receive benefits such as insurance and retirement. Even with a union, full-time temporary faculty members rarely earn more than a beginning assistant professor regardless of their service to the university and their experience. Indeed, experience, work record, and credentials may not count for any difference in pay for temporaries, though good teaching is at a premium in many departments. Several respondents said that long-term service to an institution should be honored. For example, one person wrote that "administrators could work harder to retain temporary faculty who demonstrate their commitment and ability as opposed to simply rotating people through . . . positions."

Finally, temporary faculty members who are not geographically mobile are subject to being stigmatized as local. Many feel they are penalized when "real" jobs open up because they are already there and are unlikely to move (even if opportunities were available). Being defined as local particularly disadvantages women, whose families may limit their ability to leave an area.

The lack of attention given temporaries in academic sociology reflects poorly on more fortunate (and fully employed) scholars. In the long run, the strength and vitality of sociology relies on providing reasonably sound opportunities for effective teaching, research, or practice. Thus, for example, sociologists at leading research institutions should be interested—both morally and academically—in what is happening to their former students in the temporary market. Additionally, temporaries need assistance from nationally based educational and professional organizations, including the American Sociological Association.

Sociologists off the tenure track are a social problem and one that will be heightened unless a concerted effort is made to reverse current trends. Viewing sociology from the bottom up, we gain a better understanding of the discipline than currently exists. We need to know more about temporaries and the secondary labor market that selects its members based on generation and gender; we also need to examine how temporaries affect the quality of teaching and research at our universities and colleges. Based on this research, it seems reasonable to hypothesize that teaching and research are undermined, rather than enhanced, by exploiting qualified persons who are, in turn, alienated from their workplace. As sociologists, we are especially culpable because one of the differences between sociology and other, less structurally inclined disciplines is that we know when a relationship compromises one party and exploits the other.

Acknowledgements

*I want to thank Dean Judith A. Hunt of the Office of the Chancellor for the California State University and Sherna Gluck, vice-president for lecturers in the California Faculty Association, for their help. Joel Best, Marcia Bedard, and

Richard Freimuth made helpful comments on earlier drafts of this manuscript. I especially want to thank the sociologists who responded to my questions, who corresponded with me, and who sent news clippings.

Notes

1. In 1970 the average full-time faculty salary was $13,100. For assistant professors in public institutions, the average salary was $10,900 (Statistical Abstract of the United States 1990:160).

2. This seems a good place to mention that I have personal knowledge of the temporary market for academics. I was a temporary lecturer for two years after finishing my Ph.D. at Southern Illinois University, Carbondale.

3. In the early 1980s, a concerned group of sociologists headed by Edna Bonacich formed an *ad hoc* committee to the American Sociological Association on unemployment and underemployment in the discipline. They recommended providing resources to underemployed and unemployed sociologists. They also recommended that graduate programs take more responsibility for placing their graduates and providing information about nonacademic careers in sociology (*Ad Hoc* Committee on Un- and Underemployment in the Discipline 1988).

4. Blalock contends that the quality of sociology students has declined over the past 30 years. If this is so, he casts aspersions on current graduate students as well as the former graduate students who now instruct them.

5. As of fall 1989, there are 20 CSU campuses.

6. A third contacted me in 1990 about a tenure-track job she was beginning in a midwestern state.

7. A background note: The number of minority Ph.D.s increased through the 1980s. Between 1977 and 1985, minority students receiving Ph.D.s grew from 7 to 9 percent. Most of those Ph.D.s were awarded in education, with the social sciences a distant second. Seventy-five percent of Ph.D.s graduated are white (see Bjork and Thompson, 1989:347-48).

REFERENCES

Abel, E.. 1984. *Terminal Degrees: The Job Crisis in Higher Education.* New York: Praeger.
"*Ad Hoc* Committee on Unemployment and Underemployment in the Discipline." 1988. American Sociological Association unpublished report, Washington, D.C.: January 13.
Adler, P.A., P. Adler, C.R. Ahrons, M.S. Perlmutter, W.G. Staples, and C.A.B. Warren. 1989. "Dual-Careerism and the Conjoint-Career Couple." *American Sociologist* 20:207–26.
Aisenberg, N. and M. Harrington. 1988. *Women of Academe: Outsiders in the Sacred Grove.* Amherst: University of Massachusetts Press.

Arden, E. 1989. "How to Help Adjunct Professors: Academe's Invisible People." *Chronicle of Higher Education* 35(May 17):A48.

Berger, J. 1989. "Sociology's Long Decade in the Wilderness." *New York Times* May 28, 6E.

Bjork, L. G. and T. E. Thompson. 1989. "The Next Generation of Faculty: Minority Issues." *Education and Urban Society* 21:341–51.

Blalock, H. M. 1989. "The Real and Unrealized Contributions of Quantitative Sociology." *American Sociological Review* (June):447–60.

Bowen, W.G. 1981. "Graduate Education in the Arts and Sciences: Prospects for the Future." *Change* 13:40–44.

California Commission on Higher Education. 1987. *Background Papers: The Master Plan Renewed.* Sacramento, Calif. August.

Cartter, A.M. 1976. *Ph.D.s and the Academic Labor Market.* New York: McGraw Hill.

Collins, R. 1986. "Is 1980s Sociology in the Doldrums?" *American Journal of Sociology* 91:1136–55.

———. 1987. "Looking Forward or Looking Back: Reply to Denzin." *American Journal of Sociology* 93:180–84.

Coyle, S.L. 1986. *Science, Engineering, and Humanities Doctorates in the United States: 1984 Profile.* Washington, D.C.: National Academy Press.

Denzin, N. K. 1987. "The Dean of Sociology in the 1980s: Comment on Collins." *American Journal of Sociology* 93:175–80.

Doeringer, P. and M. Piore. 1971. *Internal Labor Markets and Manpower Analysis.* Lexington, Mass.: Lexington Books.

Franklin, P., D. Laurence and R.D. Denham. 1988. "When Solutions Become Problems: Taking a Stand on Part-Time Employment." *Academe* 74:15–19.

Gans, H. J. 1989. "Sociology in America: The Discipline and the Public." *American Sociological Review* 54:1–16.

Gee, E. G. 1988. "A Lost Generation in Higher Education." *U.S. News & World Report* 104(April 4):6.

Hartung, B. 1985. "The Matter of Degree: Underemployed Academics and Labor Market Segmentation." Ph.D. dissertation, University of Nebraska-Lincoln.

———. 1987. "Academic Women and Underemployment." Paper presented at the Society for the Study of Social Problems, Chicago.

Heinzelman, K. 1986. "The English Lecturers at Austin: Our New M.I.A.'s." *Academe* 72:25–31.

Katovich, M. A. and M. J. Hardesty. 1986. "The Temporary." *Studies in Symbolic Interaction* 7:333–52.

Kauffman, D. R. and F. J. Perry. 1989. "Institutional Sexism in Higher Education: The Case of the Geographically Bound Academic Woman." *NWSA Journal* 1:644–59.

Mumford, L.S. 1986. "The Painful Process of Letting Go." *Chronicle of Higher Education* 33(November 19):A104.

National Center for Education Statistics (NCES). 1990. *Digest of Education Statistics.* Washington, D.C.: U.S. Department of Education.

Reese, W. A. and M. A. Katovich. 1989. "Untimely Acts: Extending the Interactionist Conception of Deviance." *Sociological Quarterly* 30:159–84.

Roemer, R.E. and J.E. Schnitz. 1982. "Academic Employment as Day Labor: The Dual Labor Market in Higher Education." *Journal of Higher Education* 53:514–31.

Rosenblum, G. and B. R. Rosenblum. 1990. "Segmented Labor Markets in Institutions of Higher Learning." *Sociology of Education* 63:151–164.

Shenfelt, M. 1989. "Pity the Serfs at Our Medieval Universities." *New York Times* (January 13), A31.

Skelley, M. E. 1990. "There's No Quick Fix for the Ph.D. Shortage." *School and College* 20:13.

Smart, M. S., and R. C. Smart. 1990. "Paired Prospects: Dual Career Couples on Campus." *Academe* 76:33–37.

"Sociology in Bloom." 1965. *Time*. 86(October 29):64, 66.

Statistical Abstract of the United States. 1990. 110th ed. Washington, D.C. U.S. Department of Commerce, Bureau of the Census. p. 160.

Tuchman, B.H., and H.P. Tuchman. 1980. "Women as Part-Time Faculty Members." *Higher Education* 10:169–79.

Van Arsdale, G. 1978. "Deprofessionalizing a Part–time Teaching Faculty: How Many, Feeling Small, Seeming Few, Getting Less, Dream of More." *American Sociologist* 13:195–201.

Wallace, M.E., ed. 1984. *Part-Time Academic Employment in the Humanities*. New York: Modern Language Association of America.

Wilke, A.S., ed. 1979. *The Hidden Professorate*. Westport, Conn.: Greenwood Press.

Chapter 9
IDEOLOGY AND THE CELEBRATION OF APPLIED SOCIOLOGY

Thomas A. Lyson and Gregory D. Squires

> For the social sciences are parts of culture, and it so happens that they are carried forward predominantly by college and university professors, who in turn are hired by businessmen trustees. The stake of these last in the status quo is great.
>
> Robert Lynd

In the mid-1970s the bottom dropped out of the academic job market in sociology. Ph.D. programs were turning out new doctorates in unprecedented numbers at a time when job openings in colleges and universities were declining sharply. In 1971, for instance, there were over a thousand academic job openings, while graduate programs were turning out only about 500 new Ph.D.s. By 1974, the number of academic positions had declined to only 166, but the number of new doctorates had increased to over 600. Such realities lead Richard Freeman (1976:91) to conclude that the 1970's produced "the worst job market for Ph.D.s in America's academic history."

Although the academic job market has brightened considerably in recent years and the supply of new Ph.D.s has decreased a bit, it is clear that the halcyon days of the late 1960s and early 1970s are gone forever. In view of the academic employment problems that have plagued sociology during the late 1970s and early 1980s, many looked to positions in nonacademic or applied settings as an alternative to employment in academic settings (Freeman and Rossi 1984; Freeman et. al. 1983; Huber 1982; Flynn 1982; Wright-Isak 1989). In many respects this is a welcome trend, and not only for the new jobs that are being created. For too long, the sociological community has ignored the nonacademic marketplace.

The creation of new employment alternatives outside academia, the plaudits directed to applied sociology, and the emphasis on training graduates to fit available job opportunities, however, embody potentially serious costs to the

289

profession and ignore critical changes that are occurring in the labor market that may not serve either the long-run development of the discipline or the immediate needs of its practitioners. While efforts to create nonacademic job opportunities for sociologists might temporarily bolster the employment prospects of a few social scientists, in the long run they may lead to a de-skilling of the sociological profession, the homogenization of the nonacademic labor markets open to social scientists, and a diminution of the contributions that sociology can make to society.

The sociological community historically has taken a reductionist, neoclassical approach to issues pertaining to employment opportunities for sociologists. Whether times were good or bad, little attention has been paid to the structural factors that underlie the supply of and demand for sociologists. And until the mid-1970s virtually no attention had been directed at nonacademic employment alternatives.

Given the general indifference of the sociological community to employment issues in the profession, it is not surprising that when employment prospects turn bad, as they did in the mid-1970s, the profession has been unable to offer any sociological explanation of why the demand for sociologists would fall so dramatically, nor suggest any real alternatives to diminishing employment opportunities. Instead, most sociologists have adopted reactionary stances when unemployment rises and have blamed the unemployed and underemployed for not better preparing themselves for the job market or for not seeking out alternative employment opportunities. To alleviate problems of unemployment and underemployment, the sociological community has responded with agendas to equip sociologists better for the rigors of a more competitive marketplace (i.e., the "dress for success" approach) and with a willingness to sanction almost any nonacademic employment as appropriate work for its members.

The latent ideology that has shaped the sociological professions's response to its labor market reflects broader intellectual currents in the discipline. Almost half a century ago, C. Wright Mills (1959) acknowledged some of the limitations of this ideology when he described the bureaucratization of the discipline that evolved from the emerging abstracted empiricism that characterized the research of many of his contemporaries. Subsequent advances in the technological apparatus for survey research and statistical analysis, sociology's continuing efforts to secure a more "scientific" stature and "relevant" role in human affairs, in conjunction with the celebration of applied sociology in recent years, have magnified the pitfalls Mills discussed. Human-capital theory with its emphasis on the characteristics of individual actors in social systems favored by economists, and the sociological counterpoint, status-attainment theory (Horan 1978), lend themselves to such an approach while proffering a false sense of scientific security to sociologists by mimicking a more established social science.

Today, the manifestations of this ideology are apparent in many so-called applied sociological projects where advanced survey research techniques are couched in "scientific" terms and the relevance of the sociological enterprise to human affairs is reduced to the responses of a few hundred individuals on a survey instrument. Herbert Gans recently referred to the "mindlessness" of this work in his 1988 ASA Presidential Address and lamented that the importance of social context, historical antecedents, and theory, the very essence of sociology, are too often ignored by sociologists today (Gans 1989).

In this essay, we discuss the history of unemployment in sociology, previous attempts to move the discipline out of the academy, and the ideological framework (i.e., neoclassical, human-capital/status-attainment) that has been utilized to analyze these developments. We examine current efforts by the American Sociological Association, other professional organizations, and academic departments to expand nonacademic employment opportunities, efforts that have been limited by the theoretical lens through which the problems have been seen. We conclude with a discussion of the costs and benefits to the discipline as it expands into nonacademic arenas.

Too Many Sociologists: The Past as Prologue

The most recent job crunch and research into its causes are not without precedent. During the depths of the Great Depression, when few employment opportunities existed anywhere in the economy, F. Stuart Chapin, president of the American Sociological Society (ASS), and Elsworth Faris, chairman of the sociology department at the University of Chicago (the leading producer of sociology Ph.D.s at the time), exchanged views on the state of the job market for new sociology doctorates. Writing in the *American Journal of Sociology*, Chapin (1934:506) opened the debate with the question, "Are the graduate departments of sociology overproducing trained personnel?" Basing his comments on the view that academic employment was the best, and perhaps the only, suitable employment for sociologists, he concluded, using the meager labor market data available at the time, that sociology graduate departments indeed were producing almost twice as many qualified applicants as there were jobs available.

Faris (1934:510) responded to this narrow view of the sociology job market by stating: "The need for sociologists is not static. If sociologists have produced that which is of high value, the students in American colleges and universities have as much right to it as biology, mathematics or history." He continued, "Sociology as a subject merely to be taught is a parasite: sociology as a profession to be practiced may have indispensable social utility."

As Chapin and Faris debated the need for more sociologists, the American Sociological Society organized a Committee on Opportunities for Trained

292   A CRITIQUE OF CONTEMPORARY AMERICAN SOCIOLOGY

Sociologists (Rhodes 1980). The purpose of this committee was to examine non-
teaching job opportunities for sociologists. The committee's formation appears
to be the first attempt to move sociology out of the academy and into a broader
labor market where the skills and techniques learned in graduate school could be
applied to social problems in the "real world."

Despite this apparent concern for expanding job opportunities for sociologists during the 1930s, one need only look at the employment status of
professional sociologists during the following decades to see that Faris's advice
and the recommendations of the American Sociological Society Committee
went virtually unheeded (Riley 1960). After riding out the economic downturn
of the 1930s, the post World War II years saw a steadily growing demand for
academic talent. Not surprisingly, the opportunity structure for new sociologists
in the 1950s and 1960s was defined in terms of current supply and demand within
academia.

Although systematic examination of the sociology job market emerged only
in the 1960s, personal observations about employment practices regularly
appeared in sociology journals throughout the 1950s and 1960s. For example,
Emory Bogardus (1953:39) noted that occupational opportunities for sociologists "are better than at any time since the beginning of sociology as an academic
discipline." And although sociology departments in the 1950s were turning out
record numbers of new doctorates, the best could expect to "secure satisfactory
positions immediately" (Bogardus 1953:39). Not surprisingly, Bogardus noted
that the most suitable positions were in large universities. Next in order of
acceptability were positions in smaller colleges, then government, and finally
private industry.

The academic job market for sociologists experienced a sustained period of
growth during the 1950s and 1960s, fueled in part by the postwar baby boom and
large increases in NSF and NIMH support for sociological research (Ferriss
1964). In 1964 Abbott Ferriss forecast a shortfall of Ph.D. production into the
1970s. And as late as 1970, Ernest Campbell (1970:36) noted that "one of the
pressing problems facing us in sociology today is the inadequate number of
sociologists in the marketplace."

Throughout this era, virtually without exception, the labor market opportunity
structure for new sociology Ph.D.s was defined almost solely in terms of the
supply and demand for academic employment. Faris's cry for broadening the
employment prospects for sociologists went unnoticed, and the 1930s crunch, if
remembered at all, was seen merely as a function of economic hard times and a
decline in college enrollments. These conditions were assumed to be temporary
aberrations in a generally healthy economic system. The continued growth of the
academic marketplace into the foreseeable future was assumed implicitly, and
little, if any, regard was paid to developing and seeking out nonacademic, or

applied, employment opportunities or explaining employment of Ph.D.s in other than a human-capital/supply-and-demand perspective.

The tenor of the times was summarized neatly in two research reports that appeared in the *American Sociological Review* during this era. Matilda White Riley (1960) presented data that showed no relative growth between 1950 and 1959 in the proportion of sociologists employed in nonacademic settings. In both years, about 5 percent were employed by government and 5 percent in business and industry. In terms of absolute increases, however, the number of sociologists employed in liberal arts institutions increased from 1466 to 2381. This net increase prompted one ASA council member to comment: "A proper pattern. The need for educators will be great in the years ahead and it is well that the majority of members work in liberal arts to breed a larger generation as scholars for the future" (cited in Riley 1960:920).

The second report discussed ways to make sociologists more attractive for hiring by the federal government. The most telling suggestion was this recommendation (Medalia and Mason 1963:287):

> The main responsibility for improving the status of sociologists under Civil Service regulations lies with the sociologists themselves who work in government agencies [at that time there were about 200 such sociologists] rather than with the Civil Service Commission, or with officers of the ASA who might from time to time address themselves to it . . . As sociologists in federal agencies demonstrate the value and importance that sociological analysis holds for development of agency programs, their officials will in turn request the Commission to facilitate recruitment and retention of sociologists in government.

Clearly if employment opportunities for sociologists were to expand beyond the confines of academic circles, the official arms of the sociology profession had no role to play in that endeavor.

In the early 1970s dark clouds gathered on the academic horizon. Demerath (1971) observed the beginnings of constricted employment opportunities in graduate sociology faculties and predicted a period of slow growth throughout academia. Using Allan Cartter's (1976) research on the Ph.D. labor market as a benchmark, Demerath suggested that sociologists broaden their outlook and seek out nonacademic jobs. As conditions rapidly deteriorated, the call for a nonacademic, applied sociology was echoed by McGinnis and Soloman (1973), Finsterbusch (1973, 1974), and others.

In recognition of the need to seek out new and applied employment alternatives rapidly, the ASA organized a committee on employment in 1971. The formation of this committee marked the first attempt since the 1930s to come to grips collectively with the realities of nonacademic employment and to compile systematically information on the factors and conditions that affect the supply and demand for sociologists. Not until 1975, however, when Panian and Defluer (1976) published their ASA-sponsored study "Sociologists in Nonacademic Employment," did a comprehensive assessment of the nature and scope of nonacademic employment for sociologists appear.

Applied Sociology and the Nonacademic Marketplace[1]

Unlike the American Sociological Society-sponsored study in the 1930s that recommended broadening job opportunities for sociologists beyond the confines of colleges and universities, the Panian and Defluer report served as a springboard for action. Beginning in the late 1970s and continuing to the present, the case for expanding nonacademic opportunities and the concomitant emphasis on applied sociology in graduate training are topics that have generated considerable debate. Peter Rossi, for example, argued that applied social research could take sociology out of the employment trouble it was in if the profession would diligently and flexibly exploit the opportunities it represented (Anonymous 1980). Albert Gollin (1977:8) asserted there may be "a need to develop substantial retraining programs to provide or upgrade skills specifically identified as career enhancing." Ron Manderscheid, a sociologist with the National Institute of Mental Health, stated, "by updating and expanding the definition of sociology used by the Classification Standard in federal positions, in the future a broader range of sociologists should find employment opportunities in this setting" (Buff 1988:1). And Doris Wilkinson (1980:6) claimed that the significant questions for sociology in the 1980s are simply "What skills do sociologists possess which are currently marketable outside of the academic complex? What curricula changes are necessary in order to prepare sociologists for meaningful careers? Where will the demand for sociologists come from in the 1980s and 1990s?"

Despite the seeming diversity of questions raised and responses offered to widening employment opportunities for sociologists, virtually all discussions have been rooted firmly in a neoclassical/human-capital perspective in which current demand for sociologists is accepted as a given to which supply must be adjusted. According to this perspective, candidates seeking nonacademic employment are seen as possessing skills or marginal productivities that they offer to prospective employers. Job seekers who are unable to secure work are deemed to have inadequate or inappropriate training. Structural determinants of job opportunities are either ignored or accepted as given. Yet to understand fully current or historical employment situations, human-capital variables must be examined in relation to the larger context in which supply-demand exchanges are negotiated. Such structural factors as cuts in federal financial support for social science research, reductions in state allocations to higher education, changing student enrollment patterns, and the extent to which sociologists are organized to protect their job rights are critical pieces of the job puzzle that cannot be altered with increases in human capital or personnel management techniques aimed at helping individuals package and sell themselves more effectively to employers.

As the push toward taking sociology into the nonacademic marketplace has intensified, however, the focus continues to be on various agendas to enhance the human capital of job seekers (Lambert 1978; Wilkinson 1978). Drawing on the recommendations in Panian and Defluer's study, Wilkinson (1978:212-13) provided the following suggestions:

1. Nonacademic sociologists need more training in methods, data analysis, statistics and mathematics.

2. Nonacademic sociologists need a broader conceptual framework within which to work. This may mean more course work in other departments; a reduction in the number of areas in which a student may specialize; and the requirement of specialization in general sociology.

3. More attention should be given to practical skills—proposal writing, writing and editing, small group leadership, and policy formation.

4. Research experience should be provided either through intern programs or developing research capabilities within the department.

5. Theory courses should be modified to include practical consequences.

At the same time, job candidates are offered an expanding array of literature on how to write a better résumé, how to prepare for an interview, and how to more effectively "network" in order to find the right job. Such "dress for success" job clinics are now standard fare at the annual meeting of the American Sociological Association.

The attraction of applied sociology and the rush to modify graduate training to prepare sociologists for jobs outside academia has not gone without criticism. Demerath (1981:90), for example, stated that sociologists are caught in a "temporal dialectic" between short-term professional priorities (i.e., helping people find jobs) on the one hand and long-term disciplinary needs (i.e., advancing and passing along knowledge in the field) on the other. Blalock (1978:219) has warned that "many kinds of research sponsored by `outsiders' will detract from the cumulative development of theory." And Freeman (1980:2) has noted the possibility that applied sociology can result in "work dominated by governmental groups narrow in political and social outlooks." Such warnings, however, have not stood in the way of the applied-side celebration.

Perhaps the most thorough and scholarly treatment of the potential benefits of applied sociology and the consequences for graduate training was published in the *American Sociological Review* by Howard Freeman and Peter Rossi in 1984. They make the case that "there are qualitative differences between applied and conventional academic work . . . including the educational preparation required, the criteria for student selection, the ways faculty are evaluated and the kinds of work that are valued" (1984:571). There is much to applaud in Freeman and Rossi's article. Indeed, we agree entirely with their description of nonacademic work environments. Our concern is with the implications of their recommendations for sociology as an independent, critical, intellectual enterprise. We are particularly troubled by the narrow personnel management/human-capital perspective with which they analyze current jobs problems and the role for nonacademic jobs in resolving them. Three particular problems stand out in their position.

First, their vision of the applied side of sociology emphasizes technical and administrative skills at the expense of substantive sociological expertise. While paying lip service to the need for theoretical training ("if for no other reason than to awaken and build community interest among sociology students within the discipline" [Freeman and Rossi 1984:577]), they continue: "It is especially critical, however, that applied sociologists be conversant with and well grounded in the range of research methods that constitute our craft . . ." (1984:577). According to Freeman and Rossi, these methods should include everything from evaluating structural equation models to participant observation techniques. While an array of methodological competencies ideally are part of any sociologist's repertoire, a proliferation of jobs that emphasize these dimensions in the name of applied sociology would turn sociologists into narrowly defined technicians and result in a de-skilling of the sociological profession. Graduate programs that tailor their programs to meet the perceived statistical and methodological needs of nonacademic employers reduce sociology to the status of a mere service station for groups with relatively narrow political and social outlooks, particularly, as we observe later, given the proper location for applied sociology according to Freeman and Rossi.

Second the applied side of sociology, according to Freeman and Rossi, also requires that "the applied modeler must perforce be multi-disciplinary. Clients could not care less whether their problems are solved with theories from psychology, from sociology or from any other discipline" (1984:576). If this is the case, and we believe it is, then the range of nonacademic employment opportunities open to sociologists is open to Ph.D.s in other disciplines as well. Indeed, our own research (Lyson and Squires 1984) showed that most nonacademic employers had recruited or planned to recruit persons with other kinds of educational experiences for positions normally held by sociologists. By accepting as given, or at least unchangeable, a nonacademic labor market in which sociologists are interchangeable with other social scientists, Freeman and Rossi have greatly devalued the unique skills and abilities that sociologists bring to the job market. Rather than advocate a course of action that ultimately will lead to a homogenization of the nonacademic labor markets open to applied sociologists, Freeman and Rossi would have better served both the short-term professional interests of sociologists and the long-term intellectual interests of the discipline by outlining nonacademic opportunities that would encourage independent, creative research geared toward enhancing knowledge of the public about the workings of society. In other words, we should bring sociology, as well as sociologists, to nonacademic settings.

Finally, throughout their article Freeman and Rossi comment on the locus of control in applied sociological work. They note, for example, that applied practitioners are "hired or supported by extra-disciplinary stakeholders and their [sociologists] rewards are primarily based on satisfactory performance as judged by their sponsors" (1984:572). Consequently, "applied sociologists are more narrowly constrained to comply with the demands placed upon them by their employers as sponsors and failure to do so restricts their opportunities to perform and be rewarded in the future" (1984:573). In perhaps their most revealing statement, they assert, "Although in principle it should be possible to identify and make use of politically 'liberal' settings such as women's rights groups, minority organizations, and the like, in practice most sites would (and should) be in the worlds of business, commerce, and government" (1984:578).

This is the most troublesome part of their argument. In effect, they advocate an increasingly limited and more ideological setting for the conduct of sociology. Yet if sociology is first and foremost an intellectual discipline, then its distinguishing trademark is, as Paul Baran (1961) argued, intellectual activity in general, the development of knowledge about the workings of society and its constituent elements for the purpose of attaining a more humane and rational social order. In contrasting "intellect worker," which he described as one concerned with a particular job in hand (e.g., contract research) with the intellectual, Baran emphasized the responsibility of the latter to confront questions of value formation (e.g., goals) and to be social critics. Failure to do so, even in the name of "ethical neutrality," is to abdicate this responsibility to the "charlatans, crooks, and others whose intentions and designs are everything but humanitarian" (Baran 1961:15).

The Selling of the Sociologist: Applied Sociology in the Years Ahead

The booming academic job market for sociologists in the 1950s and 1960s went bust in the 1970s. In view of the broader history of American sociology, however, the 1950s and 1960s constituted more an aberration than the norm in terms of employment opportunities. In the 1990s we may experience a more normal job market (Sovern 1989). Today, employment issues continue to be a concern to both recent recipients of sociology Ph.D.s and sociology graduate programs. In an effort to improve job prospects for members of the sociological community, the profession is looking to applied sociology and to the creation of employment opportunities in nonacademic settings. To date, however, most of these opportunities generally are technical or administrative positions that require little substantive expertise in sociology and, in fact, are open to individuals from a variety of backgrounds (Lyson and Squires 1984). Such positions offer promising careers for some individuals, and there is no reason sociologists should not get their fair share. At the same time, reorienting the training of sociologists or graduate programs in sociology in response to the current demands of nonacademic employers poses potentially serious costs to the discipline.

Technical and administrative skills constitute an increasingly important set of attributes in today's labor market. But a proliferation of jobs that emphasize these dimensions exclusively (in the name of applied sociology) would constitute a de-skilling of the sociological profession and a homogenization of at least the nonacademic labor markets open to social scientists. A de-professionalization of this sort may be one of the costs associated with the current emphasis on so-called applied sociology. Carried to the logical extreme, graduate programs that fit their training to meet the perceived needs of the nonacademic community would reduce the discipline of sociology to a mere servant of a relatively narrowly defined clientele. The short-term economic benefits may be accompanied by more permanent political and intellectual costs.

Already some graduate departments have moved toward separate training programs for nonacademic and academic careers (Freeman and Rossi 1984). All students, of course, seek training that meets their particular needs. Sociology departments and individual job seekers need to develop more effective formal and informal ties with nonacademic employers to open up communication and expand such job opportunities. But sociologists have much to offer nonacademic employers over and above technical and administrative abilities. For example, Rosabeth Moss Kanter (1977) has demonstrated how the social structure of organizations influences the productivity of individuals within them, while Robert Rosenthal and Lenore Jacobson (1968) have documented how a teacher's perceptions of student abilities influence academic performance.

Developing a broader set of technical and administrative skills and learning to market those abilities more effectively are certainly appropriate objectives. At the same time, in order to develop a more comprehensive understanding of the nature of employment problems in sociology and the role of applied sociology, and to act more effectively on those concerns, we must move beyond the human-capital/personnel-management framework and address the structural dimensions of problems that have for far too long been accepted as unalterable givens.

One place to begin is to respond more effectively to recent efforts to cut back on social science research, education, and the provision of public goods in general. The efforts of the Consortium of Social Science Associations (COSSA) to dissuade Congress from further cuts in federal support of social science research have been an important step in this direction. Declining student enrollments should be viewed as an opportunity to improve quality of instruction, rather than a justification for cutting budgets. Given growing illiteracy problems as we enter the postindustrial age, educators of virtually every discipline should be able to make a compelling case for maintaining and expanding educational opportunities (Gorelick 1983).

As wage laborers, sociologists should remove any remaining elitist blinders and take a lesson from our blue-collar counterparts. Formation of strong academic unions can prevent further erosion of academic working conditions for educators and learning conditions for students (Dowdell and Dowdell 1978).

Several steps can be taken by individual departments, colleges, universities, and other academic organizations. They could provide unemployed and underemployed sociologists with access to libraries, computers, and other resources. Unaffiliated scholars could constitute a source of funds for such institutions. Universities, or various arms within them, could serve as institutional sponsors of research proposals for unaffiliated scholars, with costs to be covered by overhead dollars so that such services would be revenue enhancing for the institution. The American Sociological Association and other social science organizations could establish similar services (Ad Hoc Committee 1988).

Again, none of this is intended to replace the development of new skills, more effective marketing of human capital, or the pursuit of more nonacademic job opportunities. What is evident is the need to complement such individualistic tactics with more collective approaches. It is time for the sociological community to recognize the sociological dimensions of its labor market and to deal with it at that level.

In 1988, the ASA Council voted to establish a standing Committee on Employment. The charge of this committee is to address all issues that pertain to the employment of sociologists including assessing the supply of sociologists in the marketplace and examining the nature and range of employment opportunities open to sociologists (Official Reports and Proceedings 1988). This is a step in the right direction toward arriving at a more robust understanding of the dynamics of the sociology job market. To the extent that this new committee can direct attention away from dealing only with the individual characteristics of job seekers and focus instead on the structural factors and conditions that effect the demand for sociological talent, it will serve to bring a more balanced and more sociological approach to studies of the job market.

Sociology for What?

Sociology remains primarily a scholarly discipline, one whose principal pursuit is the discovery of knowledge. At the same time, the utility of sociological knowledge in nonacademic settings clearly has been demonstrated. An elementary awareness of basic sociological concepts can help us understand as well as influence the behavior of individuals and families, social institutions such as schools and government agencies, economic organizations ranging from family businesses to multinational corporations, local communities, and national cultures. A sociological perspective and the knowledge that flows from it, not just the methods of social science research, can have ever greater "real world" implications, if we let them (Johnson et al. 1988).

Obviously, participation by sociologists in applied settings does not inevitably compromise the intellectual standing of the discipline. Sociological tools and knowledge can be applied to practical problem-solving efforts, often as part of an interdisciplinary team including other social scientists and people outside the social sciences altogether (Whyte 1981, 1986). In virtually all the land-grant universities and in many other public and private colleges and universities in the United States, for example, there are sociologists whose major responsibilities lie in applying the basic research of their colleagues. Many of these individuals are part of the Cooperative Extension Service of the U.S. Department of Agriculture; in other instances, these sociologists are affiliated with institutes, programs, and task forces that focus on solving the everyday, practical problems of neighborhood groups, local governments, and other constituencies in rural and urban communities.

Despite the role sociologists play in solving social problems, it is equally true that if sociology is to retain its status as a major intellectual enterprise, its practitioners must critically analyze, rather than accept as a given, structural forces that shape human behavior. We constantly must ask the question posed by Becker (1967) in his Presidential Address to the Society for the Study of Social Problems over twenty years ago, and more recently by Gans (1989) in his Presidential Address to the ASA: "Whose side are we on?" This is true particularly in efforts to understand those factors that are altering the nature of work in many occupations, including the social sciences, frequently in the direction of de-skilling, homogenization, and de-professionalization.

The reductionist, neoclassical paradigm that characterizes much sociological theory generally, and its approach to labor market issues in particular (e.g., the human-capital/status-attainment theory), has retarded efforts to understand the employment problems facing the profession. While the intention may be to pursue objective research into some of the central problems of our age, such approaches feed the technocratic orientation and bureaucratic ethic that has emerged while impeding achievement of the stated objective—that being the discovery of new and socially useful knowledge. Sociology's ability to address its own employment problems, and its pursuit of knowledge generally, have been hindered by these ideological blinders shaping much sociological work.

Clearly there is a need for sociologists in applied settings. But that role involves far more than data analysis, modeling social phenomena, or program evaluation. This does not imply any denigration of the technical components of sociological research or suggest that sociologists should participate only in activities in which they have final decision-making authority. At the same time, sociologists cannot ignore the changing contours of the discipline for fear, as John Madge warned, that "if sociology is the docile handmaiden of adminstration, unable to question the assumptions of administrative decisions, [it will lead] only to the bureaucratization of science" (Madge 1967:517). The potential contributions of sociology as an intellectual enterprise, not the vagaries of the academic job market, are the principal justification for an expansion of applied work on the part of sociologists.

Notes

1. Applied sociological research is conducted in both academic and nonacademic settings. And much valuable theoretical and substantive work is done in both environments. The growth of independent and university-affiliated research institutions in recent years also blurs distinctions between theoretical and applied research work environments. For the purposes of this essay, the term *applied sociology* refers primarily to work that is conducted by employees of government agencies, private businesses, nonprofit organizations, and sociologists employed in outreach and extension programs in colleges and universities.

REFERENCES

Ad Hoc Committee on Unemployment and Underemployment. 1988. "Report of the American Sociological Association's Ad Hoc Committee on Unemployment and Underemployment in the Discipline." American Sociological Association, Washington, D.C.

Anonymous. 1980. "Rossi Cites Opportunities in Applied Social Research." *ASA Footnotes* 8:20.

Baran, Paul. 1961. "The Commitment of the Intellectual." *Monthly Review* 13:8–18.

Becker, Howard S. 1967. "Whose Side Are We On?" *Social Problems* 14:239–47.

Blalock, Hubert M. 1978. "Debate on a Proposed `Solution' of Employment Problems (Comment on Kay, TAS November 1978)." *The American Sociologist* 13:227–29.

Bogardus, Emory S. 1953. "Obtaining a Position in Sociology." *Sociology and Social Research* 38:38–45.

Buff, Stephen A. 1988. "Breakthrough: Feds Adopt New Job Description." *ASA Footnotes* 16:1, 6.

Campbell, Ernest Q. 1970. "Recruiting Tomorrow's Sociologists." *The American Sociologist* 5:36–37.

Cartter, Allan M. 1976. *Ph.D.'s and the Academic Labor Market*. New York: McGraw-Hill.

Chapin, F. Stuart. 1934. "The Present State of the Profession." *American Journal of Sociology* 39:506–8.

Demerath, Jay. 1971. "Notes on a Nervous Job Market." *The American Sociologist* 6:187–88.
——. 1981. "Assaying the Future: The Profession vs. the Discipline." *The American Sociologist* 16:87–90.
Dowdall, Jean A. and George W. Dowdall. 1978. "Debate on a Proposed `Solution' of Employment Problems (comment on Kay, TAS November 1978)." *The American Sociologist* 13:223–24.
Faris, Ellsworth. 1934. "Too Many Ph.D.'s?" *American Journal of Sociology* 39:509–12.
Ferriss, Abbott L. 1964. "Sociological Manpower." *American Sociological Review* 29:103–4.
Finsterbusch, Kurt. 1973. "The 1973 Academic Job Market for Sociologists." *ASA Footnotes* 1:4.
——. 1974. "Academic Job Market Reports: Some Good News and Some Bad News." *ASA Footnotes* 2:7.
Flynn, Cynthia. 1982. "An Alternative Approach to Discipline's Funding Problems." *ASA Footnotes* 10:2.
Freeman, Howard. 1980. "Freeman Outlines Major Issues Related to Applied Sociology." *ASA Footnotes* 8:1–2.
Freeman, Howard, Russell Dynes, Peter Rossi, and William F. Whyte. 1983. *Applied Sociology*. San Francisco: Jossey-Bass.
Freeman, Howard, and Peter Rossi. 1984. "Furthering the Applied Side of Sociology." *American Sociological Review* 49:571–80.
Freeman, Richard B. 1976. *The Overeducated American*. New York: Academic Press.
"From Campus to Corporation." 1978. *Time* 76(August 14):76.
Gans, Herbert J. 1989. "Sociology in America: The Discipline and the Public." *American Sociological Review* 54:1–16.
Gollin, Albert E. 1977. "ASA Committee Makes Recommendations for Expanding Employment Opportunities." *ASA Footnotes* 5:1, 8.
Gorelick, Sherry. 1983. "Boom and Bust in Higher Education: Economic and Social Causes of the Current Crisis." *Insurgent Sociologist* 11:77–90.
Horan, Patrick M. 1978. "Is Status Attainment Research Atheoretical?" *American Sociological Review* 43:534–41.
Huber, Bettina. 1982. *Mastering the Job Market: Using Graduate Training in Sociology for Careers in Applied Settings*. Washington, D.C.: American Sociological Association.
Johnson, D. Paul, et. al. 1988. "The Challenge of Training in Applied Sociology." *The American Sociologist* 18:356–68.
Kanter, Rosabeth Moss. 1977. *Men and Women of the Corporation*. New York: Basic Books.
Lambert, Richard D. 1978. "Debate on a Proposed `Solution' of Employment Problems (Comment on Kay, TAS November 1978)." *The American Sociologist* 13:227–29.
Lieberson, Stanley. 1980. *A Piece of the Pie: Blacks and White Immigrants Since 1880*. Berkeley: University of California Press.
Lynd, Robert S. 1939. *Knowledge for What? The Place for Social Science in American Culture*. Princeton: Princeton University Press.
Lyson, Thomas A., and Gregory D. Squires. 1983. "Oversupply or Underutilization? The Sociology Job Market in the 1980's." *Sociological Focus* 16:275–83.
——. 1984. "The Promise and Perils of Applied Sociology: A Survey of Nonacademic Employers." *Sociological Inquiry* 54:1–15.
McGinnis, Robert and Louise Solomon. 1973. "Employment Prospects for Ph.D. Sociologists during the Seventies." *The American Sociologist* 8:57–63.
Madge, John. 1967. *The Origins of Scientific Sociology*. New York: Free Press.
Medalia, Nahum Z. and Ward S. Mason. 1963. "Positions and Prospects of Sociologists in Federal Government." *American Sociological Review* 28:280–87.
Mills, C. Wright. 1959. *The Sociological Imagination*. New York: Oxford University Press.
Official Reports and Proceedings. 1988. *ASA Footnotes* 16:21–24.

Panian, Sharon K., and Melvin L. Defluer. 1976. *Sociologists in Nonacademic Employment.* Washington, D.C.: American Sociological Association.

Riley, Matilda White. 1960. "Membership of the American Sociological Association." *American Sociological Review* 25:914–26.

Rhodes, Lawrence J. 1980. "Society Experienced Major Social Change in Turbulent '30's." *ASA Footnotes* 8:1, 4–5.

Rosenthal, Robert, and Lenore Jacobson. 1968. *Pygmalion in the Classroom.* New York: Holt, Rinehart and Winston.

Rossi, Peter H. 1980. "The Presidential Address: The Challenge and Opportunities of Applied Social Research." *American Sociological Review* 45:889–904.

Sovern, Michael J. 1989. "Higher Education-The Real Crisis." *New York Times Magazine*, January 22, 24–25, 56.

Squires, Gregory D., and Thomas A. Lyson. 1981. "Some Planned to Be Sociologists: The Changing Fortunes of New Ph.D.'s in Today's AcademicLabor Market." *Rural Sociologist* 1:139–45.

Wilkinson, Doris Y. 1978. "Exchange on Part-time Employment (comment on Tuckman, Caldwell and Vogler, TAS November 1978)." *The American Sociologist* 13:212–13.

———. 1980. "A Synopsis: Projections for the Profession in the 1980's." *ASA Footnotes* 8:6–7.

Wright-Isak, Christine. 1989. "More on Sociological Practice." *ASA Footnotes* 17:4.

Whyte, William F. 1981. "The ASA from Now until the Centennial." *The American Sociologist* 16:116–18.

———. 1986. "The Uses of Social Science Research." *American Sociological Review* 51:555–63.

Chapter	**10**	WESTERN SOCIOLOGY AND THE THIRD WORLD: ASYMMETRICAL FORMS OF UNDERSTANDING AND THE INADEQUACY OF SOCIOLOGICAL DISCOURSE

Moustapha Diouf

This chapter examines the practice of Western sociology in the Third World and discusses its implication for international development policies from a Third World perspective. My central contention is that Western sociology, which reflects the wisdom of the dominant ideology and culture of the advanced industrial nations, in fact reproduces these features in its study of Third World societies.

At the base of this situation are major epistemological issues that relate to the taken-for-granted assumption that sociology has a universal character, and ontological issues that deal with how sociological scholarship understands Third World social reality. Such epistemological and ontological problems reveal asymmetrical forms of understanding across different cultures and social structures and lead to a situation where comparative studies often are made to the disadvantage of Third World societies. Another dimension in the relation between Western sociology and the Third World is the instrumental function of the discipline in fostering a conception of development that becomes synonymous with westernization. Indeed, consciously or unconsciously, sociology, as illustrated by its intervention in international development projects, constitutes a vehicle in the perpetuation of Western capitalist hegemony in the Third World (Ake 1979; Park 1988; Gareau 1988).

Divorce between Western Sociological Discourse and Third World Social Reality

The early conceptualization of sociology has allowed a very narrow (possibly nonexistent) space to approach the discipline from a Third World perspective given its exclusive focus on the Western world. Indeed, the intellectual tools provided by Durkheim's notion of mechanical and organic solidarity and Tönnies' *Gemeinschaft/Gesellschaft* dichotomy laid the foundations for an

304

account of the distinctions between advanced societies and backward ones. It also provided a set of explanatory assumptions regarding the historical evolution of Western societies that moved from traditional social systems characterized by a mechanical solidarity, or a *Gemeinschaft* situation, to modern industrial nations, which features the characteristics of organic solidarity or a *Gesellschaft* situation.

This intellectual tradition was substantially integrated and refined by Parsons (1971), who combined both evolutionary and comparative schemes to develop a theory of the evolution of societies from primitive to intermediate to modern ones. As Parsons indicated (1977:231): "My perspective involves evolutionary judgments-for example, that intermediate societies are more advanced than primitive societies, and modern societies are more advanced than intermediate societies. I have tried to make my criterion congruent with that used in biological theory, calling more advanced the systems that display greater generalized adaptive capacity." In Parsons's thought, societies evolved from an archaic stage to a more advanced state in which the values of modernity, especially economic development, education, political independence, and some form of democracy constitute the building blocks of the modern society. These basic philosophical tenets constitute the cornerstone of modernization theory or what became known as the sociology of development.

This received tradition profoundly shaped by the early orientation of sociology has remained the theoretical corpus within which African social formations have been approached. Several factors can explain this situation. A very weak social science infrastructure in Africa, which remained tailored according to Western ideology, inhibited any attempt to conceive and implement sociological investigation from within the continent. The deficiency in social infrastructure (i.e., the small number of universities) pushed many Africans to expatriate to Western countries for university training. And the small number attending African universities were enrolled in academic programs profoundly dominated by European and American educational models and political interests. These are some of the factors that have blocked the emergence of a sociology directly conceptualized within the African continent.

Thus, sociology in Africa initially was geared to fostering Western cultural imperialism and reinforcing this ideological domination as it appeared in the early conceptualization of African development projects basically aimed at displacing the burden of sociocultural barriers against the introduction of Western civilization and the modernization of the continent. The role assigned to sociology was that of modernizing and bringing about social change in these traditional societies. This role was carried out by classical anthropology, especially during the precolonial and colonial periods, and this discipline played a key role in helping colonialism invade and perpetuate its domination, while sociology would mostly emerge during the postcolonial era. Nevertheless, it should be stated that both anthropological and sociological studies were carried out in support of economic development. The work of Bohannan and Dalton (1962) constitute an illustration of the subservient role assigned to social science study: that of justifying colonialism and its civilizing and emancipatory historical mission.

The growth of sociology as a discipline has been related to the sociopolitical context that prevailed in the aftermath of independence in Africa. In Latin America and Asia (especially India), sociology blossomed in the realm of the development/underdevelopment debate backed by empirical data provided by various schools of thought (modernization, neomodernization, dependency, world system) to reinforce their assumptions. In Africa, a weak social science infrastructure and the inability of scholars to free themselves from the dominant structure of reasoning imposed by imperialism through institutions such as the Economic Commission of Africa of the United Nations rendered virtually impossible a sociological approach emanating from within the African nations, which aspired to independence and sovereignty (Blomstrom and Hettne 1984).

In this context, Western sociology generally has displayed an ethnocentric view of the Third World and, following its mainstream tradition, has been insensitive to the social implications resulting from the implementation of modernization policies. In many cases, through its subdiscipline, rural sociology, it has been instrumental in the perpetuation of Western ideology throughout the Third World by uncritically accepting a research agenda already defined by international donor agencies and one that, despite its declared intent, in fact reinforces dependency in Third World social formations (Gruhn 1983). The issue to be addressed here is that of the technicist orientation dominating American sociology, which has transformed the discipline into a "soul selling" enterprise (Gouldner 1970) in which moral issues tend to be overlooked. Here, international development becomes an arena for lucrative market opportunities and research grants over which sociology departments compete and whose objectives and goals in many cases do not reflect the aspirations and needs of the dispossessed.

Thus, the sociological enterprise in Africa was geared toward the developmentalist doctrine, with modernization theory used as an instrument for cultural and technological change. As Goldthorpe (1984:134) points out, "It is perhaps not unfair to remark that in such a view, modernization seems to mean becoming more like the United States."

Identifying research topics that fit the African context generally has been neglected with a few exceptions such as identifying sociocultural constraints impeding people's participation in development projects. Such research has been directed to understanding people's behavior in response to change and the social impact of technology in African societies. In this sense, research topics have paralleled the overall interest in increased productivity. In other words, "identifying those obstacles and helping to remove them, was seen as a contribution which social scientists might usefully make to the process of development" (Goldthorpe 1984:133).

Since it is believed in the tradition of Durkheimian reasoning that technological change along with the division of labor will provide the infrastructure needed to induce development, the sociologist's role is that of providing the knowledge that helps bring about and further such change. As Blomstrom and Hettne (1984) indicate, the production of knowledge about African development remains to a substantial degree in the hands of expatriates who dominated planning agencies and social science research institutes in Africa throughout the 1960s and most of the 1970s.

As I have endeavored to explain, the framework that guides Third World studies from a Western perspective remains oriented primarily toward the preservation of the status quo. The value-free conception of positivist sociology that dominates the discipline has paid very little attention to the sociological relevance of research themes while continuously searching for financial support to determine its object of inquiry. It appears that the dominant trend in Western sociology is to work under the guidance and objectives set by the donor community, which emphasizes more the technical procedures to reach its objectives than the ethical dimensions its policy might entail.

In sum, the rules and objectives of the intervention of the sociologist are defined primarily by the funding institutions, as illustrated by the U.S. Agency for International Development's (USAID) "Required Format for Technical Proposal" (RFTP) for Agricultural Development in Burkina Faso and in Zaire (1989), in which sociologists have marginal input in the conceptualization and implementation of the projects.

Another dimension of the inadequacy and irrelevance of the approach of sociology to Third World societies is in the training aspect of Third World scholars in Western universities in general. Third World sociologists are trained under the assumption that sociology is a universal science that can be applied everywhere. But since this universalism is equated with Western sociology's principles, procedures, and techniques of investigation, such training produces a Western intellectual hegemony and dependency in which the Third World scholar is developed in the context of Western intellectual categories and cultural contexts that exhibit socioeconomic and political realities structurally different from the Third World. Futhermore, this intellectual dependency tends to put Third World scholars in a situation where they frequently have relied on Western sociological explanation and analytical models to study their own societies.

The Divorce between Understanding and Action

The practice of Western sociology in the Third World has raised controversial issues regarding its relevance and some moral concerns that derive from its involvement in international development programs. Grounded in a developmentalist model that relies exclusively on Western social science concepts and Euro-American ethnocentrism, the discipline has failed to capture the essence and peculiarities of Third World societies and to take into consideration their needs and concerns for development.

The implications of these trends have been scrutinized in Edwards's (1989) influential work *The Irrelevance of Development Studies*. A factor contributing to the irrelevance of developmental studies, in Edwards's view, is the domination of a technocratic approach to development that leads to the devaluation of indigenous knowledge and to the formulation of external solutions for specific local problems encountered by indigenous populations. Thus, argues Edwards (1989:117): "Many of us who are involved in the field of development have become part of the problems of underdevelopment, rather than being part of the solution to these problems." Furthermore, Edwards (1989:121) contends: "Expert oriented views of development distance the researcher from reality, create barriers which promote ignorance and perpetuate inappropriate models based on the views of outsiders."

Indeed, in Edwards's (1989:118) view, "people are treated as objects to be studied rather than as subjects of their own development; there is therefore a separation between the researcher and the object of research, and between understanding and action." He also discusses the notion of research, education and knowledge and their monopoly by experts in the development process. Edwards (1989:118) argues that ". . . in the transmission of information, usually of a technical kind from one person to another, the transmitter and the receiver of information are distanced from each other by a basic inequality in the amount of technical knowledge they each possess." Such a monopoly of knowledge by the elite prevents people from thinking for themselves, "analyzing, designing, implementing and evaluating their work in a critical fashion" (Edwards 1989:119) in order to achieve their objectives.

For this very reason, development studies will continue to be irrelevant as long as this technocratic approach continues to dominate the field. For greater relevance in development studies, Edwards (1989:119) calls for "bringing together research and practice, or understanding and change, into a single unitary process, an alternative model of research which is fully participatory." Edwards's conception of development strategies can be located within the indigenous knowledge approach (Brokensha et al. 1980; Richards 1985) through his advocacy of the use of "people's science" (a term coined by Richards [1985]), that is, local knowledge to explore local solutions to local problems. He also advocates the notion of participatory research first conceptualized by Paulo Freire and "whose purpose is to allow people to become subjects rather than objects, to control their own destinies rather than be the victims of the desires and social processes of others" (Edwards 1989:128). Edwards (1989:128) goes on to indicate that "the Freirean approach is revolutionary in its implications for development studies, and this is why it has been resisted, rejected or ignored by so many."

Nonetheless, Edwards feels it is necessary to distinguish between genuinely participatory research, as described earlier, and the way it has been misused by the World Bank, the United Nations, and many multilateral agencies in their call for more participation of people in the development projects. This type of participation, in Edwards's (1989:129) words, "tends to be used as a technique to improve the efficacy of research or programming, rather than as a means of facilitating people's own development efforts. Used in this way, it becomes merely another form of exploitation, serving the purpose of outsiders who have their own agenda but who know they cannot gain a complete picture of the problems that interest them through conventional methods alone."

Basically, participation here is seen as a means to reach predetermined objectives. In contrast, the participatory research advocated by Edwards and a body of researchers such as Richards (1985), Oakley and Marsden (1984), and Morgan (1985) starts at the grassroots level and establishes a link between local knowledge and science through a permanent contract between the subjects under study and the researcher. This participatory research represents a viable alternative to the irrelevance of current development studies and constitutes a "basic building block of a successful development strategy" (Edwards 1989:128).

The above discussion raises relevant issues in the current impasse of development sociology. In my view, reflection on the present crisis in development sociology should go beyond the narrow focus of Edwards's analysis. Such a crisis embodies a fundamental dimension: the instrumental function sociology in general exercises, that of defending the status quo (Frank 1969; So 1990). In the following elaboration, I take the case of rural sociology, which is basically involved in development policies, to illustrate my contention.

Rural Sociology as an Illustration of the Crisis

A preliminary appraisal of the state of rural sociology should help clarify its current crisis. What was characterized as a "sleeping crisis" of rural sociology (Lowry 1977) derived from a lack of clear theoretical delineation of a subdiscipline located in between agricultural economics (rural sociology being viewed as agricultural economics with a social emphasis) and the sociology of development (especially the focus on the urban-rural continuum). Thus, the discipline initially was grounded in the study of an agrarian capitalism thought to be following the same patterns as those of industrial development.

Several rural sociologists have described this crisis in diverse terms. Newby and Buttel (1980:4) indicated that "rural sociology has been [either] characterized by its atheoretical, even antitheoretical nature or has attempted to develop a specifically rural sociological theory inductively without reference to general sociological theories." Newby and Buttel (1980:3) also view this crisis as similar to a Kuhnian crisis, "something which is manifested in the persistence of a very basic problem, indeed: the definition of what constitutes rural sociology in the first place." This lack of a theoretical basis has been pointed out as one fundamental reason for the failure of rural sociology to provide a response to either the current decline of the family farm in the United States or to the massive agrarian transitions that followed the penetration of capitalism into the countryside (Rodefeld 1974).

Newby and Buttel (1980) also have indicated the absence of macrosociological theories that would help explain the emergence of particular "rural, spatial and social forms" as factors leading to the current crisis of rural sociology.

In my view, the current crisis in rural sociology originated from the early empiricism that guided that subdiscipline: Rural sociology was supposed to describe the conditions of rural poverty, but was largely used as a means of communication between policy makers and rural communities. This empiricism redirected the role of rural sociologists to the enumeration of constraints and the formulation of suggestions for policy making for the purpose of rural development. In a sense, the current crisis derived from its "theoretical closure and method-ological monism," to put it in Picou's terms (1978:558), which placed the subdiscipline under the "monopoly of structural-functional theory, survey methods, and quantitative analysis" (Gilbert 1982:613).

From a historical perspective, rural sociology has been very much a product of the land-grant system, and its organizational location has continuously influenced its orientation. The theme of the land-grant college could be summarized as a "science with practice" (Hobbs 1980), and in this context rural sociology as a science was to be applied to the study of rural populations who were basically farmers. This organizational context might explain why much work in rural sociology was positivist in nature and applied to relatively small-scale social and economic problems. In general, rural sociology has been relatively noncontroversial politically because the kind of research it has done strongly reinforced major political values of a capitalist system.

This situation demonstrates the vulnerability of rural sociology in its inability to free itself from the restrictions of the USDA and preserve its autonomy. The dilemma faced by rural sociology is summarized by Friedland (1982:591) in these terms:

> An analysis of the institutional location of rural sociology and the development of an agenda that might make it more central argue that the subdiscipline must begin a major reallocation of research priorities. Such reallocation could place the subdiscipline in one of two unattractive positions: either it will become an ideological exponent

and justifies the final destruction of family based agriculture in the United States and a supporter of corporate agribusiness or it will undertake a gadfly, critical role that could lead to its expulsion from the land grant complex.

Friedland contends that rural sociology faces a continuing crisis of identity because of its failure to develop a sociology of agriculture. His main argument is that there is no such thing as rural society since the dominant capitalist economy has invaded the rural areas. In fact, for Friedland, there is no clear reason to use the term "rural society." Therefore, there is little intellectual rationale for rural sociology. Friedland (1982:) argues that "there is little rural society left in the United States, although there are many high, medium and low density population locations; and hence, there is no longer any basis in the United States if there ever was in the past, for a rural sociology." Friedland concludes by arguing that the only legitimate practical issue of rural sociology is a concern with the sociology of agriculture.

Then again, these trends are a mere reflection of the global dilemma facing the broader discipline of sociology—that of its independence. In his essay titled "American Sociological Hegemony", Chekki (1987:24) contends that

> universities, the sociology department, research institutions and bureaucracies where sociological activities take place are closely tied to the interests of corporations and governments. An overwhelming majority of sociologists working in bureaucratic institutions cannot be value-free, especially in the analysis of data and problems, as far as research programs supported by corporation and government agencies are concerned.

In general, these contentions synthesize what often is referred to as a mainstream orientation in American sociology (a domination of structural-functionalist and positivist sociology) that favors a technocratic orientation and conceives its role as that of market researcher for the welfare state (Gouldner 1970). Overall, the ideological features of American sociology remain embedded within the dominant ideology of capitalist society. In such a context, the role of the sociologist becomes, in many cases, that of reproducing through his or her work the mechanisms perpetuating this ideological hegemony. In fulfilling this role, American sociology has become increasingly intertwined with the welfare state. As Park (1988:167) indicates: "Sociology has succeeded in promoting a view of social life which is supportive of the domination interest of the capitalist mode of production and producing a kind of knowledge which serves the interests of the dominating classes."

312   A CRITIQUE OF CONTEMPORARY AMERICAN SOCIOLOGY

A Case Study: Applied Rural Sociology in the Third World

Western sociology has, by and large, remained dominated by a modernization orientation as its strategy for developing Third World societies. A typical example of an application of modernization strategy in agricultural development is the diffusion model. This model derived from extensive research efforts of American rural sociologists to promote rapid introduction and adoption of agricultural technology at the farm level. Later this model was transplanted into Third World farming contexts.

In the field of applied rural sociology, one of the major theoretical contributions to the diffusion model has been Everett Rogers's work on diffusion of innovations (1983, 1988). The importance of Rogers's work lies in the fact that it pioneered what currently is labeled the diffusion model, and it still represents the dominant paradigm in strategies of technology transfer in the field of rural sociology (Fliegel and Van Es 1983).

The interpretation of the data collected by interviews of a random sample of 259 Iowa farmers regarding their formal education, age, farm size, income, travel, readership of farm magazines, mass media exposure, and contact with change agents led to the conclusion that the category of farmers who adopted innovations at their earliest stage (the knowledge stage) were (1) those who were cosmopolitan and highly exposed to mass media, and (2) those whose influence furthered the rate of adoption in their social system after they had adopted the recommended packages. The basic assumption here is that at the early stage of the diffusion of new practices or ideas, the innovators and the early adopters in a community constitute the first category of people to be interested in adopting the recommended packages because of their receptiveness and openmindedness to change. Rogers split the farming population into five adopter categories: the innovator, early adopter, adopter, late adopter, and laggard. From these empirical cases, he derived his model of diffusion. At the early stage of the diffusion process, the progressive farmers, innovators, and early adopters are likely to constitute 10 to 15 percent of the farmers; there follows a situation of "takeoff" with an accelerated rate of adoption. The adopter, late adopter, and laggard will follow.

From this deduction, he mainly stressed that rural sociologists, extensionists, or "change agents," when transferring research findings or introducing new technological packages, primarily should identify the category of innovators or progressive farmers, in the sense that their influence within a social system will create a trickle-down effect that will increase the rate of adoption. To quote Rogers (1983:23):

When the number of individuals adopting a new idea is plotted on a cumulative frequency basis over time, the resulting distribution is an S-shaped curve. At first, only a few individuals adopt the innovation each time, such as a year or a month; these are the innovators. But soon the diffusion curve begins to climb, as more and more individuals adopt. Finally, the S-shaped curve reaches its asymptote, and the diffusion process is finished.

The practical implication of Rogers's conventional approach for rural sociology is that once the category of progressive farmers is identified and starts adopting the recommended new practices, the rest of the rural population is likely to follow and adopt the technological innovations because of a trickle-down effect.

Within this perspective, farmers are depicted as objects that have to put into use the agricultural research findings rather than being participants in the research process. Rogers's basic strategy is reduced to one dependent variable, innovativeness (which refers to modernism), and therefore all farmers who do not fulfill this characteristic are left out in the early stages of the diffusion process. As Busch (1984:290) rightly points out: "The literature on the diffusion of agricultural innovations (e.g., Rogers and Schumacher) has concerned itself almost entirely with who adopts what scientific and technical innovations under what conditions. It has largely ignored the possible differential value of the products of science and technology to different groups and individuals." Indeed, the diffusion model is based on a technological determinism as the major cause of social change in society (Rogers et al. 1988; Vandergeest and Buttel 1986).

Analysis of the activities of rural sociologists deriving from Rogers's approach in many developing countries shows that they tend to focus attention on the few progressive farmers who have adequate resources necessary to afford risking new technologies. This situation has been pointed out by scholars such as Elliot R. Morse (1976) as a factor increasing inequality among farmers due to its elitist conception of diffusion.

Rogers's model has not paid much attention to the social consequences of innovation (Busch 1984). This model has been inattentive to the issue of how the socioeconomic benefits of innovation are distributed within a social system. Because of the discriminative approach (the target being the progressive farmers or innovators), the model, when applied in developing nations, tends to increase socioeconomic inequalities.

Cross-cultural application of the diffusion model in developing nations has generated primarily negative consequences because of its incompatibility with indigenous production systems (Taylor 1979; Busch 1984). A primary reason for such failure is that the model is based on the concepts of modernization that mainly contend that development will occur through an acculturation process, with the diffusion of cultural norms and values from the modern to the backward or traditional social system.

My opposition to this reasoning is that if we apply this model to African nations, innovativeness as a dependent variable cannot be measured solely by independent variables such as cosmopolitanism or mass media exposure. The main factor in Africa will more likely be the characteristics of the innovation: Farmers are likely to react to innovations in terms of other facets of their living conditions. If they view the innovations as suitable to their conditions, they are likely to adopt them, whether they are large or small farmers. In contrast, if they identify the innovation as unsuitable to their means and carrying capacities, they will legitimately reject it (Nair 1979).

A case study conducted by Havens and Flinn (1975) on the diffusion of new coffee production technology (new varieties, fertilizers, and herbicides) in a region in Colombia illustrates this situation. In this study, they found that it was not the personal characteristics of the farmers that explained the adoption decision, but the institutional constraints. The adoption of the new technology required financial assistance, but access to credit depended on formal education, which many farmers did not have. Consequently, those who did not have equal access to credit did not adopt. Here, according to Havens and Flinn (1975), lack of adoption was due partly to the institutional constraints and real blocks to credit availability.

Much current academic reasoning on Third World farmers' behavior as shaped by presumptions of irrationality, ignorance, or inefficiency is grounded in Western criteria of modernity, and it reflects some abstract and misguided intellectual concepts ethnocentrically transferred to the developing nations. An ignorance of the sociocultural and political realities of developing nations has characterized, for instance, policies aimed at transferring Western technology in these societies. Indeed, technology transfer seen as a key strategy of the modernization enterprise has usually been conceived as a unilateral and one-dimensional process in which the recipient Third World countries had no initial input concerning the transferability and adaptability of the technological packages. The emphasis on "appropriate" technology did indicate a recognition of the shortcomings of "inappropriate" technology and a necessity to overcome them (Morrison 1983), but the damaging effects of technology transfer on the indigenous structures have been so ruinous that their resurrection has become highly problematic (Wiarda 1990, 1992).

Another dimension of technology transfer in the Third World is that, to put it in Busch's terms (1984:308): "Technology was transferred to the Third World as a deliberate part of the colonial expansion process." In Busch's (1984:308) view, Western countries, in addition to exporting technology, have provided technical assistance and trained large numbers of Third World scientists, who then become a powerful instrument perpetuating the status quo in the Third World. Busch (1984:308) puts his argument as follows: "Upon returning to their native country, they have often found themselves in a situation in which science and technology are practiced not because they contribute to resolving the problems of everyday life (however defined), but rather because they are seen as the necessary accoutrements for a modernizing country." Busch finally contends that Western technologies are in many cases largely incompatible with indigenous production systems. They often are irrelevant and dysfunctional to the needs of farmers.

Beyond the African Food Crisis: A Case Study of the Commercialization of Agriculture Versus Subsistence Farming

In Senegal, the imposition of a modernization policy of development has been in some cases counterproductive, particularly in the agricultural sector where its emphasis on commercialization as a way to diversify and improve farm production led to a disequilibrium between subsistence farming and cash-crop agriculture, thus creating a food crisis in the rural areas. Certainly a poor natural resource base, an expanding desertification, and degradation of the environment resulting from intensive shifting cultivation, overgrazing, and deforestation are objective factors contributing to the present crisis in many sub-Saharan African countries.

In the case of Senegal, however, much of this crisis has its roots in the push toward increasing commercialization of agriculture at the expense of food production. The rationale of this policy lies in the assumption that subsistence agriculture generates low productivity, given the few inputs available for production and the fact that agricultural activity tends to be strictly oriented toward producing barely enough to meet the basic needs of the family farm. Compared to commercial farming, subsistence farming appears to be a cause of stagnation in agricultural productivity, maintaining the family farm in a semiregressive state with a sole reliance on its two basic inputs: land and labor-intensive methods.

On the other hand, it is believed that commercial farming tends to tear the family farm from the highly traditional setting of subsistence economy and to integrate it into a kind of market economy through which the producer can acquire cash and diversify one's own consumption. Indeed, commercial farming provides farmers with a range of inputs (fertilizer, seeds, pesticides, and in certain cases, technological tools) that are likely to increase agricultural productivity. By virtue of its potential for cash returns, commercial farming constitutes an attractive practice to peasants. It also plays a primary role in the transitional process from a subsistence, purely indigenous, economy to a more efficient, diversified, and productive economy. Commercial farming is a far more viable and profitable agricultural strategy for the majority of farmers in the Third World. Yet, even given the empirical support for this statement (Barker, 1986; Crummey and Steward 1981), we should not stress an agricultural development strategy based solely on the promotion of commercialization at the expense of subsistence farming. This has led to a food deficiency on one hand and increasing inequality and dependency of cash producers on the vagaries of the market system on the other (Cliffe, 1976).

An inquiry into the development policy concerning cotton as a commercial production promoted by SODEFITEX (Societé de Development des Fibres Textiles) in Senegal reflects the food production gap resulting from this agency's intensive policy of commercialization aimed primarily at satisfying the needs of the French textile industry. Historically, cotton production in Senegal was controlled by the French development agency CFDT (Compagnie Francaise de Development des Textiles). CFDT exercised a monopoly over the crop and supervised its promotion as a cash crop for export to the French market. In the early 1970s (in the aftermath of the indigenization that dominated Africa), the Senegalese government nationalized CFDT, assigning to it the mandate of improving agricultural marketing and distribution channels, as well as increasing the incomes and standards of living of the rural population. In addition, SODEFITEX inherited the national extension service infrastructure from CFDT, which is responsible for the production and commercialization of cotton.

But the "Senegalization" of CFDT did not bring major changes to the existing development strategy, a strategy conceptualized and directed by a significant body of expatriate agricultural scientists (mainly French) still concerned with the export of cotton to France. Thus, despite attempts by the Senegalese government to carry out its agenda of nationalization, SODEFITEX is still a stronghold of French influence.

SODEFITEX's policy of promoting and developing cotton cultivation is rooted within the tradition of the diffusion model, and it is based on a strategy that prioritizes the individual approach rather than focus on the household as a unit of production and consumption. SODEFITEX's policy supports the belief that the individual planter is responsible for production, and this is the most efficient way to accelerate cotton cultivation. This approach is also dictated by transitions occurring in the structure of agriculture where the traditional family farm is moving from large and collective patterns to smaller units of production. SODEFITEX's individualization approach has indeed exacerbated these trends internal to the family group by promoting cotton as a cash production, which appeals to individual interests rather than those of the collectivity. In the upper southern region of Senegal, this approach has contributed significantly to the disintegration of the traditional family farm (Archestraat 1983, Ange, 1984).

The peasants' reactions toward SODEFITEX strategy varied according to the interests being defended by each special category in the peasant society. For the household head, cotton cultivation should operate under one's own control, while for the individual dependents growing cotton, the promotion as implemented by SODEFITEX responds to their growing desire for autonomy

(Archestraat 1983). Indeed, individual agriculture appears to be more efficient and stimulating than traditional collective agriculture. Individuals growing their own crops feel more responsibility, knowing they will be held accountable for success or failure, instead of being just a physical component of the collective production process (Ange 1984). SODEFITEX has taken advantage of this inclination toward commercial farming and the need for cash flow, which, in the eyes of the individual dependents, can be satisfied only through cotton adoption.

Tied to this cash motivation is the role played by the extensionist working for SODEFITEX. The main objective of the extension service is to help individual planters increase their yield and fulfill contractual agreements with SODEFITEX. To this end, planters supervised by extension workers are required to prepare the land early for a precocious sowing and devote a significant part of their time to the weeding operation in their cotton plots. SODEFITEX's extension agent has the power to decide whether to continue providing the necessary inputs and supervision or to refuse any assistance when the planter deviates from his recommendation. Such pressure generates a crucial contradiction in labor allocation between cereal cultivation (millet, maize, sorghum) for consumption by the family group and cotton production that reflects an individual interest.

Individual planters are confronted with two problems: on the one hand, since they are not yet capable of holding an autonomous household, the only way to remain in the family group is to participate in the collective cultivation of cereals (the priority of the family farm), thus submitting themselves to the agricultural calendar designed by the household head. On the other hand, they are also exposed to the constant pressure of the SODEFITEX extensionist, who requires them to place cotton production ahead of cereal production.

By orienting its strategy on the individual planter, SODEFITEX "has favored the individual interests, at the expense of the collective ones" (Ange 1984) and hence appeared as the major reason for social dissension within the family farm. As Ange (1984:320) indicates:

> The planters interest is to produce as much cotton as possible with a minimum labor investment, while the interest of the agency distributing the factors of production is to valorize at a maximum level the production of such imports. We find here a second contradiction of the system which obliges the development agency (SODEFITEX) to sharpen its pressures on the peasants in order to make them respect the norms of the use of the inputs.

Another problem area for SODEFITEX is its lack of efficiency in and commitment to developing cereal production, despite the fact that the supervision of cereal production has been an assigned agency objective since 1981. Although SODEFITEX's primary objective is the promotion of cotton, each extension agent supervises 25 hectares of maize, millet, and sorghum in one's respective work area. Still, the extension worker implementing SODEFITEX strategy in the field first must fulfill the objectives assigned for cotton production if one is to expect any substantial reward or promotion. Indeed, SODEFITEX does not provide the same inputs and the necessary technical supervision for cereal cultivation as it does for cotton production, nor does it offer extension workers any bonus or incentive for promoting cereal production. This situation is best summarized by a SODEFITEX extensionist who stated (in Archestraat 1983:38): "We never ask a farmer to show us his cereal plot, we only ask to see his cotton plot."

This disequilibrium between cereal production and cotton as a cash-crop activity promoted by SODEFITEX is one of the major factors leading to the present food production gap accompanying the intensive commercialization of agriculture. Such a disequilibrium has reinforced food import in Senegal where more than 65 percent of the labor force is in agriculture, forcing the government to continue to import nearly 60 percent of its food, wł ile commercial farming is not generating sufficient income to allow the peasants to make up this deficit (World Bank Development Report 1989, Barker 1989). Certainly one way to deal with this dilemma is to reinforce SODEFITEX's responsibility concerning cereal production. SODEFITEX has been efficient in promoting cotton. Transferring its strategy to cereal production (mainly maize and sorghum), SODEFITEX could provide the necessary inputs and technical assistance for the development of these crops. An increase in SODEFITEX's responsibility toward cereal production would likely help alleviate peasants' reluctance toward decreasing cotton production, since the agency would be involved in both cereal and cotton production. This would also contribute to establishing an equilibrium between the two production systems. Such a change in policy would require a change in how extensionists approach food production. To facilitate this shift, SODEFITEX might, for instance, extend its bonus system for cotton production to cereal cultivation.

Additionally, any significant change in agricultural development strategy in Senegal will require profound changes in policy orientation at the state level. The World Bank vice-president for Africa, Edward Jaycox (1988) is certainly right when he contends that the main cause of hunger in Africa is not drought or crop failure but the inability to generate sufficient income to acquire food. But, as Barker (1986) argues, the dramas of African countries are not merely economic and demographic, they involve policy orientations that are still influenced by a colonial legacy. A policy of agricultural development oriented toward commercialization, as in Senegal, where the country's dependency on food importation is not under control, is likely to increase such dependency. Indeed, the continued emphasis on cash-crop cultivation at the expense of food-crop production has been one of the major factors involved in the current food deficit facing African nations in general and Senegal in particular. The issues at hand are how to promote food self-sufficiency and how to extend commercial farming in order to reach a balanced agricultural development that can improve the welfare of the Senegalese small landholders. To do this, a redesign of current agricultural development policy, as it is at present conducted by the government and applied by its agencies, must be undertaken.

The Moral Dilemma Facing Western Sociology

So far, I have explored the irrelevance and inadequacy of Western sociological discourse and its attempt to channel social, economic, and political change and development perspectives in the Third World. The origin of Western sociology ethnocentrism is not simply a problem of malcomprehension or naiveté, but a problem grounded in the global cultural hegemony imposed by Western imperialism on the Third World. The domination of the modernization paradigm in the field of international development, and more specifically in applied rural sociology, illustrates this trend. Advocates of the modernization paradigm have been more successful in gaining access to the lucrative market of international development projects than those who value the ethical and moral dimensions of development policies and use a critical perspective in their approach to international development.

The moral dilemma facing Western sociology is how to articulate issues of human rights with its participation in international development projects that turn out to be elitist in nature and exclude the powerless poor from the major arena of decision making and from formulating their needs. Such participation without a critical stance conceals the real nature of the agenda being pursued by the developers, which fundamentally deviates from the concerns of the powerless in the Third World. A sociological perspective more attuned to indigenous social structures, knowledge, and culture has to be developed.

There is a need to dismantle the ideological foundation on which the sociological enterprise was traditionally based and still continues to carry Western ethnocentric models of development to the Third World on a general basis. This dismantling does not mean calling for an indigenization of the sociological enterprise as Loubser (1988) advocates, which is more likely to duplicate the same ethnocentrism that characterizes Western sociology. But, it does indicate that Western sociology has to account for the moral implications of its participation in international development, and it should use its knowledge to empower the powerless, rather than serve the interests of oppressive forces.

Any effort to bring about change and development must start with the fundamental assumption that human agents are capable of dismantling this oppressive social reality for the purpose of reconstructing a better and freer existence. Although no preconceived scheme can predict the stages through which human beings reconstruct this new social order, or how they engage in an emancipatory process, they remain a cardinal driving force for such change.

Therefore, we need to look first at the concrete social forces and the political circumstances that surround them in a particular situation. Also, we must integrate the dimension of indigenous culture that is largely overlooked by the dominant currents in development sociology. As Worsley (1984:332) points out, "economic and political domination of the Third Word is accompanied by a new, more intensive and more extensive cultural imperialism." Alongside the constitution of a world economic system in which Third World countries are located, the emergence of a world culture dominated by Western ideology continues to affect the Third World. Thus, in the struggle for development, it is imperative to call for a cultural emancipation of dependent nations as well as for their political and economic liberation.

In order to overcome underdevelopment in the Third World, we must articulate and fashion an essentially nonethnocentric approach that deals with Third World societies in their own cultural and institutional terms. Such an approach must be geared toward praxis, however, since underdevelopment will be overcome only by the actions of those currently suffering from it. As Freire (1970) contends, genuine development will come about only when the mass of people recognize their oppression and consciously act to change it.

My attempt to respond to the irrelevance and inadequacy of Western sociological discourse and practice in the Third World, and to formulate an alternative theoretical framework, is constructed around the basic tenets of the Freirean tradition. This alternative theoretical framework is humanistic in content and embodies an emancipatory project for the dispossessed. It refers to Freire's advocacy of a radical pedagogy that brings an empowering and humanist dimension to the development process. In order to reach this emancipatory project, it is necessary to engage in critical activity, discourse, dialogue, and persuasion in order to convince people to end technocratic and bureaucratic domination in their daily existence and to make them understand that they can construct a social reality different from the oppressive one that enslaves them.

REFERENCES

Ake, Claude. 1979. *Social Science as Imperialism: The Theory of Political Development*. Ibadan: University of Ibadan Press.

Ange, Alain. 1984. "Les contraintes de la Culture Cotonniere dans les Systemes Agraires de la Haute Casamance au Seneigal." Ph.D. dissertation, Institute National Agronomique. Paris Grignon.

Archestraat, Alexandre. 1983. "Agriculture d'auto Subsistence au Agriculture de Rente?" Technical report, Universite Libre d' Amsterdam.

Arnon, Itzhak. 1981. *Modernization of Agriculture in Developing Countries*. New York: Wiley.

Barker, Jonathan. 1986. *Rural Communities under Stress: Peasant Farmers and the State in Africa.* New York: Cambridge University Press.

Bellah, Robert. 1983. "Social Science as Practical Reason." In Daniel Callahan and Bruce Jennings, eds. *Ethics, the Social Sciences and Policy Analysis.* New York: Plenum Press.

Blomstrom, Magnus, and Bjorn Hettne. 1984. *Development Theory in Transition.* London: Zed Books.

Bohannan, Paul, and George Dalton, eds. 1962. *Markets in Africa.* Evanston: Northwestern University Press.

Brokensha, David, D.M. Warren, and Oswald Werner, eds. 1980. *Indigeneous Knowledge Systems and Development.* Washington, D.C.: University Press of America.

Busch, Lawrence. 1984. "Science, Technology, Agriculture and Every Day Life in Research." Pp. 289–314 in Harry K. Schwarzweller, ed. *Rural Sociology and Development.* Greenwich, Conn.: JAI Press.

Buttel, Frederick, and Howard Newby. 1980. *The Rural Sociology of the Advanced Societies: Critical Perspectives.* Montclair: Allanheld, Osmun.

Chekki, Danesh A. 1987. *American Sociological Hegemony: Transnational Explorations.* Lanham, MD: University Press of America.

Cliffe, Lionel. 1976. "Rural Political Economy of Africa." Pp. 112–30 in Immanuel Wallerstein and Peter C. H. Gutkind, eds. *Political Economy of Africa.* Beverly Hills: Sage.

Crummey, Donald, and C.C. Steward. 1981. *Mode of Production in Africa: The Precolonial Era.* Beverly Hills: Sage.

Edwards, Michael. 1989. "The Irrelevance of Development Studies." *Third World Quarterly* 11: 117–35.

Fliegel, Frederick, and J. C. Van Es. 1983. "The Diffusion-Adoption Process in Agriculture: Changes in Technology and Changing Paradigms." Pp. 13–28 in Gene Summers, ed. *Technology and Social Change in Rural Areas.* Boulder. Colo.: Westview Press.

Frank, Andre Gunder. 1969. *Sociology of Development and Underdevelopment of Sociology in Latin America: Underdevelopment or Revolution.* New York: Monthly Review Press.

Freire, Paulo. 1970. *Pedagogy of the Oppressed.* New York: Continuum.

Friedland, William. 1982. "The End of Rural Society and the Future of Rural Sociology." *Rural Sociology* 47:589–608.

Gareau, Frederick H. 1988. "Another Type of Third World Dependency: The Social Sciences." *International Sociology* 3:171–78.

Gilbert, Jess. 1982. "Rural Theory: The Grounding of Rural Sociology." *Rural Sociology* 47:609–33.

Goldthorpe, J.E. 1984. *The Sociology of the Third World.* New York: Cambridge University Press.

Gouldner, Alvin W. 1970. *The Coming Crisis of Western Sociology.* New York: Basic Books.

Gruhn, Isebill. 1983. "The Recolonization of Africa: International Organizations on the March." *Africa Today* 30:37–48.

Havens, Eugene, and William Flinn. 1975. "Green Revolution Technology and Community Development: The Limits of Action Programs." *Economic Development and Cultural Change* 23:32–43.

Jaycox, Edward. 1988. "Ending Hunger in Africa." *Africa Report* September-October, 15–18.

Hobbs, Darryl J. 1980. "Rural Development: Intentions and Consequences." *Rural Sociology* 45:7–25.

Loubser, Jan J. 1988. "The Need for the Indigenization of the Social Sciences." *International Sociology* 3:179–87.

Lowry, Sheldon C. 1977. "Rural Sociology at the Crossroads." *Rural Sociology* 42:461–75.

Mid-America International Agricultural Consortium (MIAC). 1989. *Agricultural Research and Training Support Project in Burkina Faso.* Stillwater, Okla:

Morgan D. 1985. "The Crisis of Research." *West Africa,* October 14, 165–78.

Morrison, Denton. 1983. "A Social Movement Analysis of Appropriate Technology." Pp. 197–216 in Gene Summers, ed. *Technology and Social Change in Rural Areas*. Boulder, Colo.: Westview Press.

Morse, Elliot. 1976. *Strategies For Small Farmers' Development*. Boulder, Colo.: Westview Press.

Nair, Kusum. 1979. *In Defense of the Irrational Peasant*. Chicago: University of Chicago Press.

Newby, Howard and Frederick Buttel. 1980. "Toward a Critical Rural Sociology." Pp. 1–35 in Frederick Buttel and Howard Newby, eds. *The Rural Sociology of the Advanced Societies: Critical Perspectives*. Montclair: Allanheld, Osmun.

Oakley, P., and D. Marsden. 1984. *Approaches to Participation in Rural Development*. Geneva: International Labor Organization.

Park, Peter. 1988. "Toward an Emancipatory Sociology: Abandoning Universalism for True Indigenization." *International Sociology* 3:161–70.

Parsons, Talcott. 1977. *The Evolution of Societies*. Englewood Cliffs, N.J.: Prentice-Hall.

Picou, J. Steven, Richard H. Wells, and Kenneth L. Nybert. 1978. "Paradigms, Theories and Methods in Contemporary Rural Sociology." *Rural Sociology* 43:559–83.

Richards, Paul. 1985. *Indigenous Agricultural Revolutions*. Boulder, Colo.: Westview Press.

Rodefeld, Richard, Jan Flora, Donald Voth, Isao Fujimoto, and Jim Converse, eds. 1978. *Change in Rural America: Causes, Consequences, and Alternatives*. St. Louis: Mosby.

Rogers, Everett. 1983. *Diffusion of Innovations*. New York: Free Press.

———. 1988. *Social Change in Rural Societies*. Englewood Cliffs, N.J.: Prentice-Hall.

Rogers, Everett, Rabel Burdge, Peter Korsching, and Joseph Donnermeyer. 1988. *Social Change in Rural Societies*. Englewood Cliffs, N.J.: Prentice-Hall.

So, Alvin. 1990. *Social Change and Development*. Newbury Park, Calif.: Sage.

Taylor, John. 1979. *From Modernization to Modes of Production*. London: Macmillan.

Vandergeest, Peter, and Frederick Buttel. 1988. "Marx, Weber and Development Sociology: Beyond the Impasse. *World Development* 16:683–94.

Wiarda, J. Howard. 1990. "Technocentrism and Third World Development." Pp. 11–20 in Jeffrey Elliot, ed. *Third World*. Guilford, Conn.: Dushkin Publishing.

———. 1992. "Toward a Nonethnocentric Theory of Development: Alternative Conceptions from the Third World." Pp. 55–79 in Charles Wilber and Kenneth Jameson, eds. *The Political Economy of Development and Underdevelopment*. New York: McGraw-Hill.

World Development Report. 1989. Washington, D.C.: World Bank.

Worsley, Peter. 1984. *The Three Worlds*. Chicago: University of Chicago Press.

Chapter **11** THE RISE AND FALL OF THE
AMERICAN SOCIOLOGIST

John F. Galliher and David Nelson

The American Sociologist (TAS), sponsored by the American Sociological Association (ASA), was started through the efforts of the distinguished Harvard sociologist Talcott Parsons, who assumed editorship in 1965. *The American Sociologist* was published for seventeen years and was discontinued in 1982. We ask here what there was about *TAS*, its history, or its publications that can explain its demise when in other associations such as the American Psychological Association, a similar journal, *The American Psychologist*, continues to thrive.

The rise and fall of *TAS* is used in this chapter to illustrate how the discipline handles intellectual dissent and deviance. Ironically, given its history, intellectual deviance and dissent could not have been further from the original motivations for starting the journal. There is no evidence, for example, that it was intended to be an avenue for criticism of the profession. When *TAS* was started in the mid-1960s, no one anticipated that by the late 1960s and early 1970s there would be such a large protest against the war in Vietnam on American campuses that it would spill over into the profession. Thus, an unintended consequence of the creation of this journal was that it was available to serve as a convenient vehicle for the expression of newfound intellectual dissent. And dissent now had a legitimate, official, and slightly prestigious outlet with the imprimatur of the professional association.

This criticism of the discipline in an ASA journal must have been especially galling, since the critics were usually not from high-prestige universities, unlike the leaders of the profession, who generally were affiliated with leading American universities. Now the association was providing these academic upstarts from the backwaters of higher education with the means for public criticism of their professional betters. As we see, the editors who allowed the journal to be used in this manner were not typically the focus of attack, but the journal itself was discredited. In a futile attempt to save the journal, later editors instituted controls on what could be considered for publication, but the journal was still scuttled.

A History of the Journal

The first editorial statement of *TAS*, written by Parsons, shows his high hopes for its success and begins as follows (Parsons, 1965:2):

The decision of the Executive Committee and Council of the American Sociological Association to publish *The American Sociologist* is a landmark in the development, not only of the Association, but of sociology as a discipline, if this is to be understood to include not only the scientific character of sociology, but also the social organization of its activities.

Parsons (see table 11.1) went on in this initial editorial to advocate the publication of research on the relations between the various disciplines, as well as on teaching, and concluded (Parsons 1965:3): "The welfare of the Association and the profession depend on *the opportunity for all important points of view to receive adequate expression* and to become known throughout the profession" (italics added). The next year, Parsons emphasized the need to publish accounts of the "development of sociology in other countries" (Parsons 1966:238). The year after that, he added to this list of priorities the examination of the profession's relation to the federal government and the conditions attached to funding.

Table 11.1.
Priorities of *The American Sociologist* Editors

Topics	Parsons	Mack	Pfautz	Mayhew	Grimshaw	McCartney	Totals
Teaching	Yes	—	Yes	Yes	No	Yes	4
Funding	Yes	—	Yes	—	Yes	Yes	4
Conflict	Yes	—	—	Yes	Yes	—	3
Social org.	Yes	Yes	—	—	—	Yes	3
Interdisc.	Yes	—	—	—	—	—	1
Internatnl.	Yes	No	—	—	—	—	1
Hierarchy	—	—	—	Yes	No	—	1
Publishing	—	—	—	Yes	—	—	1
Ethics	—	—	Yes	—	Yes	Yes	3
Employment	—	—	—	—	Yes	Yes	2
Theory	—	—	—	—	Yes	Yes	2
Methods	—	—	—	—	Yes	Yes	2

In 1968 Ray Mack assumed the editorship and emphasized the importance of publications on the effects of the "social environment" of both the profession and discipline of sociology. In his first editorial, Mack concluded: "With less than a year in office, we have been threatened with a libel suit, [and] a letter to the Council demanding a change in the editorship" (Mack 1968:332). Less than a year after Parsons's departure, storm clouds were gathering. After another year, Mack (1969) reported that statements on sociology in other countries would be discontinued and noted that he had solicited the especially heated remarks of a critic of the discipline to be published in the journal together with a rejoinder.

In 1970 Harold Pfautz became editor and reported that the journal would emphasize such topics as teaching (including graduate training), research funding, the relation of the profession to government, sociologists in private industry, and professional ethics (Pfautz 1970:400). By October 1971 it was announced in *Socio-Log*, then the Association's newsletter, that *The American Sociologist* would be merged with this newsletter and assume a throwaway newspaper format. As of January 1972 the "new" *The American Sociologist* debuted. The journal was obviously in considerable trouble. Pfautz (1972c:26) referred to this as a "precipitous decision of Council." He concluded that "it is our hope that the fate of TAS as a scholarly journal will ultimately and properly be decided by a referendum of the membership, without the consideration of 'costs' and the preferences of the executive office" (Pfautz 1972c:26). He was referring to the demands of Jay Demerath, the ASA Executive Officer, who in turn referred to a "recent publications survey [that] attests to the dissatisfaction within both Council and the Committee on Publications" and concluded: "Hopefully, *The American Sociologist* will become increasingly identified as a teachers' publication," and he referred to his close work with the new section on Teaching Sociology, chaired by Hans Mauksch, and threatened to "jettison . . . [certain] journals altogether" (Demerath 1972:25). This pressure to emphasize teaching foreshadowed things to come, for a decade later the ASA Council indeed would "jettison" *TAS* and replace it almost immediately with a journal devoted to teaching. If all these problems were not enough, also in November 1972 Martin Bulmer (1972:4) criticized the journal's emphasis on academic stratification as a "bizarre kind of navel-gazing."

But *TAS* was not dead yet. Apparently as a consequence of a letter-writing campaign, in January 1973 it was announced that TAS would return to its former quarterly format with a new editor, Leon Mayhew. As a part of this campaign, Richard Hessler collected twenty-eight signatures from University of Missouri sociologists on a petition to the ASA Publications Committee protesting the change in format. One of the leading officers of the association responded to the petition and defended the decision in a letter to Hessler (1971) claiming that the journal "did not print very many articles which related to professional concerns, but rather operated as a very third rate ASR [American Sociological Review]. Finally, it has become an archive for preserving articles that ought to be printed on disposable paper . . . [it] turned into a bad parody of the ASR."

Demerath (1971), on the other hand, attempted to be more conciliatory, even if patronizing. He attempted to mollify Hessler by writing that the new publication would be printed on "considerably better stock [than most newspapers], and this should discourage throw-aways to some extent. . . . Finally, we aim to take another step to discourage throw-aways; namely, the provision of binders at cost for our members." Mayhew (1972) also wrote to one of the petition signers that others shared their distress: "Your concern about the format of *The American Sociologist* is shared by many of our colleagues around the country. Harold Pfautz left me quite a sheaf of inquiries and complaints."

The question of publication costs was especially puzzling to Pfautz, for he wrote to Hessler (Pfautz 1972a):

> Last year, the Council in a mindless fashion asked me to bring out a special issue [on public policy] to solve a political problem with the Committee on Freedom, etc. I don't know whether this costly step figured in Council's subsequent decision to downgrade TAS. I do know that I asked Jay for the cost data on various alternatives and that he refused to share them with me on the premise that it was not an editor's business.

In a later letter Pfautz indicated a willingness to fight (Pfautz 1972b): "I plan to insist that the economics of the past and current operations be revealed (including the increased costs of the Washington operation) [the executive office], for none of these figured in the discussions."

In *Footnotes* in March 1974, it was reported that *TAS* had 14,528 subscribers but all except 1063 of these (7.3 percent) got the publication automatically with ASA membership. The corresponding percentage for the *ASR* was 30.4. In other words, almost all those receiving *TAS* were forced to take it. This would soon change. In August 1974, Mayhew (1974:99) published "An Amended Statement" of editorial policy. He apparently ignored criticisms such as Bulmer's and indicated plans to emphasize research on the "profession—its status system, barriers and mobility within the system, sociological associations, and the politics of teaching, research, and publication" as well as professional ethics. A year later (1975:13', he stressed that the journal was a "vehicle for new ideas about our discipline and our profession and a voice for *a wide variety of points of view*" (italics added). This had been precisely Parson's position nearly a decade earlier. In the December 1974 *Footnotes*, the appointment of Allen Grimshaw as the new TAS editor was announced.

In his first editorial in August 1975 (1975:192), Grimshaw proclaimed that "sociology is, or should be, exciting" and encouraged submission on "'ideological' issues" and "'hard' *versus* `soft' data" as well as the impact of government funding and "what research *should* sociologists do and for whom should they do it." This suggested an interest in ethical issues and encouraged a *wide range* of opinion. Grimshaw also encouraged pieces on topics such as "discrimination or exploitation . . . tenure . . . [and] collective bargaining." Undoubtedly wary of threats from the association and perhaps smarting from Bulmer's criticism of the journal, he explicitly discouraged submission of research on the professional stratification system. He said it was "disheartening . . . [that in the journal] matters of the stratification, mobility, and productivity . . . [were] almost *the* principal 'professional concern.'" He said, "As editor . . . I want to declare a moratorium on introspective self-analyses of the stratification system of the discipline" and said he felt the same should apply to papers on teaching. Not surprisingly, in his editor's annual reports in *Footnotes* in March 1977 and March 1978 he noted decreased submissions of "prestige" and teaching studies. This deemphasis on stratification is not what Mayhew had proposed and the deemphasis on teaching was contrary to the demands of Demerath and the plans of Parsons, Pfautz, and Mayhew. By February 1979, Grimshaw noted that submissions to *TAS* fell into two clusters (1979:6): "practical professional concerns," dealing with such things as employment, and "intellectual" issues, dealing with theoretical or substantive problems of the discipline.

By November 1976, the ASA had adopted an optional journal plan with membership, and *TAS* was again in jeopardy. Grimshaw wrote (1976:1): "The fate of TAS depends, to some substantial extent, on our ability to 'win back' subscribers who dropped the journal under the new journal options of the Association." In May 1978, he noted (1978:3) that the "TAS is only slowly recovering from the change in Association subscription policies."

In January 1979, James McCartney was introduced as the new editor of *TAS*. He announced his intention of continuing Grimshaw's (1979:1) emphasis on "topics of 'practical professional concern,'" such as affirmative action, collective bargaining, tenure, employment, professional ethics," as well as "'intellectual' questions" involving new or developing theoretical perspectives. McCartney also noted the importance of teaching and funding for research, and thus it was not unexpected that he devoted a special issue to each topic. He also devoted two issues to the ASA. This latter emphasis was probably what Parsons had in mind in urging publication on the "social organization" of sociology and what Mack meant by an emphasis on the profession's and discipline's "social environment." McCartney optimistically concluded that "the battle for the survival of TAS seems to be behind us." By March 1982, he was not so sure. In his annual report, he noted (1982:11): "As of the date of this report, the fate of TAS again hangs in the balance." His concern was grounded on the report in October 1981 that the ASA council had begun a review of association publications including in its deliberations "financial considerations" and "escalating costs of publications" and the "widest possible dissemination" of knowledge, but "that it may be important to maintain a specifically sociological outlet in certain fields (i.e., health, social psychology)." Furthermore, "the [Publications] Committee recommended that the ASA cease to sponsor *The American Sociologist, Socio-*

logical Methodology, the yet to be published *Sociological Theory*, and *Sociology of Education.*" Clearly something other than "financial considerations" and the "widest possible dissemination" of knowledge were paramount. In the 1981 statements of circulation, published in each journal, it was reported that *TAS* had a paid circulation of 3129, more than the *Sociology of Education* (*SOE*) at 3050, just less than the *Social Psychology Quarterly* (*SPQ*) at 3616, and the *Journal of Health and Social Behavior* (JHSB) at 4156. The publications managers of the ASA largely confirmed these figures for 1981, showing various ASA journals clustered together with *TAS* at 3307, *SOE* at 3135, *SPQ* at 3373 (Edwards 1988): "These figures are exact, since they are the actual mailing counts from our printer ... [but still claims that dropping TAS] was due, in no small part, to the declining circulation." If circulation had been a prime consideration, *SOE* would surely have been dropped rather than *TAS*, but it was not.

These figures notwithstanding, by February 1982 the Publications Committee voted to phase out *TAS* (*Footnotes* February 1982). In May 1982 it was reported that each member of the committee had reviewed the "most recent volumes of TAS, JHSB, SPQ and SOE" (*Footnotes*, May 1982:8) in preparing this recommendation. Ultimately, as reported in August 1982, only *TAS* was to be discontinued, at the end of McCartney's term as editor in November 1982, exactly seventeen years after it had begun (*Footnotes* August 1982). Another petition campaign was started to save the journal by T.R. Young. He recalled (1988) that he "drafted a petition, sent it to the chair of every department listed in the ASA guide to graduate programs, and requested that the Chair circulate it among the faculty there and mail it into the Chair of the Publications Committee (1988)." But unlike the letter-writing efforts of 1972, this effort failed to achieve its objectives. Scarcely two years after dropping *TAS*, the association had again found the funds to support an additional journal: "The ASA Council has approved creating a new, ASA-sponsored journal on teaching sociology" (*Footnotes* 1984) and the search was begun for an editor. Such a switch must have been what Demerath had in mind in 1972. If the demise of the journal was related to what it did or did not publish, as the reviews by the Publications Committee suggests, its specific objectionable qualities may become clearer through an examination of the themes and focus of all of its published articles and research notes.[1]

Themes of Published Articles

Topics Suited to Conflict and Dispute

1. Criticism and defense of the discipline. One paper claimed that many felt that the profession must take a stand on public issues such as the war in Vietnam

(Bart 1970). Another writer explained the consequences of silence: "Our brightest and most articulate graduate students think much that the profession produces is fraudulent. Moreover, the center of much student revolt is, not surprisingly, found in sociology departments" (Gamberg 1969:115). Finally, a writer concluded (Hoult 1968:6): "Although greed and sloth may account for a significant number of those who choose to remain on what they *think* is dead center so far as controversial social issues are concerned, I am personally convinced that *cowardice* is the most important single explanation."

Pease et al. (1970:129) wrote: "For the first time, [during the 1930s] American sociologists appeared to be disposed to abandon adherence to the liberal *laissez-faire* ideology and to be willing to examine the economic and political underpinnings of institutionalized stratification. But the inclination to look hard at the structural sources of institutionalized inequality didn't last long."

Others argued that any genuine reform's objective should be to redistribute wealth (Miller and Roby 1971). The statement solicited by Mack reads in part: "Sociology has risen to its present prosperity and eminence on the blood and bones of the poor and oppressed; it owes its prestige in this society to its putative ability to give information and advice to the ruling class of this society about ways and means to keep the people down" (Nicolaus 1969:155).

Others disagreed. One writer observed that radical sociology blurs the necessary distinction between scientific truth seeking and political activism (Wrong 1974). Another claimed that sociology is not really a liberating discipline for "the sociologist has no doctrine of redemption to bring into the political arena" (Berger 1971:5). Another angry observer felt that the sociological liberation movement should do less sloganeering and more rigorous thinking about strategies for social change (Robbins 1969). Yet another paper noted that the natural scientist "provides means to ends that are given outside the profession or science. He takes no fundamental responsibility to distinguish between better or worse applications of his knowledge but relies on the market or political system to make this distinction . . . It could be argued that . . . it is presumptuous for social scientists to set up their own values as superior to those of democracy or the market" (MacRae 1971:3).

Such value judgments, MacRae concluded, belong in philosophy and not sociology. While the possibility of a value-free sociology was being rejected by the radical and black caucus of ASA as moral irresponsibility, one critic of their stance countered: "We must choose . . . between the ideal of objectivity and intellectual anarchy" (Sibley 1971:16). Some argued in utilitarian terms that if sociology takes stands on moral issues, it will become perceived as ideology and not science, will drive those away from the discipline who do not agree with the dominant ideology, and will make access to certain people needed in our research impossible—as in stands against military operations (Gove 1970). While the articles that were *generally critical* of the discipline were few in number, they nonetheless seemed to set the tone for many other papers critical of *one facet* of the discipline.

2. *Social stratification and hierarchy*. There are more studies of social stratification than any other topic (see table 11.2).

For example, several studies involve the ranking of sociology departments on the basis of the number of faculty and graduates' publications in major journals (Knudsen and Vaughan 1969; Glenn and Villemez 1970); and departments whose work is most frequently cited in journals and textbooks (Oromaner 1980). But other articles claimed that this system is maintained not so much by merit alone but by an "old boy" network. The editors of *American Sociological Review* usually were found to hold Ph.D.s from a few top-ranked departments (Yoels 1971). And another study found that the prestige of institutions influenced whether one's books were reviewed favorably (Snizek 1979). Also, it was noted that departments may have high prestige because of one or two stars in the department or because of being private institutions rather than faculty or graduate publications (Lewis 1968).

Other research observed that in this highly stratified system women were completely excluded during the early part of this century (Deegan 1981), and until 1968 to 1970 women and minorities did not participate in the American Sociological Association (Wilkinson 1981). Women were still underrepresented in the senior ranks and elite departments (Rossi 1970), another publication reported. As late as 1977, sex bias was demonstrated to exist in placement (Welch and Lewis 1980). Thus, the overall impression we are left with is that the stratification system in sociology is sexist, racist, elitist, and not necessarily based on merit.

3. *Theory*. There are multiple paradigms in sociology (Ritzer 1975); including the presuppositions of the Chicago School (Faught, 1980). Typically sociology is hopeful rather than realistically pessimistic (Killian 1971:284): "The typical sociological treatise is like a late, late movie produced in the forties. The problems are complex, the situation grows desperate, but there is hope at the end." And Marxist theory has been ignored by American sociologists (Sallach 1973). Another essay noted that deviance studies have focused on the poor and not the powerful (Thio 1973). It also was observed that labeling theory incorrectly views actors as totally passive (Schervish 1973). Gouldner criticized labeling theorists for taking sides against only low-level officials while ignoring oppressive social institutions (1968:107): "Insofar as this school of theory has a critical edge to it, this is directed at the caretaking institutions who do the mopping-up job, rather than at the master institutions that produce the deviants' suffering."

4. *Professional ethics*. The Code of Ethics of the American Sociological Association was presented (Schuler 1969). It was criticized for giving inadequate attention to the special needs of the poor, the powerless, and students (Galliher 1973; 1975). Another paper noted that both the risk of damage and

potential benefit to research subjects must be considered in determining ethical standards in fieldwork (Cassell 1978). It was also observed that fictitious names of research sites do not really protect the identity of respondents, for it often is easy to see what community is being discussed (Gibbons 1975). Questions about the consequences of covert Central Intelligence Agency (CIA) funding, consequent misrepresentation, and potential violation of anonymity of subjects were discussed (Stephenson 1978:131): "Respondents seemed to speak quite freely and frankly of their activities prior to and during the [Hungarian] revolution . . . [T]hey well may not have been so candid in the interviews if they had known of the CIA involvement."

Table 11.2.
Topics of Articles Published by Editors of *TAS*

Editors

Conflict-Oriented Topics	Parsons	Mack	Pfautz	Mayhew	Grimshaw	McCartney	Totals
Hierarchy	6	18	28	22	3	8	85
Theory	4	6	9	15	21	19	74
Ethics	0	1	2	5	6	5	19
Funding	4	0	2	2	1	3	12
Employment	0	2	2	2	10	4	20
Criticism & Defense	1	8	12	4	1	1	27
	15	35	55	50	42	40	237

Mundane Topics							
Teaching	8	17	22	12	4	10	73
Methods	4	18	18	10	16	7	73
Subfields	6	9	5	6	11	4	41
Applied	1	1	9	5	3	4	23
Publishing	0	5	5	3	9	1	23
Prof. Char.	4	6	5	7	7	20	49
	23	56	64	43	50	46	282

Grand Total 519

5. *Research funding.* Some of the history of funding of the social sciences was discussed. The Rockefeller Memorial Foundation at the University of Chicago during the 1920s was very important, since for the first time large-scale support for social science research was offered (Bulmer 1982). But Roth (1966:195) discussed "hired hand research" where the research dollar buys less than a quality product because a hired hand "has no stake in the research that he is working on, that he is simply expected to carry out assigned tasks and turn in results which will 'pass inspection.'" Another problem relating to funding was discussed. The National Institute of Law Enforcement and Criminal Justice distorted the research process by insisting that funded research represent the "prejudices of the Administration rather than any consensus of professional opinion" (Furstenberg 1971:59). But another prominent writer noted that sociologists must serve the interests of elites in gathering information for control or sociologists will be rejected as irrelevant (Gibbs 1979:80-81): "Similarly, legislators change statutory penalties, supposedly to prevent criminality. . . . [T]hose who seek power will look to the social sciences for an answer to the question: How can we control human behavior in the aggregate? If sociologists provide no answer, those who operate the purse strings will decide that they can do without us."

6. *Employment.* Empirical studies were conducted of the present and future needs for sociologists. Shortages were noted in 1968 (Ferriss) and a surplus in 1973 (McGinnis). The tenure process was discussed (Francis and Pratto 1982) and described as "a dehumanizing, demeaning, and debilitating process" (Scimecca 1976:199). The de-professionalization of part-time teachers was bemoaned (Van Arsdale 1978), as were quotas in hiring (van den Berghe 1971:43): "[A] quota system—of necessity based on the recognition of the very barriers that are to be eliminated—is self-defeating." Criticism was leveled against affirmative action as reverse discrimination (Borgatta 1976:63-64): "There are many examples of violation of the value of equal opportunity involving reverse discrimination that can be documented. Here we focus first on one especially relevant to sociologists, the American Sociological Association's program of Graduate Fellowships for Minority Students."

Mundane Professional Concerns

Table 11.2 demonstrates that more papers were published on mundane professional concerns than on topics that could directly generate conflict. Various *teaching techniques* were discussed in several essays, including such ideas as using small-group discussions to supplement class lectures (Baker and Behrens 1971; Dunphy 1967), and the use of computers in introductory sociology (Sokol 1968). *Methods of sociological research* were discussed, including the historical perspective (Erikson 1970), participant observation (Whyte, 1979), ethnomethodology (Zimmerman 1978), Marxist methods (Applebaum 1978), path analysis (Nygreen 1971), and the uses and limitations of tests of significance (Winch and Campbell 1969). *Subfields of the discipline* appeared in numerous papers describing the state of sociology in various foreign nations. Developments in various specialty areas also were described, including rural sociology (Haller and Borgatta 1968; Newby 1982), black sociology (Watson 1976), environmental sociology (Catton and Dunlap 1978), collective behavior (Quarantelli and Weller 1974), the sociology of education (Karabel 1979), and symbolic interaction (Vaughan and Reynolds 1968). Finally, the rise and decline of areas of specialization in sociology was described (Stehr and Larson 1972). *Applied sociology* was also discussed, including the notion that sociologists might serve as social and economic forecasters (Stimson and Stimson 1976), or investigate issues of crime and public policy (Glaser 1971; Ross and Blumenthal 1975). *Publication* was discussed in papers such as those analyzing the review process (Rodman 1970; Freese 1979); as was the need to evaluate faculty on objective standards of publication productivity (Lewis 1977). The *profession's characteristics* were covered in many publications, including pieces dealing with the demographic characteristics of sociologists (Glenn and Weiner 1969), their beliefs (Moskos and Bell 1967; Granberg 1973), and the nature of their professional associations (Rosenberg 1971; Moore 1981).

Conclusions and Implications

We set out to answer the question: What led the American Sociological Association to cease publication of *The American Sociologist*? In addressing this question, we have explored the turbulent history of *TAS*. We have paid special attention to the policies and overall responses of its editors. In addition, we have analyzed the nature of the kinds of articles printed in *TAS*. One facet of our discussion has dealt with the relationship between the stated policies of various editors and the nature of the articles published. We found that there often were inconsistencies between the formal policies of editors and the articles actually accepted for publication.

The founding editor, Talcott Parsons, never mentioned stratification within the discipline as a topic for publication, but accepted several papers on this topic. Parsons claimed to be interested in publishing "all important points of view," but no criticism of the discipline appeared during his term as editor. Presumably "important" points of view did not include criticism. Mack, Pfautz, and McCartney made no mention of stratification, but published numerous articles on this topic. Pfautz made no mention of criticism of the discipline, nor did he encourage a diversity of views, yet he published more of these items than any other TAS editor. Grimshaw claimed to be interested in a diversity of views, including those dealing with ideological issues, but published only one article of this type and none on funding even while claiming to give it special emphasis. Only with Mayhew is there a close match between editorial statements and published articles. Mayhew claimed to be interested in publishing papers on stratification and teaching and expressly solicited a wide diversity of views (presumably including criticism), and that is what was emphasized in the articles published during his tenure. All editors are constrained by the articles they receive, but they can and do solicit articles they believe should be represented in the journal, as Ray Mack did in 1969.

Most *TAS* editors did not make a claim to being interested in publishing on stratification. Even so, except for Grimshaw, they accepted many papers on this topic. It is evident that many sociologists were very interested in this topic and produced a lot of such research. Academic professionals live in a stratified world and make career decisions with such considerations in mind. Stratification, in short, is a little like sex. Everybody is interested in it, including most *TAS* editors, but many apparently choose not to admit it. The significance of research on academic stratification is that it indicates quite clearly those qualities that the discipline values. If departments emphasizing statistical research cluster at the top, as they do, this demonstrates the priorities of contemporary sociologists.

Although the analysis of editorial policies and the nature of the articles published are informative in their own right, the resulting patterns provide us with indirect clues as to why *TAS* ceased to be sponsored by the American Sociological Association. Our analysis suggests that the "official reasons" concerning the actions regarding *TAS* are not in accord with existing data. One of the main reasons for targeting *TAS* (and, early on, *Sociological Methodology*) as publications that should be terminated was because of financial exigencies, but we have taken note of various limitations of this justification. The discrepancies between the "official reasons" for the demise of *TAS* and what actually occurred required a tentative explanation.

At this point we shall use the data we have uncovered as a foundation for some reasoned judgments as to why we believe *TAS* was deemed unworthy of sponsorship by the leadership of the ASA. We hypothesize that there was a convergence of "interests" among strategic groups in the ASA that led to the cessation of the one journal that permitted a relatively wide expression of analysis and views to be aired concerning the state of the discipline.

One reason for the actions of the Council of the ASA, which led to the demise of *TAS*, was that it provided a forum for the publication of articles that were critical of the discipline and on occasion of the powers that be. Yet if we look at the overall nature of the publications, we discover that the number of critical articles was relatively small. Moreover, when Grimshaw was editor he was true to his word and reduced very sharply this kind of publication.

Nonetheless, articles such as those by Nicolaus stand out in a symbolic sense even to this day. We cannot imagine that his article would have been published in any other publication sponsored by the ASA except *TAS*. At the same time, we would strongly emphasize that these kinds of articles were not representative of those published in *TAS*. In fact, a number of well-established "scientific sociologists"—Jack Gibbs, Herbert Costner, H.M. Blalock, among others, published articles in *TAS*. Today, when we look back on the late 1960s and early 1970s, we find it ironic that Ray Mack, who by all criteria was an establishment figure in sociology (he held a high administrative position at Northwestern University), should have been so open- minded and yet sharply criticized in some quarters for upholding an ideal that most sociologists would acknowledge as an integral part of the discipline's mission.

A second plausible (and interrelated) reason for the failure of the ASA to support *TAS* was that it made it possible for sociologists such as T.R. Young, Jack Roach, and Martin Nicolaus to publish in a journal that had the official imprimatur of the association. Although such authors are in a distinct minority, they did not appear in other ASA-sponsored publications, such as the *ASR*. Yet if a journal is to be open to a wide range of perspectives as some editors promised, then the views of the aforementioned kinds of sociologists must be aired.

A third reason for the cessation of the publication of *TAS* was that it did not publish articles that were in keeping with rigorous scientific standards. If we compare the articles in *TAS* with those in the *ASR* and *Social Psychology Quarterly*, we will find that more articles in *TAS* were of a qualitative nature. Moreover, the quantitative articles that were published—and they were numerous—did not employ the latest quantitative techniques. Thus, as one former association officer claimed, when compared to the *ASR* and judged by these standards, *TAS* was "a very third rate ASR" and a "bad parody of the ASR." Although the nature of the articles made them accessible to a wide range of sociologists, they were not in keeping with the general trend of the discipline, which stressed "rigorous scientific procedures"—particularly the use of the latest quantitative techniques. In one sense, *TAS* compromised sociology's claim to being like the "natural sciences."

Fourth, it is evident that *TAS* had no "power base" in the discipline. Early on, *Sociological Methodology* was singled out by the committee to review ASA publications as another publication that should be terminated for financial reasons. But it seems apparent that such an effort would have placed the Council on a collision course with some of the most prominent members of the sociological establishment who were active members of the methodology section. It seems reasonable to assume that the members of the Council were in no position to take on some of the "elite" members of the discipline who view their activities as essential for furthering the development of scientific sociology.

Our thesis is that none of the aforementioned reasons would have been sufficient in and of themselves to have led to the cessation of *TAS*. Some members of the profession were opposed to *TAS* on certain grounds, while other members emphasized other reasons. What seems to have occurred was a confluence of "divergent interests," which led to the cessation of the one publication that offered an alternative perspective within the discipline. That an "outsider" such as T.R. Young led a letter-writing campaign to revive *TAS* perhaps reinforced the suspicions about *TAS* held by members in leadership roles in the ASA.

Today, about a decade after the decision of the Council to terminate the ASA sponsorship of *TAS*, we can evaluate their decision in a larger context. We are led to conclude that it is highly unfortunate that a number of intellectual issues cannot now be analyzed and debated within an ASA-sponsored publication. One of these relates to the ethics of social research. During the 1980s, the ASA's Code of Ethics was revised. But this was done on the basis of little theoretical or empirical investigation regarding the impact of the code on the research process. And now that the changes have been made, what are their implications for sociological activities?

Numerous other significant scholarly topics are deserving of attention. For example, the controversial issue of the changing stratification system within the discipline requires renewed attention. This kind of research is not only relevant to the sociology of sociology but also to the study of professions and occupations. Still other issues have come to the fore because of the massive changes in the political and economic structure on the world scene. The relationship of American sociologists to their colleagues in Europe and Japan and in the developing nations is worthy of sustained analysis. But how is it possible for American sociologists or their colleagues in other countries to react to the theoretical and methodological trends in the discipline when there is no journal outlet for addressing these questions within the ASA?

Theoretical and methodological issues relating to the discipline should be open to a wide range of reasoned debate. But there are also pressing practical problems that face the discipline of sociology. The administration's decision to terminate the Department of Sociology at Washington University is a serious matter. While now apparently safe, the Department of Sociology at Yale University had been reported in the national media as under siege. Here is a department that traces its roots to William Graham Summer—one of the founders of sociology in America. Yet this department was targeted for drastic cuts, which faculty members were able to reverse. The crisis for sociology that these actions illustrate should be debated within the ASA in a scholarly manner. But no publication is available for focusing on these compelling matters. *Teaching Sociology* does not serve this purpose. And *Footnotes* at best offers only lengthy letters, or articles that look like letters, to the editor as a mode of expression. This is hardly the basis for a systematic analysis of practical problems that affect all sociologists and their students.

In our judgment, the actions of the ASA Council relating to *TAS* will in the long haul be viewed as shortsighted. We believe that there is room for intellectual expression of a wide range of views in publications sponsored by the ASA. But until a journal like *TAS* is restored to its rightful place in the discipline, this is unlikely to occur. We hope our analysis of the demise of *TAS* has placed the role of intellectual dissent and debate within a framework on which other sociologists can build in a constructive manner.

Postscript

The American Sociologist returned for a third time. After protracted negotiations, Irving Louis Horowitz convinced the ASA to allow Transaction Publishers to produce the journal under the editorship of James McCartney. As with its predecessors, however, the future of *TAS* is uncertain. As of this writing, it is still not at all certain that the journal has sufficient subscriptions to survive. The very lucrative library subscriptions, which produce approximately twice the funds of individual subscriptions, are especially difficult to secure in this era of tight university budgets. For example, even at the University of Missouri-Columbia, where McCartney edited the journal, the library has not subscribed.

Notes

1. The database for the analysis of the major themes of the articles appearing in the *The American Sociologist* includes all the articles and research notes published in the *The American Sociologist* between 1965 and 1982 plus relevant articles that appeared in *Socio-Log*, which briefly combined with the *The American Sociologist* in 1971. In this essay, we have referred to selected articles from the population for illustrative purposes. These numerous illustrations are not fully cited in the references; we have, however, indicated each author's name and year of publication in the text. Our investigation located a total of 519 articles and research notes. We began our analysis by locating abstracts of every published piece. In most instances, coding the topic of a piece was easy from this abstract. In difficult cases, the entire article was read. The coding of all publications was done independently by each author and the few cases of initial difference of opinion were easily resolved by reading the entire article. In a few instances, the publication in truth had more than one focus, but even here publications were coded only once. We made a collective judgment as to the primary thrust of the publication. To code and include all the issues raised in each

publication would have been misleading and would have diluted the impact of any given publication. Some may feel that in dealing with events that are so recent, we should have relied on the memories of the major players involved in these developments, such as former *TAS* editors and members of the council at the time when important decisions were made. But we decided to rely on the printed record, much as I.F. Stone has done in attempting to understand the operations of the Pentagon. He has reasoned over the years that with such a controversial topic, this is a better solution than relying on the memory and veracity of the participants. And so did we. After completing a draft of this manuscript, however, it was sent to all former *TAS* editors, members of the ASA Council, and any others who had some visible role in the short history of this journal, to help check the accuracy of the written records as well as our interpretation of them.

REFERENCES

Anonymous. 1973. "A Note on *Footnotes*." *ASA Footnotes* 1(January):1.
———. 1974. "ASR Leads ASA Publication Circulation in 1973." *ASA Footnotes* 2(March):5.
———. 1974. "New Editors Appointed for Three ASA Journals; Begin Terms in 1976." *ASA Footnotes* 2(December):1–12.
———. 1979. "Editors Named for Methodology, *TAS*." *ASA Footnotes* 7(January):5.
———. 1981. "Council to Review Publications." *ASA Footnotes* 9(October):1–2.
———. 1984. "New ASA Journal Seeks Editor." *ASA Footnotes* 12(November):1.
Bonjean, Charles M.. 1982. "Publications." *ASA Footnotes* 10(May):8.
Bulmer, M.I.A. 1972. "Falling ASA Membership." *The American Sociologist* 7:4.
Costner, Herbert L. 1982. "Minutes of the 1982 ASA Council Meeting." *ASA Footnotes* 10(February):4–5.
———. 1982. "Minutes of the ASA Council Meeting." *ASA Footnotes* 10(August):12–14.
Demerath, Jay. 1971. Letter to Richard Hessler in possession of the authors. December 15.
———. 1972. "Report of the Executive Officer." *The American Sociologist* 7:25.
Edwards, Karen Gray. 1988. Letter in possession of the authors, April 12.
Grimshaw, Allen D. 1975. "A Note from the Incoming Editor." *The American Sociologist* 10:192.
———. 1976. "Editor's Page" *American Sociologist* 11:1.
———. 1977. "Report of the Editor of *The American Sociologist*" *ASA Footnotes* 5(March):9.
———. 1978. "Report of the Editor of *The American Sociologist*." *ASA Footnotes* 6(March):9.
———. 1979. "*The American Sociologist*." *ASA Footnotes* 7(February):6.
Hagan, Robert A.. 1988. Letter in possession of the authors.
Hessler, Richard M.. 1971. Letter in possession of the authors. December 8.
Letter to Richard Hessler. 1971. In possession of the authors. December 28.
Mack, Raymond W.. 1968. "Report of the Editor of *The American Sociologist*." *The American Sociologist* 3:331–32.
———. 1969. "Report of the Editor of *The American Sociologist*." *The American Sociologist* 4:349–50.
Mayhew, Leon. 1972. Letter to Stephen Turner in possession of the authors. October 23.

————. 1974. "The Task of *The American Sociologist*: An Amended Statement." *The American Sociologist* 9: 99–100.

————. 1975. "Report of the Editor of *The American Sociologist*." *ASA Footnotes* 3(August):13.

McCartney, James L. 1979. "Editor's Page." *The American Sociologist*. 14:Cover 1 and 3.

————. 1982. "*The American Sociologist*." *ASA Footnotes* 10(March):11.

"New 'American Sociologist' Debuts." 1972. *The American Sociologist* 7:1.

Parsons, Talcott. 1965. "*The American Sociologist*: Editorial Statement." *The American Sociologist* 1:2–3.

————. 1966. "The Editor's Column." *The American Sociologist* 1:238–40.

————. 1967. "The Editor's Column." *The American Sociologist* 2:62–64.

Pfautz, Harold W.. 1970. "Report of the Editor of *The American Sociologist*." *The American Sociologist* 5:400.

————. 1972a. Letter to Richard Hessler in possession of the authors. January 14.

————. 1972b. Letter to Andrew Twaddle in possession of the authors. February 18.

————. 1972c. "Report of the Editor of *The American Sociologist*." *The American Sociologist* 7:26.

Socio-Log. 1971. "*The American Sociologist* and *Socio-Log* to Merge Beginning January 1972," October, 1.

Young, T.R. 1988. Letter in possession of the authors. May 2.

EDITORS AND CONTRIBUTORS

Diouf, Moustapha. Department of Sociology, University of Vermont.

Galliher, John F. Department of Sociology, University of Missouri-Columbia.

Hartung, Beth. Department of Sociology, California State University-Fresno.

Knottnerus, J. David. Department of Sociology, Oklahoma State University.

Littrell, Boyd. Department of Sociology, University of Nebraska at Omaha.

Lyson, Thomas A. Department of Rural Sociology, Cornell University.

Reynolds, Larry T. Department of Sociology, Anthropology, and Social Work, Central Michigan University.

Nelson, David. Police Department, Columbia, Missouri.

Saxton, Stanley L. Department of Sociology, University of Dayton.

Sjoberg, Andrée F. Department of Oriental and African Languages and Literatures, University of Texas at Austin.

Sjoberg, Gideon. Department of Sociology, University of Texas at Austin.

Squires, Gregory D. Department of Sociology, University of Wisconsin-Milwaukee.

Vaughan, Ted R. Department of Sociology, University of Missouri-Columbia.

Williams, Norma. Department of Sociology and Social Work, University of North Texas.

INDEX